CAMBRIDGE
EDUCATIONAL SERVICES

AMERICA'S PREMIERE TESTING READINESS PROGRAM

The Complete Non-Negotiable Skills™
for College and Career Success

Level 1

Student Text

ACT® • PLAN® • EXPLORE® • ACT Aspire™ • SAT® • PSAT/NMSQT® • PSAT™ 8/9 • PSAT™ 10 • WorkKeys® • GRE® • GMAT® • LSAT® • GED® • TASC™ • HiSET® • ITBS • MCAT®
PRAXIS® Stanford • EOC and State Tests • Analytics • Classroom Texts • Teacher Curriculum • Professional Development • Web Courses • Question Writing
Online Services • CollegePrep™ • Guidance Services • Motivation/Admissions Workshops • Learning Styles • Career Interest Inventory
Non-Negotiable Skills™ • Essential Skills • Cambridge iFlara™ eBooks

The above-cited marks are the property of their respective owners.

Cambridge Educational Services, Inc. offers and scores tests from ACT, Inc., The College Board, and other testing companies. These are retired tests, intended for practice purposes only and not for official administration, and are based on high school curriculum as of the copyright dates of the tests. Cambridge's products and services, including its score reports, are not approved or endorsed by ACT, Inc., The College Board, or the other companies that develop the tests, and Cambridge has no affiliation with any of those entities.

Our Mission: Progress Through Partnership
Cambridge Educational Services partners with educators who share the significant mission of educational advancement for all students. By partnering together, we can best achieve our common goals: to build skills, raise test scores, enhance curriculum, and support instruction. A leading innovator in education for over twenty years, Cambridge is the nation's premiere provider of school-based test preparation and supplemental curriculum services.

Cambridge Publishing, Inc.
www.CambridgeEd.com

©2003, 2004, 2005, 2011, 2016 by Cambridge Publishing, Inc.
All rights reserved. First Edition 2003.
Sixth edition 2016

Printed in the United States of America
19 18 17 16   1 2 3 4 5

ISBN: 978-1-58894-227-2

© 2016 by Cambridge Educational Services
All rights reserved.

© 2016 by Thomas H. Martinson
All rights reserved

TABLE OF CONTENTS

Course Overview vii

PRE-ASSESSMENT

PRE-ASSESSMENT ADMINISTRATION..2
HOW TO USE THE PRE-ASSESSMENT REPORTS..2
PREPARING FOR THE FUTURE: BUILDING NON-NEGOTIABLE SKILLS........................5

NON-NEGOTIABLE SKILLS

ENGLISH.. 9

PRODUCTION OF WRITING 11
    Unit 1 | Topic Development 11
    Unit 2 | Transition Words and Phrases 27
    Unit 3 | Practice 39

KNOWLEDGE OF LANGUAGE 51
    Unit 4 | Clarity in Sentences 51
    Unit 5 | Clarity in Noun and Pronoun Usage 65
    Unit 6 | Practice 73

CONVENTIONS OF STANDARD ENGLISH 83
    Unit 7 | Conjunctions and Punctuation 83
    Unit 8 | Verb Tense 99
    Unit 9 | Practice 107
    Unit 10 | Past Participles 119
    Unit 11 | Adjectives.. 131
    Unit 12 | Commas... 141
    Unit 13 | Practice 153

ENGLISH MASTERY TEST 1 163
ENGLISH MASTERY TEST 2... 171

MATH **177**

NUMBER AND QUANTITY 179

Unit 1 | Basic Manipulations 179
Unit 2 | Fractions 187
Unit 3 | Number Lines 199

ALGEBRA AND FUNCTIONS 209

Unit 4 | One- and Two-Step Problems 209
Unit 5 | Basic Expressions 219
Unit 6 | Basic Equations 227
Unit 7 | Practice 237
Unit 8 | Pattern Identification 243

GEOMETRY 251

Unit 9 | Length and Distance 251
Unit 10 | Unit Conversions 267

STATISTICS AND PROBABILITY 277

Unit 11 | Averages 277
Unit 12 | Charts and Tables 285
Unit 13 | Practice 303

MATH MASTERY TEST 1 309
MATH MASTERY TEST 2 313

READING **317**

KEY IDEAS AND DETAILS 319

Unit 1 | Main Idea 319
Unit 2 | Specific Details 335
Unit 3 | Practice 347
Unit 4 | Events and Relationships 357

CRAFT AND STRUCTURE 375

Unit 5 | Vocabulary 375
Unit 6 | Practice 391
Unit 7 | Implied Ideas and Conclusions 403
Unit 8 | Purpose of Sentences 423
Unit 9 | Practice 443

Unit 10 | Practice 459
Unit 11 | Practice 471

INTEGRATION OF KNOWLEDGE AND IDEAS 483

Unit 12 | Analyzing Arguments 483
Unit 13 | Analyzing Paired Passages 495

READING MASTERY TEST 1 509
READING MASTERY TEST 2 519

SCIENCE 529

INTERPRETATION OF DATA 531

Unit 1 | Tables 531
Unit 2 | Tables Practice 545
Unit 3 | Bar Graphs 557
Unit 4 | Bar Graphs Practice 571
Unit 5 | Line Graphs 583
Unit 6 | Line Graphs Practice 597
Unit 7 | Practice 609

SCIENTIFIC INVESTIGATION 623

Unit 8 | Describing Experiments 623
Unit 9 | Describing Experiments Practice 641
Unit 10 | Experimental Tools and Methods 651
Unit 11 | Experimental Tools and Methods Practice 669

EVALUATION OF MODELS, INFERENCES, AND EXPERIMENTAL RESULTS 681

Unit 12 | Understanding Models 681
Unit 13 | Understanding Models Practice 695

SCIENCE MASTERY TEST 1 707
SCIENCE MASTERY TEST 2 725

POST-ASSESSMENT

POST-ASSESSMENT ADMINISTRATION 742
HOW TO USE THE POST-ASSESSMENT REPORTS 744

Appendix A: Answer Key 745
Error Correction and Suggestion Form 761

Course Overview

INSIDE THIS UNIT:
– How to Use This Book – – The Non-Negotiable Skills Series –

How to Use This Book

This book is all about non-negotiable skills. What are non-negotiable skills and what makes them "non-negotiable"?

As the name suggests, "non-negotiable" means not subject to negotiation—something that is absolute, not open to compromise. In other words, the skills covered in this book are essential.

Essential for what? The skills taught in this book have been identified as necessary for college and career readiness. If you hope to go to college or get a good job following graduation from high school, you have to know what's in this book.

Your teacher may teach through each subject one unit at a time, or your teacher may focus on some units and not others.

The three steps of a successful course are briefly explained below.

Pre-Assessment

At the beginning of this course, you will take a pre-assessment to measure your knowledge. Your teacher will use your pre-assessment score to identify specific topics he or she should target throughout your course.

Skill Building

This book is divided into four major parts: English, Math, Reading, and Science. Each major part is divided into units. The units feature:

- discussion of a targeted non-negotiable skill or skills explaining and illustrating the key concepts you need to learn.

- exercises for completion in class or at home.

- two Mastery Tests per subject to help you measure your progress and reinforce what you learned.

Post-Assessment

At the end of this course, you may take a post-assessment similar to your pre-assessment. If your course includes a post-assessment, you and your teacher will use your post-assessment reports to identify how much you grew during your course.

With this overview in mind, it's time to begin building non-negotiable skills and paving the way to success. Good luck!

Pre-Assessment

INSIDE THIS UNIT:
– Pre-Assessment Administration – – How to Use the Pre-Assessment Reports – – Preparing for the Future: Building Non-Negotiable Skills –

Pre-Assessment Administration

At the beginning of the course, you will take a pre-assessment. By taking the test, you will gain important information about your current skill level in the areas covered on the test. It is important that you take this pre-assessment seriously, since it will help both you and your teacher know which areas you are already strong in and which areas you need to focus on for improvement.

Before you take the pre-assessment, ask your instructor what you should bring to the classroom, such as sharpened No. 2 pencils, a calculator, or a watch.

If your program has ordered pre-assessment reports, you will receive one of these reports with your pre-assessment results. These reports will help you determine the areas in which you need the most study.

How to Use the Pre-Assessment Reports

Approximately six business days after you take the pre-assessment, you will receive student reports, including both a Student Summary and a Student Item Analysis, that explain your test results. These reports provide details about your performance and help you to recognize your individual strengths and weaknesses. Having this valuable information will allow you to set goals and monitor your progress toward achieving them. Review the details of the sample reports on the next two pages. The sample reports are based on a previously administered EXPLORE® test.

Student Summary

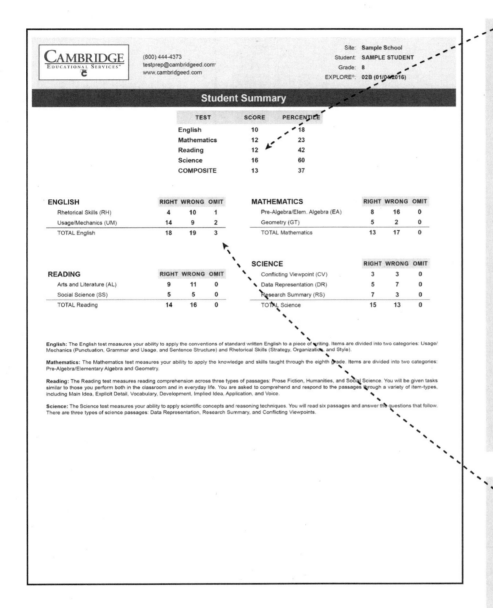

Each individual subject test on the EXPLORE® test has a benchmark score that indicates whether a student is making satisfactory progress toward college readiness in that subject. These benchmark scores for eighth graders are 13 for English, 17 for Mathematics, 16 for Reading, and 18 for Science. This student's score of 12 on the Reading test indicates that she is NOT on track for college readiness in reading. While the EXPLORE® test score is only one indicator, it provides a useful analysis of a student's progress.

On average, for every four to five items omitted, the student could have gained one more correct answer simply by guessing. So, be sure not to leave any questions blank!

Student Item Analysis

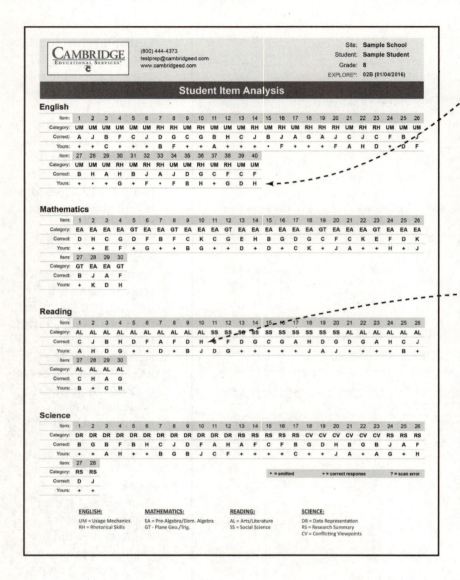

Preparing for the Future: Building Non-Negotiable Skills

Congratulations for participating in a program that will grow your potential to reach your academic and career goals. By starting now, you will have time to increase your scores on the ACT®, SAT, or other standardized tests. In fact, we believe that the earlier you start to learn, review, and hone the skills that are tested, the greater your potential for achieving the scores on standardized tests that will make you proud.

As a high school or middle school (junior high) student, a significant hurdle for you in reaching your academic and career goals is applying to and getting accepted into a college or university. For some high school students, this admissions activity is just around the corner, while for some middle school students, it may be a few years into the future. In either circumstance though, it is important to anticipate and prepare for this exciting and important step. This section of the book prepares you to take significant practical steps toward thinking about the future in terms of college or university admission. You should see this program as a tool to grow your academic skills, reach your college ambitions, and prepare for your future career.

Determine to Elevate Your Test Score and Your GPA

Most colleges use both a student's grade point average and ACT (or SAT) test score to help determine his or her viability as a future student. Schools differ, though, on how they rely on these numbers. Many schools use a complex formula that blends the two together into what is called an index. It is not important right now that you understand the intricacies of this index formula. Just know that both your grade point average and your test scores are examined, and your admission into college is tied directly to those numbers.

Using the materials in this book, you can learn the core skills that are evaluated on the ACT (or SAT) test. In addition, reviewing these core skills might help you perform better in your middle school or high school classes, which should boost your grade point average. Again, your focus should be to grow your skills that boost your test scores and your grade point average, so work hard as you review the material in this book.

Appreciate the Cost of College or University Attendance

These days, attending college or university is extremely expensive. The cost of a private college or university can exceed $40,000 per year. When the expense of room and board for four years is taken into account, the expense to obtain your college degree could easily exceed $200,000. (Fortunately, there are many more affordable options, such as state colleges and universities.) The costs accompanying a college education can be broken down into the following major components. Your own personal needs may differ depending on your situation.

- **Tuition**: Tuition is the cost for providing instruction at a college or university.

- **Room and Board**: Room and board is the expense charged for college housing and meals.

- **Fees**: Fees are special costs assigned for services, activities, or projects that are not covered by tuition, such as technology enhancements, laboratory needs, student activities, health services, etc.

- **Books and Supplies**: Books and supplies include required textbooks, class resources, materials, etc.

- **Incidentals**: Other costs to you as a student might include various general living expenses, transportation, health insurance, clothing, recreation, etc.

Most colleges provide a breakdown of these expenses for prospective students. Financial aid departments can communicate a detailed estimate of these various costs. This discussion of the financial cost of attending a college or university is meant to dramatize a point—namely, that the decision to apply to college has significant financial implications for you as an individual and perhaps for your family. But for many, the investment in a college or university education will be rewarded by four years of rich college experiences, deep new learning, and a great start on a rewarding career path.

Consider Your Academic, Career, and Personal Goals

Choosing a college is often directly associated with choosing a career or profession. Even in high school or middle school, you should begin to gather information about careers that interest you. An element of this information is the salary levels associated with various careers.

The following chart displays a range of salaries (low, average, high) for several occupations.[1]

---

[1]Bureau of Labor Statistics, "May 2014 National Occupational Employment and Wage Estimates," May 2014, United States Department of Labor, http://www.bls.gov/oes/current/oes_nat.htm (accessed October 29, 2015).

	Occupation/Salary Ranges (in USD/year)		
Occupation	25th Percentile	Median	75th Percentile
Pharmacist	$106,520	$120,950	>$138,010
Lawyer	$75,630	$114,970	$172,540
Marketing Manager	$90,630	$127,130	$171,390
Human Resources Manager	$78,310	$102,780	$138,320
Electrical Engineer	$72,470	$91,410	$115,470
Registered Nurse	$54,620	$66,640	$81,080
Technical Writer	$53,080	$69,030	$88,230
Accountant	$51,130	$65,940	$87,530
Librarian	$44,230	$56,170	$70,590
Police Patrol Officer	$42,260	$56,810	$74,870
Secondary School Teacher	$44,990	$56,210	$71,320
Graphic Designer	$34,600	$45,900	$61,740
Administrative Assistant	$27,960	$35,970	$46,820
Customer Service Representative	$24,620	$31,200	$39,970
Construction Laborer	$24,740	$31,090	$42,230

Note that higher-paying occupations often require a college or university degree. Recent US Census Bureau information indicates that individuals with a bachelor's degree earn on average almost twice as much annually as high school graduates without further education.[2] Be aware that job location also plays a major role in determining salary. For additional salary information, visit www.salary.com or www.payscale.com.

REFLECTION

On a separate sheet of paper, write down some thoughts about what academic, career, and personal successes you'd like to achieve in the next 20 years of your life.

List 5–7 careers that currently interest you.

List some ways that getting into a college or university of your choice might help you achieve these academic, career, and personal goals.

---

[2]Julian, Tiffany and Robert Kominski. "Education and Synthetic Work-Life Earnings Estimates." *United States Census Bureau* (Sept. 2011) http://www.census.gov/prod/2011pubs/acs-14.pdf (accessed October 29, 2015).

Determine a Path toward Paying for College

Even though the cost of attending college is high, there are avenues for you to pursue to help pay the expenses. Yes, colleges and universities often expect both you and your parents to contribute some money toward the tuition, room and board, and fees of college, but they also provide a variety of ways for you to find additional money. This is generally referred to as financial aid, which may come from the college itself or from federal government or state government funding. Financial aid includes grants, scholarships, waivers, assistantships, loans, and work-study opportunities.

The following terms often appear in the context of financial aid:

- *Grants:* Grants do not have to be repaid and are generally awarded based on financial need demonstrated by the family and/or student.

- *Scholarships:* Scholarships do not have to be repaid and are presented based on accomplishments in academics, athletics, or extracurricular activities; musical or artistic talent; or leadership.

- *Loans:* Loans are funds used for education that are repaid to the lending institution, usually with interest. A Stafford Loan is administered by the federal government.

- *Employment:* College students can earn funds by working in exchange for wages. Work-study programs may be subsidized by colleges or by governmental agencies.

One significant reason for doing well on tests like the ACT or SAT exams is that scholarship committees often use these type of test scores to determine to whom they will offer valuable college scholarships.

Preparing for the Future

College and career dreams may seem a long distance in the future for you, but know that the future will come more quickly than you can imagine. Set high goals for yourself. Dream big dreams. And use this program to begin to grow the skills to make those dreams come true.

Level 1
ENGLISH

PRODUCTION OF WRITING

UNIT 1 | TOPIC DEVELOPMENT.................................11
Staying on Topic..12
Exercise..16

UNIT 2 | TRANSITION WORDS AND PHRASES..........27
What Is a Conjunctive Adverb?..........................28
Table of Conjunctive Adverbs...........................29
Getting It Right..32
Exercise..33

UNIT 3 | PRACTICE...39
Exercise..40

KNOWLEDGE OF LANGUAGE

UNIT 4 | CLARITY IN SENTENCES 51
Arrangement of Sentence Elements 53
Avoid Awkward and Confusing Sentences 54
Exercise..58

UNIT 5 | CLARITY IN NOUN AND PRONOUN USAGE 65
An Important Tip on Nouns and Pronouns..........66
Exercise 68

UNIT 6 | PRACTICE...73
Exercise..74

CONVENTIONS OF STANDARD ENGLISH

UNIT 7 | CONJUNCTIONS AND PUNCTUATION 83
Building Sentences...84
Exercise..89

UNIT 8 | VERB TENSE...99
Consistent Tenses...100
Exercise..101

UNIT 9 | PRACTICE...107
Exercise..108

UNIT 10 | PAST PARTICIPLES 119
What Are Principal Parts?.................................120
Principal Parts of Some Common Verbs 120
Principal Parts of Some Common Irregular Verbs............121
Exercise..127

UNIT 11 | ADJECTIVES.......................................131
Degrees of Adjectives 132
Exercise..137

UNIT 12 | COMMAS 141
Why Use Commas? 142
When to Use Commas.......................................143
Exercise 148

UNIT 13 | PRACTICE...153
Exercise..154

MASTERY TESTS

English Mastery Test 1 163
English Mastery Test 2 171

English **Production of Writing**

Unit 1 | **Topic Development**

INSIDE THIS UNIT:
– Staying on Topic – – Exercise –

Non-Negotiable Skill:

Delete material that obviously does not relate to the topic of the essay.

Staying on Topic

The starting point for most writing, including essays, reports, and research papers, is choosing your subject matter. Often, your teacher will assign a subject. Other times, you may be given complete freedom to choose a topic that interests you.

Once you have a topic, the process of finding a focus for the paper moves from the general to the specific. You have to focus your writing on a specific theme that is manageable in terms of the number of pages required and the time you're given. A topic that is overly ambitious (too broad) can't be covered in a paper with a limited number of pages in the time you're given. This is why teachers are constantly saying, "Narrow it down."

When we talk about this process, we usually use the term "topic" to refer to the general subject matter of the paper and the term "focus" to refer to the specific, manageable scope after you've narrowed the topic. For example, topics might include "Early American Documents," "Battles of the Civil War," and "Important Scientific Discoveries." These are not really suitable for papers because they are so broad. You'd need to write an entire book to cover even the most important battles of the Civil War. So once assigned such a topic, you'd narrow it down. For example:

"The First Amendment: Freedom of Speech"

"The Civil War Battle of Atlanta"

"Dr. Jonas Salk and the Polio Vaccine"

You must define the focus of your writing so that your essay or paper is unified—so that it doesn't wander off in many directions.

As a writer, you are in control of the paper. You decide what ideas should be included and how they should be organized. You must be careful, however, to avoid including ideas that are only slightly related to your focus or that are completely irrelevant to your topic. The following examples illustrate ideas that are irrelevant to the stated topic.

Example:

Topic: The First Amendment: Freedom of Speech

> Irrelevant Sentence: Although many animals make sounds, human beings are the only species that have the capacity of speech.

Topic: The Civil War Battle of Atlanta

> Irrelevant Sentence: One of the most important battles of World War II was the Battle of the Bulge fought between the Allies and the Germans in the winter of 1944.

Topic: Dr. Jonas Salk and the Polio Vaccine

> Irrelevant Sentence: Marie Curie, who was the first woman to receive a Nobel Prize in science, died of aplastic anemia caused by her exposure to the radiation that she studied for most of her life.

Your teacher, in reviewing your writing, will indicate when an idea is too far removed from the topic or focus to be relevant. Sometimes an idea may fall into a gray area—may be relevant but may not be relevant. An idea that is not too far removed, yet not clearly in the focus, could be included depending on what you, the writer, hope to accomplish.

Example:

[1]

[1] Two songbirds seen frequently in North Dakota are the eastern kingbird and the western kingbird. [2] Both species are also called flycatchers because they catch insects for food directly from the air. [3] Flycatchers are members of the family *Tyrannidae*, which is taken from the Greek word *tyrannus*, meaning "lord or ruler." [4] <u>The Latin word for "king" is *rex*.</u> As suggested by the name, flycatchers are the most aggressive of the primitive songbirds.

[2]

[1] Most flycatchers, of which the eastern and western kingbirds are typical, are plain brown, gray, olive-green, or yellow in color. [2] They have large heads and prominent bristles at the base of the bill. [3] The male and the female of the species are generally very similar in appearance. [4] It is now generally accepted that birds evolved from dinosaurs and that the *Archaeopteryx* was the intermediate link.

14 • ENGLISH PRODUCTION OF WRITING

[3]

[1] The eastern kingbird has a black head, slate gray back, and white underparts. [2] It can be easily distinguished by a broad white band across the end of the tail feathers. [3] The eastern kingbird feeds on insects but will also eat berries as a secondary food source. [4] The main mode of hunting is to fly from a perch and catch insects out of mid-air. [5] The eastern kingbird will also land on the ground to eat insects or pluck them from the surface of the water. [6] The eastern kingbird builds a cup-shaped nest about 5 inches in diameter and lays three to five eggs marked irregularly with small blotches of brown. [7] Eastern kingbirds can be found in open country from April through September.

[4]

[1] The western kingbird is similar in size and shape to the eastern kingbird. [2] It differs only in color by having a bright yellow belly, pale gray throat and breast, dark wings, and a gray back tinged with olive. [3] It too is an insect eater and feeds by darting out from a tree, low brush, a fence post, or other structure to catch bees, wasps, dragonflies, and butterflies. [4] The western kingbird will often drop to the ground to eat caterpillars, grasshoppers, crickets, and occasionally a tree frog. [5] The bird lives in open country around ranches and towns but avoids large tracts of forest. [6] The female builds a nest in trees or other structures and lays three to seven white eggs speckled with brown spots. [7] The western kingbird is very aggressive and will attack hawks, crows, and ravens that come close to its nest. [8] This bird has even been known to attack humans, though there are no reports of any serious injuries resulting from a western kingbird attack.

1. Assuming that each of the following statements is true, which change to Sentence 4 in Paragraph 1 would be the most appropriate for the topic and development of the selection?

   A. NO CHANGE
   B. The Latin word for "lord" is *dominus*.
   C. Scientific categories use Latinized endings for names.
   D. DELETE

   The correct answer is (D). The underlined sentence is irrelevant.

2. Deleting which of the following sentences in Paragraph 2 would most improve the focus of this essay?

F. Sentence 1
G. Sentence 2
H. Sentence 3
J. Sentence 4

The correct answer is (J). The passage describes the appearance and behavior of two kinds of birds, but the subject matter is not the evolutionary history of birds. Sentence 4 should be omitted entirely.

3. Which of the following would be the most effective change for Sentence 2 in Paragraph 3?

A. NO CHANGE
B. Move the sentence to follow Sentence 4 in Paragraph 3.
C. Move the sentence to follow Sentence 5 in Paragraph 3.
D. DELETE

The correct answer is (A). The author is discussing the physical appearance of one of the subject birds, so this sentence is relevant. Its positioning is correct for this discussion.

4. Which of the following would be the most effective change for Sentence 8 in Paragraph 4?

F. NO CHANGE
G. Move to before Sentence 1 in Paragraph 4.
H. Move to after Sentence 2 in Paragraph 4.
J. DELETE

The correct answer is (F). The sentence is relevant to the discussion of the behavior of the western kingbird. It adds a nice "stinger" at the end of the passage and a bit of drama to close the discussion.

Summary

- Before you begin writing, define your topic and your focus.

- A focus is a specific, manageable theme that depends on the length of time you have to write and the targeted length of your finished work.

- When you proofread your writing, look for any sentences that are irrelevant to your topic or focus and delete them.

EXERCISE

DIRECTIONS: In each of the following passages, sentences are underlined and numbered. For each of the corresponding items, select the answer that BEST answers the question. Answers are on page 746.

Questions 1–4

The Underground Railroad

In the early nineteenth century, abolitionists and former slaves organized a network of escape routes and safe houses for runaway slaves. The routes originated in the slave states of the South and ran north to Canada, where slavery had been abolished in 1833, or north and west to states and territories where slavery was illegal. The network is now generally referred to as the Underground Railroad. While there were "conductors," such as Harriet Tubman, who led slaves to freedom, [1] most runaway slaves found their way alone along these routes. [1]

People making their escapes generally traveled at night and rested during the day. The routes typically included "stations" or "depots" 20 to 25 miles apart where escapees could rest and refresh themselves. Stations were often located in bars, under church floors, in caves, or in hollows in riverbanks. The manager of the [2] station, often the owner of the property, was called the "stationmaster." [2] While the fugitives rested, word was sent on to the next stop on the route to expect the arrival of one or more fugitives.

The Fugitive Slave Act was passed in 1850, making it illegal to harbor runaway slaves even in states that outlawed slavery. As a result, traffic on the Underground Railroad was heaviest from about 1850 to 1860. Overall, however, it is estimated [3] that even at the height of the Underground Railroad, fewer than 1,000 slaves per [3] year, from all slave-holding states, were able to escape. [3]

UNIT 1 | TOPIC DEVELOPMENT • 17

The natural birthrate actually caused the number of enslaved people to increase more than the number of people who escaped from slavery. <u>Still, although the number of escapes was comparatively small, the psychological influence of an effective network to assist escaped slaves was immense.</u>
₄

1. The underlined sentence should be
    A. left where it is because it expands the understanding of "Underground Railroad," the focus of the essay.
    B. left where it is because it shows that historical figures such as Harriet Tubman played key roles in the abolitionist movement.
    C. removed from the essay because it tends to undermine the idea that the Underground Railroad provided effective escape routes.
    D. removed from the essay because it may lead the reader to think that the "railroad" was an actual train with passengers who were escaping slaves.

2. The underlined sentence should be
    F. left unchanged.
    G. replaced with "A few unscrupulous individuals betrayed the Underground Railroad and returned slaves to the South."
    H. replaced with "Many escaped slaves settled in Ontario, Canada."
    J. DELETED.

3. The underlined sentence should be
    A. deleted because it states that the Underground Railroad was not important.
    B. deleted because it focuses on only one period of the Underground Railroad.
    C. left where it is because it helps the reader to assess the importance of the Underground Railroad.
    D. left where it is because it develops the analogy between a railroad and the escape network.

4. The underlined sentence should be
    F. left unchanged because it contains the writer's evaluation of the significance of the Underground Railroad.
    G. left unchanged because it provides a transition to a new paragraph discussing the causes of the Civil War.
    H. deleted because it helps to explain the underlying economic conditions that led to the establishment of slavery.
    J. deleted because it fails to mention the Underground Railroad by name.

Questions 5-10

Early Settlers in Olympic National Park

   About 12,000 years ago, the vast continental glaciers that had covered large parts of North America were melting. As they retreated, they left behind rounded hills and marshy meadows in what is now known as Olympic National Park in Washington State. <u>Although Olympia is the capital of Washington, the largest city in Washington is Seattle.</u> There were no dense forests yet. Elk, bison, wolves, and even larger animals roamed the land, and humans roamed with them.

   In 1977, a farmer digging a pond just outside Olympic National Park unearthed remains of a mastodon. <u>(The mastodon was a huge elephant-like mammal that grazed Ice Age grasslands.)</u> A broken piece of antler resembling a spear point was embedded in one of the mastodon's ribs. The spear point is the earliest evidence of human presence in this region, and proof that the residents 12,000 years ago were hunters.

   Hunter and gatherer groups followed the early big game hunters. From 3,000 to 10,000 years ago, they hunted deer and elk and gathered plants to survive. <u>Today's big game hunters like to go after moose and bighorn sheep as well.</u> Their stone tools, left across the peninsula, show that they spread across the rugged terrain of the entire Olympic ecosystem.

   By about 3,000 years ago, as the human population increased, early inhabitants shifted their focus to lowland rivers and lakes. Fishing, hunting sea mammals, and gathering shellfish formed the foundation of rich and complex maritime cultures for which the Pacific Northwest is known. <u>Other examples of maritime peoples include the Vikings and the Romans.</u>

   <u>The maritime peoples also relied extensively on the surrounding forests for food, fibers, medicine, and shelter.</u> They used red cedar trunks to build longhouses

UNIT 1 | TOPIC DEVELOPMENT • 19

as shelter from the relentless rain and canoes for hunting seals and whales. They made baskets, clothing, tools, and bentwood boxes for cooking and storage. The skilled workmanship of the artifacts reveals the intimate connection between the artisans, the land, and the sea.

Archaeological sites have yielded thousands of wood, shell, and bone artifacts that helped modern scholars piece together a picture of the inhabitants over time. <u>The evidence shows that the region was first inhabited by big game hunters, then hunter-gatherers, and finally a maritime people with a rich and varied culture.</u>
10

5. The underlined sentence should be

   A. deleted because it is not relevant to the discussion of the early inhabitants of the region.
   B. deleted because the size comparison belongs in the final paragraph, not the first paragraph.
   C. left unchanged because both Olympia and Seattle are cities that now have large populations.
   D. left unchanged because the reader learns how the maritime peoples established cities.

6. The underlined sentence should be

   F. deleted because the mastodon is only one of the animals mentioned in the passage.
   G. deleted because the evidence does not prove that the mastodon was killed by a spear.
   H. left unchanged because the sentence ensures that the reader understands that a mastodon was a large animal.
   J. left unchanged because the mention will encourage tourists to visit the region.

7. The underlined sentence should be

   A. left unchanged because it mentions other animals that are considered big game.
   B. left unchanged because it mentions animals that were not alive in the Ice Age.
   C. deleted because it mentions animals that may not be familiar to the average reader.
   D. deleted because it is not relevant to the time period that is discussed in the essay.

8. The underlined sentence should be

   F. left unchanged because the Vikings and the Romans are historically important peoples.
   G. left unchanged because it creates a comparison between the early inhabitants of Washington State and those of Scandinavia and Italy.
   H. deleted because the focus of the essay is the inhabitants of Washington State.
   J. deleted because Viking and Roman cultures were not thriving 3,000 years ago.

9. The underlined sentence should be

   A. deleted because it repeats the information that comes immediately after it.
   B. deleted because forests are mentioned in connection with only one of the three groups discussed.
   C. left unchanged because the writer is explaining why it is important to conserve natural resources.
   D. left unchanged because it describes the lifestyle of the third group of inhabitants discussed by the writer.

10. The underlined sentence should be

    F. left unchanged because it summarizes the development of the passage.
    G. left unchanged because Olympic National Park is an important archaeological site.
    H. deleted because big-game hunting and gathering are discussed much earlier in the passage.
    J. deleted because the evidence does not provide a complete picture of the cultures of the inhabitants.

UNIT 1 | TOPIC DEVELOPMENT • 21

Questions 11–16

Albert Einstein

It took six minutes and fifty-one seconds for Albert Einstein to become world famous. That's how long the solar eclipse of May 29, 1919, lasted. <u>Every couple of years, there is a total solar eclipse.</u>
11

Success did not come easily to Einstein. He did not receive any job offers upon graduating from college in 1900, and even after publishing the papers that laid the foundations for special relativity and deriving $E = mc^2$, it took him four more years to find work as a physicist.

Einstein was also personally dissatisfied with his scientific work. His 1905 paper on special relativity had unified Galileo's laws of motion and Maxwell's laws of electricity and magnetism, but Newton's theory of gravity had resisted integration. Einstein labored for another decade to solve the problem of gravity. <u>Even then, critics complained that there was no proof that it corresponded to reality.</u>
12

So Einstein proposed a way for scientists to test his theory. Relativity predicts that gravity should bend light. As a result, light from distant stars should curve as it passes by the sun. This, in turn, would make the stars' positions in the sky appear shifted compared with their true positions. <u>Of course, the sun's brightness makes this shift impossible to observe because the stars can't be seen during the day.</u>
13

Einstein proposed that the stars be observed during an eclipse, when stars could peek out from behind the sun's shadow.

In May 1919, English astronomer Arthur Eddington set up telescopes and cameras on Príncipe, an island off western Africa. <u>World War I had just ended, and the idea of spending British money to test a German scientist's theories upset some people.</u> Rain almost ruined the experiment, but just an hour before the eclipse, the
14

22 • ENGLISH PRODUCTION OF WRITING

clouds lifted. Eddington scrambled to take sixteen pictures, and only two were useful. Nevertheless, they revealed enough: the stars had shifted!

Newspapers worldwide jumped on the story, running headlines such as, "REVOLUTION IN SCIENCE—NEW THEORY OF THE UNIVERSE," "LIGHT ALL ASKEW IN THE HEAVENS," and "MEN OF SCIENCE MORE OR LESS AGOG." <u>Later that year, newspaper headlines announced that the 1919 World Series had been fixed.</u>
[15]

Even those who couldn't grasp relativity's nuances knew that Einstein had rewritten the fundamentals of science. From that day on, Einstein became the world's most prominent symbol of genius. <u>Even today "Einstein" is used to refer to someone considered extremely smart.</u>
[16]

11. The underlined sentence should be

A. deleted because the essay focuses only on the particular eclipse used to test Einstein's theory.
B. deleted because the writer should be more precise in a paper that deals with a scientific topic.
C. left unchanged because some readers will wonder about the frequency of solar eclipses.
D. left unchanged because the essay discusses the conditions causing a solar eclipse.

12. The underlined sentence should be

F. deleted because it contains negative information about Einstein.
G. deleted because the critics were ultimately proved wrong.
H. left unchanged because it explains the need for the experiment.
J. left unchanged because Einstein had not yet achieved fame.

13. The underlined sentence should be

A. deleted because it is unnecessarily complex and may cause confusion.
B. deleted because the passage is about relativity and not the stars.
C. left unchanged because the main focus of the passage is solar eclipses.
D. left unchanged because it tells the reader why the experiment was important.

UNIT 1 | TOPIC DEVELOPMENT • 23

14. The underlined sentence should be

F. deleted because the attitudes mentioned were not relevant to the scientific facts discovered.
G. deleted because attitudes immediately following a war are likely to be exaggerated.
H. left unchanged because it explains why Eddington chose the location.
J. left unchanged because it provides an interesting detail about the experiment.

15. The underlined sentence should be

A. deleted because it doesn't contribute anything to the description of the success of the experiment.
B. deleted because newspaper headlines can be misleading.
C. left unchanged because it contrasts scientists and corrupt sports officials.
D. left unchanged because it provides historical context.

16. The underlined sentence should be

F. deleted because most people already know that Einstein was a genius.
G. deleted because Einstein's intelligence is not questioned in the essay.
H. left unchanged because it dramatizes the point that the experiment brought Einstein fame.
J. left unchanged because the essay is a tribute to Einstein.

24 • ENGLISH PRODUCTION OF WRITING

Questions 17–20

A Medical Mystery

In 1918, dozens of sick passengers and sailors arrived aboard ships coming into the Port of New York City, and on September 12, the port was put under quarantine. Despite the quarantine, in a few weeks it became clear that New York and other parts of the northeastern United States were moving toward an influenza epidemic.

In New York, health officials worked to prevent the spread of contagion by separating healthy New Yorkers from those who were infected. A large-scale health education campaign began. Schools and theaters were regulated, and health measures, such as those prohibiting spitting, were adopted. <u>Some of the new</u>

17

<u>measures were compulsory but others were only voluntary.</u>

17

In Boston, the health commissioner closed the public schools, theaters, and dance halls, but so many people were sick that makeshift hospitals had to be built to accommodate them. <u>Even then, there was an acute shortage of civilian medical</u>

18

<u>personnel because many doctors and nurses had been called up to serve in the war.</u>

18

Military installations were also crippled by sickness and death. At Camp Devens, about thirty-five miles from Boston, the Army was training men for the war in Europe. Inexplicably, the disease was more devastating to people between twenty and forty, a group that does not generally die of flu as readily as the very young and old, so Camp Devens was devastated by the disease. <u>William Henry Welch, a</u>

19

<u>pathologist from Johns Hopkins, was asked to help find a solution.</u>

19

Approximately 675,000 people died of flu or pneumonia in the United States in the fall of 1918 and the winter of 1919. Globally, fifty million people or more succumbed during the pandemic. <u>Today, there is fear that H1N1 could become as</u>

20

<u>deadly as the 1918 pandemic.</u> The doctors of the time were still working with a

20

UNIT 1 | TOPIC DEVELOPMENT • 25

fairly primitive germ theory; they had no idea they were fighting a virus. Their vaccines were useless. The influenza pandemic that swept the globe in 1918 was the most acute crisis handled by public health officials in modern times.

17. The underlined sentence should be

A. left unchanged because it explains the working of the health regulations.
B. left unchanged because it explores how the flu virus reached New York.
C. deleted because it is so general that it does not add any information to the essay.
D. deleted because it fails to address the problems of the city of Boston.

18. The underlined sentence should be

F. deleted because the fact that a war was being fought was not relevant to the problem of the epidemic.
G. deleted because it fails to specify how many doctors and nurses were assigned to the war effort.
H. left unchanged because it is expected that a war will require both doctors and nurses to treat wounded.
J. left unchanged because it helps to explain why the epidemic was difficult to control.

19. The underlined sentence should be

A. deleted because the reference to William Henry Welch does not help to explain why the flu epidemic was so devastating.
B. deleted because many health care professionals were involved in fighting the flu epidemic.
C. left unchanged because the mention of a pathologist is needed to show the reader that the flu was a medical problem.
D. left unchanged because the writer points out that the disease mostly affected the strong.

20. The underlined sentence should be

F. deleted because the threat of a modern epidemic is not relevant to the discussion of the influenza epidemic of 1918.
G. deleted because the possibility of a modern epidemic has not yet become a reality.
H. left unchanged because it underscores the loss of life during the flu epidemic of 1918.
J. left unchanged because it helps modern scientists understand the urgency of treating H1N1.

English **Production of Writing**

Unit 2 | **Transition Words and Phrases**

INSIDE THIS UNIT:
– What Is a Conjunctive Adverb? – – Table of Conjunctive Adverbs – – Getting It Right – – Exercise –

Non-Negotiable Skill:

Use conjunctive adverbs to express the proper order, sequence of events, or logical connection between clauses or sentences.

What Is a Conjunctive Adverb?

A **conjunctive adverb** is a combination of a conjunction and an adverb. Like a conjunction (*and, but, since, while*, etc.), it joins clauses (a group of related words containing a subject and a verb) or sentences. And like an adverb (*carelessly, gladly, peacefully, slowly*, etc.), it modifies a verb.

The most important functions of conjunctive adverbs are to show a connection between clauses or sentences and to help explain how the ideas expressed are connected to each other in terms of order or sequence.

Examples of Conjunctive Adverbs:

In the basketball play called the "give and go," you pass the ball to a teammate, *then* you break for the basket.

Initially we thought Ellen went to study in the library; *later,* we found out she was in the cafeteria.

The team scored early but fell behind in the middle innings. *Finally*, they won in extra innings on a grand slam homer.

Ask Marvin to put the hamburgers on the grill. *Meanwhile*, I'll make the potato salad.

In each example the conjunctive adverb joins two clauses or sentences and tells you the order or sequence of the events.

Table of Conjunctive Adverbs

CONJUNCTIVE ADVERBS (showing order or time)		
additionally after afterwards again before elsewhere finally further furthermore generally	in addition instead just as meanwhile moreover next now once otherwise prior to rather	so sometimes soon still subsequently then thereafter usually while yet

Here are some sample sentences to illustrate the use of common conjunctive adverbs:

additionally
> We each had a salad, and all of us ate the chicken dish. *Additionally*, some of us had dessert.

after
> The principal led the school in the Pledge of Allegiance. *After* the pledge, the graduating class
> received their diplomas.

afterwards
> We had a big pep rally in the gym. *Afterwards*, some of us went to the park to play some football.

again
> Twenty years ago, we fought a war to maintain the freedoms our grandparents had bestowed upon us. *Again*, we find ourselves facing an enemy who can take away what we hold dear.

before
> The team is scheduled to play in an exhibition game against Sothby High. *Before* that, there is one more regular game to be played.

finally
> Jamal chose a topic for his paper. He went to the library, where he read articles and a book and did research on the web. *Finally*, he sat down to write.

further
> An average student does most of the homework assignment. A good student does all of it. A really good student goes *further* and does the extra-credit assignment.

generally
> *Generally*, we go straight from English class to lunch, but yesterday we had an assembly.

in addition
> The tour includes the firing range and the mess hall, but, *in addition,* we'll get to take a ride in a Humvee.

instead
> I like the burger combination the best, but I think I'll order the fish sandwich *instead*.

just as
> *Just as* the band was finishing its first set, there was a loud pop, and the arena went completely dark.

meanwhile
> Jose will go to the grocery store and pick up some snacks, and Tyra will get some sodas. *Meanwhile*, I'll set up the table and chairs on the lawn.

next
> First, I'll take out the garbage. *Next*, I'll sweep the kitchen. If there's any time left over, I'm going to relax.

now
> I've been working hard since early this morning. *Now* I'm going to take a break.

otherwise
> If the weather is good this weekend, we'll go to the baseball game. *Otherwise*, we'll go to the movies.

UNIT 2 | TRANSITION WORDS AND PHRASES • 31

prior to

Once everyone was seated, the program began. *Prior to* announcing the winner of the essay contest, the mayor thanked all of the students who had submitted entries.

rather

Most of my friends will be going away to college. I'd *rather* live at home for my first two years and then transfer.

sometimes

The practices usually last 90 minutes. *Sometimes* the coach lets the players go early.

soon

My older sister has been in the Gulf region for two years. *Soon* she'll be coming home and getting out of the service.

still

The champ has taken some punishment during this round, but he's *still* on his feet and fighting back.

subsequently

Bart was suspended from school twice during the first semester. He was *subsequently* expelled for good when he committed a third infraction.

then

You have to remove the shells; *then* you roast the peanuts.

thereafter

Students are required to finish the test. *Thereafter*, they are free to leave the classroom quietly.

usually

The bus *usually* runs every ten minutes during the day. Today, it seems to be running late.

while

While Calvin was in front of the school meeting people and shaking hands, Ann was alone in the classroom working on her speech.

yet

Oh, say does that star-spangled banner *yet* wave?

Getting It Right

Conjunctive adverbs can help a reader understand the order of events, but you want to be sure to choose a word or phrase that has the right meaning.

Examples:

Thirty-five years ago, home computers were toys for playing primitive video games. *Then*, everyone uses them for a variety of daily tasks, such as writing and doing research. **(Incorrect.)**

Thirty-five years ago, home computers were toys for playing primitive video games. *Now*, everyone uses them for a variety of daily tasks, such as writing and doing research. **(Correct.)**

In the story, the two students met when they were only seventeen. They married five years *before*. **(Incorrect.)**

In the story, the two students met when they were only seventeen. They married five years *later*. **(Correct.)**

Hussein applied a pressure bandage to control the bleeding; *first*, Hannah dialed 9-1-1 for an ambulance. **(Incorrect.)**

Hussein applied a pressure bandage to control the bleeding; *meanwhile*, Hannah dialed 9-1-1 for an ambulance. **(Correct.)**

Using a conjunctive adverb is often a good idea, but it is important to use one that communicates the right meaning. Everything depends on choosing a word or phrase that expresses the proper order or sequence of events.

Summary

- A conjunctive adverb, which is a combination of a conjunction and an adverb, joins clauses or sentences and modifies a verb.

- Conjunctive adverbs show a connection between clauses or sentences and help to explain how ideas are connected to each other in terms of order or sequence.

UNIT 2 | TRANSITION WORDS AND PHRASES • 33

EXERCISE

DIRECTIONS: In each of the following items, a word or phrase is underlined. Following each sentence or sentences are alternative suggestions for rewriting the underlined part. If you think the original is correct, choose NO CHANGE. Otherwise, choose the best alternative. Answers are on page 746.

Example:

First you sand the surface until it's smooth; <u>meanwhile</u> you apply the new coat of paint.

A. NO CHANGE
B. once
C. initially
D. then

The correct answer is (D).

1. <u>For a long time</u>, my older sister thought she wanted to become a lawyer, but she finally decided to be a doctor instead.

   A. NO CHANGE
   B. Before long
   C. Until then
   D. At last

2. <u>Eventually</u>, the police suspected a thief had taken the diamond from the desk. Later, they found the jewel in a small crack in the bottom of the drawer.

   F. NO CHANGE
   G. One night
   H. At first
   J. Recently

3. Frederick Douglass escaped from slavery in 1838. He <u>later</u> chose his new, free name from the novel *Lady of the Lake*.

   A. NO CHANGE
   B. once
   C. one time
   D. ever after

34 • ENGLISH PRODUCTION OF WRITING

4. We came to a fork in the road with no sign and didn't know which way to go. By using a compass and a map, we <u>suddenly</u> were able to figure out which direction was east and took the right road.

F. NO CHANGE
G. usually
H. eventually
J. first

5. Lawn mowers and other gasoline-powered machinery can be very dangerous. Be sure that before operating them you <u>finally</u> put on goggles and protective clothing.

A. NO CHANGE
B. then
C. afterward
D. first

6. After an hour of hard work, we were finished stacking the hay bales in the loft of the barn; <u>during that time</u>, the farmer told us we were supposed to load them on the wagon.

F. NO CHANGE
G. afterward
H. for once
J. each time

7. The thunderstorm was very brief, and <u>all the while</u> we were enjoying the bright sunshine and warm breeze.

A. NO CHANGE
B. forever
C. soon
D. some day

8. Several years after Clara died, the museum presented an exhibit of her paintings; so <u>today</u>, people were able to see the genius in her work.

F. NO CHANGE
G. one time
H. forever
J. at last

9. Early in his career, the composer Donizetti was influenced by Rossini's operas, but <u>before</u> he developed his own style.

A. NO CHANGE
B. once
C. occasionally
D. later

UNIT 2 | TRANSITION WORDS AND PHRASES • 35

10. <u>As soon as</u> the linemen realized that handoff was a fake; but by then, the quarterback had completed a pass to a receiver in the end zone.

   F. NO CHANGE
   G. Eventually
   H. Once
   J. At first

11. In July, the ground was dry and hard; a few days <u>since</u>, the heavy rains produced a carpet of green.

   A. NO CHANGE
   B. before
   C. later
   D. past

12. When the plane was 300 miles from the coast, the captain sent an emergency message. Two hours <u>before</u>, the fuel tanks were completely empty, and the crew crash-landed in a pasture just five miles from the shore.

   F. NO CHANGE
   G. later
   H. since
   J. beforehand

13. East Side lost the final game; <u>still</u>, the team's record was so good that the team continued to lead the league.

   A. NO CHANGE
   B. next
   C. once
   D. afterward

14. It was clear that the roller coaster was everyone's favorite ride; <u>as soon as</u> it was over, we got in line to ride it again.

   F. NO CHANGE
   G. then
   H. next
   J. initially

15. I met Eleanor only once, for dinner; <u>every evening</u>, she was wearing a scarf over her henna-red hair.

   A. NO CHANGE
   B. every time
   C. that evening
   D. since evening

36 • ENGLISH PRODUCTION OF WRITING

16. <u>Long before</u> the Spanish colonized the New World, the Pre-Columbian inhabitants had built elaborate civilizations with truly impressive achievements.

    F. NO CHANGE
    G. Before long
    H. Then
    J. At last

17. For the science fair, we <u>once</u> made a small track using clear plastic tubing, then we marked the distances using a marking pen, and finally we rolled the marble through the tubing making notes of the time it passed each distance mark.

    A. NO CHANGE
    B. eventually
    C. first
    D. lastly

18. It was a warm summer's evening, and we watched the full moon rise over the mountains in the east. <u>Next</u>, the fireflies were flickering in the trees.

    F. NO CHANGE
    G. Evermore
    H. All the while
    J. Ultimately

19. The number of contestants was reduced to only eight; <u>at the same time</u>, they each performed a final dance number for the judge.

    A. NO CHANGE
    B. in turn
    C. once in a while
    D. initially

20. At first, the parties couldn't agree on some of the key provisions; <u>before that</u>, they all signed the document and shook hands.

    F. NO CHANGE
    G. in the end
    H. generally
    J. in the past

21. For a real Chesapeake crab boil, pour spices into a big pot of water. Let it come to a vigorous boil for at least 10 minutes. <u>Sometimes</u>, add the crabs.

    A. NO CHANGE
    B. Then
    C. Suddenly
    D. In a minute

UNIT 2 | TRANSITION WORDS AND PHRASES • 37

22. The Republicans are worried that they will lose the governor's race this fall; <u>before that</u>, the Democrats are hoping to win the Senate seat.

    F. NO CHANGE
    G. meanwhile
    H. as long as
    J. one year

23. The referees spent 10 minutes reviewing the video tape of the challenged play; <u>still</u>, the call on the field was overruled.

    A. NO CHANGE
    B. second
    C. ultimately
    D. instead

24. Auctions are fascinating. I watched a bidding war between a grandmotherly woman in a print dress and a man who looked like a Wall Street tycoon. She bid; he bid more; she bid more; he bid again; and she bid even more. <u>Secondly</u>, she won. The winning bid was $12 for an old glass milk bottle.

    F. NO CHANGE
    G. Once more
    H. Then again
    J. In the end

25. Last autumn, we took a ride in a hot air balloon. We floated over pastures and farms, villages with homes, and even a college. The trip lasted almost two hours, and we were disappointed that it had to end. <u>Immediately</u>, we had a bird's eye view of the world.

    A. NO CHANGE
    B. In a moment
    C. Before that
    D. For a while

English **Production of Writing**

Unit 3 | **Practice**

INSIDE THIS UNIT:
– Exercise –

40 • ENGLISH PRODUCTION OF WRITING

EXERCISE

DIRECTIONS: In each of the following passages, sentences are underlined and numbered. For each of the corresponding items, select the answer that BEST answers the question. Answers are on page 746.

Questions 1–5

How Racing Pigeons Navigate

Pigeon racing is a big sport that dates back almost 2,000 years. All over the world, hobbyists train and race a special kind of homing pigeon. They take their caged pigeons to a spot that is a carefully measured distance from their home. Then they open the cages and time how long it takes for the pigeons to fly home. The pigeon with the shortest time wins the prize—or rather its owner wins the prize. The pigeon gets tired, since it has flown as fast as it could for 600 miles or more!

1

But how do the pigeons know where home is? Scientists have studied this

2

phenomenon extensively, but some questions are still unanswered. One thing that

2

seems certain is that the pigeons can detect Earth's magnetic field lines. Earth is like a big magnet, with lines of magnetic force that loop around Earth from one magnetic pole to the other. A compass needle will line up along the magnetic lines of force. That's how humans can know which way is north. The pigeons seem to have a

3

compass too, but it is "built in," so they always know in which direction they are flying.

We know they are not navigating by the position of the sun in the sky, because they fly straight home even at night or in cloudy conditions when they can't see the sun. While the pigeons don't use the sun for navigation, the sun does affect their ability to navigate. When the sun is in a stormy mood, it blasts charged particles into space at high speeds. If the blast of particles hits Earth, it shakes up Earth's protective magnetic field. When this happens, the magnetic field that the pigeons use for navigation will change direction and the pigeons' navigation system will get

confused and send the pigeon the wrong way. <u>The anxious owner may never see his</u>
<u>4</u>

<u>expensive champion racing pigeon again.</u>
4

For that reason, some pigeon racers contact the Space Weather Prediction Center before a big race to learn the "space weather" forecast. <u>The Space Weather</u>
<u>5</u>

<u>Prediction Center is part of the National Weather Service in Boulder, Colorado.</u> The
5

scientists who work at the center keep an eye on the sun using satellites with special instruments that monitor the sun's x-rays and ultraviolet light output. They can detect the beginnings of a storm that might send bad space weather toward Earth. If bad space weather is on the way, the pigeon race is postponed. No one wants to lose a prized pigeon!

1. The underlined sentence should be

  A. deleted because it is not directly related to the mechanism by which pigeons navigate.

  B. deleted because it makes a statement that should be obvious to the reader.

  C. left unchanged because it provides a statistic about pigeon racing.

  D. left unchanged because it could be used to introduce information about the number of pigeons that are raced.

2. The underlined sentence should be

  F. deleted because it states that the way pigeons navigate is not fully understood by scientists.

  G. deleted because it introduces some specific questions about pigeon racing that the writer will answer.

  H. left unchanged because it states the writer's position that science has only partial and not complete answers about pigeon navigation.

  J. left unchanged because it decreases the reader's confidence in the accuracy of scientific studies.

ENGLISH PRODUCTION OF WRITING

3. The underlined sentence should be

A. deleted because it refers to humans, not pigeons.
B. deleted because pigeons feel the earth's magnetic field.
C. left unchanged because it clarifies the idea of a "built in" compass.
D. left unchanged because it shows that humans are more advanced than pigeons.

4. The underlined sentence should be

F. deleted because the passage does not discuss in detail the cost of racing pigeons.
G. deleted because it overlooks the possibility that the pigeon may eventually return home.
H. left unchanged because it shows that the owners of racing pigeons care for them deeply.
J. left unchanged because it illustrates the extent of the navigational interference caused by the sun.

5. The underlined sentence should be

A. left unchanged because the weather is an important factor in pigeon navigation.
B. left unchanged because the government is the official source for weather information.
C. deleted because a forecast is sometimes wrong.
D. deleted because the geographical location of the center is not relevant to the navigation mechanism.

Questions 6–10

Water Produces Electricity

When you look at rushing waterfalls and rivers, you may not immediately think of electricity. But hydroelectric (water-powered) power plants are responsible for lighting many of our homes and neighborhoods. On September 30, 1882, the world's first hydroelectric power plant began operation on the Fox River in Appleton, Wisconsin. <u>The plant, later named the Appleton Edison Light Company, was initiated</u>

6

<u>by Appleton paper manufacturer H.J. Rogers, who had been inspired by Thomas</u>

6

<u>Edison's plans for an electricity-producing station in New York. Unlike Edison's</u>

6

<u>New York plant, which used steam power to drive its generators, the Appleton</u>

6

<u>plant used the natural energy of the Fox River.</u> When the plant opened, it produced

6

enough electricity to light Rogers' home, the plant itself, and a nearby building. Hydroelectric power plants today generate a lot more electricity. By the early twentieth century, these plants produced a significant portion of the country's electric energy. <u>The cheap electricity provided by the plants spurred industrial</u>

7

<u>growth in many regions of the country.</u>

7

To get even more power out of the flowing water, the government started building dams. <u>In 1933, the US government established the Tennessee Valley</u>

8

<u>Authority (TVA), which introduced hydroelectric power plants to the South's</u>

8

<u>troubled Tennessee River Valley. The TVA built dams, managed flood control and</u>

8

<u>soil conservation programs, and more. It greatly boosted the region's economy. This</u>

8

<u>development happened in other places as well.</u> Soon, people across the country

8

were enjoying electricity in homes, schools, and offices. <u>Before then, people had</u>

9

<u>been forced to read by candlelight or kerosene lamps.</u> New electricity-powered

9

44 • ENGLISH PRODUCTION OF WRITING

technologies entered American homes, including electric refrigerators and stoves, radios, televisions, and can openers. Today, people take electricity for granted. <u>One day, we may actually travel to distant planets in our own personal spacecraft.</u>
10

6. The underlined selection should be

F. left unchanged because it provides the reader with a contrast to show that hydroelectric power was an important development.
G. left unchanged because it mentions that the Appleton plant used a natural source of energy to produce electricity.
H. deleted because steam-powered electric plants are not discussed in detail in the passage.
J. deleted because steam-powered generators were already in use when hydroelectric power was introduced.

7. The underlined sentence should be

A. left unchanged because it shows the economic state of the country.
B. left unchanged because it shows that industrial growth is important.
C. deleted because the focus of the passage is hydroelectric power, not industry.
D. deleted because the writer does not show that hydroelectric power is cheap.

8. The discussion of the Tennessee Valley Authority in the final paragraph should be

F. left in the passage because it shows the effect the government has on the environment.
G. left in the passage because dams are important in soil conservation and other environmental projects.
H. deleted because other hydroelectric dams and projects are not mentioned by name.
J. deleted because the dam projects were not built just for hydroelectric power.

9. The underlined sentence should be

A. left unchanged because it provides a clear contrast to show the advances of electricity.
B. left unchanged because it discusses the history of science and technology.
C. deleted because it refers to candlelight and kerosene devices, not electrical appliances.
D. deleted because it doesn't refer specifically to people living in the Tennessee Valley region.

10. The underlined sentence should be

    F. left unchanged because the passage talks about important advances in technology.

    G. left unchanged because it suggests that the reader should do further reading on electricity.

    H. deleted because the passage discusses electricity, not space travel.

    J. deleted because it refers to events that belong to the distant future.

Questions 11–15

Across Country Cheaply by Car

[1]

It used to be that if you wanted to travel, you had to plan for a long stagecoach or train ride, but the automobile changed all that. Although at first considered a luxury, the car quickly became an American necessity. Between 1908 and 1926,

                                             11

Ford Motor Company sold more than 15 million Model T automobiles.
                       11

[2]

Almost from the beginning, people liked to use their cars to go on vacation. Gas

                                           12

was cheap and traveling by car was an affordable way to see the country. With so
                       12

many people taking to the road, the United States had to create a national highway system to support all that traffic. Gas stations began to dot the scenery. An increased demand for rubber tires caused the rubber industry to flourish. Roadside diners and drive-ins catered to auto tourists.

[3]

People also needed information on interesting places to visit and how to reach them, so road atlases and travel guides were developed. *Popular Mechanics Auto Tourist Magazine* was first published in 1924. It offered suggestions on everything 13 from camping equipment to car repairs to portable radios.

[4]

In the early days of car travel, people often went "autocamping." Mainly they camped outdoors in parks. But even in the days before trailers and Winnebagos, some people turned their cars into mobile homes. Eventually, motels, or "motor hotels," sprang up along the highways that crisscrossed the country. 14

[5]

Families with cars could go places far from where they lived. If a family lived in a warm area, they could pack up the car and go to the mountains to ski; if they lived in a cold place, they could drive to the beach. Cars made it possible to do what had 15 not been easy for most people before: explore America affordably on their own 15 schedules.
15

11. The underlined sentence should be

A. deleted because the passage is not discussing automobile manufacturing.

B. deleted because the reference is restricted to a limited time period.

C. left unchanged because it shows the rapid growth in automobile usage.

D. left unchanged because the practice of identifying automobiles by state-issued license plate originated in Massachusetts in 1903.

12. The underlined sentence should be

F. deleted because the price of gasoline today is much higher than 75 or 100 years ago.

G. deleted because it talks about sightseeing trips rather than regular automobile usage.

H. left unchanged because many people today use airplanes for vacation travel.

J. left unchanged because it helps to explain why automobile travel was popular.

13. The underlined sentence should be

A. left unchanged because it cites a timely example to show the growth of automobile travel.
B. left unchanged because it cites an authority on the history of the automobile.
C. deleted because the date of first publication of the magazine is not relevant to the history of automobile travel.
D. deleted because the writer does not discuss other publications devoted to automobiles.

14. The fourth paragraph should be

F. left unchanged because it describes an important way of traveling cheaply by car.
G. left unchanged because it could interest the reader in camping.
H. deleted because "autocamping" has been replaced by travel in recreational vehicles.
J. deleted because it doesn't help to explain why people traveled by car.

15. The underlined sentence should be

A. left unchanged because it summarizes the development of the passage.
B. left unchanged because it shows that Americans are price-conscious.
C. deleted because automobiles were used for purposes other than vacation travel.
D. deleted because it fails to state how many people traveled by automobile.

48 • ENGLISH PRODUCTION OF WRITING

DIRECTIONS: In each of the following items, a word or phrase is underlined. Following each sentence or sentences are alternative suggestions for rewriting the underlined part. If you think the original is correct, choose NO CHANGE. Otherwise, choose the best alternative. Answers are on page 746.

Example:

First, you sand the surface until it's smooth; <u>meanwhile</u>, you apply the new coat of paint.

A. NO CHANGE
B. once
C. initially
D. then

The correct answer is (D).

---

16. One hundred and fifty runners started the race; five miles <u>then</u>, only twenty-five remained.

F. NO CHANGE
G. before
H. more
J. later

17. First, we need to pick about three quarts of strawberries. <u>At the same time</u>, we will buy some stalks of rhubarb.

A. NO CHANGE
B. Later
C. Once
D. Sometimes

18. Ted Williams played for the Boston Red Sox from 1939 to 1960. <u>Afterward</u>, he managed the Washington Senators from 1969 until 1972.

F. NO CHANGE
G. At long last
H. All the while
J. Before long

19. The rain fell for several hours. <u>At first</u>, the sky cleared, and we saw a beautiful rainbow.

A. NO CHANGE
B. Meanwhile
C. Before then
D. At last

UNIT 3 | PRACTICE • 49

20. If you heat a solid to a high enough temperature, it will <u>once</u> melt and form a liquid.

   F. NO CHANGE
   G. at last
   H. until then
   J. so far

21. A star does not live on forever. <u>Then</u> it will consume the last of its fuel and die out.

   A. NO CHANGE
   B. Next
   C. Afterward
   D. Eventually

22. When we moved into our apartment, it was very dark. We cleaned everything and repainted. <u>So next</u>, it is bright and cheery.

   F. NO CHANGE
   G. So then
   H. So now
   J. In the beginning

23. Once called Ceylon, the island nation off the tip of southern India is <u>today</u> known as Sri Lanka.

   A. NO CHANGE
   B. afterwards
   C. beforehand
   D. still

24. Every July my family packs up and goes to the beach for a whole week. It's almost always great fun, but I remember that <u>for a year</u> it rained every day we were there.

   F. NO CHANGE
   G. yearly
   H. year in and year out
   J. one year

25. The Fourth of July parade was the biggest and best ever in our town. <u>At the time of</u> the color guard, we had a drum and bugle corps, a Marine Corps rifle drill team, and eight floats.

   A. NO CHANGE
   B. Following
   C. Once
   D. Then

26. The steam piston engine played a major role in the Industrial Revolution. <u>Today</u>, we use more efficient devices such as the steam turbine and the internal combustion machine.

   F. NO CHANGE
   G. Following that
   H. Over the years
   J. After a while

50 • ENGLISH PRODUCTION OF WRITING

27. According to Greek mythology, the Greeks laid siege to Troy for nine years. The Greeks <u>next</u> won the war by pretending to withdraw, leaving behind a hollow wooden horse filled with soldiers who attacked once inside the city walls.

   A. NO CHANGE
   B. eventually
   C. first
   D. occasionally

28. Where I live, corn is planted just before the end of May, when the danger of frost has passed. Once the plants are up and have been fertilized, there's nothing more to be done <u>during</u> the fall when the corn is harvested.

   F. NO CHANGE
   G. after
   H. before
   J. until

29. Have you ever watched a robin? It hops a few feet, and then it stops and cocks its head. <u>At that point</u>, it is waiting for tiny vibrations in the ground to tell it that it has found a worm or an insect. It continues in this way until it has found its lunch.

   A. NO CHANGE
   B. Again
   C. Originally
   D. Lastly

30. All summer long, we watched the watermelons growing in our neighbor's garden. <u>The following</u> night we slipped over the fence and stole the biggest one we could find.

   F. NO CHANGE
   G. One
   H. At
   J. Every

English **Knowledge of Language**

Unit 4 | **Clarity in Sentences**

INSIDE THIS UNIT:
– Arrangement of Sentence Elements – – Avoid Awkward and Confusing Sentences – – Exercise –

Non-Negotiable Skill:

Change sentence order, adverbs,
or modifiers to improve clarity.

According to Herodotus, the ancient Greek historian, Croesus, who was the king of Lydia from about 560 BCE to 546 BCE, was worried that the Persians, led by Cyrus the Great, were a military threat to his kingdom. He was debating whether to launch a preemptive attack on the Persians. In addition to consulting his other advisors, Croesus put the question to the Oracle at Delphi. When asked by Croesus what he should do, the Oracle responded, "If you go to war, a mighty empire will be destroyed."

Croesus interpreted the Oracle's answer as the go-ahead and attacked. In the decisive battle, Croesus lost; Cyrus won. And it became clear that the Oracle had meant "a mighty empire—namely yours, Croesus—will be destroyed."

As would be expected, Croesus took the loss pretty hard, especially since Cyrus captured him and tried to burn him at the stake. Croesus escaped, but that's another story. The point here is that Croesus would have been spared a lot of trouble if the Oracle had spoken clearly.

The same principle is true of your writing. You need to avoid ambiguity, and that's what you'll be working on in this unit.

There are two areas that we'll be concentrating on. First, we'll see how the order of sentence elements helps to determine the meaning of a sentence. Second, we'll look at nouns and pronouns that can create misunderstandings.

Arrangement of Sentence Elements

Order Matters

Obviously, the order of the elements of a sentence is important. This sentence makes no sense:

And meal walk a large and John Ellen then took a ate.

But this version does:

John and Ellen ate a large meal and then took a walk.

So the order of the elements of the sentence is very important. Of course, no one is likely to write a bunch of gibberish. The problem of meaning is more likely to come up when the elements are pretty much in order but one or two are out of place, creating the possibility of misunderstanding.

Example:

The doctor told Janet that the test confirmed that nothing was wrong with a reassuring smile.

Most of us would probably agree that there is nothing wrong with a reassuring smile. But that is not what the speaker means to say. The speaker means to say:

With a reassuring smile, the doctor told Janet that the test confirmed that nothing was wrong.

Now the sentence makes it clear that the doctor is using the smile to reassure Janet that the test result was good.

Example:

Barbara and Ken returned yesterday from their honeymoon in a plane from Cancun, Mexico.

Not impossible but unlikely. Perhaps a newly married couple could spend their honeymoon in a plane that came from Cancun, but more than likely the speaker means that they spent their honeymoon in Cancun and returned home from there in a plane:

Barbara and Ken returned yesterday in a plane from Cancun, Mexico, where they spent their honeymoon.

Avoid Awkward and Confusing Sentences

Although there are many different ways of being unclear, three problems occur often. If you watch out for these three errors in your writing, you will catch most of your mistakes of this kind.

Certain Adverbs, Such as Only, Just, Even, Almost, and Nearly, Are Used Differently in Conversation and Writing

The rules for conversation are generally more relaxed than those for writing. When writing, you have to be more exact. There are a few words that you can be careless with in conversation because you can quickly correct any misunderstanding. But when you are writing, you have to make sure that you communicate clearly with your readers.

Example:

By hybridizing various strains of squash, the researchers almost grew a pumpkin that weighed 123 pounds.

> Did the researchers almost grow a pumpkin that weighed 123 pounds? Or did the researchers grow a pumpkin that weighed almost 123 pounds? In conversation, you can make it clear which you mean. But in writing, order makes a difference:

By hybridizing various strains of squash, the researchers grew a pumpkin that weighed almost 123 pounds.

Example:

The string section at least needs one more rehearsal before the performance on Sunday, but the rest of the orchestra is already prepared to play.

> The speaker seems to say that the string section and some other unnamed parts of the orchestra need more practice, but this statement is inconsistent with the rest of the sentence. What the speaker really means to say is:

The string section needs at least one more rehearsal before the performance on Sunday, but the rest of the orchestra is already prepared to play.

> Now the whole sentence makes sense.

Make Sure the Modifier Clearly Modifies

A modifier can be a single word, a phrase, or a dependent clause. To avoid confusion, you need to make sure that your modifier clearly refers to the words they should modify.

Example:

For her science project, Alice looked for a book on how to grow beans without success.

> The sentence implies that Alice was looking for a book that would explain how to grow beans unsuccessfully. The confusion is created by the placement of the phrase "without success" close to "how to grow beans." The ambiguity can be eliminated by rearranging the elements:

For her science project, Alice looked, without success, for a book on how to grow beans.

> Or even rewriting it:

For her science project, Alice looked for a book on how to grow beans, but she couldn't find one.

Example:

On my trip to Kenya, I saw many different kinds of animals; and one morning, I even saw an elephant in my pajamas.

> The speaker must have had a very large pair of pajamas because the sentence implies that the elephant was in the speaker's pajamas. The problem is created by placement of "in my pajamas." The proximity of the phrase to "elephant" makes it seem as though "in my pajamas" is supposed to modify "elephant." Of course, the phrase is supposed to apply to the speaker:

On my trip to Kenya, I saw many different kinds of animals; and one morning while in my pajamas, I even saw an elephant.

> The new position of the modifier makes it clear that "in my pajamas" refers to "I," the speaker, rather than the elephant.

Avoid the Dangerous Dangling Modifier

You may have heard of this grammar problem before. The phrase "dangling modifier" is used to refer to an introductory modifier that is not directly associated with a noun or pronoun that comes almost immediately after the modifier.

Example:

Trimmed to the proper size, fastened securely to the side of the building with heavy bolts, and brightly illuminated, the storeowner admired the sign that announced the opening of her new business.

> Ouch! The sentence seems to say that the storeowner was attached to the side of the building. The modifier "dangles" because it isn't really connected to the word "storeowner," so the reader has to work to figure out what the speaker means. Of course, the sentence is supposed to say that the sign, not the storeowner, was attached:

Trimmed to the proper size, fastened securely to the side of the building with heavy bolts, and brightly illuminated, the sign that announced the opening of her new business was admired by the storeowner.

> This version corrects the dangling modifier by making the first important noun following the introductory modifier the noun that the modifier is supposed to modify: sign.

> Unfortunately, even though not technically incorrect, the sentence is still somewhat awkward and should probably be completely rewritten:

The storeowner admired the sign announcing her new business; the sign had been trimmed to the proper size, fastened securely to the side of the building with heavy bolts, and brightly illuminated.

Example:

Washed, heavily starched, and steam pressed, the soldier proudly wore the full-dress uniform at the awards ceremony.

> A brave soldier indeed, for the sentence says that he was washed, then starched, and then ironed. It must have been quite painful.

> The problem with the sentence is that the first introductory modifier, "washed, starched, and pressed," seems to refer to the first important noun that follows it. But in this sentence, that noun is "soldier." So the sentence seems to be saying that the soldier was washed, starched, and pressed.

To correct the sentence, we need to move the modifier closer to what it is supposed to modify: uniform. So we might have:

At the awards ceremony, the soldier proudly wore the full-dress uniform, which had been washed, heavily starched, and steam pressed for the occasion.

Summary

When writing or revising, avoid awkward and confusing sentences by:

- Correctly using certain adverbs, such as *only, just, even, almost,* and *nearly*;

- Making sure the modifier clearly modifies; and

- Avoiding the dangling modifier (an introductory modifier that is not directly associated with the noun or pronoun that comes almost immediately after the modifier).

ENGLISH KNOWLEDGE OF LANGUAGE

EXERCISE

> **DIRECTIONS:** In each of the following items, a word or phrase is underlined. Following each sentence or sentences are alternative suggestions for rewriting the underlined part. If you think the original is correct, choose NO CHANGE. Otherwise, choose the best alternative. Answers are on page 746.

1. Cassie was <u>old enough barely</u> to remember when her family moved from the farm to the apartment in the city.

   A. NO CHANGE
   B. enough old barely
   C. barely enough old
   D. barely old enough

2. <u>Encrusted in a thick coat of sea salt and covered with ashes, we cooked the fish</u> in the hot coals until it was tender and juicy.

   F. NO CHANGE
   G. We encrusted the fish in a thick coat of sea salt, covered it with ashes, and cooked it
   H. The fish was encrusted in a thick coat of sea salt and covered with ash by us, cooking
   J. Encrusted by us in a thick coat of sea salt and covered with ashes, we cooked the fish

3. Although he had tripped the silent alarm, the robber was able to escape <u>when he saw the security guard by jumping from a second-floor window</u>.

   A. NO CHANGE
   B. when he saw the security guard jumping from a second-floor window
   C. by jumping from a second-floor window when he saw the security guard
   D. from the security guard he saw jumping from a second-floor window

4. Martin does not like to write letters, so I doubt <u>that even he will send us</u> a postcard from Tangiers.

   F. NO CHANGE
   G. even that he will send us
   H. that he even will send us
   J. that he will send us even

UNIT 4 | CLARITY IN SENTENCES • 59

5. <u>The principal congratulated the soccer team on winning the division title in the cafeteria during the lunch hour.</u>

A. NO CHANGE
B. The principal in the cafeteria congratulated the soccer team on winning the division title during the lunch hour.
C. During the lunch hour, the principal congratulated the soccer team on winning the division title in the cafeteria.
D. In the cafeteria during the lunch hour, the principal congratulated the soccer team on winning the division title.

6. <u>Waving majestically in the breeze at the top of the pole, the soldiers snapped to attention and sharply saluted the flag.</u>

F. NO CHANGE
G. The soldiers, waving majestically in the breeze at the top of the pole, snapped to attention and sharply saluted the flag.
H. The soldiers snapped to attention and sharply saluted the flag, which was waving majestically in the breeze at the top of the pole.
J. Waving majestically in the breeze at the top of the pole, a sharp salute was given by the soldiers to the flag after they snapped to attention.

7. The medical team determined that the patient's condition was critical, and <u>they persuaded the surgeon eventually to do the operation</u>.

A. NO CHANGE
B. they eventually persuaded the surgeon to do the operation
C. they persuaded the surgeon to do the operation eventually
D. the surgeon was persuaded to eventually do the operation

8. According to the law, the judge can impose a fine <u>after only the parties</u> have had an opportunity to present their case.

F. NO CHANGE
G. only after the parties
H. after the parties only
J. after the only parties

9. <u>Having read O. Henry's "The Gift of the Magi," the ending</u> wasn't a great surprise, as it was fairly obvious all along what the author had in mind.

A. NO CHANGE
B. Reading O. Henry's "The Gift of the Magi," the ending
C. While reading O. Henry's "The Gift of the Magi," the ending
D. The ending of O. Henry's "The Gift of the Magi"

60 • ENGLISH KNOWLEDGE OF LANGUAGE

10. <u>The prankster ran across the stage while the famous opera singer was performing wearing only his undershorts.</u>

   F. NO CHANGE
   G. The prankster, wearing only the famous opera singer's undershorts, ran across the stage while he was performing.
   H. The prankster, wearing only his undershorts, ran across the stage while the famous opera singer was performing.
   J. The only prankster wearing his undershorts ran across the stage while the famous opera singer was performing.

11. Arriving fashionably late and dressed in a stunning evening gown with a faux fur wrap, <u>the red ribbon was cut by the movie star opening the new bridge</u>.

   A. NO CHANGE
   B. the movie star cut the red ribbon, opening the new bridge
   C. the new bridge was opened by the movie star cutting the red ribbon
   D. the opening of the bridge was done by the movie star with the cutting of the red ribbon

12. Arriving at the bottom of Heartbreak Hill, <u>only the race leader realized that</u> a little over two miles remained in the grueling fifty-mile cross-country bicycle race.

   F. NO CHANGE
   G. the race leader only realized that
   H. the race leader realized that only
   J. the only race leader realized that

13. Georgette performed her routine <u>flawlessly nearly to win the bronze medal</u> and almost the silver medal.

   A. NO CHANGE
   B. flawlessly to win nearly the bronze medal
   C. flawlessly to win the bronze medal nearly
   D. nearly flawlessly to win the bronze medal

14. Dentists advise their patients that <u>brushing frequently helps</u> to prevent cavities and keeps teeth looking healthy.

   F. NO CHANGE
   G. frequently brushing helps
   H. brushing helps frequently
   J. frequent brushing help

15. After soaking overnight in turpentine and hung on hooks to dry, I carefully arranged the brushes according to size in the workbench drawer.

    A. NO CHANGE
    B. After soaking overnight in turpentine, I carefully arranged the brushes according to size in the workbench drawer and hung them on hooks to dry.
    C. After I had soaked them overnight in turpentine and hung them on hooks to dry, I carefully arranged the brushes according to size in the workbench drawer.
    D. Soaked overnight in turpentine, hung on hooks to dry, and arranged according to size, I placed the brushes in the workbench drawer.

16. Shortly after pulling out of the driveway, both front tires suddenly went flat.

    F. NO CHANGE
    G. Shortly after the car pulled out of the driveway
    H. Pulling out of the driveway shortly after
    J. After shortly pulling out of the driveway

17. While running the obstacle course, several of the recruits became extremely tired and almost fell into the muddy water.

    A. NO CHANGE
    B. fell almost into the muddy water
    C. fell into the muddy water almost
    D. fell into the almost muddy water

18. The City Council met on Wednesday to discuss demolishing the abandoned municipal building with the mayor.

    F. NO CHANGE
    G. to discuss demolishing the abandoned municipal building with the mayor on Wednesday
    H. on Wednesday to discuss with the mayor demolishing the abandoned municipal building
    J. to discuss with the mayor demolishing the abandoned municipal building on Wednesday

19. Bouncing, sliding, and struggling to remain upright, we rode our trail bikes down the roughest part of the ravine.

   A. NO CHANGE
   B. Bouncing, sliding, and struggling to remain upright, the roughest part of the ravine is where we rode down our trail bikes.
   C. Bouncing, sliding, and struggling to remain upright down the roughest part of the ravine, we rode our trail bikes.
   D. Bouncing, sliding, and struggling to remain upright, our bikes were ridden by us down the roughest part of the ravine.

20. Ringing loudly, Jacob was startled by the alarm clock, jumped out of bed, and mistakenly hurried to answer the door in his pajamas.

   F. NO CHANGE
   G. the alarm clock startled Jacob jumping out of bed, and he
   H. Jacob jumped out of bed startled by the alarm clock and
   J. the alarm clock startled Jacob, who jumped out of bed and

21. Wearing heavy gloves and a hat draped with mesh, the bees did not sting the beekeeper as she extracted honey from several of the boxes.

   A. NO CHANGE
   B. The bees, wearing heavy gloves and a hat draped with mesh, did not sting the beekeeper
   C. Wearing heavy gloves and a hat draped with mesh, the beekeeper was not stung by the bees
   D. The beekeeper was not stung by the bees wearing heavy gloves and a hat draped with mesh

22. Calvert was not a very experienced golfer, but after a few lessons only he was able to make a hole in one playing in the annual charity tournament.

   F. NO CHANGE
   G. after only a few lessons he was
   H. only after a few lessons he was
   J. after a few lessons he was only

UNIT 4 | CLARITY IN SENTENCES • 63

23. Out of the entire graduating class, <u>only Susan was the student</u> who had earned straight A's throughout her entire four years in high school even though she took a very demanding course of study.

   A. NO CHANGE
   B. Susan only was the student
   C. Susan was the student only
   D. Susan was the only student

24. <u>Almost half of the shipment was</u> salvaged from the shipwreck and sold before the fruit could spoil, and the insurance company reimbursed the ship's owner for the rest of it.

   F. NO CHANGE
   G. Half almost of the shipment was
   H. Half of the shipment was almost
   J. Half of the shipment almost was

25. Behind by just three points in the closing seconds of the game, <u>the ball was lofted by the quarterback over the defenders into the hands of the receiver in the end zone to give the home team a stunning upset victory</u>.

   A. NO CHANGE
   B. the home team won a stunning upset victory when the quarterback lofted the ball over the defenders into the hands of the receiver in the end zone
   C. the quarterback lofted the ball over the defenders into the hands of the receiver to give the home team a stunning upset victory in the end zone
   D. the quarterback lofted the ball over the defenders to give the home team a stunning upset in the hands of the receiver in the end zone

English **Knowledge of Language**

Unit 5 | **Clarity in Noun and Pronoun Usage**

INSIDE THIS UNIT:

– An Important Tip on Nouns and Pronouns –
– Exercise –

ENGLISH KNOWLEDGE OF LANGUAGE

Non-Negotiable Skill:

Change nouns and pronouns
that introduce ambiguity.

An Important Tip on Nouns and Pronouns

Nouns and pronouns can introduce ambiguity into a sentence. Below are two important tips for making sure that your nouns and pronouns do not create misunderstanding.

You can avoid ambiguity if you make sure that your nouns mean what you intend and your pronouns clearly refer to some other noun or some other pronoun.

Example:

The exhibit includes works by 12 students; they were executed over a two-year period.

> As written, the sentence is not clear whether the "works" (noun) were executed over a two-year period or the students were. The ambiguity can be corrected by eliminating the "they" (pronoun):

The exhibit includes works by 12 students. The works were executed over a two-year period.

> Or:

The exhibit includes works executed over a two-year period by 12 students.

Example:

Persons are prohibited from placing flowers on any grave except their own.

> The sentence seems to say that no one may put flowers on any grave except the grave that the person himself or herself is buried in, and that would be impossible. The sentence can be revised:

Persons are prohibited from placing flowers on any grave except those of loved ones.

Example:

If you are a non-swimmer, you can learn to be one in the summer classes.

> If someone is already a non-swimmer, why would it be necessary to learn to be one? The problem is that the pronoun "one" doesn't refer to anything in the sentence. The speaker intends for "one" to refer to "swimmer," but that word doesn't appear. The sentence can be corrected by resolving the ambiguity:

If you are a non-swimmer, you can learn to swim in the summer classes.

Summary

- Avoid ambiguity by making sure nouns mean what you intend them to mean.

- Avoid ambiguity by making sure pronouns clearly refer to the nouns or pronouns they are intended to represent.

EXERCISE

DIRECTIONS: In each of the following items, a word or phrase is underlined. Following each sentence or sentences are alternative suggestions for rewriting the underlined part. If you think the original is correct, choose NO CHANGE. Otherwise, choose the best alternative. Answers are on page 747.

1. The technician determined that safety switches had not been installed correctly on two of the units at the factory, so to correct <u>it</u>, she ordered the appropriate parts and installed them in the repair shop.

   A. NO CHANGE
   B. them
   C. these
   D. the problem

2. The choir director plans to buy ten robes because of the addition of five new members and the deterioration of <u>some robes</u>.

   F. NO CHANGE
   G. some
   H. others
   J. some others

3. Because powerful prescription drugs pose a serious threat to children, it is important to keep <u>them</u> locked securely in a medicine cabinet.

   A. NO CHANGE
   B. some
   C. some of them
   D. medicines

4. Victoria planned to use the empty jelly jar filled with marbles as an ornament, but when she put it on her glass table, <u>it</u> broke, and she had to buy another.

   F. NO CHANGE
   G. the table
   H. the marbles
   J. the jar

5. Management wishes to announce <u>for parents who don't know that there is a daycare facility for their children</u>.

   A. NO CHANGE
   B. that there is a daycare facility for parents who don't know it but have children
   C. that there is a daycare facility for children of parents who don't know it
   D. that there is a daycare facility for parents who have children but don't know it

Unit 5 | Clarity in Noun and Pronoun Usage • 69

6. The sergeant received a medal for his bravery and a promotion, but he was always modest about <u>it</u>.

F. NO CHANGE
G. his heroism
H. that
J. that thing

7. Peter had no brothers or sisters, and <u>it made growing up</u> both interesting and difficult.

A. NO CHANGE
B. growing up an only child was
C. growing up made it
D. they made growing up

8. Newspapers, civic leaders, commentators, and everyone else condemns dishonesty in government, but we never seem to elect politicians <u>who have it</u>.

F. NO CHANGE
G. with it
H. who are honest
J. having it

9. A newly approved medication for the treatment of depression may produce adverse side effects when used with either of two other very widely used prescription medicines, and <u>this</u> presents a serious problem for doctors treating patients for depression.

A. NO CHANGE
B. that
C. those side effects
D. these

10. The company's president successfully covered up the financial problems of the business for years, and <u>this</u> prevented investors from predicting the company's eventual failure.

F. NO CHANGE
G. the deception
H. it
J. they

11. The final skier <u>failed to complete the course and was disqualified</u> from the time trial.

    A. NO CHANGE
    B. failed the completion of the course and because of it was disqualified
    C. failed to complete the course and because of that was disqualified
    D. failed to complete the course and because of it was disqualified

12. When he returned from the grocery store, Mark forgot to put the ice cream in the freezer, and <u>because of it,</u> the ice cream melted into a puddle on the kitchen table.

    F. NO CHANGE
    G. so it caused
    H. it was the cause that
    J. OMIT

13. <u>With the line we threw the man in the disabled boat and towed it to the dock.</u>

    A. NO CHANGE
    B. We threw the man in the disabled boat and used the line to tow it to the dock.
    C. We threw the man in the disabled boat a line and used it to tow the disabled boat to the dock.
    D. We threw a line to the man in the disabled boat and towed it to the dock.

14. To show the effect of air pressure, the experimenter places a thin board on a table with several inches protruding over the edge, covers the board with a single sheet of newspaper, and strikes the protruding portion sharply with a hammer, so that <u>it</u> holds the board firmly in place while the protruding end snaps off.

    F. NO CHANGE
    G. air pressure
    H. this
    J. OMIT

15. Our family dog is really great; she's well behaved, and she'll eat <u>anything and is particularly fond of</u> children.

    A. NO CHANGE
    B. anything and is fond of particular
    C. anything fond of particular
    D. anything, and she is particularly fond of

16. The nature photographer took dozens of pictures of the <u>tadpoles that are still not developed</u>.

    F. NO CHANGE
    G. tadpoles still not yet developed
    H. tadpoles, but the film is still not developed
    J. tadpoles which were not developed

17. As your neighborhood bank, we are anxious to explain our many different plans <u>for you to own your home</u>.

    A. NO CHANGE
    B. for owning your home
    C. for owning homes
    D. to own your home

18. The owner's manual explains that the car's oil should be changed every 5,000 miles because clean oil is needed to minimize friction and wear <u>and it can cause</u> engine failure.

    F. NO CHANGE
    G. that can cause
    H. because it can cause
    J. that are caused by

19. The designers of the toasters included an overload cutout switch so that <u>it wouldn't start a fire</u> if it overheated.

    A. NO CHANGE
    B. a unit wouldn't start a fire
    C. they wouldn't start a fire
    D. the fire wouldn't be started

20. The driver, who was not wearing a seat belt at the time of the accident, was thrown from the car and found <u>unconscious in the pasture by some cows</u>.

    F. NO CHANGE
    G. unconsciously in the pasture by some cows
    H. unconscious in the pasture near some cows
    J. in the pasture by some cows, unconscious

21. Lara was deceptive about her spending habits for years, and after her husband hired an accountant to manage the family's finances, it was discovered that it had not improved.

    A. NO CHANGE
    B. the family
    C. the accountant
    D. her dishonesty

22. The mechanic checked the motor and found that the rattling was being caused by the failure of the factory to install a bracket.

    F. NO CHANGE
    G. a bracket that was never installed at the factory
    H. the factory's missing bracket
    J. the missing bracket that was never installed at the factory

23. Because of an illness, Jeffrey had to spend three days in the hospital that made him dizzy.

    A. NO CHANGE
    B. Because of an illness that made him dizzy, Jeffrey had to spend three days in the hospital.
    C. An illness caused Jeffrey to spend three days in the hospital that made him dizzy.
    D. The hospital that made him dizzy for three days is where Jeffrey spent his time for illness.

24. Cities like New York, Washington, DC, and Chicago all have world-renowned botanic gardens; they are credited for exposing young people to the wonders of nature.

    F. NO CHANGE
    G. these cities
    H. this city
    J. these gardens

25. The Art Institute, home to the largest collection of Impressionist paintings in the US, employs many docents who know a great deal about their significance.

    A. NO CHANGE
    B. them
    C. the significance of the paintings
    D. themselves

English **Knowledge of Language**

Unit 6 | **Practice**

INSIDE THIS UNIT:
– Exercise –

74 • ENGLISH KNOWLEDGE OF LANGUAGE

EXERCISE

DIRECTIONS: In each of the following items, a word or phrase is underlined. Following each sentence or sentences are alternative suggestions for rewriting the underlined part. If you think the original is correct, choose NO CHANGE. Otherwise, choose the best alternative. Answers are on page 747.

1. Although literary critics <u>almost unanimously all regarded</u> Smithwicke's novels as simplistic and poorly written, his books regularly appeared at or near the top of various best seller lists.

   A. NO CHANGE
   B. unanimously almost regarded all
   C. almost regarded unanimously all
   D. unanimously regarded almost all

2. Pretending to fall off the miniature bicycle, <u>the clown wearing oversized shoes, an orange wig, and a bright red nose caused the audience to laugh uproariously</u>.

   F. NO CHANGE
   G. the crowd laughed uproariously at the clown wearing oversized shoes, an orange wig, and a bright red nose
   H. the oversized shoes, an orange wig, and a bright red nose worn by the clown caused the audience to laugh uproariously
   J. the clown caused the crowd wearing oversized shoes, an orange wig, and a bright red nose to laugh uproariously

3. While many commuters rely on trains and busses to get to work each day, others still drive and don't take advantage of it.

   A. NO CHANGE
   B. public transportation
   C. trains
   D. them

4. The principal of the local high school determined that the state test results were not accurate, so she made them retake it.

   F. NO CHANGE
   G. the students retake it
   H. them retake the test
   J. the students retake the test

5. The taxi driver told the passenger that the trip to the airport only would take about 20 minutes so that there would be no problem in making the flight.

   A. NO CHANGE
   B. would take only about 20 minutes
   C. would take about only 20 minutes
   D. would take about 20 minutes only

6. Used in the manufacture of crystal methamphetamine, the distribution of pseudoephedrine, which is found in common over-the-counter cold remedies, has been severely restricted.

   F. NO CHANGE
   G. Used in the manufacture of crystal methamphetamine, pseudoephedrine's distribution, which is found in common over-the-counter cold remedies, has been severely restricted.
   H. Used in the manufacture of crystal methamphetamine, pseudoephedrine, which is found in common over-the-counter cold remedies, has been severely restricted in its distribution.
   J. The distribution of pseudoephedrine, which is used in the manufacture of crystal methamphetamine and found in common over-the-counter cold remedies, has been severely restricted.

7. Wanted for the murder of the store clerk, the sheriff arrested the suspect identified by the eyewitness as the shooter.

    A. NO CHANGE
    B. the eyewitness identified the shooter as the suspect who was arrested by the sheriff
    C. the suspect identified by the eyewitness as the shooter was arrested by the sheriff
    D. the shooter arrested by the sheriff was identified by the eyewitness as the suspect

8. Growing up, the boys down the street never shared their bikes with us because they said they were too valuable.

    F. NO CHANGE
    G. the bikes
    H. the boys
    J. the streets

9. The 1905 San Francisco earthquake was one of the worst natural disasters that California residents have experienced.

    A. NO CHANGE
    B. they
    C. people
    D. them

10. Many fish remain on the endangered species list, but recently a rare species of small minnow was taken off it in Oregon.

    F. NO CHANGE
    G. was taken off in Oregon
    H. in Oregon was taken off
    J. found in Oregon was taken off of the list

11. Children can often dart into the street in front of cars in the blink of an eye, which is why it's important for them to always keep them in sight.

    A. NO CHANGE
    B. for parents to keep them
    C. for them to keep children
    D. for parents to keep their children

12. A coordinated denial-of-service attack on a web site is an attempt to shut down the site by bombarding it with data requests from multiple <u>computers exceeding</u> the capacity of the servers to respond.

    F. NO CHANGE
    G. computers which exceed
    H. computers, thus exceeding
    J. computers which are exceeding

13. By the time that the volunteer fire department arrived at the scene, <u>nearly all of the animals had been rescued from the burning barn</u> and the firefighters were able to save the few that remained inside.

    A. NO CHANGE
    B. all of the animals had been rescued from the nearly burning barn
    C. all of the animals had nearly been rescued from the burning barn
    D. the animals all had been nearly rescued from the burning barn

14. Despite earning an A in the class, she didn't feel that her half-hearted attempts throughout the semester merited <u>it</u>.

    F. NO CHANGE
    G. earning such a high grade
    H. that
    J. that grade

15. Roaring out of turn four, the <u>driver of the lead car jammed the accelerator to the floor</u> and, picking up speed, crossed the finish line a half second in front of the second place finisher.

    A. NO CHANGE
    B. accelerator of the lead car was jammed to the floor by the driver
    C. accelerator was jammed to the floor by the driver of the lead car
    D. driver jammed the accelerator of the lead car to the floor

16. Organic vegetable farmers don't realize that, in many stores, <u>they</u> are being mixed with non-organic products.

    F. NO CHANGE
    G. their vegetables
    H. the farmers
    J. products

17. When I was a child, my mother made my sister and me share clothes, much to her dislike.

    A. NO CHANGE
    B. my mother's
    C. my sister's
    D. its

18. Built on the foundation of an earlier fortress, the later palace dominates the surrounding landscape, inspiring awe and respect in visitors from other regions.

    F. NO CHANGE
    G. the palace later dominated the surrounding landscape, inspiring awe and respect in visitors from other regions.
    H. the awe and respect of visitors from other regions was inspired by the later domination of the surrounding landscape by the palace.
    J. the surrounding landscape is dominated by the later palace, inspiring awe and respect in visitors from other regions.

19. The school's new guidelines for washroom environmental responsibility say that students should save hot water and waste paper in designated containers.

    A. NO CHANGE
    B. use designated containers to save hot water and waste paper
    C. save hot water and put waste paper in designated containers
    D. save hot water in designated containers and waste paper

20. Although she conscientiously prepared for the final, Tanya suffered the bad student's dream that the exam asked questions on topics not covered in class.

    F. NO CHANGE
    G. the student's bad dream
    H. badly the dream of students
    J. the dream of bad students

21. After her bike accident, Melissa promised her father she would always wear her helmet.

    A. NO CHANGE
    B. it
    C. them
    D. those

22. Peter had five brothers growing up and they always put on comedy acts together; in fact, he credits them for making him decide to become a stand-up comedian.

    F. NO CHANGE
    G. his brothers
    H. those
    J. his childhood

23. Following a furious closing sprint, Ellie finished second and first nearly, barely beaten by the best high school miler in the entire state.

    A. NO CHANGE
    B. nearly finished second and first, barely
    C. finished second and nearly first, barely
    D. finished second and first, nearly barely

24. Suspended from the highest point in the center of the ballroom ceiling, the maintenance worker carefully cleaned each crystal of the chandelier using a 30-foot stepladder.

    F. NO CHANGE
    G. The maintenance worker carefully cleaned each crystal of the chandelier using a 30-foot stepladder suspended from the highest point in the center of the ballroom ceiling.
    H. Using a 30-foot stepladder, the maintenance worker carefully cleaned each crystal suspended from the highest point in the center of the ballroom ceiling of the chandelier.
    J. Standing on a 30-foot stepladder, the maintenance worker carefully cleaned each crystal of the chandelier which was suspended from the highest point in the center of the ballroom ceiling.

25. <u>After finishing the yard work during the heat of the day, the landscaping crew was very appreciative of the cold lemonade served by the homeowner.</u>

    A. NO CHANGE
    B. After finishing the yard work during the heat of the day, the cold lemonade served by the homeowner was very much appreciated by the landscaping crew.
    C. After the yard work was finished, the homeowner served very much appreciated lemonade to the landscaping crew during the heat of the day.
    D. The landscaping crew was very much appreciative of the cold lemonade served by the homeowner during the heat of the day after finishing the yard work.

26. Ms. Boyle received the Golden Apple award and a $5,000 bonus for her exemplary teaching, but she reminded her supporters she didn't get into <u>teaching for the money</u>.

    F. NO CHANGE
    G. it for that
    H. it for the money
    J. teaching for that

27. Jeffrey's mother determined that he had serious math deficiencies that were making high school calculus near impossible, so to address <u>it</u> she hired a math tutor.

    A. NO CHANGE
    B. the issue
    C. math
    D. high school

28. After the collapse of the building, emergency workers used search and rescue dogs <u>to look for possible</u> victims.

    F. NO CHANGE
    G. to possibly look for
    H. possibly to look for
    J. to look for

29. Noise pollution in the ocean produced by motor boats and military sonar has been shown to adversely affect whale and dolphin behavior, making the marine animals travel outside of their normal migration patterns.

   A. NO CHANGE
   B. them
   C. these
   D. the boats

30. While still relatively rare, bear attacks have been increasing recently as humans are becoming more brazen about camping and hiking in territories where they live.

   F. NO CHANGE
   G. bears live
   H. there's bears
   J. they are

English **Conventions of Standard English**

Unit 7 | **Conjunctions and Punctuation**

INSIDE THIS UNIT:
– Building Sentences – – Exercise –

Non-Negotiable Skill:

Combine simple clauses using appropriate conjunctions or punctuation.

Building Sentences

When you first learned to talk, you talked "baby talk." You used short, simple sentences like "Samantha is going to the store" and "I am going with her." As you grew up and developed a greater mastery of language, you used longer, more complex sentences, such as "Samantha is going to the store, and I am going with her."

The two simple sentences are not grammatically wrong, but combining the two into a single sentence is a more sophisticated use of language. Joining the two short sentences with the conjunction "and" shows that there is a connection between the idea of Samantha's going to the store and the speaker's going with her.

Similarly, more mature and sophisticated writers know how to combine two or more simple clauses into a single sentence.

Example:

Simple: The temperature had dropped to 28° Fahrenheit. The snow was beginning to fall.

More sophisticated: The temperature had dropped to 28° Fahrenheit, and the snow was beginning to fall.

The first version is not wrong, but the second version shows that there is a connection between the two ideas expressed. Additionally, short, choppy sentences sound harsh to the reader's ear, so the second version will read better.

Example:

Simple: The Scopes "Monkey Trial" matched two legal giants against each other in the courtroom. William Jennings Bryan was the prosecutor. Clarence Darrow was the defense lawyer.

UNIT 7 | CONJUNCTIONS AND PUNCTUATION • 85

More sophisticated: The Scopes "Monkey Trial" matched two legal giants against each other in the courtroom. William Jennings Bryan was the prosecutor, and Clarence Darrow was the defense lawyer.

Example:

Simple: *Walden* evokes a picture of isolated, independent living. Thoreau actually lived close to town and even sent his laundry out to be done.

More sophisticated: *Walden* evokes a picture of isolated, independent living, but Thoreau actually lived close to town and even sent his laundry out to be done.

Example:

Simple: The last of the ballots were not counted until 1:30 a.m. The editor waited to print the morning edition of the paper in order to include the results.

More sophisticated: The last of the ballots were not counted until 1:30 a.m., but the editor waited to print the morning edition of the paper in order to include the results.

Example:

Simple: It is only about 21 inches wide and 30 inches high. The *Mona Lisa*, the painting by Leonardo da Vinci, is famous throughout the world.

More sophisticated: Though it is only about 21 inches wide and 30 inches high, the *Mona Lisa*, the painting by Leonardo da Vinci, is famous throughout the world.

The rules for combining simple clauses into longer sentences are fairly easy:
- Combine two simple clauses with a coordinating conjunction and a comma.
- Combine two simple clauses with a semicolon.
- Combine two simple clauses with a subordinating conjunction and a comma.

The method that a writer chooses will depend on the exact sense of the sentences and, to a certain extent, on style.

Combine two simple clauses with a coordinating conjunction and a comma.

Example:

Simple: We invited Ellen to join us. She sat down.

Combined: We invited Ellen to join us, and she sat down.

Simple: We hurried to the theater. The movie had already started.

Combined: We hurried to the theater, but the movie had already started.

Combine two simple clauses with a semicolon.

Example:

Simple: We invited Ellen to join us. She sat down.

Combined: We invited Ellen to join us; she sat down.

Simple: We hurried to the station. The train had already left.

Combined: We hurried to the station; the train had already left.

Combine two simple clauses with a subordinating conjunction and a comma.

Example:

Simple: We invited Ellen to join us. She sat down.

Combined: Because we invited Ellen to join us, she sat down.

Simple: We hurried to the station. The train had already left.

Combined: Although we hurried to the station, the train had already left.

The rules for joining two clauses into a single sentence can be summarized as follows:

When the two clauses have equal status, use *and*, *but*, *or*, and *neither/nor*, preceded by a comma.

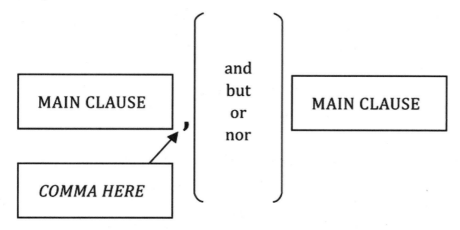

When the two clauses have equal status, and no conjunction is used, separate the clauses with a semicolon.

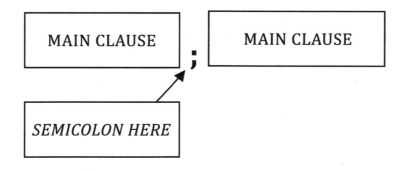

When one clause depends on the other, use a subordinating conjunction and separate the two clauses with a comma.

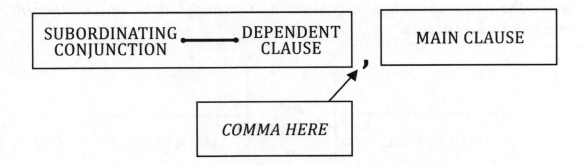

Summary

- Combining two or more simple clauses into a single sentence using conjunctions or punctuation shows that there is a connection between or among the ideas expressed.

- Two simple clauses can be combined into one sentence using a coordinating conjunction and a comma, a semicolon, or a subordinating conjunction and a comma.

- A writer may use different methods of combining simple clauses, depending on sentence structure and writing style.

EXERCISE

DIRECTIONS: In each of the following items, select the choice that most effectively combines the sentences. Answers are on page 747.

1. We forgot to water the plants. They died.

   A. We forgot to water the plants, they died.
   B. We forgot to water the plants, and they died.
   C. We forgot to water the plants they died.
   D. We forgot to water the plants and, they died.

2. Mark washed the dishes. Linda dried them.

   F. Mark washed the dishes, and Linda dried them.
   G. Mark washed the dishes and; Linda dried them.
   H. Mark washed the dishes Linda dried them.
   J. Mark washed the dishes, Linda dried them.

3. The mail carrier delivered the package. We opened it immediately.

   A. The mail carrier delivered the package, and we opened it immediately.
   B. The mail carrier delivered the package we opened it immediately.
   C. The mail carrier delivered the package, we opened it immediately.
   D. The mail carrier delivered the package and, we opened it immediately.

4. We hurried to the station. The train had already left.

   F. We hurried to the station, the train had already left.
   G. We hurried to the station the train had already left.
   H. We hurried to the station, or the train had already left.
   J. We hurried to the station, but the train had already left.

5. I must return the books to the library by Friday. I will pay $3 in late fees.

   A. I must return the books to the library by Friday I will pay $3 in late fees.
   B. I must return the books to the library by Friday and, I will pay $3 in late fees.
   C. I must return the books to the library by Friday, or I will pay $3 in late fees.
   D. I must return the books to the library by Friday if I will pay $3 in late fees.

6. Three students were assigned to sweep the gym. The rest were told to report to the coach.

   F. Three students were assigned to sweep the gym, or the rest were told to report to the coach.
   G. Three students were assigned to sweep the gym; the rest were told to report to the coach.
   H. Three students were assigned to sweep the gym the rest were told to report to the coach.
   J. Three students were assigned to sweep the gym, the rest were told to report to the coach.

7. At the banquet, Frank chose the fish. I chose the chicken.

   A. At the banquet, Frank chose the fish I chose the chicken.
   B. At the banquet, Frank chose the fish; I chose the chicken.
   C. At the banquet, Frank chose the fish, I chose the chicken.
   D. At the banquet, Frank chose the fish, if I chose the chicken.

8. Our anchor unleashed a furious sprint on the last lap and gained 30 yards on the leader. He finished second by inches.

   F. Our anchor unleashed a furious sprint on the last lap and gained 30 yards on the leader but, he finished second by inches.
   G. Our anchor unleashed a furious sprint on the last lap and gained 30 yards on the leader but he finished second by inches.
   H. Our anchor unleashed a furious sprint on the last lap and gained 30 yards on the leader, he finished second by inches.
   J. Our anchor unleashed a furious sprint on the last lap and gained 30 yards on the leader, but he finished second by inches.

UNIT 7 | CONJUNCTIONS AND PUNCTUATION • 91

9. Alberta had hoped to receive the scholarship award. Her best friend, Anita, won it.

   A. Alberta had hoped to receive the scholarship award, but her best friend, Anita, won it.
   B. Alberta had hoped to receive the scholarship award, or her best friend, Anita, won it.
   C. Alberta had hoped to receive the scholarship award but, her best friend, Anita, won it.
   D. Alberta had hoped to receive the scholarship award her best friend, Anita, won it.

10. The batteries eventually were exhausted. The flashlight grew dimmer and finally went dark.

   F. The batteries eventually were exhausted, the flashlight grew dimmer and finally went dark.
   G. The batteries eventually were exhausted the flashlight grew dimmer and finally went dark.
   H. The batteries eventually were exhausted, but the flashlight grew dimmer and finally went dark.
   J. The batteries eventually were exhausted, and the flashlight grew dimmer and finally went dark.

11. Irene operated the chopper, cutting the corn plants into small pieces for silage. Trish drove the dump truck back and forth from the field to the barn.

   A. Irene operated the chopper, cutting the corn plants into small pieces for silage Trish drove the dump truck back and forth from the field to the barn.
   B. Irene operated the chopper, cutting the corn plants into small pieces for silage, Trish drove the dump truck back and forth from the field to the barn.
   C. Irene operated the chopper, cutting the corn plants into small pieces for silage, while Trish drove the dump truck back and forth from the field to the barn.
   D. Irene operated the chopper, cutting the corn plants into small pieces for silage and, Trish drove the dump truck back and forth from the field to the barn.

12. The storm produced violent winds. A tree blew down on the wires and disrupted electrical service to our neighborhood.

F. The storm produced violent winds, and a tree blew down on the wires and disrupted electrical service to our neighborhood.
G. The storm produced violent winds a tree blew down on the wires and disrupted electrical service to our neighborhood.
H. The storm produced violent winds and, a tree blew down on the wires and disrupted electrical service to our neighborhood.
J. The storm produced violent winds, a tree blew down on the wires and disrupted electrical service to our neighborhood.

13. In *The Thomas Crown Affair*, Pierce Brosnan played the male lead. Rene Russo played the female lead.

A. In *The Thomas Crown Affair*, Pierce Brosnan played the male lead but, Rene Russo played the female lead.
B. In *The Thomas Crown Affair*, Pierce Brosnan played the male lead Rene Russo played the female lead.
C. In *The Thomas Crown Affair*, Pierce Brosnan played the male lead, Rene Russo played the female lead.
D. In *The Thomas Crown Affair*, Pierce Brosnan played the male lead; Rene Russo played the female lead.

14. When the final gun sounded, the score was tied. The game went into overtime.

F. When the final gun sounded, the score was tied the game went into overtime.
G. When the final gun sounded, the score was tied, the game went into overtime.
H. When the final gun sounded, the score was tied, and the game went into overtime.
J. When the final gun sounded, the score, was tied the game, went into overtime.

15. The senator had already committed to speak at the high school's graduation. She declined the invitation to attend the dedication ceremony for the new park.

    A. The senator had already committed to speak at the high school's graduation, or she declined the invitation to attend the dedication ceremony for the new park.
    B. Because the senator had already committed to speak at the high school's graduation, she declined the invitation to attend the dedication ceremony for the new park.
    C. The senator had already committed to speak at the high school's graduation she declined the invitation to attend the dedication ceremony for the new park.
    D. The senator had already committed to speak at the high school's graduation, she declined the invitation to attend the dedication ceremony for the new park.

16. The original superhero comic books did not use humor very much. Spiderman comics, which came later, often used tongue-in-cheek dialogue.

    F. The original superhero comic books did not use humor very much Spiderman comics, which came later, often used tongue-in-cheek dialogue.
    G. The original superhero comic books did not use humor very much, and Spiderman comics, which came later, often used tongue-in-cheek dialogue.
    H. The original superhero comic books did not use humor very much, but Spiderman comics, which came later, often used tongue-in-cheek dialogue.
    J. The original superhero comic books did not use humor very much, Spiderman comics, which came later, often used tongue-in-cheek dialogue.

17. Very popular television shows may run for many years. Some even produce related programs called spin-offs.

    A. Very popular television shows may run for many years some even produce related programs called spin-offs.
    B. Very popular television shows may run for many years, some even produce related programs called spin-offs.
    C. Very popular television shows may run for many years; some even produce related programs called spin-offs.
    D. Very popular television shows may run for many years, or some even produce related programs called spin-offs.

18. The storm dropped nearly two feet of snow on the city. The mayor declared a state of emergency.

    F. The storm dropped nearly two feet of snow on the city the mayor declared a state of emergency.
    G. The storm dropped nearly two feet of snow on the city, and the mayor declared a state of emergency.
    H. The storm dropped nearly two feet of snow on the city, the mayor declared a state of emergency.
    J. The storm dropped nearly two feet of snow on the city because the mayor declared a state of emergency.

UNIT 7 | CONJUNCTIONS AND PUNCTUATION • 95

19. The emcee announced that the Outstanding Player Award was won by Scott. Scott had left the banquet early because he was feeling ill.

    A. The emcee announced that the Outstanding Player Award was won by Scott but, Scott had left the banquet early because he was feeling ill.

    B. The emcee announced that the Outstanding Player Award was won by Scott Scott had left the banquet early because he was feeling ill.

    C. The emcee announced that the Outstanding Player Award was won by Scott, Scott had left the banquet early because he was feeling ill.

    D. The emcee announced that the Outstanding Player Award was won by Scott, but Scott had left the banquet early because he was feeling ill.

20. For the party, everyone showed up in costume. Mark came as Batman. Sophia dressed as Catwoman.

    F. For the party, everyone showed up in costume. Mark came as Batman Sophia dressed as Catwoman.

    G. For the party, everyone showed up in costume. Mark came as Batman, Sophia dressed as Catwoman.

    H. For the party, everyone showed up in costume. Mark came as Batman, and Sophia dressed as Catwoman.

    J. For the party, everyone showed up in costume. Mark came as Batman and, Sophia dressed as Catwoman.

21. The morning after the blizzard, there wasn't a cloud in the sky. Icicles hanging from the eaves of the house refracted the light like enormous jewels.

A. The morning after the blizzard, there wasn't a cloud in the sky, and icicles hanging from the eaves of the house refracted the light like enormous jewels.
B. The morning after the blizzard, there wasn't a cloud in the sky and icicles hanging from the eaves of the house refracted the light like enormous jewels.
C. The morning after the blizzard, there wasn't a cloud in the sky icicles hanging from the eaves of the house refracted the light like enormous jewels.
D. The morning after the blizzard, there wasn't a cloud in the sky, but icicles hanging from the eaves of the house refracted the light like enormous jewels.

22. The conductor raised her baton high in the air. The musicians picked up their instruments and waited for the baton to fall.

F. The conductor raised her baton high in the air but, the musicians picked up their instruments and waited for the baton to fall.
G. The conductor raised her baton high in the air the musicians picked up their instruments and waited for the baton to fall.
H. The conductor raised her baton high in the air, the musicians picked up their instruments and waited for the baton to fall.
J. When the conductor raised her baton high in the air, the musicians picked up their instruments and waited for the baton to fall.

UNIT 7 | CONJUNCTIONS AND PUNCTUATION • 97

23. The police responded to the 911 call and arrived on the scene within three minutes. The suspects had already fled.

    A. The police responded to the 911 call and arrived on the scene within three minutes, but the suspects had already fled.
    B. The police responded to the 911 call and arrived on the scene within three minutes, when the suspects had already fled.
    C. The police responded to the 911 call and arrived on the scene within three minutes the suspects had already fled.
    D. The police responded to the 911 call and arrived on the scene within three minutes, the suspects had already fled.

24. The old printing presses of the Department of the Treasury cannot handle the process that produces the security features for the new $100 bills. Billions of dollars of misprinted currency will have to be destroyed.

    F. The old printing presses of the Department of the Treasury cannot handle the process that produces the security features for the new $100 bills, so billions of dollars of misprinted currency will have to be destroyed.
    G. The old printing presses of the Department of the Treasury cannot handle the process that produces the security features for the new $100 bills billions of dollars of misprinted currency will have to be destroyed.
    H. The old printing presses of the Department of the Treasury cannot handle the process that produces the security features for the new $100 bills, billions of dollars of misprinted currency will have to be destroyed.
    J. The old printing presses of the Department of the Treasury cannot handle the process that produces the security features for the new $100 bills, when billions of dollars of misprinted currency will have to be destroyed.

25. The pilot vectored around the towering thunderhead. Once clear, she resumed her original course heading.

   A. The pilot vectored around the towering thunderhead and, once clear, she resumed her original course heading.

   B. The pilot vectored around the towering thunderhead once clear, she resumed her original course heading.

   C. The pilot vectored around the towering thunderhead and once clear, she resumed her original course heading.

   D. The pilot vectored around the towering thunderhead; once clear, she resumed her original course heading.

English Conventions of Standard English

Unit 8 | Verb Tense

INSIDE THIS UNIT:
– Consistent Tenses –   – Exercise –

Non-Negotiable Skill:

Use the correct verb tense between simple clauses and adjoining sentences.

Consistent Tenses

When you write, you tell a story. An essay on "My Summer Vacation" is obviously a story. A history paper or a book report is a story. Even the directions you write down for a friend saying how to get to your home is a story—the story of how to get to where you live. And one of the important elements of any story is the timeline.

A good storyteller (and a good writer) makes sure that the timeline of events is consistent and easy to understand. One of the tools for creating the timeline is verb tense.

Example:

Last Monday, I went to the library and checked out a copy of *Pride and Prejudice*. (The event has already taken place.)

I am almost finished reading the book. (The event is occurring in the present.)

I will return the book to the library on Friday. (The event will happen in the future.)

If you use these tools carefully, the result is a coherent story:

Last Monday, I went to the library and checked out a copy of *Pride and Prejudice*. I am almost finished reading the book. I will return the book to the library on Friday.

However, if you are not careful with verb tenses, the story can get very confusing:

I will go to the library to check out a copy of *Pride and Prejudice*. I was almost finished reading the book. I am returning it to the library on Friday.

This second version makes absolutely no sense. So make sure that your tenses reflect the logic of the story.

UNIT 8 | VERB TENSE • 101

Summary

- Use the correct verb tense between simple clauses or adjoining sentences to ensure that the timeline of events is consistent and easy to understand.

EXERCISE

DIRECTIONS: In each of the following items, select the choice that expresses the correct verb tense. Answers are on page 747.

1. During the season, the field hockey team practices every Tuesday and Wednesday, and they <u>played</u> a match every other Friday evening.

   A. NO CHANGE
   B. play
   C. playing
   D. have played

2. With the finish line in sight, the coxswain picked up the tempo. The rowers <u>will respond</u>, pulling decisively ahead of the other boat.

   F. NO CHANGE
   G. respond
   H. responded
   J. would respond

3. The board met in an executive session yesterday to decide whether to renew the coach's contract. Their decision <u>is</u> announced tomorrow.

   A. NO CHANGE
   B. was
   C. will be
   D. had been

4. Kevin backed the trailer down the ramp to unload the boat into the water. He <u>forgets</u> to put the car in park, and it rolled into the lake.

   F. NO CHANGE
   G. forgot
   H. will forget
   J. has forgotten

102 • ENGLISH CONVENTIONS OF STANDARD ENGLISH

5. The jazz ensemble will perform Sunday afternoon. They <u>will play</u> several Gershwin numbers as well as some swing and bebop.

    A. NO CHANGE
    B. play
    C. played
    D. would play

6. Our flight <u>is</u> delayed because of bad weather on the East Coast. It left as soon as the plane was refueled and the new crew arrived.

    F. NO CHANGE
    G. was
    H. will be
    J. has been

7. The extremely cold weather would cause the logs to freeze into a jam, and the lumberjacks <u>will dislodge</u> them with dynamite.

    A. NO CHANGE
    B. dislodge
    C. have dislodged
    D. would dislodge

8. Crop rotation is an important conservation measure. If the same crop is planted year after year, essential nutrients in the soil <u>have been</u> depleted.

    F. NO CHANGE
    G. were
    H. <u>will be</u>
    J. had been

9. Milfoil is a weed that grows on the bottom of many lakes. It is a nuisance because it <u>grows</u> in thick mats and interferes with recreational activities such as boating, fishing, and swimming.

    A. NO CHANGE
    B. grew
    C. was growing
    D. has grown

10. On weekends, the N train <u>will</u> not run between 36th Street and Coney Island. Instead, it is routed along 4th Avenue to 95th Street.

    F. NO CHANGE
    G. had
    H. has
    J. does

UNIT 8 | *VERB TENSE* • **103**

Questions 11–15

Edward Hopper, who <u>lives</u> from 1882 to
₁₁
1967, was a prominent American painter. He is
best known for his depictions of modern
American life. Hopper mainly painted the
common features of American life, such as gas
stations, motels, restaurants, theaters, and
railroads. He painted his best-known work,
Nighthawks, in 1942. It shows customers sitting at
the counter of a diner in New York City. The time
is night, and the bright electric lights inside the
diner <u>created</u> a stark contrast with the darkness
₁₂
outside. As in many Hopper paintings, the people
in the painting don't seem to interact with one

another. Instead, each <u>appeared</u> to be alone in his
₁₃
own world. The sense of isolation that

<u>fills</u> the painting is a defining element of Hopper's
₁₄
view of modern life.

Many people think that the painting was
inspired by a real diner in Greenwich Village. Over
the years, researchers <u>have found</u> photographs,
₁₅
descriptions, and even architectural plans of
various diners that might identify the depicted
diner. Hopper himself did not provide any help on
this issue. When asked about the inspiration for
any of his paintings, he would invariably answer,
"The whole answer is there on the canvas."

11. A. NO CHANGE
B. lived
C. will live
D. will be living

12. F. NO CHANGE
G. create
H. will create
J. has created

13. A. NO CHANGE
B. has appeared
C. appears
D. was appearing

14. F. NO CHANGE
G. filled
H. had filled
J. would fill

15. A. NO CHANGE
B. will find
C. find
D. will have found

16. Kyle <u>forgets</u> to take the box of chocolates out of the car, and the heat of the sun melted them.

    F. NO CHANGE
    G. is forgetting
    H. will forget
    J. forgot

17. Jan's blog contains some really insightful comments about movies, but sometimes his remarks <u>seem</u> to be insensitive to the feelings of some people who submit comments to the site.

    A. NO CHANGE
    B. seemed
    C. will seem
    D. has seemed

18. The recent flooding in Australia has covered an area equal in size to France and Germany combined. Entire towns are under water, and residents <u>were</u> dependent on airdrops for essential supplies.

    F. NO CHANGE
    G. will be
    H. had been
    J. are

19. The governor of New Mexico was considering granting Billy the Kid a posthumous pardon for some crimes committed over a century ago, but he <u>will decide</u> against the pardon because it was opposed by descendants of Pat Garrett, the sheriff who killed the Kid.

    A. NO CHANGE
    B. decides
    C. decided
    D. was deciding

20. Reunions between returning soldiers and family are almost always depicted as joyous affairs, but it often <u>took</u> family members months to re-establish the comfortable feeling that existed before deployment.

    F. NO CHANGE
    G. had taken
    H. was taking
    J. takes

UNIT 8 | VERB TENSE • 105

21. To emphasize that the new administration will be watching expenditures closely, the governor-elect has decided against a pre-inaugural ball. Instead, a pre-inaugural dinner <u>will include</u> only the governor's family, a few close friends, and the governor's most important associates. Some of the governor's inner staff will not be on the guest list.

   A. NO CHANGE
   B. has included
   C. included
   D. did include

22. A new restaurant chain called Kura is serving sushi, but there are no sushi chefs with razor sharp knives behind a sushi bar displaying different cuts of fish. Instead, at Kura, robots prepare the sushi, and conveyor belts <u>served</u> the sushi with diners simply taking what they want.

   F. NO CHANGE
   G. will serve
   H. serve
   J. have served

23. Every year as the clock nears midnight on December 31st, the eyes of the world turn to the dazzling lights and bustling energy of Times Square. The world <u>held its breath and cheered</u> as the clocks strike twelve. New Year's Eve at the symbolic center of New York City is more than just a celebration—it's a global tradition.

   A. NO CHANGE
   B. held its breath and will cheer
   C. holds its breath and would cheer
   D. holds its breath and cheers

24. On average, 20 school-age children die each year in school bus–related crashes or incidents. Of these 20, 15 <u>were</u> struck either by the bus itself or by other vehicles. So only five children out of 23.5 million who ride school buses might be saved by school bus seat belts.

   F. NO CHANGE
   G. are
   H. have been
   J. could be

25. The Huskies were undefeated this season until losing to the Tigers last night in the Frampton Arena. The height of the Tigers' players <u>prove</u> too much for the smaller Huskies players, who were out-rebounded and out-scored.

   A. NO CHANGE
   B. proved
   C. was proving
   D. will prove

English **Conventions of Standard English**

Unit 9 | **Practice**

INSIDE THIS UNIT:
– Exercise –

108 • ENGLISH CONVENTIONS OF STANDARD ENGLISH

EXERCISE

DIRECTIONS: For each of the following items, choose the best way to write the underlined part of the passage. Answers are on page 747.

Questions 1–5

A wood burning fireplace makes a dramatic room <u>accent. It</u> is not particularly useful for
₁

heating purposes. The fire requires <u>oxygen, and</u>
₂
<u>the</u> oxygen is drawn from the room that is being
₂
heated. Thus, a lot of heated air goes up the chimney. Perhaps as much as 70 percent of the heat produced is lost in this way. A fireplace insert woodstove is more efficient. The stove

<u>is</u> essentially an airtight steel box with intake
₃
vents that can be adjusted to let in more or less air. Controlling the air intake makes it possible to reduce the amount of heat lost to the outside to 20 or 25 percent of the amount produced.

1. Which of the following is the most effective way to join the two sentences?

   A. accent it
   B. accent, it
   C. accent, but
   D. accent, and

2. Which of the following is NOT an acceptable way of writing the underlined part?

   F. NO CHANGE
   G. oxygen. The
   H. oxygen, the
   J. oxygen; the

3. A. NO CHANGE
   B. was
   C. will be
   D. has been

Equipped with a glass door, the insert <u>will have</u>
4

<u>had</u> the beauty of a traditional masonry
4

<u>fireplace. It</u> is an efficient device for producing
5

heat with a renewable resource.

4. F. NO CHANGE
    G. had
    H. has had
    J. has

5. Which of the following is the most effective way to join the two sentences?

    A. fireplace, and it
    B. fireplace, it
    C. fireplace it
    D. fireplace, but it

DIRECTIONS: For each of the following items, choose the most effective way of combining the underlined sentences. Answers are on page 747.

Questions 6–15

6. <u>This will be the tenth year that I have traveled to Ethiopia to work on the large dig. I am still filled with excitement and anticipation.</u>

    F. This will be the tenth year that I have traveled to Ethiopia to work on the large dig, but I am still filled with excitement and anticipation.
    G. This will be the tenth year that I have traveled to Ethiopia to work on the large dig I am still filled with excitement and anticipation.
    H. This will be the tenth year that I have traveled to Ethiopia to work on the large dig, I am still filled with excitement and anticipation.
    J. This will be the tenth year that I have traveled to Ethiopia to work on the large dig and, I am still filled with excitement and anticipation.

7. Coal ash can be disposed of by recycling it into products such as cement. It can be stored in special containment facilities supervised by the government.

   A. Coal ash can be disposed of by recycling it into products such as cement, it can be stored in special containment facilities supervised by the government.
   B. Coal ash can be disposed of by recycling it into products such as cement, but it can be stored in special containment facilities supervised by the government.
   C. Coal ash can be disposed of by recycling it into products such as cement it can be stored in special containment facilities supervised by the government.
   D. Coal ash can be disposed of by recycling it into products such as cement, or it can be stored in special containment facilities supervised by the government.

8. A group of teachers opposed the appointment of the new superintendent on the grounds that she did not have classroom experience. The School Board approved the appointment because the candidate had considerable experience managing a large textbook publishing company.

   F. A group of teachers opposed the appointment of the new superintendent on the grounds that she did not have classroom experience the School Board approved the appointment because the candidate had considerable experience managing a large textbook publishing company.
   G. A group of teachers opposed the appointment of the new superintendent on the grounds that she did not have classroom experience, the School Board approved the appointment because the candidate had considerable experience managing a large textbook publishing company.
   H. A group of teachers opposed the appointment of the new superintendent on the grounds that she did not have classroom experience, but the School Board approved the appointment because the candidate had considerable experience managing a large textbook publishing company.
   J. A group of teachers opposed the appointment of the new superintendent on the grounds that she did not have classroom experience, or the School Board approved the appointment because the candidate had considerable experience managing a large textbook publishing company.

9. Last week, jazz musician and composer Dr. Billy Taylor died of heart failure. He was 89 years old and lived in Riverdale.

A. Last week, jazz musician and composer Dr. Billy Taylor died of heart failure; he was 89 years old and lived in Riverdale.
B. Last week, jazz musician and composer Dr. Billy Taylor died of heart failure, and he was 89 years old and lived in Riverdale.
C. Last week, jazz musician and composer Dr. Billy Taylor died of heart failure and he was 89 years old and lived in Riverdale.
D. Last week, jazz musician and composer Dr. Billy Taylor died of heart failure he was 89 years old and lived in Riverdale.

10. The Public Theater has created a new Mobile Unit that will perform Shakespeare's plays in venues such as churches, prisons, and community centers. The first performance will be *Measure for Measure.*

F. The Public Theater has created a new Mobile Unit that will perform Shakespeare's plays in venues such as churches, prisons, and community centers the first performance will be *Measure for Measure.*
G. The Public Theater has created a new Mobile Unit that will perform Shakespeare's plays in venues such as churches, prisons, and community centers, but the first performance will be *Measure for Measure.*
H. The Public Theater has created a new Mobile Unit that will perform Shakespeare's plays in venues such as churches, prisons, and community centers, or the first performance will be *Measure for Measure.*
J. The Public Theater has created a new Mobile Unit that will perform Shakespeare's plays in venues such as churches, prisons, and community centers; the first performance will be *Measure for Measure.*

11. <u>When I stepped off the train from Chengdu, I imagined I was one of the hundreds of thousands of migrants who flock from the countryside to the city's crowded streets every year. I was energized and terrified, awed and optimistic all at the same time.</u>

　　A. When I stepped off the train from Chengdu, I imagined I was one of the hundreds of thousands of migrants who flock from the countryside to the city's crowded streets every year and I was energized and terrified, awed and optimistic all at the same time.
　　B. When I stepped off the train from Chengdu, I imagined I was one of the hundreds of thousands of migrants who flock from the countryside to the city's crowded streets every year, I was energized and terrified, awed and optimistic all at the same time.
　　C. When I stepped off the train from Chengdu, I imagined I was one of the hundreds of thousands of migrants who flock from the countryside to the city's crowded streets every year I was energized and terrified, awed and optimistic all at the same time.
　　D. When I stepped off the train from Chengdu, I imagined I was one of the hundreds of thousands of migrants who flock from the countryside to the city's crowded streets every year; I was energized and terrified, awed and optimistic all at the same time.

12. <u>Auto-Train passengers traveled in upscale comfort with a nightclub car and live entertainment for adults. Actors dressed up as Disney characters entertained children.</u>

　　F. Auto-Train passengers traveled in upscale comfort with a nightclub car and live entertainment for adults actors dressed up as Disney characters entertained children.
　　G. Auto-Train passengers traveled in upscale comfort with a nightclub car and live entertainment for adults; actors dressed up as Disney characters entertained children.
　　H. Auto-Train passengers traveled in upscale comfort with a nightclub car and live entertainment for adults, actors dressed up as Disney characters entertained children.
　　J. Auto-Train passengers traveled in upscale comfort with a nightclub car and live entertainment for adults, even actors dressed up as Disney characters entertained children.

13. As new applications are developed, cell phones are rapidly cannibalizing other devices. They may soon completely replace alarm clocks, medical alert bracelets, digital cameras, and navigational systems.

    A. As new applications are developed, cell phones are rapidly cannibalizing other devices but they may soon completely replace alarm clocks, medical alert bracelets, digital cameras, and navigational systems.

    B. As new applications are developed, cell phones are rapidly cannibalizing other devices they may soon completely replace alarm clocks, medical alert bracelets, digital cameras, and navigational systems.

    C. As new applications are developed, cell phones are rapidly cannibalizing other devices, they may soon completely replace alarm clocks, medical alert bracelets, digital cameras, and navigational systems.

    D. As new applications are developed, cell phones are rapidly cannibalizing other devices; they may soon completely replace alarm clocks, medical alert bracelets, digital cameras, and navigational systems.

14. The company was known for its extravagant parties. The full-sized, ice sculpture copy of Michelangelo's *David* spouting a cold beverage was completely unexpected.

    F. The company was known for its extravagant parties; the full-sized, ice sculpture copy of Michelangelo's *David* spouting a cold beverage was completely unexpected.

    G. The company was known for its extravagant parties, but the full-sized, ice sculpture copy of Michelangelo's *David* spouting a cold beverage was completely unexpected.

    H. The company was known for its extravagant parties the full-sized, ice sculpture copy of Michelangelo's *David* spouting a cold beverage was completely unexpected.

    J. The company was known for its extravagant parties, the full-sized, ice sculpture copy of Michelangelo's *David* spouting a cold beverage was completely unexpected.

114 • ENGLISH CONVENTIONS OF STANDARD ENGLISH

15. <u>Critics of the planned expansion complained that it commercializes a historic site. The architect explained that the accommodations are intended to make the memorial more accessible to a greater number of people.</u>

A. Critics of the planned expansion complained that it commercializes a historic site, but the architect explained that the accommodations are intended to make the memorial more accessible to a greater number of people.

B. Critics of the planned expansion complained that it commercializes a historic site the architect explained that the accommodations are intended to make the memorial more accessible to a greater number of people.

C. Critics of the planned expansion complained that it commercializes a historic site, the architect explained that the accommodations are intended to make the memorial more accessible to a greater number of people.

D. Critics of the planned expansion complained that it commercializes a historic site, or the architect explained that the accommodations are intended to make the memorial more accessible to a greater number of people.

UNIT 9 | PRACTICE • 115

DIRECTIONS: In each of the following items, a word or phrase is underlined. Following each sentence or sentences are alternative suggestions for rewriting the underlined part. If you think the original is correct, choose NO CHANGE. Otherwise, choose the best alternative. Answers are on page 747.

Question 16–20

16. Mark's dad is crazy about airplanes. He has dozens of models that he <u>will build</u> himself and displays in his den.

   F. NO CHANGE
   G. will have built
   H. built
   J. had built

17. Contrary to popular opinion, darker coffee beans have less caffeine than lighter beans because the darker beans roast longer, and the caffeine <u>will have cooked</u> away.

   A. NO CHANGE
   B. will cook
   C. cooks
   D. cooked

18. Pink bathrooms were common in homes built in mid-century America. But by the 1970s they <u>are</u> as artificial as no-sugar sweetener.

   F. NO CHANGE
   G. were
   H. will be
   J. had been

19. Plasma TVs use more energy than LCD models, but LCD sets <u>worked</u> better in bright rooms because they have higher bright settings than plasmas.

   A. NO CHANGE
   B. work
   C. are working
   D. have worked

20. Survivalist television <u>featured</u> so-called experts stranded in desolate places with few or no supplies and only their own resourcefulness to turn to for help. These survivalists build their own shelter, search for water, and forage for food.

   F. NO CHANGE
   G. will feature
   H. has featured
   J. feature

Questions 21-27

The Supreme Court of the United States first met <u>in 1790. One</u> legal historian has called it "the
₂₁
longest sitting Court." As would be expected given its long history, the Court has many traditions.

In American courts, it is customary for judges to be seated according to seniority. When the Supreme Court sits, the Chief Justice <u>will have</u>
₂₂
<u>occupied</u> the center <u>chair. The</u> senior Associate
₂₂ ₂₃
Associate Justice sits to his right, the second senior to his left, and so on, alternating right and left by seniority.

Since at least 1800, the Justices have worn black robes while in Court. The first Chief Justice,

John Jay, <u>wore</u> a robe with a red facing, somewhat
₂₄
like those of early colonial and English judges. The Jay robe of black and salmon is now in the possession of the Smithsonian Institution.

For many years, attorneys dressed in formal "morning clothes" when appearing before the

21. Which of the following would be the most effective way to join the two sentences?

   A. in 1790 one
   B. in 1790, one
   C. in 1790, and one
   D. in 1790 and, one

22. F. NO CHANGE
    G. occupied
    H. has occupied
    J. occupies

23. Which of the following would be the most effective way to join the two sentences?

    A. chair the
    B. chair, the
    C. chair; the
    D. chair, but the

24. F. NO CHANGE
    G. wears
    H. was wearing
    J. will wear

Court. Senator George Wharton Pepper of Pennsylvania often told friends of the incident he caused when, as a young lawyer in the 1890s, he <u>arrives</u> to argue a case in "street clothes." Justice
25

Horace Gray was overheard whispering to a colleague, "Who is that beast who dares to come in here with a gray coat?" The young attorney was refused admission until he borrowed a "morning coat." Today, the tradition of formal dress is observed by only the Department of Justice and other government lawyers.

Quill pens have remained part of the Courtroom scene. White quills are placed on counsel tables each day that the Court sits, as was done at the earliest sessions of the Court. The "conference handshake" has been a tradition since the days of Chief Justice Melville W. Fuller in the late nineteenth century. When the Justices assemble to go on the Bench each day and at the beginning of the private conferences at which they <u>discussed</u> decisions, each Justice shakes
26

hands with each of the other eight. Chief Justice Fuller instituted the practice as a reminder that differences of opinion on the Court did not preclude overall harmony of purpose.

The Supreme Court uses electronic equipment to record arguments, but the Justices still <u>do not allow</u> television coverage of
27

proceedings. Most of the Justices apparently believe strongly that television cameras would undermine the dignity of the Court.

25. A. NO CHANGE
B. arrived
C. has arrived
D. will arrive

26. F. NO CHANGE
G. discuss
H. had discussed
J. have discussed

27. A. NO CHANGE
B. did not allow
C. were not allowing
D. had not allowed

Questions 28–30

Molds are microscopic fungi that <u>lives</u> on
plant or animal matter. No one knows how many species of fungi exist. Estimates range from tens of thousands to perhaps 300,000 or more. Most fungi are threadlike organisms. The production of spores is characteristic of fungi in general. These spores can be transported by air, water, or insects.

Ordinarily, you see only part of the mold on the surface of food—gray fur on forgotten bologna, fuzzy green dots on bread, white dust on cheddar cheese, coin-size velvety circles on fruits, and furry growth on the surface of jellies. Under a microscope, the mold <u>had looked</u> like skinny mushrooms.

Some molds cause allergic reactions and respiratory problems. A few molds, in the right conditions, <u>produced</u> "mycotoxins," poisonous substances that can make you sick. In dangerous molds, poisonous substances are often contained in and around the threads. In some cases, toxins may have spread throughout the food.

28. F. NO CHANGE
    G. live
    H. lived
    J. will have lived

29. A. NO CHANGE
    B. looked
    C. was looking
    D. looks

30. F. NO CHANGE
    G. produce
    H. was producing
    J. will have produced

English Conventions of Standard English

Unit 10 | Past Participles

INSIDE THIS UNIT:

– What Are Principal Parts? –
– Principal Parts of Some Common Verbs –
– Principal Parts of Some Common Irregular Verbs –
– Exercise –

Non-Negotiable Skill:

Form the past and past participle of irregular verbs, including memorizing the principal parts of commonly used irregular verbs.

What Are Principal Parts?

In English, verbs have <u>principal parts</u>. As the name implies, these are the most important (principal) forms of the verb. The technical terminology used to describe the three parts is *present* (also *base* or *infinitive*), *past,* and *past participle*:

Principal Parts of Some Common Verbs

Verb	Present	Past	Past Participle
to believe	believe	believed	believed
to ask	ask	asked	asked
to beg	beg	begged	begged
to bring	bring	brought	brought

But what is a "participle"? Sometimes the participle is a pure verb, and sometimes it is an adjective. The word "participle" is related to the word "participate"; since the participle shares the characteristics of both a verb and an adjective, it "participates" in both parts of speech.

Most English verbs form the past and past participle forms by adding *-ed* or simply *-d* (when the base form ends in *-e*) to the main form of the verb, as illustrated above by the verbs "believe" and "ask." There are a few exceptions, such as the doubling of a final consonant, as illustrated above by *beg*.

Principal Parts of Some Common Irregular Verbs

The real problem with English verbs, however, comes with the *irregular* verbs. These are verbs that do not fit any pattern, as illustrated on the previous page by the verb *bring*. Other common verbs that are irregular are:

Verb	Present	Past	Past Participle
to blow	blow	blew	blown
to eat	eat	ate	eaten
to freeze	freeze	froze	frozen
to ride	ride	rode	ridden

The irregular verbs do not follow any set rule, so there is no alternative to memorizing their principal parts:

Present	Past	Past Participle
awake	awoke/awakened	awoken
be	was, were	been
bear	bore	born/borne
beat	beat	beaten
become	became	become
begin	began	begun
bend	bent	bent
bet	bet	bet
bid	bid/bade	bid/bidden
bind	bound	bound
bite	bit	bitten
bleed	bled	bled
blow	blew	blown
break	broke	broken
breed	bred	bred
bring	brought	brought
broadcast	broadcast	broadcast
build	built	built
burst	burst	burst
buy	bought	bought
cast	cast	cast

Present	Past	Past Participle
catch	caught	caught
choose	chose	chosen
cling	clung	clung
come	came	come
cost	cost	cost
creep	crept	crept
cut	cut	cut
deal	dealt	dealt
dig	dug	dug
dive	dived/dove	dived
do	did	done
draw	drew	drawn
drink	drank	drunk
drive	drove	driven
eat	ate	eaten
fall	fell	fallen
feed	fed	fed
feel	felt	felt
fight	fought	fought
find	found	found
fit	fit	fit
flee	fled	fled
fling	flung	flung
fly	flew	flown
forbid	forbade	forbidden
forego (forgo)	forewent (forwent)	foregone (forgone)
forget	forgot	forgotten
forgive	forgave	forgiven
forsake	forsook	forsaken
freeze	froze	frozen
get	got	gotten
give	gave	given
go	went	gone
grind	ground	ground

Present	Past	Past Participle
grow	grew	grown
hang	hung	hung
hear	heard	heard
hide	hid	hidden
hit	hit	hit
hold	held	held
hurt	hurt	hurt
keep	kept	kept
kneel	knelt	knelt
knit	knit	knit
know	knew	known
lay	laid	laid
lead	led	led
leap	leaped/leapt	leaped/leapt
learn	learned/learnt	learned/learnt
leave	left	left
lend	lent	lent
let	let	let
lie	lay	lain
light	lit	lit
lose	lost	lost
make	made	made
mean	meant	meant
meet	met	met
mow	mowed	mowed/mown
pay	paid	paid
plead	pled/pleaded	pled/pleaded
prove	proved	proved/proven
put	put	put
quit	quit	quit
read	read	read
rid	rid	rid
ride	rode	ridden
ring	rang	rung

Present	Past	Past Participle
rise	rose	risen
run	ran	run
saw	sawed	sawed/sawn
say	said	said
see	saw	seen
seek	sought	sought
sell	sold	sold
send	sent	sent
set	set	set
sew	sewed	sewed/sewn
shake	shook	shaken
shave	shaved	shaved/shaven
shed	shed	shed
shine	shone	shone
shoot	shot	shot
show	showed	showed/shown
shrink	shrank	shrunk
shut	shut	shut
sing	sang	sung
sink	sank	sunk
sit	sat	sat
slay	slayed/slew	slayed/slain
sleep	slept	slept
slide	slid	slid
sling	slung	slung
slit	slit	slit
smite	smote	smitten
sow	sowed	sowed/sown
speak	spoke	spoken
speed	sped	sped
spend	spent	spent
spin	spun	spun
spit	spit/spat	spit
split	split	split

Present	Past	Past Participle
spread	spread	spread
spring	sprang	sprung
stand	stood	stood
steal	stole	stolen
stick	stuck	stuck
sting	stung	stung
stink	stank	stunk
stride	strode	stridden
strike	struck	struck
string	strung	strung
strive	strove	striven
swear	swore	sworn
sweep	swept	swept
swell	swelled	swelled/swollen
swim	swam	swum
swing	swung	swung
take	took	taken
teach	taught	taught
tear	tore	torn
tell	told	told
throw	threw	thrown
thrust	thrust	thrust
tread	trod	trodden
understand	understood	understood
uphold	upheld	upheld
upset	upset	upset
wake	woke	woken
wear	wore	worn
weave	weaved/wove	weaved/woven
wed	wed	wed
weep	wept	wept
win	won	won
wind	wound	wound
withhold	withheld	withheld

Present	Past	Past Principle
withstand	withstood	withstood
wring	wrung	wrung
write	wrote	written

Summary

- The three principal parts of verbs are present, past, and past participle.

- With a few exceptions, most English verbs form the past and past participle by adding –*ed* or simply –*d* (when the verb's base form ends in –*e*).

- Irregular verbs do not follow any set rule when forming past or past participles, so students must memorize irregular verbs' principal parts.

UNIT 10 | PAST PARTICIPLES • 127

EXERCISE

DIRECTIONS: In each of the following items, a word is underlined. Following each sentence or sentences are alternative suggestions for rewriting the underlined part. If you think the original is correct, choose NO CHANGE. Otherwise, choose the best alternative. Answers are on page 748.

1. Before we could get to the shelter on the ninth hole, the skies opened up and it <u>begun</u> to rain.

   A. NO CHANGE
   B. began
   C. beginned
   D. begint

2. Mel did not have an air pressure gauge, and he overfilled the bike tire to the point at which it <u>busted</u>.

   F. NO CHANGE
   G. bust
   H. burst
   J. bursted

3. After several days of below-zero temperatures, the pond <u>froze</u>, and we were able to go ice skating.

   A. NO CHANGE
   B. freezed
   C. frozed
   D. freeze

4. We <u>heared</u> through the grapevine that a new dean was being appointed to fill the position left vacant when Ms. Evans retired.

   F. NO CHANGE
   G. heart
   H. hearred
   J. heard

5. When Honey first planted the tree, it was just a twig, but now you can see how big it's <u>grown</u>.

   A. NO CHANGE
   B. growed
   C. grew
   D. growt

6. On Saturday afternoon, I didn't have much to do, so I just went to the mall and <u>hung</u> out with friends.

   F. NO CHANGE
   G. hungen
   H. hangen
   J. hang

ENGLISH CONVENTIONS OF STANDARD ENGLISH

7. The most exciting ride at the fair was the Whirl-a-Gig, which <u>spunt</u> you around so fast that you were jammed into the back of your seat.

    A. NO CHANGE
    B. spinned
    C. spun
    D. span

8. In the tale by Washington Irving, Rip van Winkle dozed off under a tree and <u>sleeped</u> for 20 years.

    F. NO CHANGE
    G. slept
    H. sleepped
    J. slapt

9. At Ed's surprise party, we all hid behind the furniture in the darkened room and then <u>sprung</u> up and shouted "Welcome home!" when he turned on the light.

    A. NO CHANGE
    B. springed
    C. spring
    D. sprang

10. The truck dumped the topsoil on the garden area, and we carefully <u>spreaded</u> it out with rakes to a uniform depth.

    F. NO CHANGE
    G. spreadt
    H. spread
    J. sprode

11. The delivery driver brought the floral arrangement into the office and <u>sat</u> it down on the table in the lobby.

    A. NO CHANGE
    B. set
    C. sit
    D. setted

12. When Miguel went to court to testify as a witness about the car accident he saw, he <u>sweared</u> to tell the truth, the whole truth, and nothing but the truth.

    F. NO CHANGE
    G. sworn
    H. swore
    J. swear

13. The sun was already shining brightly when we finally <u>awokened</u>, so we had to hurry down to the dock to catch the boat.

    A. NO CHANGE
    B. awakened
    C. wokened
    D. woked

14. Exhausted, the runner nodded weakly that she <u>understood</u> that she had finished first, setting a new track record.

    F. NO CHANGE
    G. understanded
    H. understooded
    J. understand

UNIT 10 | PAST PARTICIPLES • 129

15. To begin the recipe, the chef mixed several spices together in a mortar and <u>grinded</u> them to a fine powder with the pestle.

    A. NO CHANGE
    B. grund
    C. grounded
    D. ground

Questions 16–20

In 1969, Dr. Martin Luther King <u>went</u> to
                                  16
Memphis to support the almost entirely African American sanitation workforce as they <u>striked</u> for
                                   17
union recognition, better pay, safer working conditions, and, fundamentally, respect. It was there, on April 3, that Dr. King delivered his "I've Been to the Mountaintop" speech. You would be hard-pressed to find another speech that so perfectly <u>wove</u> together the beautiful yet all too
             18
fragile fabric of the historical struggle for basic human rights. And what's so remarkable about the way Dr. King <u>telled</u> the story that day was not
              19
the pain, frustration, and violence of that endless struggle for justice, but the hope, the optimism, the nonviolent sensibility, and most profoundly, the faith that he <u>brang</u>, and urged us all to bring,
          20
to that struggle.

16. F. NO CHANGE
    G. gone
    H. goed
    J. go

17. A. NO CHANGE
    B. struck
    C. strake
    D. strucked

18. F. NO CHANGE
    G. woven
    H. wovened
    J. woved

19. A. NO CHANGE
    B. told
    C. tolded
    D. tollen

20. F. NO CHANGE
    G. brung
    H. bringed
    J. brought

Questions 21–25

Edward Kennedy Ellington, often <u>sayed</u> to be
                                        21
America's greatest composer, bandleader, and recording artist, was born on April 29, 1899, in Washington, D.C. Nicknamed "Duke" as a youngster, Ellington turned down a visual arts scholarship to focus on music. With a background in classical, popular, ragtime, and stride music, Ellington emerged as arguably the greatest single talent in the history of jazz.

Duke Ellington <u>teachen</u> himself James P.
                          22
Johnson's "Carolina Shout" by slowing down a piano roll and copying each note. When Johnson appeared in Washington, pals pushed Ellington to play for Johnson, and the two <u>becomed</u> friends.
                                              23
Ellington moved to New York in 1923 with his band, The Washingtonians. They <u>got</u> their first big
                                               24
break at the Cotton Club. During an era of strict segregation, the Club presented black performers to white audiences. They played a variety of venues and over the years <u>maken</u> some sixty
                                25
recordings. Ellington and his orchestra performed into the early 1970s.

21. A. NO CHANGE
    B. said
    C. sain
    D. sayen

22. F. NO CHANGE
    G. teached
    H. taught
    J. taughten

23. A. NO CHANGE
    B. becomen
    C. became
    D. becamen

24. F. NO CHANGE
    G. get
    H. gat
    J. getted

25. A. NO CHANGE
    B. maked
    C. makened
    D. made

English **Conventions of Standard English**

Unit 11 | **Adjectives**

INSIDE THIS UNIT:
– Degrees of Adjectives –   – Exercise –

Non-Negotiable Skill:

Form comparative and superlative adjectives.

Degrees of Adjectives

Adjectives are words that modify nouns.

Examples:

the *blue* car

a *quiet* afternoon

two *large* sodas

an *important* game

the *final* inning

In English, adjectives express one of three degrees: positive, comparative, or superlative. The degree of an adjective depends upon the number of distinct individuals or concepts being compared.

The positive degree simply makes the statement that a particular noun has the characteristic expressed by the adjective:

a *loud* noise

the *large* dog

one *ripe* apple

The comparative degree compares two nouns according to the characteristic expressed by the adjective:

The first noise was *louder* than the second. (the *louder* noise)

The black dog is *larger* than the white dog. (the *larger* dog)

The red apple is *riper* than the green one. (the *riper* apple)

The superlative degree distinguishes three or more nouns according to the characteristic expressed by the adjective:

The third noise was the *loudest.* (the *loudest* noise)

The black dog was the *largest* one in the show. (the *largest* dog)

The red apple is the *ripest* on the tree. (the *ripest* apple)

In general, the comparative form of an adjective is formed by adding *-er* to the positive form of the adjective or, in the case of adjectives ending in *e*, just an *-r*. There are some exceptions in the spelling of the comparative form, such as adjectives for which the final consonant of the adjective is doubled or a final *y* is changed to *i*:

There are *fewer* boys than girls on the debating team. (*few* → *few* + *-er* = *fewer*)

Mark is two inches *taller* than Erik. (*tall*→ *tall* + *-er* = *taller*)

The new king is *wiser* than the old one. (*wise* → *wise* + *-r* = *wiser*)

The Amazon River is *wider* at its mouth than the Mississippi River. (*wide*→*wide* + *-r* = *wider*)

Maria is *sadder* today than yesterday. (*sad*→*sad* + *-der* = *sadder*)

Margaret is *happier* today than yesterday. (*happy*→*happ-* + *i* + *-er* = *happier*)

And in general, the superlative form of an adjective is formed by adding *-est* to the positive form, though there are some peculiar spelling shifts of the sort described above:

Mark is the *tallest* boy in the class. (*tall* + *-est* = *tallest*)

Maria is the *saddest* girl in the room. (*sad* + *-dest* = *saddest*)

Margaret is the *happiest* person in the world. (*happ* + *i* + *-est* = *happiest*)

The general rules for forming the comparative and superlative of adjectives often give way to a different rule when the adjective has more than two syllables. The difficulty in pronouncing the result of adding *-er* or *-est* leads to the use of *more/less* or *most/least* to modify the positive degree form:

Positive	Comparative	Superlative
rambunctious	more/less rambunctious	most/least rambunctious
beautiful	more/less beautiful	most/least beautiful
forgetful	more/less forgetful	most/least forgetful
irritable	more/less irritable	most/least irritable

Some shorter adjectives for which the basic rule would produce pronunciation difficulties may also use the alternative comparative and superlative forms:

Positive	Comparative	Superlative
careful	more/less careful	most/least careful
stylish	more/less stylish	most/least stylish
frigid	more/less frigid	most/least frigid
precious	more/less precious	most/least precious

This is not to say that it would be grammatically incorrect to use "frigider" or "stylishest," but the construction would not sound pleasant to the ear of a fluent English speaker.

In fact, some adjectives can be formed using either the standard rule of adding -er or -est or using *more* or *most*.

Examples:

Positive	Comparative	Superlative
friendly	friendlier *or* more friendly	friendliest *or* most friendly
tacky	tackier *or* more tacky	tackiest *or* most tacky
wise	wiser *or* more wise	wisest *or* most wise

Both forms are equally correct. However, you cannot combine the two forms:

Positive	Comparative	Superlative
friendly	more friendlier (Wrong)	most friendliest (Wrong)
tacky	more tackier (Wrong)	most tackiest (Wrong)

All of this is probably very familiar to you, as you learned these rules years ago. The point that seems to give many writers trouble is the distinction between the comparative and the superlative forms of an adjective. Remember that the comparative or -er form is used to compare two things. The superlative or -est form is used to compare three or more things:

Of the three brothers, Ricardo is the *taller*. (Incorrect)

Of the three brothers, Ricardo is the *tallest*. (Correct)

German is the *faster* runner on the team. (Incorrect)

German is the *fastest* runner on the team. (Correct)

So far, the adjectives we have discussed play by the rules. Unfortunately, in English there are a handful that form the comparative and superlative forms in irregular fashion. These you have to memorize:

Positive	Comparative	Superlative
bad	worse	worst
far	further	furthest
far	farther	farthest
good	better	best
little	less	least
many	more	most

You almost surely know this already, but you need to be careful when you are writing or speaking formally.

A final point to remember about the formation of adjectives is that some adjectives do not admit to degrees of comparison. For example, one cannot be more or less *dead*, so there would be no occasion in formal writing to use *deader* or *deadest*. In informal conversation, we might use such words—*This is the deadest I've ever seen the café.*—but this usage would be slang.

Examples:

absolute	final	minor	unanimous
adequate	ideal	paramount	unavoidable
chief	impossible	perpetual	unbroken
complete	inevitable	preferable	unique
devoid	irrevocable	principal	universal
entire	main	stationary	whole
fatal	manifest	sufficient	

Summary

- Adjectives are words that modify nouns and express one of three degrees: positive (a particular noun has the expressed characteristic), comparative (compares two nouns according to the expressed characteristic), and superlative (distinguishes three or more nouns according to the expressed characteristic).

- With some exceptions, the comparative form of an adjective is formed by adding *–er* or *–r* to the positive form of the adjective.

- Also, with some exceptions, the superlative form of an adjective is formed by adding *–est* to the positive form of the adjective.

- When adjectives have more than two syllables (or when the basic rule would produce pronunciation difficulties for shorter adjectives), comparative and superlative adjectives are formed by using *more/less* or *most/least* to modify the positive adjective.

- Memorize the adjectives that form the comparative and superlative in irregular fashion.

UNIT 11 | ADJECTIVES • 137

EXERCISE

DIRECTIONS: In each of the following items, a word is underlined. Following each sentence or sentences are alternative suggestions for rewriting the underlined part. If you think the original is correct, choose NO CHANGE. Otherwise, choose the best alternative. Answers are on page 748.

1. There are four puppies in the litter, and the spotted one is the smaller.

   A. NO CHANGE
   B. small
   C. smallest
   D. smallier

2. The third and loud noise was the sound of the barn collapsing after the wind blew the structure off the foundation.

   F. NO CHANGE
   G. louder
   H. loudest
   J. louding

3. LeRoy Brown, who carried a .34 caliber gun in his pocket for fun and a razor in his shoe, was certainly the baddest man in the whole town.

   A. NO CHANGE
   B. worst
   C. badder
   D. more bad

4. Donna often said that she was the happier girl in the whole United States.

   F. NO CHANGE
   G. happiest
   H. happily
   J. more happier

5. The recipe produced a very tasty cake, but it would have been more better had we used walnuts as well as pecans.

   A. NO CHANGE
   B. more best
   C. better
   D. most best

6. The guide warned us to be more carefuller of the edge when the path narrowed as it passed the fallen boulder.

   F. NO CHANGE
   G. more careful
   H. most carefullest
   J. most carefuller

7. Profiting from the misfortune of a friend is the <u>furthest</u> thing from my mind, so I hope Alex recovers quickly.

A. NO CHANGE
B. farrest
C. further
D. more further

8. The <u>baddest</u> outcome would be for Sydney to lose her match and the opposing team's captain to win hers.

F. NO CHANGE
G. worser
H. badder
J. worst

9. <u>The most impossible</u> task was the third one: scaling a rock wall without any ropes, hammers, or other equipment.

A. NO CHANGE
B. The more impossible
C. The seemingly impossible
D. The impossiblest

10. The <u>best</u> loved of all fairy tales is *Jack and the Beanstalk* because it has a happy ending.

F. NO CHANGE
G. better
H. more better
J. most better

11. According to Benjamin Franklin, the only things in the world that are <u>most certain</u> are death and taxes.

A. NO CHANGE
B. certain
C. more certain
D. certainest

12. Nathan received a <u>higher</u> score on the test than either Jonathan or Maxwell.

F. NO CHANGE
G. more higher
H. highest
J. most high

13. Of the two wounds, the <u>more fatal was the one</u> inflicted by the spear.

A. NO CHANGE
B. most fatal was the one
C. fatal one was
D. fataller one was

14. <u>The most unique</u> solution was suggested by Peter, who said that the prize ought to be given to the entire school.

F. NO CHANGE
G. The more unique
H. The uniquest
J. A unique

UNIT 11 | ADJECTIVES • 139

15. The red-headed, saddle-backed woodpecker is the endangeredest bird of all the woodpeckers.

    A. NO CHANGE
    B. more endangered
    C. endangered
    D. most endangered

16. Between the Civil War and World War I, New England had become a major producer of textiles and other goods needed by people all across the expanding nation. Some of the nation's earliest labor disputes occurred here.

    F. NO CHANGE
    G. most earliest
    H. more earliest
    J. earlier

17. I went to the doctor, who prescribed some antibiotics for the infection, but the next morning I felt worser, so I went to the hospital emergency room.

    A. NO CHANGE
    B. more bad
    C. worse
    D. worst

18. After completing eleven of the twelve tasks, Hercules was given the most difficult task of all: capturing Cerebus.

    F. NO CHANGE
    G. more difficult one
    H. difficultest one of all
    J. harder one

19. At the end of World War II, medical science was no far along in understanding polio than it was in 1916.

    A. NO CHANGE
    B. further
    C. more further
    D. more far

20. A century and a half ago, the United States and Mexico were the two youngest nations.

    F. NO CHANGE
    G. most young
    H. more younger
    J. most youngest

21. The skies were filled with balloons, each one more colorful than the next, launched by amateur enthusiasts at the festival.

    A. NO CHANGE
    B. more colorfuller
    C. colorfuller
    D. most colorfulest

140 • ENGLISH CONVENTIONS OF STANDARD ENGLISH

22. After observing several hundred students in the college library, a psychologist concluded that those who wore earphones were <u>lesser</u> interested in enjoying music than avoiding contact with fellow students.

F. NO CHANGE
G. less
H. lesser
J. least

23. No-till field management increased the amount of organic matter in the soil and made it <u>more stabler</u>.

A. NO CHANGE
B. stablest
C. more stable
D. most stable

24. The jets on one of Saturn's moons might be erupting from near-surface pockets of liquid water at a temperature <u>more greater</u> than 0 degrees Celsius.

F. NO CHANGE
G. most greatest
H. greatest
J. greater

25. There were two puppies in the pet store window; <u>the smallest one was also the cutest</u>.

A. NO CHANGE
B. the smallest one was also the cuter
C. a smaller one was also the cuter
D. the smaller one was also the cuter

English **Conventions of Standard English**

Unit 12 | **Commas**

INSIDE THIS UNIT:
– Why Use Commas? – – When to Use Commas – – Exercise –

Non-Negotiable Skill:

Use commas to make sentences clearer and delete commas that cause confusion.

Why Use Commas?

Commas help to make sentences clearer by giving the reader signals or directions. We can compare punctuation to traffic signs. A period is like a stop sign. It says, "Come to a complete stop." A comma is like a yield sign. It says, "Slow down before proceeding."

As a general rule, commas often appear where a speaker would naturally slow down or pause.

Spoken: Camping taught me that the forest is home to biting flies [pause] mosquitoes [pause] gnats [pause] and ticks.

Written: Camping taught me that the forest is home to biting flies, mosquitoes, gnats, and ticks.

Spoken: The firefighters grilled hamburgers [pause] and the police officers brought baked beans.

Written: The firefighters grilled hamburgers, and the police officers brought baked beans.

The "speaking" test for commas can be helpful, but the test isn't completely reliable. Sometimes, we talk quickly or unclearly, so it is important to learn the rules for using commas.

When to Use Commas

In a series of three or more elements, use commas to separate the elements.

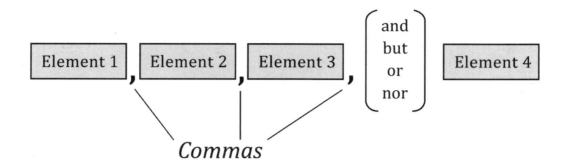

Commas are used to separate the elements of a series so that a reader can easily see where one element ends and the next begins.

> **Incorrect:** The cake contains raisins dried apricots pineapple pieces walnuts and almonds.

The sentence has a list of ingredients. Commas between the ingredients will avoid confusion.

> **Correct:** The cake contains raisins, dried apricots, pineapple pieces, walnuts, and almonds.

Examples:

Peanut oil and canola oil are low in saturated fats.
  (Only two elements so no comma.)

Peanut oil, canola oil, and safflower oil are low in saturated fats.
  (Three elements separated by commas.)

Olive oil, peanut oil, canola oil, and safflower oil are low in saturated fats.
  (Four elements separated by commas.)

The menu included *orange and grapefruit* juices.
  (Only two elements so no comma.)

The menu included *tomato, orange, and grapefruit* juices.
  (Three elements separated by commas.)

The menu included *cranberry, tomato, orange, and grapefruit* juices.
  (Four elements separated by commas.)

The team captain *grabbed the rebound and dribbled the length of the court.*
   (Only two elements so no comma.)

The team captain *grabbed the rebound, dribbled the length of the court, and shot a three-pointer* right at the buzzer.
   (Three elements separated by commas.)

The team captain *grabbed the rebound, dribbled the length of the court, pulled up sharply, and shot a three-pointer* right at the buzzer.
   (Four elements separated by commas.)

Use a comma before *and*, *but*, *or*, or *nor* when one of these words is used to join main clauses.

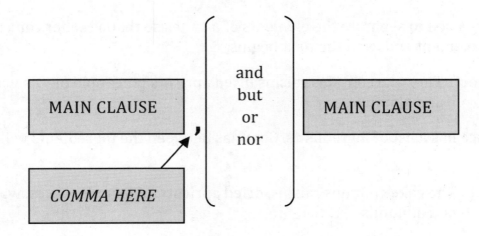

Commas are used to mark the end of one independent clause and the beginning of another independent clause when the two independent clauses are joined to make a single sentence using *and*, *but*, *or*, or *nor*.

   The coach introduced the players to the journalist. She congratulated each one on the victory.

Here you have two independent clauses each presented as its own sentence and marked at the end by a period. The two sentences can be combined to make a single sentence:

   The coach introduced the players to the *journalist, and she* congratulated each one on the victory. (The two complete thoughts—*the coach introduced* and *she congratulated*—are joined by *and*. The comma is correct.)

The fire alarm *sounded, but the people* in the office did not evacuate the building. (Two complete thoughts—*the alarm sounded* and *people did not evacuate*—are joined by *but*. The comma is correct.)

Either the governor will veto the *bill, or she* will ask the legislature to amend it. (Two complete thoughts—*the governor will veto* and *she will ask*—are joined by *or*. The comma is correct.)

Do not use a comma to separate the subject from its verb.

A comma that separates the subject of a sentence from the verb is grammatically incorrect and will only confuse the reader.

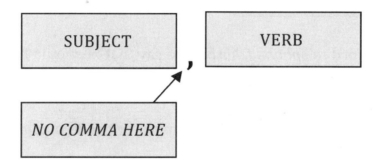

Incorrect: The express *train, arrived* at the final destination twenty minutes late.
(*Train* is the subject, and *arrived* is the verb. The comma separating the subject from the verb is a mistake.)

Incorrect: The *audience, gave* the orchestra a 5-minute standing ovation.
(*Audience* is the subject, and *gave* is the verb. The comma separating the subject from the verb is a mistake.)

Incorrect: *Alyssa, plans* to study mathematics at the state college.
(*Alyssa* is the subject, and *plans* is the verb. The comma separating the subject from the verb is a mistake.)

Incorrect: Neither *jets nor large propeller planes, can land* at the municipal airport because the runway is too short.
(*Jets nor planes* is the subject, and *can land* is the verb. The comma separating the subject from the verb is a mistake.)

146 • English Conventions of Standard English

Do not use a comma to separate the verb from the rest of the sentence.

Another common mistake is to put a comma after the verb. The comma leaves the rest of the sentence disconnected from the main body of the sentence.

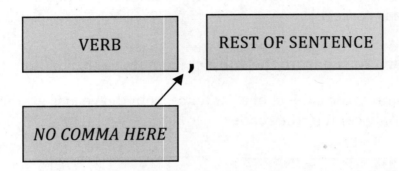

Incorrect: Clifford *telephoned, his boss* to say that he would be late for work.
(*Telephoned* is the verb, and *boss* is the direct object. The comma is a mistake.)

Incorrect: Juanita went to the office supply store and *bought, a box* of pens and a notebook.
(*Bought* is part of the verb, and *box* is part of the direct object. The comma is a mistake.)

Incorrect: The class took up a collection and *gave, their teacher* a retirement present.
(*Gave* is part of the verb, and *teacher* is the indirect object. The comma is a mistake.)

Incorrect: My friend Yuri *came, to* the United States with his family from Russia.
(*Came* is the verb, and the rest of the sentence consists of prepositional phrases explaining "where." The comma disconnects those phrases from the main part of the sentence. The comma is a mistake.)

Summary

- As a general rule, commas often appear where a speaker would naturally slow down or pause.

- In a series of three or more elements, use commas to separate the elements.

- Use a comma before *and*, *but*, *or*, or *nor* when one of these words is used to join main clauses.

- Do not use a comma to separate the subject from its verb.

- Do not use a comma to separate the verb from the rest of the sentence.

EXERCISE

DIRECTIONS: Each of the following sentences contains one error in comma usage. Select the one underlined portion that must be changed to produce a correct sentence. Answers are on page 748.

1. As a child growing up in a small town in Montana, Eleanor <u>learned, to</u> ride <u>horses, rope</u> <u>cows, hunt</u> for <u>food, and</u> survive in the wilderness.
   A — learned, to; B — horses, rope; C — cows, hunt; D — food, and

2. The architect suggested oak flooring for the living <u>room, the</u> dining <u>room, and</u> the <u>entry, but</u> the owners <u>decided, on</u> a new product made from bamboo.
   F — room, the; G — room, and; H — entry, but; J — decided, on

3. The resort advertises hiking <u>trails, an</u> Olympic swimming <u>pool,</u> <u>and</u> other outdoor <u>facilities, and</u> it offers indoor entertainment such as <u>movies, and</u> video games.
   A — trails, an; B — pool, and; C — facilities, and; D — movies, and

4. Rugby players can <u>run with</u> the <u>ball kick</u> the <u>ball, and</u> tackle an opposing <u>player, but</u> they cannot throw a forward pass.
   F — run with; G — ball kick; H — ball, and; J — player, but

5. The geologist explained that the forces are building up and will <u>cause an</u> <u>earthquake but</u> she added that it is impossible to say whether it will occur next <u>year, the</u> year <u>after, or</u> 500 years from now.
   A — cause an; B — earthquake but; C — year, the; D — after, or

6. Guillermo scraped off the peeling <u>paint, spackled</u> the <u>cracks, and</u> sanded the rough <u>areas, and</u> then he applied a <u>primer, and</u> a finish coat.
   F — paint, spackled; G — cracks, and; H — areas, and; J — primer, and

UNIT 12 | COMMAS • 149

7. The weather forecaster <u>predicts, high</u> <u>winds, freezing</u> <u>rain, driving</u> <u>sleet, and</u> snow, so we will have to leave early.
           A   B   C   D

8. Daily <u>newspapers, weekly</u> <u>magazines, monthly</u> <u>journals, and</u> other forms of print media are losing circulation <u>to, news</u> sources on the web.
        F   G   H   J

9. Fifty years ago, telephones could be <u>used only</u> for making calls, but today's cell phones are able to call from almost <u>anywhere, take</u> <u>pictures play</u> <u>music, and</u> even connect to the web.
        A   B   C   D

10. My favorite movie plot <u>is, one</u> with an action hero who is suspected of being a bad <u>guy, solves</u> the <u>mystery, beats</u> the real bad <u>guys, and</u> is treated as a hero.
         F   G   H   J

150 • ENGLISH CONVENTIONS OF STANDARD ENGLISH

DIRECTIONS: Each of the following sentences contains a part that is underlined. Choice (A) or (F) repeats the original; the other four choices are different. Choose the answer that you believe is correct. Some underlined parts may contain more than one error. Answers are on page 748.

11. My grandfather told me that when he was a boy he made skateboards out of boards and a roller skate, but the steel roller <u>skate wheels, would completely wear out</u> in one day.

    A. skate wheels, would completely wear out
    B. skate, wheels, would completely wear out
    C. skate wheels would, completely wear out
    D. skate wheels would completely wear out
    E. skate wheels would, completely wear out,

12. My friend lives in an apartment on the top floor of his <u>building and can see, the lake</u> on the other side of the valley.

    F. building and can see, the lake
    G. building, and can see the lake
    H. building and can see the lake
    J. building, and can see, the lake
    K. building and can see the lake,

13. A Waldorf salad <u>contains, diced apples,</u> pears, celery, and walnuts mixed together with a mayonnaise dressing.

    A. contains, diced apples,
    B. contains diced apples,
    C. contains, diced apples
    D. contains diced, apples
    E. contains diced, apples,

14. The high school band <u>director visited our school</u> looking for students to learn to play different musical instruments.

    F. director visited our school
    G. director, visited our school
    H. director visited, our school
    J. director visited, our school,
    K. director, visited, our school

15. Businesses, civic groups, and volunteers pitched in <u>to clean up, the mess</u> left by the flood.

    A. to clean up, the mess
    B. to clean up the mess
    C. to clean, up the mess
    D. to clean up, the mess,
    E. to clean up the mess,

16. The daily <u>chores, included walking the horses</u> mucking out the stalls, putting down clean hay, and making sure that the horses had food and plenty of clean water.

    F. chores, included walking the horses
    G. chores, included walking the horses,
    H. chores included walking the horses,
    J. chores, included walking, the horses,
    K. chores included, walking the horses,

17. Everyone who went on the trip agreed that the best rides at the adventure park <u>are, the sky toss, the death drop</u> and the roller coaster.

    A. are, the sky toss, the death drop
    B. are, the sky toss, the death drop,
    C. are the sky toss, the death drop,
    D. are the sky toss the death drop,
    E. are the sky toss the death drop

18. Eibar is a really excellent athlete, and he <u>excels at football, basketball,</u> and baseball.

    F. excels at football, basketball,
    G. excels, at football, basketball,
    H. excels, at football basketball,
    J. excels at, football, basketball,
    K. excels at football basketball,

19. The test pilots of the X-1 <u>flew faster and higher</u> than any have before them and were the first to break the sound barrier.

    A. flew faster and higher
    B. flew, faster and higher
    C. flew, faster, and higher
    D. flew faster, and higher
    E. flew, faster, and higher,

20. Every summer I <u>plant, basil and other herbs</u> in the garden and add them fresh to a variety of dishes.

    F. plant, basil and other herbs
    G. plant basil, and other herbs
    H. plant basil and other herbs,
    J. plant, basil, and other herbs
    K. plant basil and other herbs

21. Dairy cows produce milk that can be <u>bottled, made into cheese turned into ice cream, or</u> churned into butter.

    A. bottled, made into cheese turned into ice cream, or
    B. bottled made into cheese turned into ice cream or
    C. bottled made into cheese, turned into ice cream, or
    D. bottled made into cheese turned into ice cream, or
    E. bottled, made into cheese, turned into ice cream, or

22. People who observe parades from the sidelines usually do so <u>by sitting, standing or remaining, in</u> their vehicles.

    F. by sitting, standing or remaining, in
    G. by sitting, standing, or remaining in,
    H. by sitting, standing, or remaining in
    J. by sitting standing, or remaining in
    K. by sitting standing or remaining in

23. <u>Kayaking canoeing and jet skiing are</u> three enjoyable ways to spend a summer day at the lake.

    A. Kayaking canoeing and jet skiing are
    B. Kayaking, canoeing and jet skiing, are
    C. Kayaking, canoeing, and jet skiing, are
    D. Kayaking, canoeing, and jet skiing are
    E. Kayaking canoeing, and jet skiing are

24. Snowboarders can do tricks that are <u>creatively executed, fun to watch and, dangerous to</u> perform.

    F. creatively executed, fun to watch and, dangerous to
    G. creatively executed, fun to watch, and dangerous to
    H. creatively executed fun to watch and dangerous to
    J. creatively executed fun to watch and, dangerous to
    K. creatively executed, fun to watch and dangerous, to

25. The Venus flytrap <u>is, one of</u> 500 types of carnivorous or meat-eating plants.

    A. is, one of
    B. is one, of
    C. is, one, of
    D. is one of,
    E. is one of

English **Conventions of Standard English**

Unit 13 | **Practice**

INSIDE THIS UNIT:
– Exercise –

EXERCISE

DIRECTIONS: In the following passages, certain words and phrases are underlined and numbered. In the right-hand column, alternatives for the underlined parts are listed. Choose the one that best expresses the idea, makes the statement consistent with standard written English, or is most consistent with the style and tone of the entire passage. Choose "NO CHANGE" if you think the original version is best. Answers are on page 748.

Questions 1-5

Almost everyone knows the lyric that Frank Sinatra <u>singed</u> in the song *New York, New York*: "If
1
I can make it there, I can make it anywhere." Not many people, however, realize that Abraham Lincoln did make it there. Lincoln arrived in New York on Saturday, February 25, 1860, as an unknown congressman. That was the year that he <u>sought</u> the Republican nomination for president.
2
The very next day, Lincoln sat for Matthew Brady, who made a daguerreotype image of him; and on Monday evening, he delivered a passionate speech condemning slavery in the Great Hall of Cooper Union. Lincoln <u>catched</u> the attention of the entire
3
town. Horace Greeley wrote in the *New York*

Tribune that no man ever before made a <u>gooder</u>
4
impression on his first appeal to a New York

1. A. NO CHANGE
   B. sung
   C. sang
   D. sunged

2. F. NO CHANGE
   G. seekt
   H. soughted
   J. soughten

3. A. NO CHANGE
   B. catch
   C. caught
   D. caughten

4. F. NO CHANGE
   G. good
   H. better
   J. best

audience. By the time Lincoln <u>leften</u> the city, he
             5
was a national sensation, thanks to the zealous New York press and the printing of pamphlets of his speech that included Brady's image. Lincoln himself would later say, "Brady and the Cooper Institute made me President."

Questions 6–10

Larger than life itself, Ernest Hemingway <u>strided</u> across the literary landscape of his century
       6
with a tough attitude. Six feet tall and 250 pounds at his <u>heaviest</u> weight, Hemingway was an American
          7
star who vied for fame with Clark Gable, Gary Cooper, and Marilyn Monroe. He loved the outdoors, big game hunting, fishing, bullfighting, and checkered flannel shirts. He was a <u>busiest</u>
                                                      8
person and tested the limits of his physical and mental endurance. For years, his life was a movable feast as he lived in homes in Key West and Cuba and traipsed around Europe. Admirers said that he sucked all the oxygen out of a room. But up close, one could see the toll <u>taken</u> by heavy drinking and
                                9
failed marriages and physical injuries he got during his various adventures. On July 2, 1961, battling manic depression and a host of physical ailments, Hemingway died of a self-inflicted gunshot wound. Yet, even in his death, he was <u>biggest</u> than life.
                                            10

5. A. NO CHANGE
   B. leave
   C. leaved
   D. left

6. F. NO CHANGE
   G. strode
   H. stroded
   J. strodt

7. A. NO CHANGE
   B. heavier
   C. more heaviest
   D. most heaviest

8. F. NO CHANGE
   G. more busy
   H. busy
   J. busier

9. A. NO CHANGE
   B. took
   C. tooken
   D. token

10. F. NO CHANGE
    G. more big
    H. most bigger
    J. bigger

Questions 11-15

The launch of the satellite Sputnik by the Soviet Union in 1957 shocked America. America was even <u>more upset</u> when in 1961 the Soviet
         11

Cosmonaut Yuri Gagarin <u>flied</u> into space. The
                          12
assumption had been that America was scientifically superior to the Soviet Union and the

<u>most furthest</u> ahead in rocket technology. These
  13

events rudely <u>awoken</u> Americans. In reaction,
               14
President John F. Kennedy announced that, by the end of the 1960s, America would land a man on the moon. On July 20, 1969, Apollo 11 touched down on the surface of the moon in the Sea of Tranquility. Two US astronauts, Neil Armstrong and Buzz Aldrin, walked around on the frozen surface of the moon for over two hours, collecting rock samples and setting up experimental apparatus. The Apollo manned space program <u>come</u>
                                                  15
to an end in 1972 with Apollo 17, but the program was a great success.

11. A. NO CHANGE
    B. most upset
    C. upsetter
    D. upsettest

12. F. NO CHANGE
    G. flown
    H. fly
    J. flew

13. A. NO CHANGE
    B. more further
    C. furthest
    D. most further

14. F. NO CHANGE
    G. awakened
    H. awake
    J. woken

15. A. NO CHANGE
    B. comed
    C. comen
    D. came

Questions 16-20

Experts have shown that effective listening is a
            16

learned skill. More effective listening can improve
                 17
relations with your family, friends, colleagues, and even strangers. Hearing and listening are as different as night and day. Hearing is a mechanical function in which your ears process vibrations and noise. Hearing is passive. Listening is hearing plus interpretation, evaluation, and reaction. Listening is active. The experts studied listeners carefully. They noted that the goodest listeners
                                       18
maintained eye contact and sat up straight. The

baddest listeners daydreamed and slouched in
  19
their chairs. As you listen, be alert for nonverbal communication such as facial expressions, gestures, tone, and speech patterns. For example, when people talk quickly, this usually indicates an emotion such as excitement or anger, while speaking slowly may show the speaker is more thoughtful or little certain. Above all, listening
                    20
requires practice.

16. F. NO CHANGE
    G. showt
    H. showded
    J. shone

17. A. NO CHANGE
    B. Effectiver
    C. More effectiver
    D. Most effectiver

18. F. NO CHANGE
    G. gooder
    H. more good
    J. best

19. A. NO CHANGE
    B. worst
    C. badder
    D. wurst

20. F. NO CHANGE
    G. lest
    H. least
    J. less

Questions 21–25

Most teenagers enjoy pets. Some like <u>cats</u> [21] <u>and others like,</u> dogs. There are some teens [21] who like exotic or non-traditional pets such as <u>gerbils hamsters, and snakes</u>. Maintaining [22] a pet requires <u>time patience and money</u>. The [23] conscientious pet owner must find time to

21. A. NO CHANGE
B. cats, and others like
C. cats, and others, like
D. cats and, others like

22. F. NO CHANGE
G. gerbils hamsters and snakes
H. gerbils, hamsters, and snakes
J. gerbils hamsters, and, snakes

23. A. NO CHANGE
B. time, patience, and money
C. time patience, and money
D. time, patience and, money

UNIT 13 | PRACTICE • 159

play with the pet, to feed the pet, and to take
care of its medical needs. A well-cared-for pet

24. F. NO CHANGE
G. pet to feed the pet and to
H. pet to feed the pet and, to
J. pet, to feed the pet and, to

can provide, its owner with a warm body to
hug and unconditional, loyalty.

25. A. NO CHANGE
B. provide, its owner with a warm body, to hug and unconditional loyalty
C. provide its owner with a warm body, to hug and unconditional loyalty
D. provide its owner with a warm body to hug and unconditional loyalty

Questions 26–30

When you were a <u>little kid your parents,</u> chose your friends, put you in <u>playgroups and arranged playdates with</u> children they knew and liked. Now that you are older, you are the one who <u>decides who your friends are, and with</u> whom you will spend your time.

26. F. NO CHANGE
    G. little kid, your parents chose
    H. little kid, your parents, chose
    J. little, kid, your parents chose

27. A. NO CHANGE
    B. playgroups and arranged, playdates with
    C. playgroups, and arranged playdates with
    D. playgroups, and arranged playdates, with

28. F. NO CHANGE
    G. decides who, your friends are, and with
    H. decides who, your friends are and with
    J. decides who your friends are and with

Your friends—your peers—are people your age who have <u>experiences, and interests similar</u> to yours. You and your friends make
                                           29

dozens of decisions every <u>day and you</u> influence
                                    30
each other's choices and behaviors. It is human nature to listen to and learn from other people in your age group.

29. A. NO CHANGE
    B. experiences and interests similar
    C. experiences, and interests, similar
    D. experiences and interests, similar

30. F. NO CHANGE
    G. day, and you
    H. day and, you
    J. day, and, you

ENGLISH MASTERY TEST 1

> **DIRECTIONS:** In each of the following passages, sentences are underlined and numbered. For each of the corresponding items, select the answer that BEST answers the question. Answers are on page 748.

Questions 1–5

An American Hero in England

On May 28, 1877, the SS *Indiana* sailed into the harbor in Liverpool, England, carrying Civil War general and former president Ulysses S. Grant and his wife. A sea of red, white, and blue appeared as they approached the docks. Grant could hardly believe his eyes. It wasn't the Union Jack flying from the mainmast of almost every ship in port, but the Stars and Stripes. The British port was awash in American flags. And then there were the people. Young and old crammed the docks, cheering the arrival of his ship. The mayor was also there, offering a ride to the hotel in the state

carriage.[1] As the Grants made their way through the city, thousands more people lined the streets, craning their necks for a glimpse of the famous Americans.

Liverpool was the first stop on the Grants' two-and-a-half-year trip around the world.[2] After eight years in the White House, Grant and his wife, Julia, decided to take the world tour they'd long looked forward to. Additionally, by leaving the country, Grant hoped to give the incoming president, Rutherford B. Hayes, a chance to govern without reporters constantly running to his predecessor for comment.[3]

Invitations poured in from towns and individuals wanting to play host to Grant and his wife. Queen Victoria invited the Grants to stay at Windsor Castle. He breakfasted with well-known British poets Matthew Arnold and Robert Browning.[4]

Grant had worked hard during his presidency to resolve differences between England and America that lingered after the Civil War, and he characterized the warm welcome as a sign of the resumption of friendly relations between the two countries. "I appreciate the fact—and am proud of it—that the attentions I am receiving are intended more for our country than for me personally," he wrote.

164 • ENGLISH

Grant was being overly modest. The attention was not for the United States, but for him personally. He was the closest thing America had to a real, larger-than-life hero. Mathew Brady managed to capture Grant's essence in an iconic photo taken in June of 1864. Grant is standing with his right arm resting against a tree, left hip and arm thrust forward, and hat tipped slightly back. Dust covers his uniform and boots, signaling that he's no armchair general. His stance is defiant, almost cocky, yet he doesn't engage the camera. He looks off into the distance, his eyes made old by the horrors he's seen and ordered. 5

1. The underlined sentence should be

   A. deleted because a city mayor is not as important as a queen.

   B. deleted because it doesn't provide the name of the mayor.

   C. left unchanged because it adds detail to the description of Grant's arrival.

   D. left unchanged because Grant, as president, was also a political leader.

2. The underlined sentence should be

   F. left unchanged because it informs the reader that England was only one of many places Grant planned to visit.

   G. left unchanged because it shows that Grant planned to return to the United States to run for president again.

   H. deleted because the passage does not provide a detailed itinerary for Grant's trip around the world.

   J. deleted because Grant probably did not plan to stay in England for the entire two-and-a-half years.

3. The underlined sentence should be

   A. deleted because Grant chose not to run for a third term and was no longer president.
   B. deleted because the passage deals with Grant's travels, not with his presidency.
   C. left unchanged because it casts light on the relationship between Grant and Hayes.
   D. left unchanged because it helps to explain Grant's reasons for going on a long trip.

4. The underlined sentence should be

   F. deleted because the passage treats Grant as a military and political leader, not a poet.
   G. deleted because Arnold and Browning are no longer as famous as they once were.
   H. left unchanged because the detail helps to show that Grant was considered a hero.
   J. left unchanged because the detail provides an additional example of the people who hosted the Grants.

5. The description of Brady's photograph contained in the last paragraph of the passage should be

   A. left unchanged because the photograph depicts Grant as a heroic figure.
   B. left unchanged because the reader will find the description interesting.
   C. deleted because the photograph was taken before Grant began his trip.
   D. deleted because the photograph shows Grant as a soldier, not as president.

166 • ENGLISH

DIRECTIONS: In each of the following items, a word or phrase is underlined. Following each sentence or sentences are alternative suggestions for rewriting the underlined part. If you think the original is correct, choose NO CHANGE. Otherwise, choose the best alternative. Answers are on page 748.

Example:

First, you sand the surface until it's smooth; <u>meanwhile</u>, you apply the new coat of paint.

   A. NO CHANGE
   B. once
   C. initially
   D. then

   The correct answer is (D).

---

6. When he was only 19, Galileo discovered that the time needed for a pendulum to complete its swing is the same regardless of the height of the starting point. <u>Sometimes</u>, he determined experimentally that all bodies fall at the same speed regardless of their weight.

   F. NO CHANGE
   G. Just in time
   H. Some time later
   J. Time after time

7. As a child, Jonathan received allergy shots. <u>Thus</u>, he was also treated by an herbal doctor. One day, the allergies stopped, and it is impossible to say which treatment was effective.

   A. NO CHANGE
   B. In any event
   C. After all
   D. At the same time

8. Mahatma Gandhi is regarded as the father of independent India. He practiced law in South Africa, defending the rights of Indians in that country. He returned to India in 1915; and <u>by then</u>, he was already regarded as a leader in the nationalist movement.

F. NO CHANGE
G. since then
H. then
J. after then

9. In 1900, Galveston, Texas, was devastated by a hurricane, so a sea wall was built to protect the city. It has helped, but hurricanes <u>then</u> damage the city.

A. NO CHANGE
B. once
C. afterward
D. still

10. Valerie is a multi-tasking wizard. She can talk on the telephone and listen to the television news report; <u>simultaneously,</u> she can type a letter without any mistakes.

F. NO CHANGE
G. later
H. continuously
J. in any case

11. Dressed in a flame-retardant jumpsuit emblazoned with the logos of various sponsors, <u>the driver waved to the crowd and then climbed into the race car</u>.

A. NO CHANGE
B. the crowd received a wave from the driver who then climbed into the race car
C. a wave to the crowd preceded the driver's climbing into the race car
D. the race car received the driver who first waved to the crowd

12. <u>The math class had started just</u> when the teacher announced that instead of the regular lesson, there would be a pop quiz.

F. NO CHANGE
G. Just the math class had started
H. The math class had just started
J. The math class just had started

13. Between the first and second rounds of debate, we <u>barely had time to grab a snack</u> and discuss our strategy against our next opponent.

A. NO CHANGE
B. had time to grab barely a snack
C. had time to grab a snack barely
D. had time to grab a barely snack

14. The eyewitness picked out the thief <u>using a light pen pointing at a photograph</u>.

    F. NO CHANGE
    G. pointing at a photograph using a light pen
    H. by pointing at a photograph using a light pen
    J. by using a light pen that was pointing at a photograph

15. Draped with the traditional blanket of roses, <u>the winner of the Kentucky Derby was walked to the winner's circle so that pictures could be taken by all of the sports photographers covering the event</u>.

    A. NO CHANGE
    B. all the sports photographers covering the event took pictures of the winner of the Kentucky Derby walking to the winner's circle
    C. the winner's circle was used by all the sports photographers covering the event to take pictures of the winner of the Kentucky Derby
    D. pictures of the winner of the Kentucky Derby walking were taken by all the sports photographers covering the event in the winner's circle

16. The school offers intensive courses so that a student ambassador who is a non-speaker of the language of the host country can learn <u>to become one</u> in a short time.

    F. NO CHANGE
    G. to speak the language
    H. some
    J. them

17. Vicki looked through a telephone directory to find a number for a plumber who would make an emergency call on Saturday afternoon, but she could not find <u>one</u>.

    A. NO CHANGE
    B. them
    C. it
    D. a plumber

18. The campsites at Roger's Rock have no lean-tos, showers, or sanitary facilities, so <u>they are</u> really roughing it in the wild.

    F. NO CHANGE
    G. campers are
    H. everything is
    J. it is

19. In the mountains, the summer brought an uninterrupted period of dry weather with warm days and cool nights, a difference that was greatly appreciated by visitors from the city.

    A. NO CHANGE
    B. a difference in temperature
    C. a difference in seasons
    D. the difference

20. At exactly 2:00 p.m., the announcer instructed the drivers to start their engine and line up for the beginning of the race.

    F. NO CHANGE
    G. an engine
    H. their engines
    J. the engine

21. We waited two hours for the train. It never showed up.

    A. NO CHANGE
    B. We waited two hours for the train, and it never showed up.
    C. We waited two hours for the train, it never showed up.
    D. We waited two hours for the train, but it never showed up.

22. I have to renew my driver's license this week. I will get a ticket.

    F. NO CHANGE
    G. I have to renew my driver's license this week, or I will get a ticket.
    H. I have to renew my driver's license this week, so I will get a ticket.
    J. I have to renew my driver's license this week; I will get a ticket.

23. Despite the rain, we went to the beach. We had a good time anyway.

    A. NO CHANGE
    B. Despite the rain; we went to the beach, we had a good time anyway.
    C. Despite the rain, we went to the beach; we had a good time anyway.
    D. Despite the rain, we went to the beach, we had a good time anyway.

170 • ENGLISH

24. <u>The wage gap in the United States still exists. Women continue to make strides in the workplace.</u>

    F. NO CHANGE
    G. Although the wage gap in the United States still exists, women continue to make strides in the workplace.
    H. The wage gap in the United States still exists, so women continue to make strides in the workplace.
    J. The wage gap in the United States still exists; women continue to make strides in the workplace.

25. <u>I forgot to put an address on my sister's birthday card. She never received it.</u>

    A. NO CHANGE
    B. I forgot to put an address on my sister's birthday card, but she never received it.
    C. I forgot to put an address on my sister's birthday card; so she never received it.
    D. I forgot to put an address on my sister's birthday card, so she never received it.

ENGLISH MASTERY TEST 2

> **DIRECTIONS**: In each of the following items, a word or phrase is underlined. Following each sentence or sentences are alternative suggestions for rewriting the underlined part. If you think the original is correct, choose NO CHANGE. Otherwise, choose the best alternative. Answers are on page 749.

Questions 1–5

1. Robert Altman's *A Prairie Home Companion* featured a character named Asphodel, who is the Angel of Death. It <u>was</u> released five months before Altman's death.

   A. NO CHANGE
   B. is
   C. will be
   D. could be

2. In the 1960s, Laura Ashley introduced prints with reversible ground and motif colors. The fabric industry <u>used</u> the idea ever since.

   F. NO CHANGE
   G. has used
   H. will use
   J. could use

3. The editorial policy of the newspaper <u>slowly had changed</u> so that now it is virtually on the opposite end of the political spectrum from what it was several years ago.

   A. NO CHANGE
   B. will change slowly
   C. has slowly changed
   D. will have slowly changes

4. According to an anonymous source, the present director will resign tomorrow, and the board <u>appoints</u> a new director before the end of the week.

   F. NO CHANGE
   G. appointed
   H. has appointed
   J. will appoint

5. When *West Side Story* closes on Broadway next week, several dancers <u>will move</u> to a new show that is already in rehearsals.

   A. NO CHANGE
   B. moved
   C. had moved
   D. move

172 • ENGLISH

Questions 6–10

Andrew Carnegie was <u>knowed</u> as "The Richest
6

Man in the World." He was <u>born</u> in 1835 in
7

Scotland, but his family moved to America. At age thirteen, he became a stoker in a Pittsburgh textile factory, then a telegraph messenger, then an assistant to a superintendent on the Pennsylvania Railroad. He continued to climb the company ladder and by 1881 planned to retire in two more years. Then a newly developed process for making steel caught Carnegie's eye, and it <u>keeped</u> him working on building his fortune over the
8

next thirty-two years. In 1901, he <u>selled</u> his steel
9

company for 480 million dollars and began giving his money away. Carnegie's philosophy was that a man who dies rich dies in shame. And so the world's richest man became its <u>greatest</u>
10

philanthropist.

6. F. NO CHANGE
G. know
H. knowt
J. known

7. A. NO CHANGE
B. bornt
C. bored
D. bearn

8. F. NO CHANGE
G. keep
H. kept
J. kepted

9. A. NO CHANGE
B. selt
C. solt
D. sold

10. F. NO CHANGE
G. greater
H. more greater
J. most greatest

Questions 11–15

In Andrew Jackson's view, the President was the "representative" of the American people. When he <u>taken</u> the oath of office in 1829, few
11

people <u>understoodt</u> exactly what Jackson meant,
12

but by 1835, Jackson's enemies had <u>dubbed</u> him
13

"King Andrew." Jackson used the veto, the pocket veto, and executive privilege to set national above local interests and to strengthen the presidential office at the expense of Congress. The key issues of his two administrations—money, banking, internal improvements, the tariff, even the nature of the Union— <u>sat</u> much of the political agenda for
14

the remainder of the nineteenth century. Jackson's legacy to the executive branch was a framework

out of which would evolve a <u>more powerful</u>
15

presidency.

11. A. NO CHANGE
B. took
C. token
D. had taken

12. F. NO CHANGE
G. understanded
H. understood
J. understand

13. A. NO CHANGE
B. dub
C. dubbeded
D doubed

14. F. NO CHANGE
G. set
H. sit
J. setted

15. A. NO CHANGE
B. more powerfuller
C. powerfuller
D. powerfulest

174 • ENGLISH

> **DIRECTIONS:** Each of the following sentences contains a part that is underlined. Choice (A) or (F) repeats the original; the other four choices are different. Choose the answer that you believe is correct. Some underlined parts may contain more than one error. Answers are on page 749.

16. Some household items <u>such as old paint cans batteries, and weed killers are</u> considered hazmats.

   F. such as old paint cans batteries, and weed killers are

   G. such as, old paint cans batteries, and weed killers are

   H. such as old paint cans, batteries, and weed killers are

   J. such as old, paint cans, batteries, and weed killers are

   K. such as old paint, cans batteries, and weed killers are

17. Henry Ford, founder of the Ford Motor Company, <u>built, a strong, and sturdy, car.</u>

   A. built, a strong, and sturdy, car.

   B. built a strong and sturdy car.

   C. built a strong, and sturdy car.

   D. built a strong and sturdy, car.

   E. built, a strong and sturdy car.

18. When the weather starts to get chilly, some butterflies, such as the monarch, <u>migrate to warmer places.</u>

   F. migrate to warmer places.

   G. migrate, to warmer places.

   H. migrate to, warmer places.

   J. migrate to warmer, places.

   K. migrate, to warmer, places.

19. Compost piles can be made up <u>of orange rinds, coffee grounds, eggshells, leaves grass, and other material.</u>

   A. of orange rinds, coffee grounds, eggshells, leaves grass, and other material.

   B. of orange rinds coffee grounds, eggshells leaves, grass and other material.

   C. of orange rinds, coffee grounds, eggshells leaves grass, and other material.

   D. of orange rinds, coffee grounds, eggshells, leaves, grass, and other material.

   E. of orange, rinds, coffee grounds, eggshells, leaves, grass, and other material.

20. <u>Natural, gas, coal and oil are</u> all fossil fuels.

    F. Natural, gas, coal and oil are
    G. Natural gas, coal, and oil are
    H. Natural gas coal and oil are
    J. Natural gas coal, and oil are
    K. Natural gas, coal and oil are,

21. Most mammals are <u>color-blind but monkeys, apes and humans</u> can tell colors apart.

    A. color-blind but monkeys, apes and humans
    B. color-blind but monkeys, apes, and humans
    C. color-blind, but monkeys, apes and, humans
    D. color-blind, but monkeys, apes, and humans
    E. color-blind but, monkeys apes, and humans

22. Trivial Pursuit players advance on a game board by answering trivia questions <u>about sports, movies history, literature, and nature.</u>

    F. about sports, movies history, literature, and nature.
    G. about sports movies history literature and nature.
    H. about sports movies, history literature, and nature.
    J. about sports, movies, history, literature, and nature.
    K. about, sports, movies, history, literature, and nature.

23. <u>Melanin is a naturally occurring brown substance or pigment that is</u> found in everybody's skin.

    A. Melanin is a naturally occurring brown substance or pigment that is
    B. Melanin is a naturally occurring brown substance or pigment, that is,
    C. Melanin is a naturally, occurring brown substance or pigment that is
    D. Melanin is a naturally occurring brown, substance, or pigment that is
    E. Melanin is a naturally occurring brown substance, or pigment that is

24. Most people don't care where chocolate comes from as long as they can eat <u>it, chew it drink it or</u> let it melt in their mouths.

    F.   it, chew it drink it or
    G. it chew it, drink it, or
    H. it, chew it, drink it, or
    J.   it chew it drink it, or
    K. it chew, it drink, it or

25. Metamorphic <u>rocks, are sedimentary or igneous rocks</u> changed by underground heat and pressure.

    A. rocks, are sedimentary or igneous rocks
    B. rocks, are sedimentary, or igneous rocks
    C. rocks are sedimentary or igneous rocks
    D. rocks, are sedimentary, or igneous, rocks
    E. rocks are sedimentary or igneous, rocks

Level 1
MATH

NUMBER AND QUANTITY

UNIT 1 | BASIC MANIPULATIONS...........................179
Perform One-Step Computations............................180
Exercise..183

UNIT 2 | FRACTIONS...187
The Language of Fractions....................................188
The Fundamental Rule of Fractions 189
Exercise..195

UNIT 3 | NUMBER LINES.....................................199
Positive Number Line Coordinates 200
Exercise..204

ALGEBRA AND FUNCTIONS

UNIT 4 | ONE- AND TWO- STEP PROBLEMS.........209
Solve Word Problems..210
Exercise..215

UNIT 5 | BASIC EXPRESSIONS 219
Exhibit Knowledge of Basic Expressions................220
Exercise..223

UNIT 6 | BASIC EQUATIONS 227
Solve One-Step Equations.....................................228
The Fundamental Rule of Equations 229
Exercise..235

UNIT 7 | PRACTICE..237
Exercise..238

UNIT 8 | PATTERN IDENTIFICATION 243
The Features of a Sequence 244
Exercise..247

GEOMETRY

UNIT 9 | LENGTH AND DISTANCE........................251
Measurement 252
Comparing Lengths 253
Figures Drawn to Actual Size 255
Figures Drawn to Scale 257
Figures with "No-Name" Units 259
Figures "Not Drawn to Scale"................................259
Exercise..261

UNIT 10 | UNIT CONVERSIONS 267
Perform Common Unit Conversions 268
Exercise..272

STATISTICS AND PROBABILITY

UNIT 11 | AVERAGES 277
Calculate the Average of a List of Numbers............278
Exercise..280

Unit 12 | Charts and Tables 285

Tables 286

Bar Graphs 288

Line Graphs 289

Pie Charts 290

Pictographs 294

Exercise..296

Unit 13 | Practice 303

Exercise..304

MASTERY TESTS

Math Mastery Test 1 309

Math Mastery Test 2 313

Math **Number and Quantity**

Unit 1 | **Basic Manipulations**

INSIDE THIS UNIT:
– Perform One-Step Computations – – Exercise –

Non-Negotiable Skill:

Perform simple calculations, such as addition, subtraction, multiplication, and division, using whole numbers and decimals.

Perform One-Step Computations

One of the most important math skills you need is the basic ability to do simple calculations: add, subtract, multiply, and divide.

Example:

What is the sum of 6 and 48?

A. 8   C. 54   E. 288
B. 42   D. 108

    The correct answer is (C). "Sum" indicates addition: 6 + 48 = 54.

Example:

What is the difference between 81 and 27?

F. 3   H. 18   K. 108
G. 9   J. 54

    The correct answer is (J). "Difference" indicates subtraction: 81 – 27 = 54.

Example:

What is the product of 16 and 4?

A. 0.25   C. 12   E. 64
B. 4   D. 20

    The correct answer is (E). "Product" indicates multiplication: 16 • 4 = 64, or 16 × 4 = 64.

Note: The "•" and "×" are both symbols for multiplication.

Example:

What is the quotient when 60 is divided by 240?

F. 0.25 H. 144 K. 300
G. 4 J. 180

The correct answer is (F). "Quotient" indicates division:

$$60 \div 240 = \frac{60}{240} = \frac{6}{24} = \frac{1}{4} = 0.25.$$

The above computations are not difficult, and often you'll have a calculator available to make the task even easier. But there is something that a calculator cannot provide: **number sense**.

"Number sense" is the feeling that the answer the calculator gives you is either reasonable or out of line. Take a few seconds to **think** about your answer.

Example:

$24 + 16 = ?$

A. $\dfrac{3}{4}$ C. 8 E. 48

B. $\dfrac{4}{3}$ D. 40

The correct answer is (D). This is a very easy addition problem: $24 + 16 = 40$. You probably don't need a calculator. But assume that you use a calculator and happen to push a **wrong key** such as the "subtract" key:

24 [subtract key] 16 = 8

The calculator correctly did just what you told it to do. However, you told the calculator to do the **wrong** thing, so 8 is **not** the correct answer for the problem. Use some number sense. If you add 24 and 16, the answer should be greater than either 24 or 16. In this case, however, 8 is less than both 24 and 16. That makes no sense. So a few seconds **thinking** about your answer should tell you that you've made an error.

Example:

36 – 12 = ?

F. $\frac{1}{3}$ H. 24   K. 56

G. 3   J. 48

The correct answer is (H). This is another simple calculation; in this case, subtraction: 36 – 12 = 24. But suppose you use the calculator and make the mistake of pushing the "add" function instead of the "subtract." You'll get:

36 [add] 12 = 48

Again, this is a wrong answer. **Think** about your answer. Your number sense should tell you that when you subtract 12 from 36, the result has to be **less** than 36.

Number sense is very important, and you should practice using it to check whether your final answers are reasonable or not.

Summary

- "Sum" indicates addition (+).
- "Difference" indicates subtraction (–).
- "Product" indicates multiplication (• or ×).
- "Quotient" indicates division (÷).
- "Number sense" is the feeling that the answer the calculator gives you is either reasonable or out of line.

UNIT 1 | BASIC MANIPULATIONS • 183

EXERCISE

DIRECTIONS: The following items can be solved with either pencil and paper or a calculator. Before performing the indicated operation(s), eliminate any choices that violate your number sense. Answers are on page 749.

1. 12 + 24 = ?

   A. 0.5   C. 12   E. 36
   B. 2   D. 24

2. 48 + 6 = ?

   F. 0.125   H. 42   K. 288
   G. 8   J. 54

3. 68 + 33 = ?

   A. 35   C. 95   E. 2,244
   B. 91   D. 101

4. 1.002 + 0.2 = ?

   F. 0.501   H. 1.022   K. 1.220
   G. 1   J. 1.202

5. 32 − 4 = ?

   A. 0.125   C. 28   E. 128
   B. 8   D. 36

6. 144 − 72 = ?

   F. 0.5   H. 12   K. 216
   G. 2   J. 72

7. 135 − 45 = ?

   A. 3   C. 110   E. 180
   B. 90   D. 170

8. 216 − 18 = ?

   F. 12   H. 234   K. 3,888
   G. 198   J. 298

9. 24 × 3 = ?

   A. 0.125   C. 21   E. 72
   B. 8   D. 27

10. 54 × 9 = ?

    F. 6   H. 63   K. 486
    G. 45   J. 463

11. 32 × 8 = ?

    A. 4   C. 40   E. 346
    B. 24   D. 256

12. 49 × 0.3 = ?

    F. 14.7   H. 48.9   K. 147
    G. 16.3   J. 49.3

13. $156 \times 0.2 = ?$

    A. 31.2   C. 155.8   E. 780
    B. 78   D. 157.2

14. $16 \div 10 = ?$

    F. 0.625   H. 6   K. 160
    G. 1.6   J. 26

15. $182 \div 14 = ?$

    A. 12.1   C. 168   E. 2,548
    B. 13   D. 196

16. $20 \div 0.5 = ?$

    F. 0.25   H. 19.5   K. 40
    G. 10   J. 21.5

17. $22 \div 0.2 = ?$

    A. 1.1   C. 21.8   E. 110
    B. 11   D. 44

18. $0.4 \div 0.2 = ?$

    F. 0.08   H. 3.8   K. 8
    G. 2   J. 4.2

19. What is the sum of 94 and 67?

    A. 27   C. 161   E. 170
    B. 116   D. 162

20. The quotient when 234 is divided by 9 is:

    F. 26   H. 243   K. 2,106
    G. 225   J. 245

21. The product of 28 and 7 is:

    A. 4   C. 35   E. 196
    B. 21   D. 194

22. What is the sum of 32 and 19?

    F. 23   H. 51   K. 608
    G. 41   J. 141

23. The product of 63 and 3 is:

    A. 21   C. 66   E. 189
    B. 60   D. 96

24. What is the difference between 242 and 11?

    F. 22   J. 253   K. 2,662
    G. 221   H. 231

25. What is the sum of 112 and 16?

    A. 7   C. 108   E. 1,792
    B. 96   D. 128

26. The quotient when 224 is divided by 4 is:

    F. 51   H. 220   K. 896
    G. 56   J. 228

27. What is the difference between 4.09 and 0.8?

    A. 3.272
    B. 3.29
    C. 3.89
    D. 4.29
    E. 5.1125

28. The sum of 108 and 26 is:

    F. 82
    G. 92
    H. 122
    J. 124
    K. 134

29. The quotient when 162 is divided by 9 is:

    A. 18
    B. 81
    C. 153
    D. 171
    E. 1,458

30. What is the product of 12 and 24?

    F. 12
    G. 72
    H. 136
    J. 270
    K. 288

Math **Number and Quantity**

Unit 2 | **Fractions**

INSIDE THIS UNIT:

– The Language of Fractions –
– The Fundamental Rule of Fractions –
– Exercise –

Non-Negotiable Skill:

Reduce fractions to lowest terms and identify equivalent fractions.

The Language of Fractions

It's worth doing a quick review of the terminology that we use to talk about fractions.

The first numbers you learned, even before you started school, were the **natural numbers**: 1, 2, 3, etc. And later you added 0, so that you knew the **whole numbers**.

Whole numbers worked well enough in most situations, but you eventually encountered situations in which things were divided or broken up into pieces. You broke a cookie into two pieces to share with a friend, or you spent part of a dollar. Whole numbers were not adequate for describing parts, and that's when fractions became necessary.

Just as pieces of a thing are called **fragments**, pieces of a number are called **fractions**. Both words—"fragment" and "fraction"—developed in English from the old Latin word (think Roman Empire, chariots, and gladiators) *fractus*, meaning "broken." So fractions are just pieces of a whole number that has been broken apart into equal size pieces:

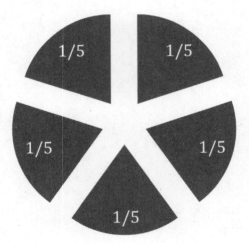

The disc is fractured into 5 equal pieces, so each piece is 1 of 5, or $\frac{1}{5}$ of the disc.

It obviously makes a big difference how large or how small the pieces are. If something is broken into two equal parts, the parts are larger than the parts of a similar object that is broken into 10 equal parts.

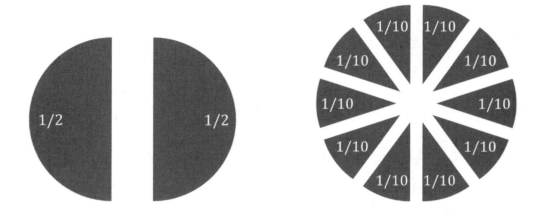

The size of the pieces that result when you break a number apart are said to be "denominated." "Denominate" is another word that comes from old Latin, and it just means "to name." So the **denominator** of a fraction names the size of the pieces, for example, halves or tenths.

Numerator also comes from old Latin and is related to the English words "number" and "enumerate." The numerator states how many of the denominated pieces are in the fraction.

If you understand the origin of these words, fractions should be a lot less mysterious than when you first memorized all those rules for them.

The Fundamental Rule of Fractions

All fractions are governed by a fundamental rule:

The Fundamental Rule of Fractions
When the numerator and denominator of a fraction are both multiplied (or divided) by the same number, the value of the fraction remains unchanged.

190 • MATH NUMBER AND QUANTITY

Examples:

$$\frac{3}{4} = \frac{3(2)}{4(2)} = \frac{6}{8} = \frac{6(3)}{8(3)} = \frac{18}{24} = \frac{18 \div 6}{24 \div 6} = \frac{3}{4}$$

$$\frac{2}{3} = \frac{2(4)}{3(4)} = \frac{8}{12} = \frac{8(2)}{12(2)} = \frac{16}{24} = \frac{16 \div 8}{24 \div 8} = \frac{2}{3}$$

In the above examples, the different forms $\frac{3}{4}$, $\frac{6}{8}$, and $\frac{18}{24}$ are equivalent to each other, and the different forms $\frac{2}{3}$, $\frac{6}{9}$, and $\frac{12}{18}$ are equivalent to each other. These equivalencies can also be demonstrated visually:

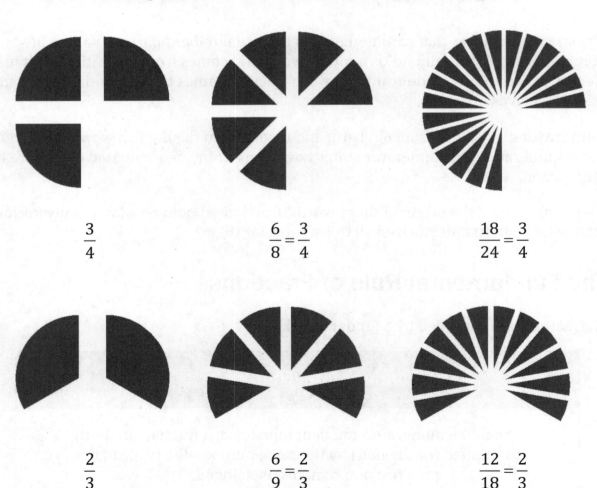

UNIT 2 | FRACTIONS • 191

Because the same fraction can have several equivalent forms, it is convenient to designate one form as the basic form. The preferred form of a fraction is the version expressed with the smallest numbers. This is the fraction in **lowest terms**.

For example, $\frac{50}{100}, \frac{30}{60}, \frac{18}{36}, \frac{7}{14}$, and $\frac{2}{4}$ can all be expressed as $\frac{1}{2}$, and $\frac{1}{2}$ is the form of the fraction that uses the smallest possible numbers.

To reduce a fraction to *lowest terms*, you must divide both the numerator and the denominator by the *largest* number that will divide both evenly.

Example:

What is $\frac{14}{21}$ expressed in lowest terms?

A. $\frac{3}{21}$ C. $\frac{2}{7}$ E. $\frac{2}{3}$

B. $\frac{1}{5}$ D. $\frac{3}{7}$

The correct answer is (E): $\frac{14}{21} = \frac{14 \div 7}{21 \div 7} = \frac{2}{3}$.

Example:

What is $\frac{24}{56}$ expressed in lowest terms?

F. $\frac{1}{60}$ H. $\frac{12}{28}$ K. $\frac{24}{32}$

G. $\frac{3}{7}$ J. $\frac{3}{4}$

The correct answer is (G): $\frac{24}{56} = \frac{24 \div 8}{56 \div 8} = \frac{3}{7}$.

Sometimes, you need to determine whether two fractions are equivalent even if they are not in lowest terms.

For example, $\dfrac{9}{15}$ and $\dfrac{6}{10}$ are equivalent fractions because both are equal to $\dfrac{3}{5}$:

$$\frac{9}{15} = \frac{9 \div 3}{15 \div 3} = \frac{3}{5}$$

$$\frac{6}{10} = \frac{6 \div 2}{10 \div 2} = \frac{3}{5}$$

And $\dfrac{3}{5}$ is the fraction in lowest terms.

The technique of **cross multiplication** gives you a procedure for testing different fractions to find whether they are **equivalent fractions**.

Example:

Is $\dfrac{27}{42}$ equivalent to $\dfrac{9}{14}$?

The solution is to assume, just for testing purposes, that $\dfrac{27}{42} = \dfrac{9}{14}$.

Cross multiply:

$$27(14) = 9(42)$$

$$378 = 378$$

Since 378 is equal to 378, this confirms that $\dfrac{27}{42}$ and $\dfrac{9}{14}$ are equivalent fractions.

Example:

Is $\dfrac{12}{18}$ equivalent to $\dfrac{2}{3}$?

$$\dfrac{12}{18} \stackrel{?}{=} \dfrac{2}{3}$$

$$12(3) \stackrel{?}{=} 2(18)$$

$$36 = 36$$

Since 36 is equal to 36, this confirms that $\dfrac{12}{18}$ and $\dfrac{2}{3}$ are equivalent fractions, and $\dfrac{12}{18}$ in lowest terms is $\dfrac{2}{3}$.

Example:

Is $\dfrac{3}{5}$ equivalent to $\dfrac{9}{12}$?

$$\dfrac{3}{5} \stackrel{?}{=} \dfrac{9}{12}$$

$$3(12) \stackrel{?}{=} 9(5)$$

$$36 \neq 45$$

Since 36 is not equal to 45, this confirms that $\dfrac{3}{5}$ and $\dfrac{9}{12}$ are not equivalent fractions, and $\dfrac{9}{12}$ in lowest terms is $\dfrac{3}{4}$, not $\dfrac{3}{5}$.

Summary

- *Fractions* are pieces of a whole number that has been broken into equal size pieces. The *denominator* of a fraction names the size of the pieces (e.g., halves or tenths), and the *numerator* names how many of the denominated pieces are in the fraction.

- The Fundamental Rule of Fractions: when the numerator and denominator of a fraction are both multiplied (or divided) by the same number, the value of the fraction remains unchanged

- The preferred form of a fraction (*lowest terms*) is the version expressed with the smallest numbers.

- To reduce a fraction to *lowest terms*, divide both the numerator and the denominator by the largest number that will divide both evenly.

- *Equivalent fractions* are those fractions that reduce to the same fraction in lowest terms.

- To test whether two fractions are equivalent, set them equal to each other and cross multiply. If the products are equal, the fractions are equivalent.

UNIT 2 | FRACTIONS • 195

EXERCISE

DIRECTIONS: Answer each of the following items about fractions. Check your answers using cross multiplication. Answers are on page 749.

1. What is $\frac{6}{9}$ expressed in lowest terms?

   A. $\frac{15}{54}$ C. $\frac{1}{9}$ E. $\frac{1}{2}$

   B. $\frac{2}{15}$ D. $\frac{2}{3}$

2. What is $\frac{10}{12}$ expressed in lowest terms?

   F. $\frac{11}{22}$ H. $\frac{1}{6}$ K. $\frac{1}{5}$

   G. $\frac{5}{6}$ J. $\frac{4}{5}$

3. What is $\frac{10}{16}$ expressed in lowest terms?

   A. $\frac{5}{16}$ C. $\frac{5}{8}$ E. $\frac{3}{5}$

   B. $\frac{5}{13}$ D. $\frac{3}{8}$

4. What is $\frac{9}{36}$ expressed in lowest terms?

   F. $\frac{9}{45}$ H. $\frac{4}{9}$ K. $\frac{1}{4}$

   G. $\frac{7}{27}$ J. $\frac{5}{6}$

5. What is $\frac{18}{20}$ expressed in lowest terms?

   A. $\frac{2}{38}$ C. $\frac{9}{10}$ E. $\frac{1}{9}$

   B. $\frac{1}{38}$ D. $\frac{1}{10}$

6. What is $\frac{63}{81}$ expressed in lowest terms?

   F. $\frac{11}{27}$ H. $\frac{7}{9}$ K. $\frac{1}{9}$

   G. $\frac{5}{18}$ J. $\frac{2}{9}$

196 • MATH NUMBER AND QUANTITY

7. What is $\dfrac{43}{86}$ expressed in lowest terms?

   A. $\dfrac{5}{6}$ C. $\dfrac{3}{4}$ E. $\dfrac{1}{2}$

   B. $\dfrac{4}{5}$ D. $\dfrac{2}{3}$

8. What is $\dfrac{112}{118}$ expressed in lowest terms?

   F. $\dfrac{112}{236}$ H. $\dfrac{6}{118}$ K. $\dfrac{2}{3}$

   G. $\dfrac{30}{236}$ J. $\dfrac{56}{59}$

9. What is $\dfrac{750}{1500}$ expressed in lowest terms?

   A. $\dfrac{2}{2250}$ C. $\dfrac{1}{750}$ E. $\dfrac{1}{2}$

   B. $\dfrac{1}{2250}$ D. $\dfrac{1}{500}$

10. Chanelle has a necklace made from 140 beads, and 80 of the beads are black. The black beads are what fraction of the total number of beads in the necklace?

    F. $\dfrac{7}{11}$ H. $\dfrac{4}{7}$ K. $\dfrac{3}{4}$

    G. $\dfrac{3}{11}$ J. $\dfrac{3}{7}$

11. In the seventh grade at Elm Street School, out of the 60 students, 45 are girls. The girls are what fraction of the total number of students?

    A. $\dfrac{1}{5}$ C. $\dfrac{1}{4}$ E. $\dfrac{1}{3}$

    B. $\dfrac{3}{4}$ D. $\dfrac{2}{3}$

12. Cedric is the star player on the basketball team. In the last game, Cedric scored 36 points out of the total of 48 points scored by the team. What fraction of the team's points did Cedric score?

    F. $\dfrac{4}{9}$ H. $\dfrac{1}{4}$ K. $\dfrac{1}{3}$

    G. $\dfrac{3}{4}$ J. $\dfrac{2}{3}$

13. A bag contains 56 marbles. If 24 of those marbles are blue, the blue marbles are what fraction of the total number of marbles in the bag?

    A. $\dfrac{3}{10}$ C. $\dfrac{5}{8}$ E. $\dfrac{3}{7}$

    B. $\dfrac{7}{8}$ D. $\dfrac{4}{7}$

UNIT 2 | FRACTIONS • 197

14. Of the 42 students in Mr. Gomez's class, 38 are going on a field trip. What fraction of the students are going on the field trip?

    F. $\dfrac{19}{40}$ H. $\dfrac{2}{21}$ K. $\dfrac{2}{19}$

    G. $\dfrac{19}{21}$ J. $\dfrac{17}{19}$

15. Maria is reading a book that is 180 pages long. She has already read 45 pages. What fraction of the book has Maria read?

    A. $\dfrac{2}{9}$ C. $\dfrac{1}{4}$ E. $\dfrac{1}{2}$

    B. $\dfrac{1}{9}$ D. $\dfrac{1}{3}$

16. At his job, Jonathan must load 120 boxes onto a truck. He has already loaded 80 boxes. What fraction of the boxes has Jonathan loaded?

    F. $\dfrac{3}{5}$ H. $\dfrac{3}{4}$ K. $\dfrac{1}{3}$

    G. $\dfrac{2}{5}$ J. $\dfrac{2}{3}$

17. Which one of the following fractions is equivalent to $\dfrac{16}{20}$?

    A. $\dfrac{4}{5}$ C. $\dfrac{3}{4}$ E. $\dfrac{2}{3}$

    B. $\dfrac{1}{5}$ D. $\dfrac{1}{4}$

18. Which one of the following fractions is equivalent to $\dfrac{15}{35}$?

    F. $\dfrac{9}{12}$ H. $\dfrac{1}{4}$ K. $\dfrac{1}{3}$

    G. $\dfrac{3}{7}$ J. $\dfrac{2}{3}$

19. Which one of the following fractions is equivalent to $\dfrac{48}{56}$?

    A. $\dfrac{8}{13}$ C. $\dfrac{6}{7}$ E. $\dfrac{1}{6}$

    B. $\dfrac{7}{13}$ D. $\dfrac{1}{7}$

20. Which one of the following fractions is equivalent to $\dfrac{75}{100}$?

    F. $\dfrac{50}{75}$ H. $\dfrac{1}{4}$ K. $\dfrac{1}{3}$

    G. $\dfrac{27}{36}$ J. $\dfrac{2}{3}$

21. Which one of the following fractions is equivalent to $\frac{16}{17}$?

   A. $\frac{32}{34}$ C. $\frac{32}{33}$ E. $\frac{6}{7}$

   B. $\frac{1}{34}$ D. $\frac{1}{33}$

22. Which one of the following fractions is NOT equivalent to $\frac{2}{3}$?

   F. $\frac{24}{36}$ H. $\frac{10}{15}$ K. $\frac{6}{9}$

   G. $\frac{24}{30}$ J. $\frac{8}{12}$

23. Which one of the following fractions is NOT equivalent to $\frac{2}{5}$?

   A. $\frac{30}{75}$ C. $\frac{10}{25}$ E. $\frac{3}{7}$

   B. $\frac{12}{30}$ D. $\frac{4}{10}$

24. Which one of the following fractions is NOT equivalent to $\frac{3}{7}$?

   F. $\frac{21}{49}$ H. $\frac{12}{28}$ K. $\frac{6}{14}$

   G. $\frac{18}{42}$ J. $\frac{18}{21}$

25. On a test, Priya answered 24 questions and got 20 correct. Priya answered the same fraction of questions correctly as which one of the following students?

   A. Eleanor answered 30 questions and got 25 correct.

   B. Sid answered 16 questions and got 12 correct.

   C. Damon answered 36 questions and got 28 correct.

   D. Neveah answered 18 questions and got 9 correct.

   E. Peter answered 28 questions and got 24 correct.

Math **Number and Quantity**

Unit 3 | **Number Lines**

INSIDE THIS UNIT:

–Positive Number Line Coordinates –
– Exercise –

Non-Negotiable Skill:

Locate points with positive coordinates
on the number line.

Positive Number Line Coordinates

A number line is a line with numbers on it. Several devices that you use almost every day are, in essence, number lines. For example, a ruler:

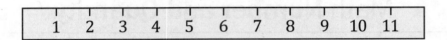

A thermometer is also, in essence, a number line:

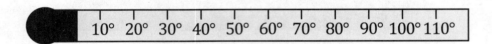

Even the mile markers on a highway are a number line:

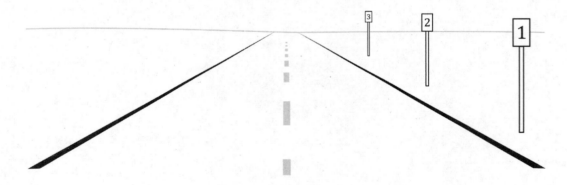

Mathematical number lines are usually presented as horizontal lines with numerical values increasing from left to right:

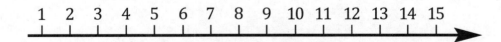

The number line of mathematics is the general case of the other examples presented. It's a little like talking about a baseball team as consisting of a pitcher, a catcher, first, second, and third base players, a shortstop, and three outfielders. That's true of every baseball team even though it doesn't mention a team such as the Atlanta Braves or the Chicago Cubs by name. So the baseball equivalent of a number line would look something like the following diagram:

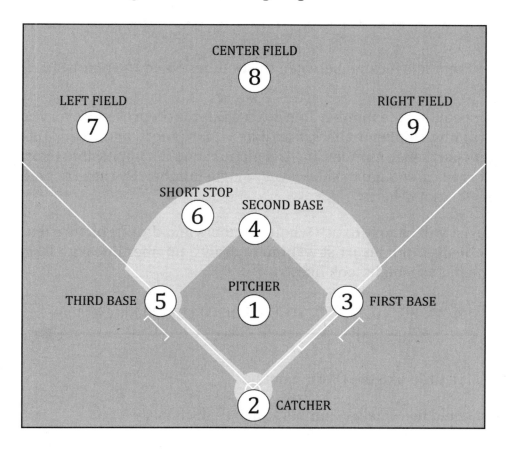

Just as you can locate or indicate a position or point on a ruler, a thermometer, a highway, or a baseball diagram, you can locate or indicate a point on the number line:

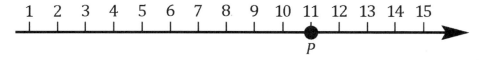

Point *P* is located at the number 11.

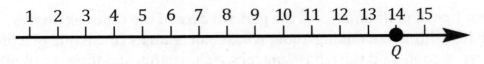

Point *Q* is located at the number 14.

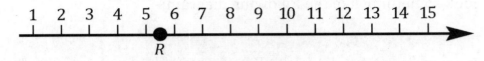

Point *R* is located between the number 5 and the number 6.

Technically speaking, the number line has a point that represents every real number, including whole numbers, fractions, square roots, and so on. But practically speaking, any particular number line is a picture, and it's impossible to draw a picture that is exact enough to show every single number. So the artist indicates some values but not others.

Often, the artist will choose to use whole numbers and draw a picture like those shown previously. But if an artist wanted to draw a number line with larger numbers, the picture might look like:

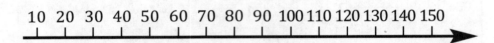

This picture is a little like the thermometer.

Or the artist could use smaller numbers such as decimals:

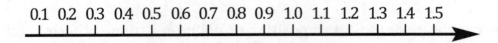

Or the artist could use fractions:

$$\frac{1}{4} \quad \frac{1}{2} \quad \frac{3}{4} \quad 1 \quad \frac{5}{4} \quad \frac{3}{2} \quad \frac{7}{4} \quad 2 \quad \frac{9}{4} \quad \frac{5}{2} \quad \frac{11}{4} \quad 3 \quad \frac{13}{4} \quad \frac{7}{2} \quad \frac{15}{4}$$

Or the artist could even decide to label some but not all marks:

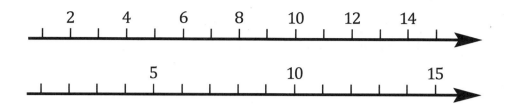

The tick marks are evenly spaced, so values that aren't labeled are still known.

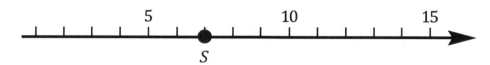

Point *S* is located at the number 7.

The procedure for reading a number line is always the same. The position or location of a point indicates the number with which it is associated.

> **Summary**
> - Mathematical number lines are usually presented as horizontal lines with numerical values increasing from left to right.
> - Number lines have points representing real numbers, such as whole numbers, fractions, square roots, and decimals.

EXERCISE

DIRECTIONS: Answer the following items using information from the corresponding number line. Answers are on page 749.

Questions 1–5

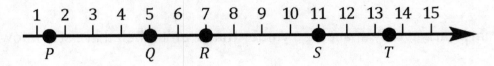

1. Which one of the points shown is located at 7 on the number line?

   A. P
   B. Q
   C. R
   D. S
   E. T

2. Which one of the points shown is located at 11 on the number line?

   F. P
   G. Q
   H. R
   J. S
   K. T

3. Which one of the points shown is located between 13 and 14 on the number line?

   A. P
   B. Q
   C. R
   D. S
   E. T

4. Which one of the points shown is located between 1 and 2 on the number line?

   F. P
   G. Q
   H. R
   J. S
   K. T

5. Which one of the points shown is located at three less than the number 8?

   A. P
   B. Q
   C. R
   D. S
   E. T

Questions 6-10

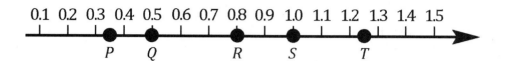

6. Which one of the points shown is located at 0.8 on the number line?

F. P   H. R   K. T
G. Q   J. S

7. Which one of the points shown is located at 1.0 on the number line?

A. P   C. R   E. T
B. Q   D. S

8. Which one of the points shown is located between 1.2 and 1.3 on the number line?

F. P   H. R   K. T
G. Q   J. S

9. Which one of the points shown is greater than 0.3 but less than 0.4?

A. P   C. R   E. T
B. Q   D. S

10. Which one of the points shown is 0.3 less than 1.1?

F. P   H. R   K. T
G. Q   J. S

Questions 11–15

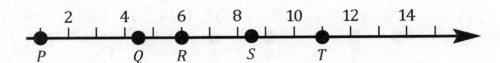

11. Which one of the points shown on the number line is located at 6?

    A. P   C. R   E. T
    B. Q   D. S

12. Which one of the points shown on the number line is located at 11?

    F. P   H. R   K. T
    G. Q   J. S

13. Which one of the points shown on the number line is located at 1?

    A. P   C. R   E. T
    B. Q   D. S

14. Which one of the points shown on the number line is greater than 4 but less than 5?

    F. P   H. R   K. T
    G. Q   J. S

15. Point S could be located at which one of the following values?

    A. 7   C. 8   E. 9
    B. 7.5 D. 8.5

Questions 16–20

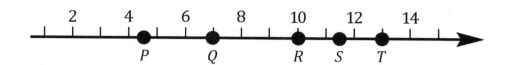

16. Which one of the points shown on the number line is located at 10?

    F. P H. R K. T
    G. Q J. S

17. Which one of the points shown on the number line is located at 7?

    A. P C. R E. T
    B. Q D. S

18. Which one of the points shown on the number line is located at 13?

    F. P H. R K. T
    G. Q J. S

19. Which one of the points shown on the number line could be 11.5?

    A. P C. R E. T
    B. Q D. S

20. Point P could be located at which one of the following values?

    F. 3.5 H. 4.5 K. 6
    G. 4   J. 5

Questions 21–25

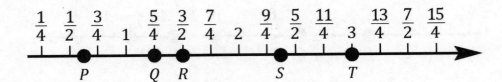

21. Which one of the points shown on the number line is located at 3?

    A. P
    B. Q
    C. R
    D. S
    E. T

22. Which one of the points shown on the number line is located at $1\frac{1}{4}$?

    F. P
    G. Q
    H. R
    J. S
    K. T

23. Which one of the points shown on the number line is located between $\frac{1}{2}$ and $\frac{3}{4}$?

    A. P
    B. Q
    C. R
    D. S
    E. T

24. Which one of the points shown on the number line is $\frac{1}{2}$ less than 2?

    F. P
    G. Q
    H. R
    J. S
    K. T

25. Point S could be located at which one of the following values?

    A. 2
    B. $2\frac{1}{4}$
    C. $2\frac{3}{8}$
    D. $2\frac{1}{2}$
    E. $2\frac{3}{4}$

Math Algebra and Functions

Unit 4 | One- and Two-Step Problems

INSIDE THIS UNIT:
– Solve Word Problems – – Exercise –

Non-Negotiable Skill:

Solve word problems involving simple
calculations in one or two steps.

Solve Word Problems

At this stage in your education, you probably won't be asked to do pure arithmetic very often. You are more likely to be asked to use your computational skills to solve word problems. Let's look at some examples.

First, a word problem requiring addition:

Example:

A customer at a bookstore selects three books, one marked $7.95, one marked $9.98, and one marked $8.52. Not including tax, how much should the customer be charged for the books?

A. $16.11   C. $18.50   E. $26.45
B. $17.57   D. $19.12

The correct answer is (E). The customer is buying three items. To determine the total cost of the three books, simply add:

$$\begin{array}{r} \$7.95 \\ \$9.98 \\ + \$8.52 \\ \hline \$26.45 \end{array}$$

Now ask whether this agrees with your number sense. Since you are adding prices that are about $8, $10, and $8.50, the result should be about $26.50. (E) is a sensible answer.

This next example is a word problem requiring subtraction:

Example:

A truck originally contained 545 cases of soda. The driver unloaded a total of 231 cases at five different stops on her delivery route. How many cases remained on the truck?

F. 214
G. 300
H. 314
J. 347
K. 776

The correct answer is (H). "Remained" signals subtraction. The driver started with 545 cases and unloaded 231. To determine how many cases are still on the truck, simply subtract:

$$\begin{array}{r} 545 \\ -231 \\ \hline 314 \end{array}$$

So 314 cases are still on the truck.

Does this answer make sense? Yes. Think about it. The truck originally contained about 550 cases and about 230 were unloaded, so the number remaining on the truck should be about 320. (H) is a sensible answer. There is no way that (K) could be correct because the answer must be less than 545, the original number of cases on the truck.

Next we have a word problem using multiplication:

Example:

Roberto is catering a dinner party for 52 guests. The place setting for each guest will include a gift bag with 6 chocolate mints. How many chocolate mints does Roberto need for the gift bags?

A. 9
B. 46
C. 58
D. 312
E. 415

The correct answer is (D). The party will have 52 guests, and each guest bag will have 6 mints. To determine how many mints are needed overall, simply multiply:

6 mints per bag × 52 bags = 312 mints

212 • MATH ALGEBRA AND FUNCTIONS

Does this answer make sense? Yes. Think about it. With about 50 guests and 6 mints for each guest, Roberto will need about 300 mints. So (D) is a reasonable answer.

And finally, here is an example that uses division:

Example:

A lake resort offers motorboat rentals for $15 per hour. A group of 5 people wants to rent a boat for 1 hour and share the cost equally. How much will each of them pay for the boat rental?

F. $3.34   H. $3.50   K. $10.00
G. $3.00   J. $7.15

The correct answer is (G). To determine the cost of the boat rental per person, simply divide the total cost for one hour by the number of people:

$$\$15.00 \div 5 = \$3.00$$

Does $3.00 make sense? Yes. If 5 people each pay $3.00, the total payment will be $5 \times 3 = 15$, or $15.

While number sense is a good strategy for checking your answers, number sense may not tell you how to get started on a problem. The procedure for solving a word problem is:

1. Read carefully. Then isolate the question asked.
2. Determine how the information given will answer the question.
3. Do the computations necessary to answer the question.

The first step is very important when solving math word problems: read slowly and carefully. In many other contexts, such as when reading a novel, one should learn to read more quickly. However, in doing math word problems, reading quickly is NOT the way to success, because each word may be very important.

Example:

Jeremiah opened a package containing 24 cookies. He ate 4 of the cookies, and Patricia ate 2 cookies. Jeremiah then resealed the package. How many cookies remained in the package?

A. 4
B. 6
C. 16
D. 18
E. 30

Step 1: Begin by focusing on the question to be answered:

How many cookies remained in the package?

The key words are: "**How many remained?**"

This indicates that there were some cookies in the package to begin with and that some were taken out. Now, a few of the original cookies remain in the package. The question is, "How many?"

Step 2: Look at the information you've been given to solve the problem:

Jeremiah opened a package containing 24 cookies. He ate 4 of the cookies, and Patricia ate 2 cookies. Jeremiah then resealed the package.

The package had 24 cookies to start with, and 4 cookies plus 2 cookies were removed.

Step 3: Subtract the **total number removed** from the original number of cookies in the package.

There was a total of 4 + 2 = 6 cookies removed.

And so the number remaining was:

24 − 6 = 18

214 • MATH ALGEBRA AND FUNCTIONS

Example:

If 6 bagels cost \$3.00, what is the cost of 1 bagel?

F. \$0.20   H. \$2.00   K. \$9.00
G. \$0.50   J. \$3.00

Step 1: What is the question to be answered?

What is the cost of 1 bagel?

Step 2: And what information is provided?

6 bagels cost \$3.00

Step 3: So divide to find the cost of 1 bagel:

$$\frac{\$3.00}{6 \text{ bagels}} = \$0.50 \text{ per bagel}$$

Summary

- Use the three-step method for solving word problems:

  1. Read carefully. Then isolate the question asked.

  2. Determine how the information given will answer the question.

  3. Do the computations necessary to answer the question.

- Don't forget your number sense; it can save you from calculator input errors.

EXERCISE

DIRECTIONS: The following items can be solved with either pencil and paper or a calculator. Before performing the indicated operation(s), eliminate any choices that violate your number sense. Answers are on page 750.

1. At 9:00 a.m., a bank's electric sign said that the outside temperature was 72°F. By 10:00 a.m., the outside temperature had risen 5°F, and by 11:00 a.m., it had risen another 8°F. What temperature was displayed on the bank's sign at 11:00 a.m.?

   A. 15°F   C. 77°F   E. 85°F
   B. 59°F   D. 80°F

2. At the end of every weekday, Todd empties his pants pockets and puts the loose money that was in his pockets into a jar. Then he uses the change for spending money on the weekend. On Monday, he put $2.18 into the empty jar, on Tuesday he added $1.08, and on Wednesday he added $3.77. How much money was in the jar after he put in the money on Wednesday?

   F. $0.56   H. $3.26   K. $7.03
   G. $1.59   J. $4.85

3. Calvin had a spool of electrical wire 150 feet long. He cut off a piece 10 feet long. How long, in feet, was the wire remaining on the spool?

   A. 15   C. 150   E. 1,500
   B. 140   D. 160

4. A 12-ounce jar was filled to capacity with water. Two ounces of water were then poured from the jar into one pail, and 3 ounces were poured into another pail. How much water, in ounces, remained in the jar?

   F. 7   H. 10   K. 17
   G. 9   J. 14

5. Mr. Umberto teaches a class with 25 students. Each student submitted 5 short essays that Mr. Umberto must grade. How many essays does Mr. Umberto have to grade?

   A. 5   C. 25   E. 125
   B. 20   D. 30

216 • MATH ALGEBRA AND FUNCTIONS

6. A computer plays a video format that displays 30 frames of video every second. How many frames of video will the computer display if a video clip lasts 6 seconds?

F. 5   H. 30   K. 180
G. 24   J. 36

7. A teacher plans to divide a class of 36 students into teams of 3 students each for an academic competition. How many 3-student teams will she have?

A. 12   C. 36   E. 108
B. 33   D. 39

8. Five students plan to share the cost of a birthday gift equally. If the gift costs $40, how much will each student pay?

F. $8.00   H. $35.00   K. $200.00
G. $12.50   J. $45.00

9. A student club is conducting a raffle to raise money to purchase an electronic sign for the school. Tickets for the raffle cost $2 each, and the students need to sell $2,000 worth of tickets. How many tickets do the students need to sell?

A. 100   C. 1,000   E. 4,000
B. 400   D. 1,998

10. Marilyn changes the oil in her car's engine every 5,000 miles. Since her last oil change, she has driven 275 miles around town and taken one long trip of 1,825 miles. How many more miles can she drive before she needs another oil change?

F. 2,900   H. 3,450   K. 7,100
G. 3,175   J. 3,950

11. One Wilderness Trail nutritional bar has 76 calories. How many total calories are contained in the 14 Wilderness Trail bars in a 3–pound bag?

A. 93   C. 1,064   E. 3,192
B. 118   D. 1,106

12. Emily makes and sells costume jewelry. She bought 2,560 beads at the craft store and used a total of 392 beads to make 8 bracelets. How many beads did she have left?

F. 2,160   H. 2,176   K. 2,278
G. 2,168   J. 2,268

UNIT 4 | ONE- AND TWO-STEP PROBLEMS • 217

13. Madison and Rachael each purchased a new pair of jeans. Madison paid $36.49 for her jeans, and Rachael paid $12.98 more than Madison did. How much did Rachael pay for her jeans?

    A. $23.51 C. $48.37 E. $49.47
    B. $24.51 D. $49.38

14. Maria bought new notebooks for school. Each notebook costs $0.40, and she spent a total of $5.20. How many notebooks did Maria buy?

    F. 0.13 H. 2   K. 21
    G. 1.3   J. 13

15. Last year, River Forks City received an average of 3.53 inches of rain per month. How much total rain, in inches, did River Forks City receive last year?

    A. 15.53 C. 35.3   E. 42.36
    B. 21.18 D. 38.83

16. David weighed 98.2 pounds at the beginning of middle school. By the end of middle school, his weight had increased by 25.46 pounds. How much did David weigh at the end of middle school?

    F. 35.28 H. 113.66 K. 123.66
    G. 72.74 J. 123.48

17. Cherries cost $2.88 per pound. What is the cost of 2.5 pounds of cherries?

    A. $1.15 C. $5.38 E. $72.00
    B. $2.63 D. $7.20

18. Mrs. Johnson divided $300 equally among her 4 grandchildren. If Marissa spent $27 of her share, how much of her original share does Marissa have left?

    F. $48 H. $102 K. $273
    G. $75 J. $269

19. A group of 5 students spent the day at an amusement park. Regular admission to the park costs $42, but each student used a coupon worth $6 off the regular price. What was the final cost in dollars of admission for the entire group?

    A. 58   D. 210 C. 204
    B. 180 E. 240

20. The cost of crude oil per barrel was $115 in March and $97 in September. How many dollars did an oil refinery save by purchasing 100 barrels of oil in September rather than March?

    F. 312   H. 2,800 K. 21,200
    G. 1,800 J. 8,550

218 • MATH ALGEBRA AND FUNCTIONS

21. Kevin had $98. He loaned Rob $40, and then Stephen paid Kevin back $10 from the week before. Kevin then spent $25. How many dollars does Kevin have left?

A. 23   C. 73   E. 103
B. 43   D. 93

22. Community High School charges $12 for each adult ticket and $6 for each student ticket to see the fall play. A ticket order totaled $54 and included a request for exactly 1 adult ticket. How many student tickets did the order request?

F. 18   H. 6   K. 3
G. 7   J. 4

23. The newspaper sells two types of advertisements. A black and white advertisement costs $35, and a color advertisement costs $60. A local business buys 7 of each type of advertisement. How much more did they pay for the 7 color advertisements than for the 7 black and white advertisements?

A. $102   C. $245   E. $665
B. $175   D. $420

24. Ava has 220 square inches of wrapping paper. She needs to wrap 3 packages that each requires 63 squares inches of wrapping paper. How many square inches of paper will Ava have after wrapping the packages?

F. 31   H. 157   K. 199
G. 154   J. 189

25. Daniel had 162 fish in his aquarium at the beginning of summer. By the end of the summer, 36 fish had died and twice the number that had died were born. How many fish did Daniel have at the end of the summer?

A. 54   C. 126   E. 198
B. 124   D. 128

Math Algebra and Functions

Unit 5 | Basic Expressions

INSIDE THIS UNIT:
– Exhibit Knowledge of Basic Expressions –   – Exercise –

Non-Negotiable Skill:

Recognize basic expressions and their components.

Exhibit Knowledge of Basic Expressions

Learning math is a lot like learning another language. Perhaps you and some of your friends already know English and another language. Or maybe you know some words and phrases in a different language. If so, the idea of translating English into another language should be familiar. And math is just another language.

Take the English phrase "Carl and Mary" as an example. In Spanish, this would be "Carlos y Maria." In French, it would be "Charles et Marie." In German, it would be "Karl und Marie." And in math it would be "$C + M$."

Of course, in math, "$C + M$" often does not refer to the actual people but instead refers to some numbers associated with those two people such as their weights, the number of marbles they have, the amount of money they have, and so on.

Example:

Let C be Charles' weight in pounds and let M be Mary's weight in pounds. Together they weigh $C + M$.

Let C be the number of marbles that Charles has and let M be the number of marbles that Mary has. Together they have $C + M$ marbles.

Let C be the number of dollars that Charles has and let M be the number of dollars that Mary has. Together the number of dollars they have is $C + M$.

In the language of math, you make statements not just about addition, but about subtraction, multiplication, and division as well.

Example:

If Charles weighs C pounds and Mary weighs M pounds, what is the difference in their weights expressed in pounds? ($C > M$) The difference is $C - M$ pounds.

If Charles has C marbles and Mary has M marbles, how many more marbles does Charles have than Mary? ($C > M$) The difference is $C - M$ marbles.

If Mary has M dollars and spends $3, how much money does Mary have left? ($M > \$3$) The amount left is $M - 3$ dollars.

Example:

The school bus has r rows of seats. If 4 students are seated in each row and the bus is full, how many students are seated on the bus? The number of students is equal to $4r$.

Pat bought 5 packages of paper plates for a picnic. If each package contains p paper plates, how many paper plates did Pat buy? The number of paper plates is equal to $5p$.

For a pancake breakfast, Doris bought c cartons of eggs. If each carton contained 18 eggs, how many eggs did Doris buy? The number of eggs is equal to $18c$.

Example:

Hillary is assigned a book to read that is p pages long. If she reads 15 pages every day, how many days will it take her to finish the book? The number of days is equal to p pages divided by 15 pages a day, or $\dfrac{p}{15}$ days.

A bag contains k pieces of candy. If the candy is to be divided equally among 6 children, how many pieces of candy will each child get? The number of pieces of candy is equal to k pieces of candy divided by 6 children, or $\dfrac{k}{6}$ pieces of candy for each child.

A group of 12 friends rents 4 bowling lanes for the evening and plan to share the cost equally. If the cost of renting the lanes is r dollars, how much will each person pay? The amount per person is equal to r dollars divided by 12 people, or $\dfrac{r}{12}$ dollars per person.

Summary

- In the language of math, we make statements about addition, subtraction, multiplication, and division.

- In math, letters, called variables, are often used to refer to unknown numbers. For example, if Carol has an unknown number of dollars, we may let x represent the number of dollars Carol has.

EXERCISE

DIRECTIONS: For each of the following items, choose the correct basic expression for the given information. Answers are on page 750.

1. Which one of the following mathematical expressions is the same as the phrase "3 added to *x*"?

   A. $\dfrac{3}{x}$ C. 3   E. $3x$
   B. $x - 3$ D. $3 + x$

2. Which one of the following mathematical expressions is the same as the phrase "the sum of *k* and *n*"?

   F. $\dfrac{k}{n}$ H. $k + n$ K. $2kn$
   G. $k - n$ J. kn

3. Which one of the following mathematical expressions is the same as the phrase "the total of *c* and *d*"?

   A. $\dfrac{c}{d}$ C. $c + d$ E. $2cd$
   B. $c - d$ D. cd

4. Peter picked *p* apples and Jane picked *j* apples. Which one of the following mathematical expressions shows the total number of apples Peter and Jane picked?

   F. $\dfrac{p}{j}$ H. $p + j$ K. $2pj$
   G. $p - j$ J. pj

5. On Monday, Glendale received 1.2 inches of rain, and on Tuesday Glendale received *x* inches of rain. How many inches of rain did Glendale receive on Monday and Tuesday in total?

   A. $\dfrac{1.2}{x}$ C. $\dfrac{x}{1.2}$ E. $1.2x$
   B. x D. $1.2 + x$

6. Germaine had *x* dollars in a savings account and deposited another *y* dollars. How much was in the savings account after Germaine made the deposit?

   F. $x - y$ H. y K. $2y$
   G. x J. $x + y$

224 • MATH ALGEBRA AND FUNCTIONS

7. Mr. Pena's class was sitting in the auditorium, and Ms. Abdul's class came in and sat down. If there are p students in Mr. Pena's class and q students in Ms. Abdul's class, how many students from these two classes are sitting in the auditorium?

A. p C. $p + q$ E. $2pq$
B. q D. pq

8. Which one of the following mathematical expressions is the same as the phrase "the difference between x and y"?

F. $\dfrac{x}{y}$ H. $x + y$ K. $2xy$
G. $x - y$ J. xy

9. Which one of the following mathematical expressions is the same as the phrase "n subtracted from m"?

A. $m - n$ C. mn E. $2mn$
B. $n - m$ D. $2(m + n)$

10. Which one of the following mathematical expressions is the same as the phrase "s take away w"?

F. $s - w$ H. $s + w$ K. $2sw$
G. $w - s$ J. sw

11. If 255 students were sitting in the auditorium, and x of them left, how many students were left sitting in the auditorium?

A. $\dfrac{x}{255}$ C. x E. $255x$
B. $x - 255$ D. $255 - x$

12. Martin received a gift of d dollars for his birthday, and he spent b dollars of it on a video game. How much money does Martin have left from the birthday gift?

F. $d - b$ H. $\dfrac{d}{b}$ K. $b + d$
G. $b - d$ J. $\dfrac{b}{d}$

13. Ben is b years old, and his younger brother Abel is a years old. Which one of the following expressions shows how much older, in years, Ben is than Abel?

A. $a - b$ C. a E. ab
B. $b - a$ D. b

14. Linda had a board that was m inches long, and she cut off and used a piece n inches long. How long, in inches, is the remaining piece of board?

F. $m - n$ H. n K. $2m$
G. m J. $m + n$

15. Al is reading a book that is p pages long. If he has already read q pages, how many pages does he have left to read?

A. $p - q$ C. p E. pq
B. $q - p$ D. q

16. Which one of the following mathematical expressions is the same as the phrase "two times x"?

F. $\dfrac{x}{2}$ H. 2 K. $(x)(x)$

G. $\dfrac{x}{x}$ J. $2x$

17. Which one of the following mathematical expressions is the same as the phrase "five times x"?

A. $\dfrac{x}{5}$ D. $5x$

B. 5 E. $(x)(x)(x)(x)(x)$
C. $5 + x$

18. George and four of his friends agreed to clean Mrs. Thomson's yard for x dollars each. How many dollars will Mrs. Thomson pay the entire group for cleaning the yard?

F. 5 H. $5x$ K. $\dfrac{5}{x}$

G. x J. $5 + x$

19. Sanjay works part time at the mailing center. One Saturday afternoon, he mailed 5 boxes of letters. If each box contained t letters, how many letters did Sanjay mail?

A. $\dfrac{5}{t}$ C. t E. $5t$

B. 5 D. $5 + t$

20. At the gym, Rod did x sets of an exercise with y repetitions in each set. How many repetitions of the exercise did Rod do?

F. $\dfrac{x}{y}$ H. $x - y$ K. xy

G. $\dfrac{y}{x}$ J. $x + y$

21. Which one of the following mathematical expressions is the same as the phrase "x divided by 2"?

A. $\dfrac{1}{2x}$ C. $\dfrac{x}{2}$ E. $2x$

B. $\dfrac{2}{x}$ D. $x + 2$

22. Which one of the following mathematical expressions is the same as the phrase "x divided by y"?

   F. $\dfrac{1}{xy}$　　H. $\dfrac{y}{x}$　　K. xy

   G. $\dfrac{x}{y}$　　J. $x - y$

23. Which one of the following mathematical expressions is the same as the phrase "m divided by 2n"?

   A. $\dfrac{m}{2n}$　　D. $m + 2n$

   B. $m - 2n$　　E. $\dfrac{2n}{m}$

   C. $2mn$

24. Todd has 10 pounds of fertilizer that he wants to spread evenly over x square yards of lawn. How many pounds of fertilizer should Todd spread on each square yard of lawn?

   F. $\dfrac{x}{10}$　　H. 10　　K. $10x$

   G. $\dfrac{10}{x}$　　J. $10 + x$

25. A group of hikers is preparing for a wilderness survival trek. The trek will last 5 days. If they carry with them x packages of prepared meals, how many meals will they have for each day?

   A. $\dfrac{x}{5}$　　C. 5　　E. $5x$

   B. $\dfrac{5}{x}$　　D. $5 + x$

Math **Algebra and Functions**

Unit 6 | **Basic Equations**

INSIDE THIS UNIT:

– Solve One-Step Equations –
– The Fundamental Rule of Equations –
– Exercise –

Non-Negotiable Skill:

Solve and check one-step algebraic equations involving whole numbers or decimals.

Solve One-Step Equations

We have already seen that math is a language that has some similarity to English. There is one other similarity that is very important.

In English, we make statements such as "Dr. Windemere is the principal," "The top student is Michelle," and "Peter Parker is Spiderman." The general form of these statements is "x is y," and they are sometimes called **identity** statements because they establish an identity between two people or objects:

Dr. Windemere = Principal (Dr. Windemere is the principal.)

Top Student = Michelle (The top student is Michelle.)

Peter Parker = Spiderman (Peter Parker is Spiderman.)

In math, we use the equal sign (=) in place of the "is," and such statements are called **equations**. An equation establishes the equality of two quantities:

3 = 3 (3 is equal to 3.)

3 + 2 = 1 + 4 (3 + 2 is equal to 1 + 4 because 5 is equal to 5.)

$x = y$ (Whatever quantity x might be, it is equal to y.)

$m + 2 = n + 1$ (Whatever quantity m or n might be, if you add 2 to m and 1 to n, the two sums are equal.)

The Fundamental Rule of Equations

You can:

- Add the same quantity to both sides.
- Subtract the same quantity from both sides.
- Multiply both sides by the same quantity.
- Divide both sides by the same quantity (except 0).

Examples:

$$3 = 3$$
$$3 + 2 = 3 + 2 \quad \text{(Add the same quantity to both sides)}$$
$$5 = 5$$
$$5 - 1 = 5 - 1 \quad \text{(Subtract the same quantity from both sides)}$$
$$4 = 4$$
$$4 \times 3 = 4 \times 3 \quad \text{(Multiply both sides by the same quantity)}$$
$$12 = 12$$
$$12 \div 4 = 12 \div 4 \quad \text{(Divide both sides by the same quantity)}$$
$$3 = 3$$

In the context of an equation, a variable (an unknown such as x) functions much like a pronoun in English:

Someone is Batman.

x is Batman.

x = Batman.

In this case, as anyone who has seen a Batman movie or read the comic books knows, x is "Bruce Wayne":

Bruce Wayne = Batman

Of course, equations are not exactly like English sentences. Equations deal with quantities:

$$x + 3 = 5$$

This is a mathematical way to say, "the sum of a number and 3 is equal to 5." And that number is 2:

$$2 + 3 = 5$$
$$5 = 5$$

You were probably able to recognize x as being 2 just by looking at the statement, but it's more difficult when the statement is complicated:

$$x + 3.41 = 6.52$$

To determine the value of x, use the Fundamental Rule of Equations. Subtract the same number from both sides:

$$x + 3.41 - 3.41 = 6.52 - 3.41$$
$$x = 3.11$$

Example:

If $x - 4 = 10$, then $x = ?$

Solve for x:

$$x - 4 = 10$$
$$x - 4 + 4 = 10 + 4$$
$$x = 14$$

Example:

If $3x = 12$, then $x = ?$

Solve for x:

$$3x = 12$$
$$3x \div 3 = 12 \div 3$$
$$x = 4$$

As just noted, an unknown in math such as *x*, which is also called a variable, functions very much like a pronoun in English:

Someone ate my sandwich. (I don't know who.)

x ate my sandwich. (I don't know who *x* is.)

John ate my sandwich. (John = *x*)

Carmen Santiago is somewhere. (But I don't know where.)

Carmen Santiago is at point *x*. (But I don't know where *x* is.)

Carmen Santiago is in Los Angeles. (*x* = Los Angeles)

This relationship sets up a really neat procedure for checking the accuracy of your work when you solve an equation: substitute your answer for the unknown in the equation, and if the equation makes a true statement, your answer is correct.

Example:

If $x + 5 = 10$, then $x = ?$

A. 0.2
B. 0.5
C. 5
D. 15
E. 50

The correct answer is (C). Solve for *x*:

$$x + 5 = 10$$
$$x + 5 - 5 = 10 - 5$$
$$x = 5$$

Now substitute 5 for *x* in the original equation:

$$x + 5 = 10$$
$$(5) + 5 = 10$$
$$10 = 10 \text{ (True)}$$

Since the statement is true, *x* is equal to 5 and (C) is indeed the correct answer.

232 • MATH ALGEBRA AND FUNCTIONS

But what if you had made a mistake? For example:

$$x + 5 = 10$$
$$x + 5 - 5 = 10 + 5 \text{ (Wrong)}$$
$$x = 15 \text{ (Wrong)}$$

Check the accuracy of the solution:

$$x + 5 = 10$$
$$(15) + 5 = 10$$
$$20 = 10 \text{ (False)}$$

The fact that the statement is <u>false</u> proves that the solution is wrong.

Example:

If $2.5 + x = 10$, then $x = ?$

F. 0.25	H. 2.5	K. 12.5
G. 4	J. 7.5	

The correct answer is (J). Solve for x:

$$2.5 + x = 10$$
$$2.5 - 2.5 + x = 10 - 2.5$$
$$x = 7.5$$

Check:

$$2.5 + x = 10$$
$$2.5 + 7.5 = 10$$
$$10 = 10 \text{ (Correct)}$$

Example:

If $2x = 20$, then $x = ?$

A. 0.1   C. 18   E. 40
B. 10   D. 22

The correct answer is (B). Solve for x:

$$2x = 20$$
$$2x \div 2 = 20 \div 2$$
$$x = 10$$

Check:

$$2x = 20$$
$$2(10) = 20$$
$$20 = 20 \text{ (Correct)}$$

Example:

If $\dfrac{x}{12} = 10$, then $x = ?$

F. 1.2   H. 12   K. 120
G. 10   J. 22

The correct answer is (K). Solve for x:

$$\frac{x}{12} = 10$$
$$\left(\frac{x}{12}\right)(12) = (10)(12)$$
$$x = 120$$

Check:

$$\frac{x}{12} = 10$$

$$\frac{120}{12} = 10$$

$$10 = 10 \text{ (Correct)}$$

Summary

- An equation uses the equal sign (=) to establish the equality of two quantities.

- The Fundamental Rule of Equations: you can add the same quantity to both sides, subtract the same quantity from both sides, multiply both sides by the same quantity, and divide both sides by the same quantity (except 0).

- To check the accuracy of your work when solving an equation, substitute the solution back into the equation. If the equation makes a true statement, your answer is correct.

EXERCISE

DIRECTIONS: For each of the following items, solve for *x*. Check your work by substituting your solution for *x* into the original equation. Answers are on page 750.

1. If $x + 1 = 3$, then $x = ?$

   A. 0   C. 2   E. 4
   B. 1   D. 3

2. If $x + 4 = 12$, then $x = ?$

   F. 3   H. 8   K. 16
   G. 4   J. 12

3. If $x + 1.2 = 3.6$, then $x = ?$

   A. 1.2   C. 3   E. 4.8
   B. 2.4   D. 3.6

4. If $5 + x = 15$, then $x = ?$

   F. 3   H. 10   K. 75
   G. 5   J. 20

5. If $18 = x + 9$, then $x = ?$

   A. 2   C. 18   E. 162
   B. 9   D. 36

6. If $10 = x - 5$, then $x = ?$

   F. 0.5   H. 5   K. 50
   G. 2   J. 15

7. If $-10 = x - 10$, then $x = ?$

   A. 0   C. 5   E. 50
   B. 2.5   D. 15

8. If $-8.5 = x - 34$, then $x = ?$

   F. 0.25   H. 25.5   K. 280
   G. 4   J. 42.5

9. If $x - 9 = 27$, then $x = ?$

   A. $\dfrac{1}{3}$ C. 18   E. 243
   B. 3   D. 36

10. If $x - 12.4 = -3.1$, then $x = ?$

    F. 0.25   H. 9.3   J. 15.5
    G. 4   K. 38.44

11. If $x = 2.1 + 2.8$, then $x = ?$

    A. 0.4   C. 0.75   E. 4.9
    B. 0.7   D. 4

12. If $x = 1.24 + 4$, then $x = ?$

    F. 0.31   H. 3.76   K. 5.24
    G. 0.84   J. 4.96

236 • MATH ALGEBRA AND FUNCTIONS

13. If $7.77 = 0.77 + x$, then $x = ?$

A. 0.1   C. 1   E. 11
B. 0.7   D. 7

14. If $4x = 32$, then $x = ?$

F. 4   H. 7   K. 128
G. 6   J. 8

15. If $2x = 36$, then $x = ?$

A. 0.8   C. 12   E. 72
B. 2   D. 18

16. If $5x = 40$, then $x = ?$

F. 0.125   H. 8   K. 200
G. 5   J. 9

17. If $3x = 63$, then $x = ?$

A. 0.048   C. 9   E. 189
B. 3   D. 21

18. If $4.5 = 1.5x$, then $x = ?$

F. $\frac{1}{3}$ H. 3   K. 6.75
G. 1   J. 6

19. If $8.64 = 3.6x$, then $x = ?$

A. 0.417   C. 3   E. 31.104
B. 2.4   D. 4.32

20. If $\dfrac{x}{3} = 5$, then $x = ?$

F. 9   H. 25   K. 60
G. 15   J. 30

21. If $\dfrac{x}{4} = 2$, then $x = ?$

A. 0.5   C. 10   E. 20
B. 8   D. 16

22. If $\dfrac{x}{5} = 30$, then $x = ?$

F. 6   H. 150   K. 1,500
G. 15   J. 600

23. If $5 = \dfrac{x}{2}$, then $x = ?$

A. 0.2   C. 3   E. 10
B. 0.4   D. 4

24. If $6.5 = \dfrac{x}{6}$, then $x = ?$

F. 1.08   H. 42   K. 390
G. 39   J. 48

25. If $2.5 = \dfrac{x}{3.5}$, then $x = ?$

A. 8.75   C. 60   E. 875
B. 24   D. 87.5

Math Algebra and Functions

Unit 7 | Practice

INSIDE THIS UNIT:
– Exercise –

238 • MATH ALGEBRA AND FUNCTIONS

EXERCISE

DIRECTIONS: The following items can be solved with either pencil and paper or a calculator. Answers are on page 750.

1. $36 + 52 = ?$

  A. 1.4   C. 16   E. 88
  B. 6   D. 44

2. $26 - 8 = ?$

  F. 3.25   H. 18   K. 208
  G. 16   J. 22

3. $14 \times 2.3 = ?$

  A. 6.09   C. 16.3   E. 322
  B. 11.7   D. 32.2

4. $58 \div 8 = ?$

  F. 0.14   H. 7.25   K. 464
  G. 7   J. 66

5. What is the sum of 202 and 191?

  A. 1.06   C. 393   E. 38,582
  B. 11   D. 404

6. What is $\dfrac{4}{100}$ expressed in lowest terms?

  F. $\dfrac{1}{104}$ H. $\dfrac{1}{25}$ K. $\dfrac{1}{20}$

  G. $\dfrac{1}{96}$ J. $\dfrac{1}{24}$

7. What is $\dfrac{26}{39}$ expressed in lowest terms?

  A. $\dfrac{2}{5}$ C. $\dfrac{1}{4}$ E. $\dfrac{1}{2}$

  B. $\dfrac{3}{4}$ D. $\dfrac{2}{3}$

8. George bought a pizza cut into 8 slices. If he ate 2 slices, what fraction of the pizza did George eat?

  F. $\dfrac{1}{8}$ H. $\dfrac{3}{8}$ K. $\dfrac{5}{8}$

  G. $\dfrac{1}{4}$ J. $\dfrac{1}{2}$

9. Marlene worked at a restaurant for 6 hours. If she worked for 2 hours in the dining room and the other 3 hours in the kitchen, what fraction of her work time did she spend in the kitchen?

   A. $\dfrac{1}{6}$ C. $\dfrac{1}{2}$ E. $\dfrac{5}{6}$
   B. $\dfrac{1}{3}$ D. $\dfrac{2}{3}$

10. Which one of the following fractions is equivalent to $\dfrac{30}{36}$?

    F. $\dfrac{24}{30}$ H. $\dfrac{15}{20}$ K. $\dfrac{2}{3}$
    G. $\dfrac{20}{25}$ J. $\dfrac{10}{12}$

Questions 11–15

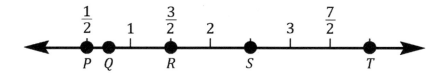

11. Which one of the points shown on the number line is located at $1\dfrac{1}{2}$?

    A. P   C. R   E. T
    B. Q   D. S

12. Point P is located at which one of the following values?

    F. $\dfrac{1}{2}$ H. $\dfrac{3}{2}$ K. 3
    G. 1   J. $\dfrac{5}{2}$

13. Which one of the points shown on the number line is located between $\dfrac{1}{2}$ and 1?

    A. P   C. R   E. T
    B. Q   D. S

14. Which one of the points shown on the number line is greater than 3?

    F. P   H. R   K. T
    G. Q   J. S

15. Point S is how many units away from Point T?

    A. $\dfrac{1}{2}$ C. 2   E. 7
    B. $1\dfrac{1}{2}$ D. 3

240 • MATH ALGEBRA AND FUNCTIONS

16. A gym teacher ordered 12 physical education uniforms consisting of shorts and shirts. The price for a pair of gym shorts is $7 and the price for a gym shirt is $9. What is the total cost of all 12 uniforms?

F. $16   H. $84   K. $192
G. $28   J. $108

17. The postage rate for a regular letter was 39¢ in 2006. The postage rate for the same letter was 46¢ in 2010. How much more did it cost to send 10 regular letters in 2010 than in 2006?

A. 7¢   C. 75¢   E. 95¢
B. 70¢   D. 85¢

18. At his summer job, Derek packs boxes of aquarium sand into shipping crates. Each shipping crate holds 30 1-pound boxes. If Derek packs 16 crates each hour, how many pounds of aquarium sand does Derek pack every 4 hours?

F. 120   H. 600   K. 1,920
G. 480   J. 720

19. A business firm flew 4 employees to a convention. The firm paid $145 in round-trip airfare for each employee and an additional $25 to check a box of equipment. What was the total cost to the firm for flying the employees and the equipment to the convention?

A. 120   C. 555   E. 605
B. 170   D. 580

20. A group of 12 girls and 6 boys spent $108 to play miniature golf. If they shared the cost equally, how much did each person pay?

F. $3   H. $9   K. $18
G. $6   J. $12

21. Which one of the following can be used to represent the phrase "the sum of r and t"?

A. r C. $t - r$ E. rt
B. $\dfrac{t}{r}$ D. $r + t$

22. Which one of the following can be used to represent the phrase "y subtracted from 5"?

F. $\dfrac{5}{y}$ H. $y - 5$ K. $5y$
G. $5 - y$ J. $5 + y$

23. Which one of the following can be used to represent the phrase "the product of b and c"?

   A. $\dfrac{b}{c}$ C. $c - b$ E. bc

   B. $\dfrac{c}{b}$ D. $b + c$

24. Which one of the following can be used to represent the phrase "the total of a, b, and c"?

   F. $a - b - c$ J. $ab + c$
   G. $a + b - c$ K. abc
   H. $a + b + c$

25. Mary had d dollars. For her birthday, her mother gave her n more dollars. What is the total number of dollars that Mary has?

   A. $\dfrac{d}{n}$ C. $n - d$ E. dn
   B. $d - n$ D. $d + n$

26. If $16 = 8 + x$, then $x = ?$

   F. -8 H. 2 K. 24
   G. -2 J. 8

27. If $x + 1.5 = 7$, then $x = ?$

   A. 2.5 C. 6.5 E. 8.5
   B. 5.5 D. 8

28. If $x - 4.5 = 6$, then $x = ?$

   F. 1.5 H. 10 K. 11.5
   G. 2.5 J. 10.5

29. If $3x = 24$, then $x = ?$

   A. $\dfrac{1}{8}$ C. 8 E. 21
   B. 6 D. 12

30. If $0.5x = 14$, then $x = ?$

   F. 7 H. 14.5 K. 28
   G. 14 J. 24

Math Algebra and Functions

Unit 8 | Pattern Identification

INSIDE THIS UNIT:
– The Features of a Sequence – – Exercise –

Non-Negotiable Skill:

For patterns exhibiting constant increase or decrease between terms, determine the next few terms that extend the pattern.

The Features of a Sequence

A **sequence** is a set of numbers that follow a pattern. Each number in the sequence is a **term**. In an arithmetic sequence, each subsequent term is found by adding the same value to the previous term. This number is called the **common difference**. For example, the groups of marbles shown below illustrate an arithmetic sequence:

Term 1	Term 2	Term 3	Term 4	Term 5
1	4	7	10	13

Notice that the same number of marbles (three) is added to each term to create the next term. Thus, the common difference in this sequence is 3.

Example:

The arithmetic sequence 3, 11, 19, ... has a common difference of 8. What is the next term in the sequence?

A. −5
B. 0
C. 8
D. 27
E. 35

The correct answer is (D). Add the common difference to the last term listed in the sequence: 19 + 8 = 27.

You will not always be given the common difference of a sequence. In some cases, you must use the given terms to determine the common difference or the next term(s) in the sequence.

Example:

What is the fifth term in the arithmetic sequence 12, 17, 22, ... ?

F. 27
G. 32
H. 37
J. 42
K. 47

The correct answer is (G). First, notice that the item stem specifies that you should find the fifth term in the sequence, not the next term in the sequence. Then find the common difference and verify it by choosing terms and subtracting their values from their previous terms. For example, 17 − 12 = 5, and 22 − 17 = 5. Thus, the common difference is 5. Now, add 5 to 22 to determine the fourth term: 22 + 5 = 27. Add 5 again to determine the fifth term: 27 + 5 = 32.

Notice that the common difference will be positive, if the sequence is increasing, or negative, if the sequence is decreasing.

Example:

What is the next term in the arithmetic sequence 99, 89, 79, ... ?

A. 54   C. 69   E. 109

B. 59   D. 74

The correct answer is (C). To find the common difference between the listed terms, choose a term and then subtract the value of its previous term: $89 - 99 = -10$. Thus, the common difference is -10. Then, to find the next term in the sequence, add the common difference, -10, to the last term listed: $79 + (-10) = 69$.

Summary

- A sequence is a set of numbers that follow a pattern.

- Each number in the sequence is a term.

- Arithmetic sequences have a common difference (the number added to each term to determine the next term in the sequence).

EXERCISE

DIRECTIONS: The following items can be solved with either pencil and paper or a calculator. Before performing the indicated operation(s), eliminate any choices that violate your number sense. Answers are on page 750.

1. The arithmetic sequence 20, 29, 38, ... has a common difference of 9. What is the next term in the sequence?

   A. 9   C. 29   E. 56
   B. 11   D. 47

2. The arithmetic sequence 8, 14, 20, ... has a common difference of 6. What is the next term in the sequence?

   F. 14   H. 26   K. 42
   G. 24   J. 32

3. The arithmetic sequence 32, 43, 54, ... has a common difference of 11. What is the next term in the sequence?

   A. 11   C. 65   E. 129
   B. 21   D. 76

4. What is the common difference for the arithmetic sequence 14, 16, 18, ... ?

   F. 1   H. 4   K. 12
   G. 2   J. 8

5. What is the common difference for the arithmetic sequence 32, 39, 46, ... ?

   A. 7   C. 18   E. 32
   B. 17   D. 25

6. What is the common difference for the arithmetic sequence 19, 42, 65, ... ?

   F. 4   H. 23   K. 61
   G. 19   J. 42

7. What is the common difference for the arithmetic sequence 22, 12, 2, ... ?

   A. −22   C. −10   E. −6
   B. −18   D. −8

8. What is the common difference for the arithmetic sequence 6, 1, −4, ... ?

   F. −24   H. −9   K. −4
   G. −14   J. −5

248 • MATH ALGEBRA AND FUNCTIONS

9. What is the common difference for the arithmetic sequence 2, –2, –6, ... ?

A. –12   C. –8   E. –4
B. –10   D. –6

10. What is the next term in the arithmetic sequence 24, 36, 48, ... ?

F. 12   H. 54   K. 72
G. 18   J. 60

11. What is the next term in the arithmetic sequence 2, 14, 26, ... ?

A. 12   C. 36   D. 38
B. 14   E. 50

12. What is the next term in the arithmetic sequence 105, 207, 309, ... ?

F. 102   H. 401   K. 411
G. 311   J. 409

13. What is the next term in the arithmetic sequence 1.5, 3, 4.5, ... ?

A. 1.5   C. 5   E. 6
B. 4   D. 5.5

14. What is the next term in the arithmetic sequence 21, 14, 7, ... ?

F. –28   H. –7   K. 0
G. –14   J. –1

15. What is the next term in the arithmetic sequence 31, 28, 25, ... ?

A. 28   C. 19   E. 3
B. 22   D. 16

16. What is the fifth term in the arithmetic sequence 7, 16, 25, ... ?

F. 9   H. 40   K. 52
G. 34   J. 43

17. What is the sixth term in the arithmetic sequence 9, 12, 15, ... ?

A. 3   C. 21   E. 27
B. 18   D. 24

18. What is the sixth term in the arithmetic sequence –12, –4, 4, ... ?

F. 8   H. 20   K. 32
G. 12   J. 28

19. What is the seventh term in the arithmetic sequence 26, 21, 16, ... ?

A. 11   C. 5   E. 1
B. 6   D. 4

20. What is the eighth term in the arithmetic sequence 49, 51, 53, ... ?

F. 2   H. 61   K. 65
G. 59   J. 63

21. Consider the following arithmetic sequence of numbers:

$$20, \underline{\quad}, \underline{\quad}, 32$$

What two numbers should be placed in the blanks?

A. 4, 8
B. 21, 27
C. 24, 28
D. 25, 30
E. 26, 31

22. Consider the following arithmetic sequence of numbers:

$$63, \underline{\quad}, \underline{\quad}, 90$$

What two numbers should be placed in the blanks?

F. 9, 18
G. 72, 81
H. 73, 83
J. 74, 85
K. 75, 86

23. Your house feels cool, so you check the thermostat. It is set to 60°F. Over the next 30 minutes, you increase the temperature a total of three times by the same number of degrees each time. If your thermostat is set to 69°F after the third time you increase the temperature, by how many degrees did you adjust the temperature each time?

A. 1°F
B. 2°F
C. 3°F
D. 6°F
E. 9°F

24. The weather station predicts that snow will begin to fall at 4 p.m. and that 2 inches will fall every hour for the next three hours. In total, how much snow, in inches, is predicted to fall by 6 p.m.?

F. 2
G. 3
H. 4
J. 6
K. 8

25. Which one of the following statements is true about the arithmetic sequence −10, −5, 0, 5, … ?

A. Every term in the sequence is divisible by 10.
B. The first term is 0.
C. The fifth term is 15.
D. The common difference is −5.
E. The sum of the first five terms is 0.

Math **Geometry**

Unit 9 | **Length and Distance**

INSIDE THIS UNIT:
– Measurement –
– Comparing Lengths –
– Figures Drawn to Actual Size –
– Figures Drawn to Scale –
– Figures with "No-Name" Units –
– Figures "Not Drawn to Scale" –
– Exercise –

Non-Negotiable Skill:

Estimate or calculate line segment lengths
in geometric figures based on
the information given.

Measurement

A very important real-world skill is determining length, distance, height, and so on. Just briefly, try to think about a world in which there were no inches, feet, miles, meters, or any such similar units. How would you know how tall you are? How would you know how far it is to your friend's home? How would you build anything? Without a unit of measure, you can't talk directly about distances. You can't say how long a stick is, how far the next town is, or how tall your friend is. Without units, the best that you can do is to say whether two lengths are equal or unequal and, if they are not equal, which one is longer and which one is shorter. But you can't say <u>how much</u> longer or <u>how much</u> shorter.

Of course, we do have inches, feet, miles, and meters, and so on, and we have tools for measuring lengths, heights, and distances. Most often we use a ruler, a meter stick, or a tape measure, but there are other more advanced, and even more precise, measuring devices. Perhaps you have a Global Positioning System (GPS), in your car or on your phone. For all the sophistication of the GPS, however, it still depends upon units of measurement, such as miles or meters.

The length of a line segment is always measured as a **linear length**. "Linear" is an adjective that comes from the noun "line," and it basically means "straight." So the kind of lengths and distances that we'll be discussing are "straight" or "straight line" lengths and distances. We will not be concerned with lengths and distances that curve as, for example, a circle does.

UNIT 9 | LENGTH AND DISTANCE • 253

Comparing Lengths

As the previous discussion makes clear, the most basic operation with lengths is just to compare them:

Are they equal?

Which is longer?

Which is shorter?

Example:

The figure below shows five straight sticks that are stored vertically in a cabinet.

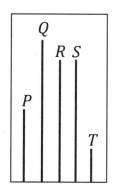

1. Which of the sticks is the longest?

   A. P   C. R   E. T
   B. Q   D. S

2. Which of the sticks is the shortest?

   F. P   H. R   K. T
   G. Q   J. S

3. Which two sticks are equal in length?

   A. P and Q
   B. Q and R
   C. Q and S
   D. R and S
   E. S and T

You can answer all three questions based on the appearance of the line segments in the figure: which looks longest, which looks shortest, which two look equal. The longest stick is Q, the shortest is T, and R and S are equal in length.

Example:

In the figure below, *PQRS* is a rectangle and $\overline{PQ}$ is longer than $\overline{PS}$. Which of the following line segments is the longest?

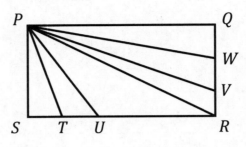

A. $\overline{PT}$
B. $\overline{PU}$
C. $\overline{PR}$
D. $\overline{PV}$
E. $\overline{PW}$

The correct answer is (H). You can see that $\overline{PR}$ is longer than $\overline{PT}$ or $\overline{PU}$, and $\overline{PR}$ is longer than $\overline{PV}$ and $\overline{PW}$. Thus, $\overline{PR}$ is the longest line segment.

Note that the figures in the examples above are drawn as accurately as possible. This is typically true of figures because the figures are intended to help the reader.

Example:

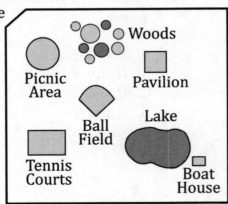

1. Which of the following features is farthest from the park entrance?

   A. Woods
   B. Ball field
   C. Pavilion
   D. Picnic area
   E. Boat house

2. Which of the following features is closest to the picnic area?

   F. Woods
   G. Pavilion
   H. Lake
   J. Boat house
   K. Tennis courts

3. Which of the following features are approximately the same distance from the park entrance?

   A. Picnic area and boat house
   B. Woods and lake
   C. Tennis courts and pavilion
   D. Ball field and picnic area
   E. Lake and picnic area

   The picture tells the entire story. The boat house is farthest from the park entrance, the woods are closest to the picnic area, and the tennis courts and pavilion are about the same distance from the park entrance.

Figures Drawn to Actual Size

The previous examples were based on comparing lengths and distances. Any units of measurement were irrelevant when answering questions such as, "Which is longer?", "Which is closest?", etc. Now we will look at problems that include units.

Sometimes a figure will be drawn to actual size. In that case, measuring tools can be used to find the lengths of the various features in common units of measurement.

Example:

The diagram below shows a pattern for a party mask to be cut from fabric. What is the value of *x*?

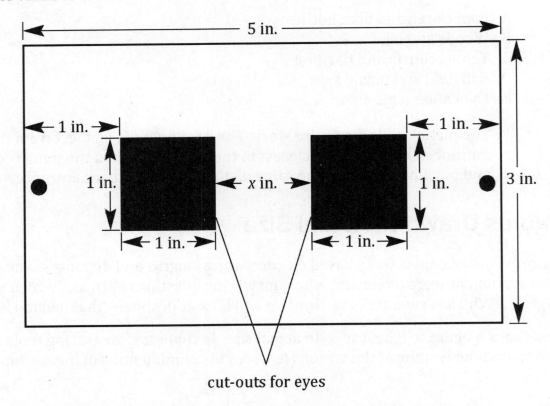

cut-outs for eyes

Note: All angles are right angles. Figure is drawn to actual size.

Of course, you can deduce the value of *x* from the information provided, but you can also just measure the distance. Since the figure is drawn to actual size, you can use a ruler to measure the distance between the two eye openings, and you'll find that the distance between the eye cut-outs is 1 inch.

It's not very often that you will find a drawing in a math book or on a test that is drawn to actual size. More often than not, the figures are "drawn to scale."

Figures Drawn to Scale

Most of the figures you encounter in books or on tests are drawn to scale. That is, the figures are rendered as accurately as possible but the lengths of the line segments shown are not the actual lengths you would find in the real world.

Example:

The figure below represents a fenced playground. All of the fences intersect at right angles. What is the value of x?

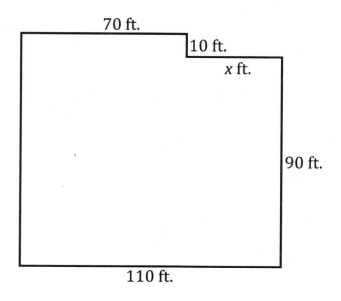

A. 30
B. 40
C. 50
D. 60
E. 80

The correct answer is (B). Since all angles are right angles, the bottom length of the figure (110 ft.) equals the sum of the two lengths at the top of the figure:

$x + 70 = 110$

$x + 70 - 70 = 110 - 70$

$x = 40$

But you can also find the value of x just by measuring, as the next example illustrates.

Example:

The figure below represents a rectangular piece of land with the dimensions given. $\overline{PR}$ is an electrical power line that runs diagonally across the property. What is the length of $\overline{PR}$?

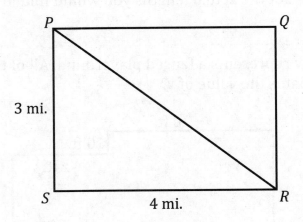

F. 1 mile
G. 2 miles
H. 3 miles
J. 5 miles
K. 7 miles

The correct answer is (J). You can find the length of $\overline{PR}$ by creating a ruler using the straight edge of a piece of paper. Using $\overline{SR}$, mark 4 units; using $\overline{PS}$ mark 3 units; the difference is 1 unit:

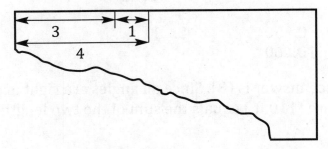

Use the ruler to measure the length of $\overline{PR}$.

UNIT 9 | LENGTH AND DISTANCE • 259

Figures with "No-Name" Units

Often you see math problems with figures using units that have no names.

Example:

In the figure below, what is the length of $\overline{AC}$?

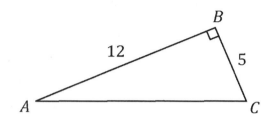

A. 5
B. 12
C. 13
D. 15
E. 17

The correct answer is (C). What units are used to describe the figure? They're not real units. They're good only for this particular figure. You can call them "no name units." Still, you can find the length of $\overline{AC}$ by creating a ruler and measuring.

Figures "Not Drawn to Scale"

Occasionally, you will see a figure with the warning note "Not Drawn to Scale" or similar wording. With such a figure, you <u>cannot</u> estimate lengths or use the ruler approach. Instead, you will have to use your knowledge of mathematics to solve the problem.

Example:

In the figure below, line segment PS has a length of 10. What is the length of line segment QR?

```
       3            3
   •───•────•───────•
   P   Q    R       S
```

Note: Figure not drawn to scale.

F. 2
G. 3
H. 4
J. 7
K. 16

The correct answer is (H). The figure is accompanied by a warning note telling you that it is not drawn to scale. Therefore, you cannot estimate or use the ruler approach to find the length of $\overline{QR}$. Instead:

$$\overline{PQ} + \overline{QR} + \overline{RS} = 10$$

$$3 + \overline{QR} + 3 = 10$$

$$\overline{QR} + 6 = 10$$

$$\overline{QR} = 10 - 6$$

$$\overline{QR} = 4$$

So even though $\overline{QR}$ seems to have a length of 3, it actually has a length of 4.

Summary

- The ability to estimate or calculate length, width, height, and distance is an important skill, both in the real world and in math class.

- Most figures in books or on tests are drawn to scale, meaning that the figures are rendered as accurately as possible but the lengths of the line segments shown are not the actual lengths one would find in the real world.

- With figures labeled "Not Drawn to Scale," you <u>cannot</u> estimate lengths or use the ruler approach. Instead, you must use your knowledge of mathematics to solve the problems.

UNIT 9 | LENGTH AND DISTANCE • 261

EXERCISE

DIRECTIONS: Answer each of the following items using information from the corresponding figure. Answers are on page 751.

1. The figure below shows a circle with center O. Which of the following line segments is the longest?

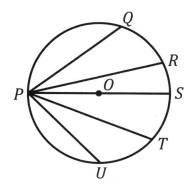

A. $\overline{PQ}$ C. $\overline{PS}$ E. $\overline{PU}$
B. $\overline{PR}$ D. $\overline{PT}$

Questions 2-3

The figure below is a drawing of a state park.

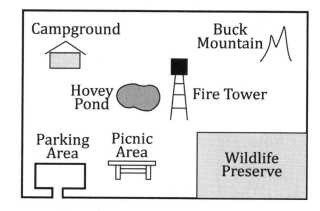

2. Which feature of the park is closest to the parking area?

   F. Picnic area
   G. Wildlife preserve
   H. Hovey pond
   J. Campground
   K. Fire tower

3. Which of the following features is farthest from the wildlife preserve?

   A. Campground
   B. Hovey pond
   C. Fire tower
   D. Buck mountain
   E. Picnic area

Questions 4–8

The figure below shows the putting area for the shot put event of a track and field meet. The lettered points indicate the landing spots of eight different throws from the putting circle, shown in gray.

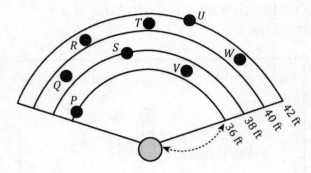

Note: Figure not drawn to scale.

4. Which of the following points indicates the longest throw?

   F. P   H. T   K. W
   G. R   J. U

5. Which of the following points indicates the shortest throw?

   A. P   C. T   E. W
   B. S   D. V

6. The distances indicated by which two of the following points are most nearly equal?

   F. P and Q   J. S and T
   G. Q and U   K. T and U
   H. R and T

7. What is the approximate distance of the throw indicated by S?

   A. 36 feet   D. 39 feet
   B. 37 feet   E. 40 feet
   C. 38 feet

8. What is the difference between the distances of the throws indicated by S and U?

   F. 1 foot   J. 38 feet
   G. 2 feet   K. 42 feet
   H. 4 feet

Questions 9–13

The figure below is a map of a town in which all of the streets run either north and south or east and west. The blocks are all the same size (the distance from one intersection to the next intersection is equal for all intersections). The lettered points indicate points of interest.

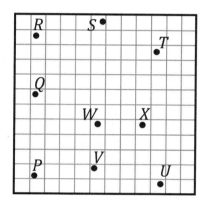

9. Using the most direct route possible along the streets, which one of the following locations is the greatest distance from *U*?

    A. *Q* C. *S* E. *V*
    B. *R* D. *T*

10. Using the most direct route possible along the streets, which one of the following locations is the greatest distance from *W*?

    F. *Q* H. *S* K. *U*
    G. *R* J. *T*

11. Using the most direct route possible along the streets, which one of the following locations is the shortest distance from *X*?

    A. *S* C. *U* E. *W*
    B. *T* D. *V*

12. Using the most direct routes possible along the streets, which two of the following locations are most nearly equal in distance from *T*?

    F. *P* and *Q*   J. *R* and *U*
    G. *P* and *W*   K. *U* and *V*
    H. *Q* and *S*

13. Traveling "as a crow flies" (in a straight line and not along the streets), what is the approximate distance, in blocks, from *P* to *T*? (The diagonal distance across a block is approximately 1.5 times the distance of one block.)

    A. 4 C. 9   E. 29
    B. 8 D. 12

14. In the figure below, ∠PRQ is a right angle. Which of the following lengths is the greatest?

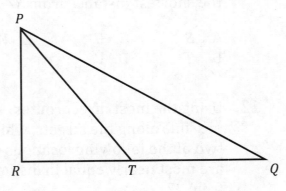

F. $\overline{PR}$
G. $\overline{PT}$
H. $\overline{PQ}$
J. $\overline{RT}$
K. $\overline{TQ}$

15. In the figure below, PQRS is a rectangle, and the segments of the dark line are parallel to either $\overline{PQ}$ or $\overline{PS}$. What is the length of the dark line?

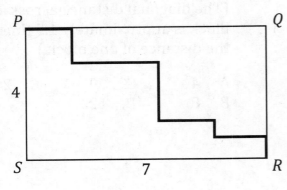

A. 3
B. 4
C. 7
D. 11
E. 28

16. The figure below shows two squares, ABCD and EFGD. What is the length of DG?

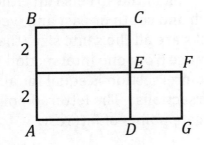

F. 2
G. 4
H. 6
J. 8
K. 12

17. In the figure below, PQRS is a rectangle and ∠PVT is a right angle. If $\overline{QR} = 5$, what is the length of $\overline{TR}$?

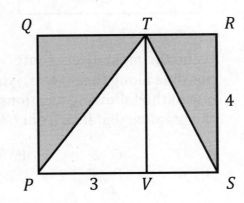

A. 1
B. 2
C. 3
D. 5
E. 7

18. The figure below shows a stack of books 14 inches tall and includes the thickness of each book. What is the value of x?

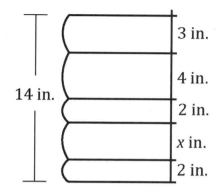

F. 2
G. 3
H. 4
J. 5
K. 11

Questions 19–20

The figure below shows a section of a floor made of boards, each 4 inches wide.

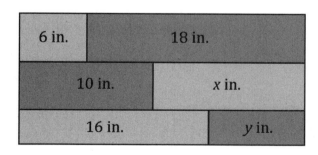

Note: Figure not drawn to scale.

19. What is the value of x?

A. 4
B. 6
C. 8
D. 12
E. 14

20. What is the value of y?

F. 4
G. 6
H. 8
J. 12
K. 14

Questions 21–22

The figure below shows a vertical light tower held in place by guy wires.

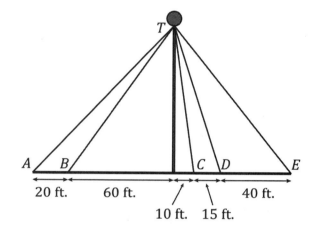

21. Which of the guy wires is the longest?

A. $\overline{AT}$
B. $\overline{BT}$
C. $\overline{CT}$
D. $\overline{DT}$
E. $\overline{ET}$

22. Which one of the following statements about the guy wires is FALSE?

F. $\overline{BT}$ is longer than $\overline{CT}$.
G. $\overline{BT}$ is longer than $\overline{DT}$.
H. $\overline{BT}$ is longer than $\overline{ET}$.
J. $\overline{CT}$ is shorter than $\overline{DT}$.
K. $\overline{CT}$ is shorter than $\overline{ET}$.

23. The figure below shows a football field with lines marking the yardage from the goal. Each of the five dark lines represents one play and shows the progress made by the team in possession of the ball. For which play did the team cover the most yards?

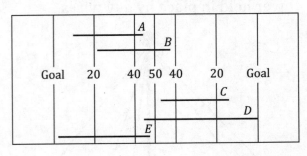

A. A   C. C   E. E
B. B   D. D

24. The figure below shows a circle with center O. Which of the five lines is the longest?

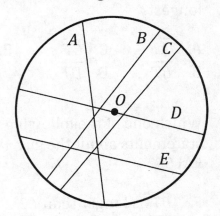

F. A   H. C   K. E
G. B   J. D

25. The figure below shows a rectangular board with equally spaced nails along the edges. Five wires are strung on the board. Each wire is attached to a nail at the top of the board, wrapped around a nail at the bottom of the board, and then attached to a different nail at the top of the board. Which of the five wires is the longest?

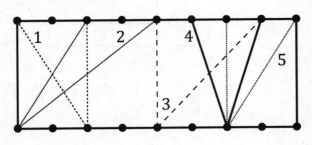

A. 1   C. 3   E. 5
B. 2   D. 4

Math **Geometry**

Unit 10 | **Unit Conversions**

INSIDE THIS UNIT:
– Perform Common Unit Conversions – – Exercise –

Non-Negotiable Skill:

Complete common unit conversions involving money, length, weight, or time, such as dimes to dollars, inches to feet, ounces to pounds, or minutes to hours.

Perform Common Unit Conversions

Some word problems require you to perform a unit conversion. For example, you might need to convert inches into feet. Always read carefully to see what units are required for the answer.

The main thing to remember when converting units is that you can multiply any expression by 1 and that expression will still be true.

$$24 \text{ eggs} \times 1 = 24 \text{ eggs}$$

To convert units, multiply by a fraction that is equal to 1, using the correct units. Remember to cancel.

$$24 \text{ eggs} \times \left(\frac{1 \text{ dozen eggs}}{12 \text{ eggs}} \right) = 2 \text{ dozen eggs}$$

Example:

Rhys sells his old baseball cards for a quarter each. He earns 35 quarters from his sales. How much money, in dollars, does Rhys make?

A. $0.25   C. $8.75   E. $140.00
B. $3.50   D. $35.00

The correct answer is (C). There are 4 quarters in 1 dollar. To find the amount of money that Rhys makes, convert 35 quarters to dollars:

$$35 \text{ quarters} \times \frac{1 \text{ dollar}}{4 \text{ quarters}} = \frac{35 \text{ dollars}}{4} = 8.75 \text{ dollars} = \$8.75$$

Example:

Brianna must read for at least 60 minutes each week during the school year and submit a reading log. Her teacher records the total number of minutes Brianna read throughout the school year. At the end of the year, Brianna has read for 2,460 minutes. How long, in hours, has Brianna read?

F. 4.1   H. 35.4   K. 246
G. 24.6   J. 41

The correct answer is (J). Convert minutes to hours:

$$2{,}460 \text{ minutes} \times \frac{1 \text{ hour}}{60 \text{ minutes}} = 41 \text{ hours}$$

If a problem requires conversion between common units such as inches and feet or minutes and hours, you should already be familiar with the units required. Sometimes you may be given a problem that involves conversion of units with which you are not familiar. In that case, the needed information will be provided.

Example:

During a car trip to visit friends, Raymond sees a road sign that reads "Montreal 200 kilometers." How far, in miles, is Raymond from Montreal? (1 kilometer = 0.62 miles)

A. 6.2   C. 124   E. 322.6
B. 12.4   D. 248

The correct answer is (C). Convert kilometers to miles using the equivalence provided:

$$200 \text{ kilometers} \times \frac{0.62 \text{ miles}}{1 \text{ kilometer}} = 124 \text{ miles}$$

Example:

Sal is flying to Spain. The airline charges passengers an additional fee for luggage that weighs more than 10 kilograms. Sal does not want to pay for his luggage. What is the maximum weight, in pounds, that Sal's luggage can weigh before Sal incurs an additional fee? (1 kilogram = 2.2046 pounds)

F. 12.2046   H. 44.092   K. 2,204.6
G. 22.046   J. 220.46

The correct answer is (G). Convert kilograms to pounds using the equivalence provided:

$$10 \text{ kilograms} \times \frac{2.2046 \text{ pounds}}{1 \text{ kilogram}} = 22.046 \text{ pounds}$$

Example:

A recipe used in a commercial kitchen calls for 6 gallons of milk. If the chef has only quart containers of milk, how many quarts of milk should be used in the recipe? (1 gallon = 4 quarts)

A. 0.67   C. 2   E. 24
B. 1.5   D. 10

The correct answer is (E). Convert gallons to quarts using the equivalence provided:

$$6 \text{ gallons} \times \frac{4 \text{ quarts}}{1 \text{ gallon}} = 24 \text{ quarts}$$

If you look again at the five items we just covered, you will notice that converting units involves multiplying and dividing. A common mistake is to invert the conversion. For example, suppose that you tried to convert 6 gallons into quarts as follows:

$$6 \times \frac{1}{4} = 1.5$$

This result is wrong. Fortunately, there is an easy way to make sure that you are doing the conversion correctly: **always include the units**. Consider the wrong conversion just shown:

$$6 \text{ gallons} \times \frac{1 \text{ gallon}}{4 \text{ quarts}} = 1.5 \frac{\text{gallons} \times \text{gallon}}{\text{quarts}}$$

But $\text{gallon} \times \frac{\text{gallon}}{\text{quarts}}$ is not a real unit. The correct solution is:

$$6 \text{ gallons} \times \frac{4 \text{ quarts}}{1 \text{ gallon}} = 24 \; \cancel{\text{gallons}} \times \frac{\text{quarts}}{\cancel{\text{gallons}}} = 24 \text{ quarts}$$

In the correct solution, the "gallons" unit in the numerator and the "gallons" unit in the denominator cancel each other out (divide to leave 1). Generally, you can be sure that you've done the conversion correctly if you include the units in your calculation.

> **Summary**
> - Some word problems require a unit conversion.
> - Always read carefully to determine what units are required for the answer to a word problem.
> - To avoid mistakes while converting units, always include the units in your conversion calculations.

272 • MATH GEOMETRY

EXERCISE

DIRECTIONS: The following items can be solved with either pencil and paper or a calculator. Remember to include units and cancel. Answers are on page 751.

1. On New Year's Eve, a clock counts down the seconds until midnight. If the clock shows 3,600 seconds remaining until midnight, how many minutes remain until midnight?

   A. 20   C. 60   E. 360
   B. 30   D. 200

2. A truckload of coal weighs 2 tons. What is the weight of the coal, in pounds? (1 ton = 2,000 pounds)

   F. 100   J. 1,000
   G. 400   K. 4,000
   H. 500

3. A commercial recipe for cookies calls for 8 pints of corn syrup. How many quarts of corn syrup does the recipe call for? (2 pints = 1 quart)

   A. 2   C. 4   E. 16
   B. 2.5   D. 6

4. The altimeter of an airplane shows the altitude of the plane as 10,000 feet. What is the approximate altitude of the plane in miles? (1 mile = 5,280 feet)

   F. 0.528   H. 1.89   K. 5.28
   G. 0.89   J. 4.72

5. In one week, Dan drives his car 120 kilometers. How many miles does he drive his car during the week? (1 kilometer = 0.62 miles)

   A. 58   C. 119.38   E. 193.5
   B. 74.4   D. 182

6. Beth buys 2.5 pounds of cheese. How much cheese, in ounces, does she buy? (1 pound = 16 ounces)

   F. 6.4   H. 15.6   K. 40
   G. 13.5   J. 18.5

7. A ship's speed is often measured in knots. Knots are nautical miles per hour. If a ship's speed is 12 knots, what is its speed in land miles per hour? (1 nautical mile = 1.15 land miles)

   A. 1.15   C. 10.85   E. 13.8
   B. 10.4   D. 13.15

8. People who raise and care for horses often measure the height of a horse in units called hands. What is the height of a horse, in inches, that stands 12 hands tall? (1 hand = 4 inches)

F. 3   H. 16   K. 52
G. 8   J. 48

9. A skier's competition jump measures 180 meters. What is the length, in feet, of the jump? (1 meter = 3.28 feet)

A. 54.87   C. 248   E. 608
B. 183.12   D. 590.4

10. A sailor determines that a boat is anchored in 6 fathoms of water. If 1 fathom is equal to 6 feet, what is the depth of the water, in feet, where the boat is anchored?

F. 0   H. 12   K. 36
G. 1   J. 18

11. Isabella needs 24 feet of electric wire to install a new outlet in her garage, but wire is sold by the yard. How many yards of wire should Isabella buy?

A. 2   C. 8   E. 288
B. 6   D. 72

12. The rules of a basketball league require teams to file a registration form for each player. The form includes a space for height in inches. A coach knows that the tallest player on the team is 6 feet 7 inches tall. What should the coach enter on the registration form for the player's height in inches?

F. 13   H. 67   K. 79
G. 25   J. 72

13. A game displays the number of minutes that each player is logged on to the game. Last week, Sophia spent 12 hours and 47 minutes logged on to the game. How many minutes should the display show?

A. 59   C. 335   E. 767
B. 191   D. 407

14. It is exactly 570 steps from Abigail's front door to the bus stop. If Abigail walks at the rate of 1 step per second, how many minutes will it take her to reach the bus stop?

F. 9.5   H. 19.0   K. 47.5
G. 12.6   J. 23.75

15. Before putting a bag of grapes into her shopping cart, Chloe weighs the fruit. The digital scale provided for customer use is set to ounces and displays the weight as 64. If the scale were set to pounds, what would the display read? (1 pound = 16 ounces)

A. 2.6   C. 4.0   E. 8.0
B. 3.5   D. 5.3

16. At the start of a logging operation, a semi-truck is loaded with a load of pulp logs weighing 9,000 pounds. When the truck arrives at the paper mill, the load is weighed again, in tons. How many tons does the load weigh at the paper mill? (1 ton = 2,000 pounds)

F. 4.5   H. 18   K. 90
G. 9   J. 45

17. A restaurant's recipe for lemonade calls for 3 dozen lemons, 10 cups of sugar, and enough water to make 18 quarts of lemonade. How many gallons of lemonade does the recipe make? (1 gallon = 4 quarts)

A. 2.5   C. 3.6   E. 9.0
B. 3.0   D. 4.5

18. A football coach is planning a series of drills for the afternoon practice. The length of the drills is calculated in minutes, and the practice is 4 hours long. How long, in minutes, is the practice?

F. 28   H. 108   K. 240
G. 72   J. 120

19. Ethan's first long jump attempt is 72 inches. How many yards does he jump?

A. 2   C. 6   E. 864
B. 3   D. 216

20. Barclay's boat is $5\frac{2}{3}$ yards long. How many feet long is his boat?

F. 5.67   H. 62   K. 204
G. 17   J. 84

21. A battery is rated to last 720 minutes before recharging is necessary. How many hours is the battery expected to last before recharging?

A. 6   C. 20   E. 120
B. 12   D. 60

22. A phone app converts minutes into seconds. Jay enters 23 minutes into the input field. How many seconds does the app indicate as the equivalent of 23 minutes?

F. 138   H. 552   K. 1,380
G. 276   J. 690

23. As an experiment, a test subject spends 6 days in a sealed biosphere with sufficient oxygen, food, and water. How many hours does the subject spend in the biosphere?

A. 72   C. 144   E. 360
B. 108   D. 180

24. In one week, a construction crew lays down 10,560 feet of blacktop on a straight road. How many miles of blacktop does the crew lay down during the week? (1 mile = 5,280 feet)

F. 2   H. 6   K. 10
G. 4   J. 8

25. Teams of two drivers participate in a cross-country road race. The winning team completes the course in exactly 96 hours. How many days does it take the winning team to complete the course?

A. 4   C. 8   E. 2,304
B. 6   D. 1,152

Math Statistics and Probability

Unit 11 | Averages

INSIDE THIS UNIT:
– Calculate the Average of a List of Numbers – – Exercise –

278 • MATH STATISTICS AND PROBABILITY

Non-Negotiable Skill:

Determine the average of a list of numbers.

Calculate the Average of a List of Numbers

The procedure for calculating the average of a list of positive numbers can be generally represented as:

$$\text{Average} = \frac{a_1 + a_2 + a_3 + \ldots + a_n}{n}$$

This is translated into English as:

"The average of n numbers is the sum of the numbers divided by n."

Example:

What is the average of 4, 8, 12, and 24?

A. 2   C. 6   E. 16
B. 4   D. 12

The correct answer is (D). The average of the 4 numbers is the sum of the numbers divided by 4:

$$\text{Average} = \frac{4 + 8 + 12 + 24}{4} = \frac{48}{4} = 12$$

Example:

Pedro's grade in English is the average of 5 test scores. If he received 85, 91, 93, 88, and 95 on the 5 tests, what is his English grade?

F. 71.4   H. 90.4   K. 95
G. 85   J. 91

The correct answer is (H). The average of the 5 tests is the sum of the tests divided by 5:

$$\text{Average} = \frac{85 + 91 + 93 + 88 + 95}{5} = \frac{452}{5} = 90.4$$

Example:

Michael buys 4 books that cost $7.95, $12.05, $8.49, and $9.99 each. What is the average cost per book?

A. $7.95
B. $9.62
C. $10.00
D. $12.05
E. $38.48

The correct answer is (B). The average cost of the 4 books is the sum of the costs divided by 4:

$$\text{Average} = \frac{\$7.95 + \$12.05 + \$8.49 + \$9.99}{4} = \frac{\$38.48}{4} = \$9.62$$

To find the average of a list of positive numbers:

Add up all the numbers in the list and divide that sum by the number of items in the list.

Summary

- The average of n numbers is the sum of the numbers divided by n.

280 • MATH STATISTICS AND PROBABILITY

EXERCISE

DIRECTIONS: The following items can be solved with either pencil and paper or a calculator. Before performing the indicated operation(s), eliminate any choices that violate your number sense. Answers are on page 751.

1. What is the average of 6 and 10?

    A. $1\frac{2}{3}$ C. 4   E. 16
    B. 2   D. 8

2. What is the average of 4 and 12?

    F. 4   H. 8   K. 16
    G. 6   J. 12

3. What is the average of 100 and 200?

    A. $\frac{1}{2}$ C. 100   E. 300
    B. 2   D. 150

4. What is the average of 3, 8, and 4?

    F. 3   H. 5   K. 15
    G. 4   J. 5.5

5. What is the average of 22, 43, and 25?

    A. 27   C. 46   E. 90
    B. 30   D. 81

6. What is the average of 26, 34, 19, and 31?

    F. 4   H. 27.5   K. 110
    G. 26.5   J. 28.5

7. What is the average of 21, 11, 11, 22, and 20?

    A. 5   C. 17   E. 85
    B. 16.5   D. 20

8. What is the average of 802, 795, 806, 801, and 796?

    F. 5   H. 800.5   K. 4,000
    G. 800   J. 801

9. What is the average of 6, 6, 8, 6, 9, 5, and 9?

    A. 4   C. 7   E. 49
    B. 6   D. 8

10. Arnie jogs on 4 consecutive days. If he jogs a total of 12 miles on the 4 days, what is the average distance, in miles, that he jogs each day?

    F. 3   H. 8   K. 48
    G. 4   J. 12

11. Amy pays a total of $48.64 for 8 collectible stamps. What is the average cost per stamp?

    A. $6.08   D. $56.64
    B. $8.00   E. $389.12
    C. $40.64

12. Emma watches television a total of 21 hours over 7 days. What is the average number of hours of television that she watches per day?

    F. 3   H. 9   K. 28
    G. 7   J. 14

13. The weights of 5 children in a boat are 83 pounds, 92 pounds, 88 pounds, 105 pounds, and 86 pounds. What is the average weight, in pounds, per child?

    A. 22   C. 90.8   E. 454
    B. 88   D. 94

14. Victor bowls 6 games and earns scores of 178, 180, 211, 191, 169, and 235. What is his average score for the 6 games?

    F. 180   H. 190.5   K. 202
    G. 185.5   J. 194

15. Debbie wins a fishing tournament by catching 5 fish with the greatest average length. If the 5 fish measure 12 inches, 18 inches, 23 inches, 14 inches, and 16 inches, what is the average length, in inches, per fish?

    A. 15   C. 17   E. 18
    B. 16.6   D. 17.5

16. On 6 tests, Nichole scores 95, 91, 86, 80, 81, and 89. What is her average score for the 6 tests?

    F. 86   H. 88.5   K. 97
    G. 87   J. 89

17. The daily high temperatures recorded in Mason City for a week were 54°F, 58°F, 64°F, 42°F, 39°F, 31°F, and 41°F. What was the average daily high temperature, in degrees Fahrenheit, for the week?

    A. 41   C. 42.5   E. 47.5
    B. 42   D. 47

18. For his first semester in college, Flynn bought 5 textbooks for $32.50, $41.35, $54.96, $18.21, and $67.43 each. What was the average cost per book?

    F. $41.35   J. $43.73
    G. $42.84   K. $214.45
    H. $42.89

282 • MATH STATISTICS AND PROBABILITY

19. James pays $11, $4, and $9 for 3 books. What is the average price per book?

A. $4   C. $6   E. $9
B. $5   D. $8

20. A swimmer completes 4 races in 31, 28, 22, and 35 seconds. What is her average time, in seconds, for per race?

F. 25   H. 29   K. 37
G. 28   J. 32

21. Ben charges $30 for each lawn he mows. Listed below are his earnings for the last 7 weeks. What is the average amount he earned per week?

Week 1	$120
Week 2	$90
Week 3	$0
Week 4	$30
Week 5	$0
Week 6	$150
Week 7	$30

A. $30   C. $84   E. $420
B. $60   D. $390

22. During her 6-day vacation, Martina hiked the following number of miles per day: 5, 7, 8, 0, 3, and 7. What is the average distance, in miles, that Martina hiked per day?

F. 5   H. 7   K. 32
G. 6   J. 30

23. The number of trash bags the Lopez family sent to the landfill each week for 4 weeks is listed below. What is the average number of trash bags that the family sent to the landfill per week?

Week 1	2
Week 2	4
Week 3	0
Week 4	6

A. 3   C. 6   E. 13
B. 4   D. 12

24. There are 9 flights leaving Chicago. The number of available seats on each flight is 7, 4, 0, 1, 6, 2, 5, 0, and 2. What is the average number of available seats per flight?

F. 2   H. 4   K. 36
G. 3   J. 27

25. A student spent 56, 59, 62, 59, 63, and 61 minutes working on homework per day during the past 6 days. What was the average number of minutes the student worked on homework per day?

A. 59   C. 72   E. 360
B. 60   D. 301

26. Ron's electric bills for the past 5 months were $240, $105, $98, $180, and $87. What was the average bill per month?

    F. $98   H. $142   K. $710
    G. $105 J. $701

27. Grace spends $15 for dinner Monday and $19 for dinner Tuesday. What is the average amount she spends for each dinner?

    A. $16   C. $19   E. $34
    B. $17   D. $27

28. Anna practices tennis 2 hours on Sunday, 3 hours on Monday, 5 hours on Tuesday, 1 hour on Wednesday, 4 hours on Thursday, 2 hours on Friday, and 4 hours on Saturday. How many hours of practice does she average per day?

    F. 2   H. 5   K. 21
    G. 3   J. 17

29. Adrian's quiz scores are 93, 75, and 81. What is Adrian's average score?

    A. 73   C. 81   E. 88
    B. 75   D. 83

30. Laura's golf scores are 48, 45, 39, 51, 43, and 38. What is Laura's average golf score?

    F. 39   H. 47   K. 54
    G. 44   J. 51

Math Statistics and Probability

Unit 12 | Charts and Tables

INSIDE THIS UNIT:
– Tables –   – Bar Graphs –   – Line Graphs –   – Pie Charts –   – Pictographs –   – Exercise –

286 • MATH STATISTICS AND PROBABILITY

Non-Negotiable Skill:

Solve one-step problems using information from a table or chart.

Tables

In Unit 4, you reviewed "word" or "story" problems. These problems require the same procedure you will need to solve problems involving tables and charts. To review, the procedure for solving a word problem is:

1. Read carefully. Then isolate the question being asked.

2. Determine how the information given will answer the question.

3. Do the computations necessary to answer the question.

The first step is very important when solving math word problems: read slowly and carefully. In many other contexts, such as when reading a novel, you can read quicker. However, in doing math word problems, reading quickly is NOT the way to success: each word may be very important.

Here is an example of a word problem:

Example:

At the bookstore, Gayle bought 3 magazines. *Runner's Weekly* cost $4.95, *Fitness and Health* cost $3.49, and *Fashion* cost $5.45. What was the total amount that Gayle spent on magazines? (No tax was charged.)

A. $4.63 C. $8.94 E. $13.89
B. $8.44 D. $10.40

The correct answer is (E). The question to be answered is "total amount." So you add the costs of the three magazines:

$4.95
$3.49
+$5.45
$13.89

UNIT 12 | CHARTS AND TABLES • 287

Now here is the same problem using a table:

Example:

At the bookstore, Gayle bought three magazines. Below is a copy of the sales slip:

Product	Price
Runner's Weekly	$4.95
Fitness and Health	$3.49
Fashion	$5.45
TOTAL	

What was the total amount that Gayle spent on magazines? (No tax was charged.)

F. $4.63   H. $8.94   K. $13.89
G. $8.44   J. $10.40

And, of course, the solution is the same as shown on the previous page:

Product	Price
Runner's Weekly	$4.95
Fitness and Health	$3.49
Fashion	$5.45
TOTAL	**$13.89**

The arithmetic needed to answer problems based on a table is the same arithmetic that is used to solve problems based on a story, but a table is usually easier to use.

Summary

- The procedure for solving a problem using information from a table or a chart is the same procedure for solving a word problem:

    1. Read carefully. Then isolate the question being asked.
    2. Determine how the information given will answer the question.
    3. Do the computations necessary to answer the question.

Bar Graphs

Graphs are "pictures" of information. Instead of "telling the story," the problem-writer "paints a picture." And just as one picture is worth a thousand words, a graph can provide information more efficiently than a narrative description of the same data.

This type of data presentation is called either a bar graph or column graph (the vertical bars look like columns of a building). In the graph, the length of the bars represent value. The longer the bar, the bigger the value. The title, axis labels, bar labels, units, and footnotes (if any) will all give you additional information.

Examples:

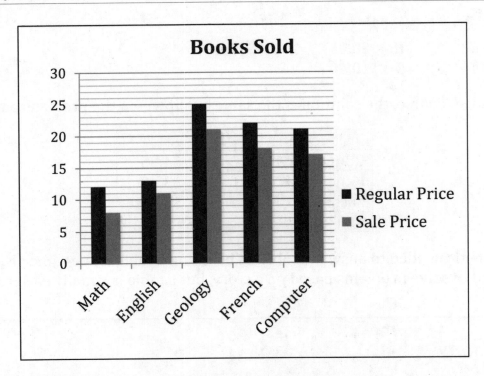

How many geology books were sold at the regular price?

A. $12   C. $18   E. $25
B. $13   D. $21

The correct answer is (E). The "Regular Price" bar for geology book sales extends to the 25 line, so 25 books were sold.

Which of the following books sold the most at the sale price?

F. Math
G. English
H. Geology
J. French
K. Computer

The correct answer is (H). The "Sale Price" bar is tallest for the geology book.

Line Graphs

To create a line graph, plot the data points on a grid and connect them with a line. Line graphs make it easy to identify trends in collected data.

Example:

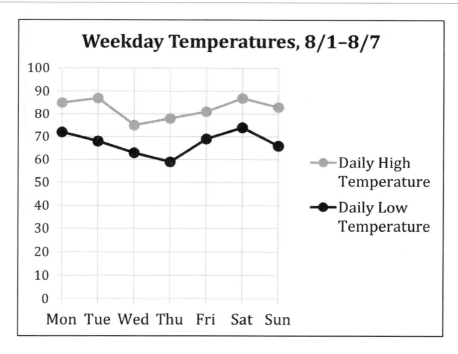

On what day did the daily low temperature first increase over the previous day?

A. Tuesday
B. Wednesday
C. Thursday
D. Friday
E. Saturday

The correct answer is (D). Daily low temperature decreases from Tuesday to Thursday, then increases on Friday and Saturday.

Pie Charts

Pie charts show the ratio of various categories of data. You can compare slices at a glance to determine which category is the largest, which is the smallest, etc.

Example:

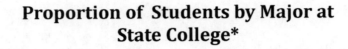

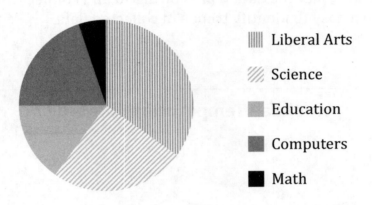

*only includes students who have declared one major

Which one of the following areas of study has the largest proportion of majors?

F. Liberal Arts
G. Science
H. Education
J. Computers
K. Math

The correct answer is (F). The "Liberal Arts" slice is by far the largest piece of the pie. It is also obvious that "Math" is the smallest piece of the pie.

Often a pie will be accompanied by percentages so that the data is more precise. With the additional precision, it is possible to answer questions about percentages.

Example:

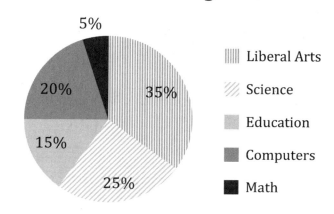

Proportion of Students by Major at State College*

*only includes students who have declared one major

What proportion of the students at State College chose either Math or Computers for a major?

A. 5% C. 20% E. 35%
B. 15% D. 25%

The correct answer is (D):

Math + Computers = Total

5% + 20% = 25%

But even with this additional information, the pie still does not tell how <u>many</u> students are represented. Without more information, you cannot answer this type of question.

Example:

Proportion of Students by Major at State College*

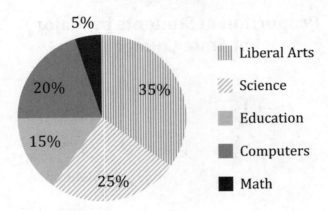

*only includes students who have declared one major

How many students chose Liberal Arts for a major?

F. 5
G. 15
H. 20
J. 30
K. Cannot be determined from the given information

The correct answer is (K). The question asks "how *many* students." The pie tells you what *proportion* (what *percent*) of the student population. The pie does not tell you how *many* students—unless you have more information.

A pie chart is often accompanied by a "total" number to tell you how many individuals are included.

Example:

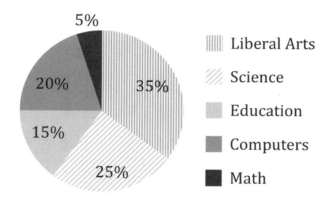

Proportion of Students by Major at State College*
Total = 1,000 students

*only includes students who have declared one major

Now you can calculate how many students are in each category:

Category	Percent	Total Students	Number
Liberal Arts	35%	1,000	350
Science	25%	1,000	250
Education	15%	1,000	150
Computers	20%	1,000	200
Math	5%	1,000	50
TOTAL	100%	1,000	1,000

Pictographs

The charts and graphs you've seen so far are widely used in science, business, and other activities that require a lot of "number crunching." Sometimes, though, it's easier to make a point with a graph of pictures—a **pictograph**. The "key" tells you how many individuals each picture represents.

Examples:

Population of Weston

Approximately how many men live in Weston?

A. 5   C. 800   E. 8,000
B. 8   D. 5,000

The correct answer is (E). Each "man" represents 1,000 men. The pictograph shows 8 men, so there are (8)(1,000) = 8,000 men in Weston.

Approximately how many children live in Weston?

F. 4.75   H. 475   K. 47,500
G. 5   J. 4,750

The correct answer is (J). Each "child" represents 1,000 children. The pictograph shows 4 complete children and 1 partial child, so there are between (4)(1,000) = 4,000 children and (5)(1,000) = 5,000 children in Weston. 4,750 is between 4,000 and 5,000.

Approximately how many women who live in Weston are not married?

A. 0.5   C. 500   E. Cannot be determined from
B. 5   D. 5,000   the given information

The correct answer is (E). The pictograph shows the number of men and women individually. It does not provide any information about the marital status of individuals.

What is the approximate total population (men, women, and children) of Weston?

F. 21.5   H. 2,150   K. 212,500
G. 215   J. 21,250

The correct answer is (J). We have already determined that there are 8,000 men and approximately 4,750 children in Weston. The pictograph shows 8 complete women and about half of one woman, so there are approximately (8)(1,000) + (1)(500) = 8,000 + 500 = 8,500 women in Weston. The total population is approximately 8,000 + 4,750 + 8,500 = 21,250.

Summary

- A bar graph uses columns to represent values (the longer the bar, the bigger the number) and provides a scale to help read the information.

- A line graph uses data points plotted on a grid and connected with lines to represent values such as time and distance.

- A pie chart uses a circle divided into "slices" to represent how large or small a share each category has of the total. Pie charts are often accompanied by a "total" number to indicate how many individual items are included.

- A pictograph uses pictures to show numerical values and includes a "key" to tell you how many individuals each picture represents.

296 • MATH STATISTICS AND PROBABILITY

EXERCISE

DIRECTIONS: Answer the following items using information from the corresponding table. Answers are on page 751.

Questions 1–5

ATTENDANCE AT W.E.B. DUBOIS MIDDLE SCHOOL Monday		
Grade	Total Enrolled	Present
6th Grade	123	116
7th Grade	117	110
8th Grade	115	105

1. Of the total number of 6th-graders enrolled, how many were not present on Monday?

   A. 6 C. 10 E. 128
   B. 7 D. 116

2. How many students are enrolled in the 7th and 8th grades combined?

   F. 115 H. 232 K. 355
   G. 215 J. 331

3. On Monday, how many 7th- and 8th-graders, combined, were present?

   A. 105 C. 116 E. 226
   B. 110 D. 215

4. How many more 6th-graders are enrolled at the school than 8th-graders?

   F. 6 H. 8 K. 11
   G. 7 J. 10

5. How many students were present on Monday?

   A. 225 C. 240 E. 355
   B. 232 D. 331

Questions 6-10

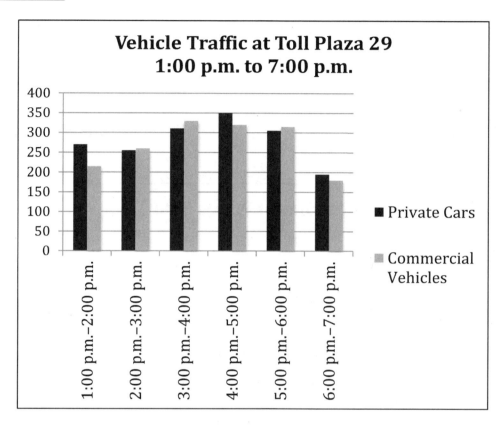

6. Approximately how many private cars traveled through Toll Plaza 29 from 4:00 p.m. to 5:00 p.m.?

   F. 195   H. 320   K. 350
   G. 310   J. 325

7. Approximately how many commercial vehicles traveled through Toll Plaza 29 from 1:00 p.m. to 2:00 p.m.?

   A. 180   C. 225   E. 330
   B. 220   D. 270

8. Approximately how many more private cars than commercial vehicles traveled through Toll Plaza 29 from 6:00 p.m. to 7:00 p.m.?

   F. 20   H. 180   K. 375
   G. 45   J. 195

9. Approximately how many total vehicles traveled through Toll Plaza 29 from 2:00 p.m. to 4:00 p.m.?

   A. 515   C. 585   E. 1,150
   B. 560   D. 635

10. What was the approximate average hourly number of private cars that traveled through Toll Plaza 29 from 1:00 p.m. to 7:00 p.m.?

   F. 225 H. 280 K. 1,680
   G. 250 J. 1,605

Questions 11–15

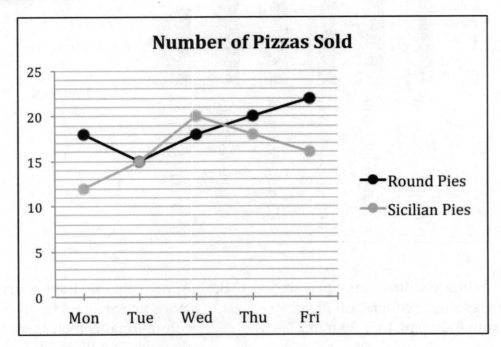

11. How many round pies were sold on Monday?

   A. 12 C. 20 E. 30
   B. 18 D. 22

12. On what day did the number of Sicilian pies sold first exceed the number of round pies sold?

   F. Monday   J. Thursday
   G. Tuesday   K. Friday
   H. Wednesday

13. How many round pies were sold on Thursday and Friday combined?

   A. 20 C. 34 E. 42
   B. 22 D. 38

14. How many more round pies than Sicilian pies were sold on Friday?

   F. 6   H. 19 K. 38
   G. 16 J. 22

15. What was the average daily number of round pies sold for the five-day period?

A. 16.2   C. 18.6   D. 23.25
B. 18   D. 23.25

Questions 16–20

The following chart shows the proportion of tree species in a section of a forest.

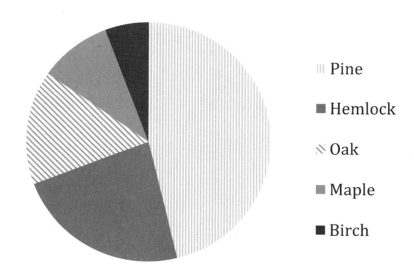

Proportion of Tree Species

- Pine
- Hemlock
- Oak
- Maple
- Birch

16. Which tree species accounts for the largest proportion of trees in the section of forest?

F. Pine   J. Maple
G. Hemlock K. Birch
H. Oak

17. Which tree species accounts for the smallest proportion of trees in the section of forest?

A. Pine   D. Maple
B. Hemlock E. Birch
C. Oak

300 • MATH STATISTICS AND PROBABILITY

18. Approximately how many pine trees are there in the section of forest?

F. 45
G. 450
H. 4,500
J. 45,000
K. Cannot be determined from the given information

19. Approximately how many more maple trees than birch trees are there in the section of forest?

A. 5
B. 50
C. 500
D. 5,000
E. Cannot be determined from the given information

20. Pine trees make up a smaller percentage of the total number of trees in the section of forest than which of the following?

F. Birch
G. Birch and Maple combined
H. Birch, Maple, and Oak combined
J. Birch, Maple, Oak, and Hemlock combined
K. Cannot be determined from the given information

Questions 21–25

Non-Commercial Vehicles Registered in Coweta County

21. Of the non-commercial vehicles registered in Coweta County, how many are pick-ups?

   A. 7 C. 70 E. 700
   B. 20 D. 350

22. Of the non-commercial vehicles registered in Coweta County, how many are SUVs?

   F. 6 H. 60 K. 600
   G. 30 J. 300

23. Of the non-commercial vehicles registered in Coweta County, how many are either cars or SUVs?

   A. 6.5 C. 65 E. 650
   B. 13 D. 130

24. Of the non-commercial vehicles in Coweta County, how many more are cars than SUVs?

   F. 1 H. 13 K. 130
   G. 5 J. 50

25. What is the total number of cars, SUVs, and pick-ups registered as non-commercial vehicles in Coweta County?

   A. 20 C. 200 E. 10,000
   B. 150 D. 1,000

Math Statistics and Probability

Unit 13 | Practice

INSIDE THIS UNIT:
– Exercise –

EXERCISE

DIRECTIONS: The following items can be solved with either pencil and paper or a calculator. Before performing the indicated operation(s), eliminate any choices that violate your number sense. Answers are on page 751.

1. The arithmetic sequence 111, 119, 127, ... has a common difference of 8. What is the next term in the sequence?

   A. 108   C. 138   E. 145
   B. 135   D. 143

2. What is the common difference for the arithmetic sequence 96, 85, 74, ... ?

   F. 9   H. 52   K. 65
   G. 11   J. 63

3. What is the next term in the arithmetic sequence −10, −1, 8, ... ?

   A. −9   C. 9   E. 26
   B. 1   D. 17

4. What is the sixth term in the arithmetic sequence 39, 35, 31, ... ?

   F. 4   H. 23   K. 29
   G. 19   J. 27

5. Which of the following statements is true about the arithmetic sequence −4, 0, 4, 8, ... ?

   A. Every term in the sequence is evenly divisible by 8.
   B. The first term is 0.
   C. The fifth term is 16.
   D. The common difference is 4.
   E. The sum of the first five terms is 0.

6. In the figure below, which of the following line segments is the shortest?

   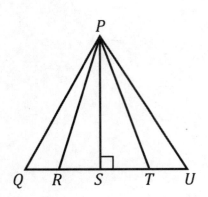

   F. $\overline{PQ}$ H. $\overline{PS}$ K. $\overline{PU}$
   G. $\overline{PR}$ J. $\overline{PT}$

Questions 7–8

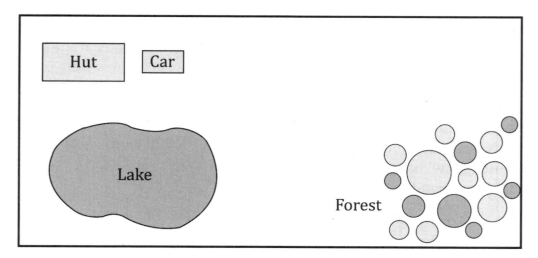

7. Which of the following objects are closest to each other?

   A. The hut and the car
   B. The car and the lake
   C. The hut and the lake
   D. The hut and the forest
   E. The lake and the forest

8. Which of the following objects are farthest from each other?

   F. The hut and the car
   G. The car and the lake
   H. The hut and the lake
   J. The hut and the forest
   K. The lake and the forest

Questions 9–10

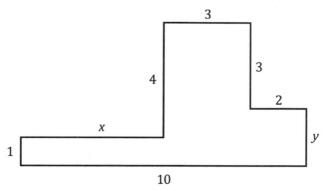

Note: All angles are right angles.

9. What is the value of x?

   A. 2   C. 4   E. 6
   B. 3   D. 5

10. What is the value of y?

    F. 1   H. 3   K. 5
    G. 2   J. 4

306 • MATH STATISTICS AND PROBABILITY

11. Two official timers each have a stopwatch to time a swimming match. One of the watches displays elapsed time as minutes and seconds. The other stopwatch displays elapsed time as seconds. If the first watch displays 3 minutes and 15 seconds as the winning time for the match, how many seconds should the second watch display?

A. 75   C. 123   E. 195
B. 105   D. 150

12. A construction crane has a maximum lifting capacity of 5.5 tons. What is the maximum lifting capacity of the crane expressed in pounds? (1 ton = 2,000 pounds)

F. 550   J. 5,500
G. 1,100   K. 11,000
H. 2,750

13. A dairy packing plant has enough milk in the cooling tank to fill 52 1-quart containers. If the plant manager decides instead to bottle the milk in 1-gallon containers, how many gallon containers will be filled by the milk? (1 gallon = 4 quarts)

A. 6.5   C. 10.4   E. 26
B. 8.6   D. 13

14. At a certain college, it is a freshman tradition to walk the entire distance of a wall that surrounds the old campus. If the wall is 1.5 miles long, how long is the walk, in feet? (1 mile = 5,280 feet)

F. 1,500   H. 4,500   K. 7,920
G. 3,000   J. 7,500

15. Wilson Elementary School is collecting dimes as part of a fundraiser. The collection jar in Mr. Beem's classroom contains 532 dimes. How much money is in the jar in Mr. Beem's classroom?

A. $5.32   D. $133
B. $26.60   E. $532
C. $53.20

16. Katie bought her lunch in the cafeteria for the past 8 school days. She spent a total of $32 for lunches in those 8 days. What was the average amount Katie spent per lunch?

F. $4   H. $5   K. $32
G. $4.50   J. $6

17. Over 6 days, a total of 660 cars were tested for safety. What was the average number of tested cars per day?

A. 107   C. 113   E. 660
B. 110   D. 558

UNIT 13 | PRACTICE • 307

18. Listed below is the number of bagels that the local bakery sold during one week. What was the average number of bagels sold per day?

BAGEL SALES AT THE LOCAL BAKERY	
Day	Number of Bagels Sold
Sunday	178
Monday	115
Tuesday	141
Wednesday	120
Thursday	102
Friday	151
Saturday	187

F. 120   H. 167   K. 994
G. 142   J. 985

19. A group of 4 friends are babysitters. One week, Ramona earned $47, Katie earned $39, Erin earned $47, and Lucy earned $71. What was the average amount earned per friend for the week?

A. $47   C. $68   E. $204
B. $51   D. $157

20. After a bookstore opened, it made profits of $300, $400, $600, and $500 each week. What was the average weekly profit for the bookstore for those weeks?

F. $300   H. $400   K. $500
G. $350   J. $450

Questions 21-25

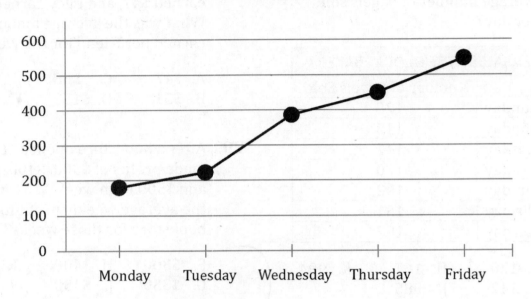

21. Approximately how many students used the library on Friday of exam week?

    A. 190 C. 390 E. 550
    B. 210 D. 450

22. On what day was the number of students using the library the greatest during exam week?

    F. Monday   J. Thursday
    G. Tuesday   K. Friday
    H. Wednesday

23. Approximately how many more students used the library on Thursday of exam week than on Wednesday?

    A. 60   C. 420 E. 840
    B. 390 D. 450

24. Approximately how many more students used the library on Friday of exam week than on Monday?

    F. 320 J. 560
    G. 360 K. 740
    H. 460

25. What was the approximate average daily number of students who used the library on Monday through Friday during exam week?

    A. 190 D. 450
    B. 210 E. 550
    C. 360

MATH MASTERY TEST 1

DIRECTIONS: The following items can be solved with either pencil and paper or a calculator. Before performing the indicated operation(s), eliminate any choices that violate your number sense. Answers are on page 752.

1. What is the difference between 155 and 87?

   A. 68   C. 78   E. 243
   B. 77   D. 242

2. $1.2 + 0.9 = ?$

   F. 1.08   H. 1.29   K. 10.2
   G. 1.1   J. 2.1

3. $342 \div 19 = ?$

   A. 18   C. 323   E. 6,498
   B. 171   D. 361

4. What is the quotient when 18 is divided by 0.06?

   F. 1.08   H. 17.94   K. 300
   G. 3   J. 108

5. $21 \times 13 = ?$

   A. 8   C. 84   E. 273
   B. 34   D. 263

6. Which of the following fractions is equivalent to $\dfrac{225}{250}$?

   F. $\dfrac{22}{25}$ H. $\dfrac{9}{10}$ K. $\dfrac{1}{2}$

   G. $\dfrac{3}{25}$ J. $\dfrac{1}{10}$

7. Which of the following fractions is NOT equivalent to $\dfrac{11}{66}$?

   A. $\dfrac{60}{360}$ C. $\dfrac{25}{150}$ E. $\dfrac{1}{6}$

   B. $\dfrac{111}{661}$ D. $\dfrac{15}{90}$

8. Which of the following fractions is NOT equivalent to $\dfrac{27}{54}$?

   F. $\dfrac{81}{216}$ H. $\dfrac{18}{36}$ K. $\dfrac{1}{2}$

   G. $\dfrac{54}{108}$ J. $\dfrac{3}{6}$

9. Six students promised to paint the 300 sections of fence that enclose a pasture, and each was assigned a different number of sections to paint. By noon, Steve had painted 40 of the 60 sections he was assigned. Which of the following students had painted the same fraction of their assignment as had Steve?

A. By noon, Marla had painted 20 of her 30 sections.
B. By noon, Allen had painted 50 of his 70 sections.
C. By noon, Ellen had painted 30 of her 40 sections.
D. By noon, Sammy had painted 10 of her 30 sections.
E. By noon, Harry had painted 60 of his 70 sections.

10. In an archery contest, Elaine scored 4 bull's-eyes out of 12 shots. Which of the following archers scored the same fraction of bull's-eyes as had Elaine?

F. John scored 12 bull's-eyes out of 15 shots.
G. Mark scored 15 bull's-eyes out of 18 shots.
H. Sally scored 18 bull's-eyes out of 25 shots.
J. Beth scored 9 bull's-eyes out of 15 shots.
K. Steve scored 6 bull's-eyes out of 18 shots.

Questions 11–15 refer to the following figure.

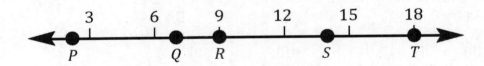

11. Point *P* could be located at which of the following values?

A. 2   C. 4   E. 9
B. 3   D. 6

12. Point *R* is located at which of the following values?

F. 3   H. 8   K. 12
G. 6   J. 9

13. Which of the following points is located at 18?

A. *P*   C. *R*   E. *T*
B. *Q*   D. *S*

14. Which of the following points could be located at 7?

F. *P*   H. *R*   K. *T*
G. *Q*   J. *S*

15. Point S could be located at which of the following values?

- A. 9
- B. 10
- C. 12
- D. 14
- E. 15

16. On his summer vacation, Charlie used his digital camera to take 25 photos at Yosemite, 8 photos at Crater Lake, and 149 photos at Yellowstone. He deleted 74 photos because of poor quality. How many photos does Charlie have left?

- F. 98
- G. 108
- H. 172
- J. 182
- K. 256

17. The cafeteria manager bought 32 boxes of broccoli for $14 each and 18 boxes of carrots for $14 each. How much did the cafeteria manager spend?

- A. $78
- B. $196
- C. $686
- D. $700
- E. $714

18. Bella bought a wallet on sale for $15.57 and gave the sales clerk a $20 bill. How much change should she have gotten back?

- F. $4.43
- G. $4.53
- H. $5.53
- J. $7.43
- K. $35.57

19. At the end of the first month of a recycling project, Daniela dropped off 3.5 pounds of metal cans at the transfer center. At the end of the second month, she dropped off 3.9 times the amount she'd dropped off the previous month. What was the weight of the cans, in pounds, dropped off by Daniela at the end of the second month?

- A. 7.4
- B. 9.4
- C. 13.65
- D. 27.3
- E. 136.5

20. Mary weighed 130 pounds at the end of May. She lost 4 pounds in June, gained 6 pounds in July, and lost 8 pounds in August. What was her weight, in pounds, at the end of August?

- F. 112
- G. 124
- H. 128
- J. 140
- K. 148

21. Which of the following can be used to represent the English phrase "five added to n"?

- A. $n - 5$
- B. $n + n + n + n + n$
- C. $5n$
- D. $5 - n$
- E. $5 + n$

22. Which of the following can be used to represent the English phrase "24 is divided by m"?

F. $\dfrac{24}{m}$ 　　 H. $24m$ 　　 K. $24 + m$

G. $\dfrac{m}{24}$ 　　 J. $24 - m$

23. Hannah received r dollars for her allowance. She bought a book that cost b dollars. How much money does she have left?

A. $\dfrac{r}{b}$ 　　 C. $r - b$ 　　 E. rb

B. $b - r$ 　　 D. $r + b$

24. Suzanne bought w cartons, each containing 1 dozen eggs. How many eggs did she buy?

F. $12 + w$ 　 H. $12w$ 　 K. $\dfrac{w}{12}$

G. $w - 12$ 　 J. $\dfrac{12}{w}$

25. Amy has k songs on her computer, and Amanda has 1,000 songs on her computer. If Amy has more songs on her computer than Amanda does, how many more songs does Amy have on her computer than Amanda?

A. $k + 1000$ 　　 D. $k - 1000$
B. k 　　　　　　 E. $1000k$
C. $1000 - k$

26. If $16 = 4 + x$, then $x = ?$

F. 4 　　 H. 12 　　 K. 64
G. 8 　　 J. 20

27. If $\dfrac{9}{x} = 3$, then $x = ?$

A. $\dfrac{1}{3}$ 　　 C. 6 　　 E. 27

B. 3 　　 D. 12

28. If $42 = 6x$, then $x = ?$

F. $\dfrac{1}{7}$ 　　 H. 8 　　 K. 48

G. 7 　　 J. 36

29. If $\dfrac{x}{0.5} = 16$, then $x = ?$

A. $\dfrac{1}{8}$ 　　 C. 8 　　 E. 32

B. 4 　　 D. 18

30. If $18 - x = 9$, then $x = ?$

F. -9 　　 H. $\dfrac{1}{2}$ 　　 K. 9

G. -2 　　 J. 2

MATH MASTERY TEST 2

DIRECTIONS: The following items can be solved with either pencil and paper or a calculator. Before performing the indicated operation(s), eliminate any choices that violate your number sense. Answers are on page 752.

1. What is the next term in the arithmetic sequence 4, 10, 16, …?

   A. 6 C. 20 E. 26
   B. 18 D. 22

2. What is the next term in the arithmetic sequence 53, 61, 69, … ?

   F. 8   H. 78 K. 87
   G. 77 J. 85

3. What is the common difference for the arithmetic sequence 19, 15, 11, … ?

   A. −15 C. −5 E. −2
   B. −7   D. −4

4. What is the fifth term in the arithmetic sequence 10, 6, 2, … ?

   F. 14 H. −2 K. −10
   G. 4   J. −6

5. Margo currently weighs 60 pounds. Her pediatrician expects her to gain 4 pounds next year and 4 pounds the following year. How many pounds will she weigh in two years if her pediatrician's predictions are correct?

   A. 8   C. 68 E. 76
   B. 64 D. 72

Questions 6–7 refer to the following figure.

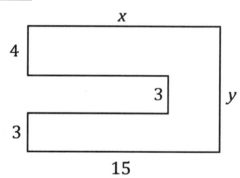

Note: All angles are right angles.

6. What is the value of x?

   F. 10 H. 15 K. 17
   G. 13 J. 16

7. What is the value of y?

   A. 7   C. 12 E. 24
   B. 10 D. 13

Questions 8–10 refer to the following figure.

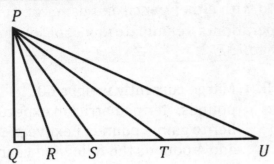

8. Which line segment is the shortest?

    F. $\overline{PQ}$ H. $\overline{PS}$ K. $\overline{PU}$
    G. $\overline{PR}$ J. $\overline{PT}$

9. Which line segment is the longest?

    A. $\overline{PQ}$ C. $\overline{PS}$ E. $\overline{PU}$
    B. $\overline{PR}$ D. $\overline{PT}$

10. Which line segment is the second longest?

    F. $\overline{PQ}$ H. $\overline{PS}$ K. $\overline{PU}$
    G. $\overline{PR}$ J. $\overline{PT}$

11. A sporting goods store sells a custom-made racing bicycle that weighs 6 pounds and 7 ounces. What is the weight of the bicycle, in ounces? (1 pound = 16 ounces)

    A. 6.7   C. 79   E. 151
    B. 13   D. 103

12. A commercial ice cream freezer uses 7 gallons of milk for a batch of ice cream. If a worker uses a 1-quart container to measure the milk, how many quarts of milk should the worker put into the ice cream freezer? (1 gallon = 4 quarts)

    F. 14   H. 35   K. 56
    G. 28   J. 42

13. Bobby has twelve $5 bills in his wallet, but no other currency. How much money does Bobby have in his wallet?

    A. $5   C. $60   E. $240
    B. $12   D. $120

14. A bag of sugar has a mass of 1.5 kilograms. What is the mass of the bag, in grams?

    F. 0.0015   J. 150
    G. 0.15   K. 1,500
    H. 15

15. The Traylor family spent a total of 144 minutes doing yard work on a Saturday afternoon. How long, in hours, did the yard work take them?

    A. 1.2   C. 6   E. 8,640
    B. 2.4   D. 144

16. Carter has a part-time job. Over a 6-week period, he worked 12 hours the first week, 18 the second week, 24 the third week, 36 the fourth week, 12 the fifth week, and 30 the sixth week. What was the average number of hours per week that he worked for those 6 weeks?

F. 12 H. 22 K. 32
G. 18 J. 24

17. Ethan received 103 text messages on Monday, 162 on Tuesday, 151 on Wednesday, and 172 on Thursday. What was the average number of text messages per day that he received for those 4 days?

A. 147 C. 162 E. 588
B. 151 D. 493

18. In Ms. Edelston's class, 18 students received a total of 108 "A" letter grades on their report cards. What was the average number of "A" letter grades on each of the report cards?

F. 4 H. 8 K. 18
G. 6 J. 12

19. The table below shows the number of traffic accidents in Center City for 3 consecutive years. What was the average number of accidents per year?

TRAFFIC ACCIDENT RECORD FOR CENTER CITY	
Year	Number of Accidents
2011	306
2012	273
2013	261

A. 273 C. 306 E. 840
B. 280 D. 739

20. The table below shows the number of students enrolled in each math class at Western Middle School. What is the average number of students enrolled in each of the math classes?

WESTERN MIDDLE SCHOOL MATH CLASSES	
Math Class	Number of Students Per Class
6th Grade	106
7th Grade	74
8th Grade	42
Pre-Algebra	115
Algebra	83

F. 74 H. 106 K. 456
G. 84 J. 420

Questions 21–23 refer to the following graph.

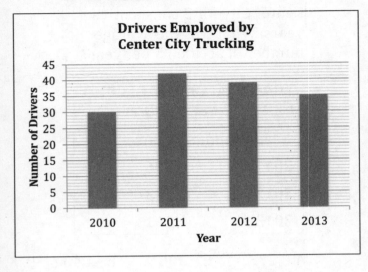

Questions 24–25 refer to the following graph.

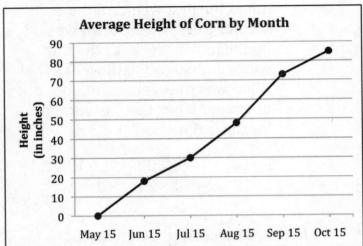

21. How many more drivers were employed by Center City Trucking in 2011 than in 2012?

    A. 3   C. 39   E. 81
    B. 12   D. 42

22. What was the increase in the number of drivers employed by Center City Trucking from 2010 to 2011?

    F. 2   H. 30   K. 72
    G. 12   J. 42

23. What was the total number of drivers employed by Center City Trucking for the years 2012 and 2013?

    A. 12   C. 36   E. 96
    B. 18   D. 74

24. What was the approximate average height of the corn, in inches, on July 15?

    F. 19   H. 48   K. 72
    G. 30   J. 60

25. During which period did the average height of the corn increase the most?

    A. May 15 to June 15
    B. June 15 to July 15
    C. July 15 to August 15
    D. August 15 to September 15
    E. September 15 to October 15

Level 1
READING

KEY IDEAS AND DETAILS

UNIT 1 | MAIN IDEA 319
Focus and Purpose 320
Exercise 321

UNIT 2 | SPECIFIC DETAILS 335
The Basic Facts 336
Read the Passage Carefully 337
Read the Questions Carefully 338
Exercise 339

UNIT 3 | PRACTICE 347
Exercise 348

UNIT 4 | EVENTS AND RELATIONSHIPS 357
When? 358
Why? 360
Exercise 363

CRAFT AND STRUCTURE

UNIT 5 | VOCABULARY 375
An Experiment 376
Be a Word Detective 377
Common Clues 378
Exercise 382

UNIT 6 | PRACTICE 391
Exercise 392

UNIT 7 | IMPLIED IDEAS AND CONCLUSIONS 403
What Is an Inference? 404
Exercise 414

UNIT 8 | PURPOSE OF SENTENCES 423
The Craft of Writing 424
Exercise 431

UNIT 9 | PRACTICE 443
Exercise 444

PRACTICE

UNIT 10 | PRACTICE 459
Exercise 460

UNIT 11 | PRACTICE 471
Exercise 472

INTEGRATION OF KNOWLEDGE AND IDEAS

UNIT 12 | ANALYZING ARGUMENTS 483
The Structure of Logical Arguments 484
Exercise 489

UNIT 13 | ANALYZING PAIRED PASSAGES 495
Relationships between Passages 496
Exercise 500

MASTERY TESTS

Reading Mastery Test 1..509
Reading Mastery Test 2..519

Reading **Key Ideas and Details**

Unit 1 | **Main Idea**

INSIDE THIS UNIT:
– Focus and Purpose –   – Exercise –

Non-Negotiable Skill:

Identify the writer's topic and purpose
for a particular passage.

Recognize a clear intent of an author
or narrator.

Focus and Purpose

Every good piece of writing has a focus and a purpose. The *focus* is the topic that the writer has chosen. The *purpose* is the writer's goal for the writing.

Taken together, focus and purpose are often referred to as the thesis, the main idea, or the primary purpose of writing. Purpose and focus are closely tied together.

Example:

Some people say that the recent cold weather proves there is no global warming. This is wrong. People are confusing "climate" and "weather." Weather is what we get on a day-to-day basis. Climate is the average weather conditions over a long period of time. So, a couple snowstorms don't mean that the climate 5 is getting colder. A couple cold spells don't prove that there is no global warming. In fact, scientists predict that climate change will cause extreme weather, including snowstorms. You have to look at the big picture. You have to think tens of thousands of years. As Mark Twain put it, "Climate is what we expect; weather is what we get."

Focus: The main idea of this paragraph is that climate and weather are not the same thing.

Purpose: The writer wants to explain the difference to the reader.

UNIT 1 | MAIN IDEA • 321

> ## Summary
>
> - The **focus** of a written passage is the writer's topic, and the **purpose** of a written passage is the writer's goal.
>
> - Together, the purpose and focus of a written passage make up the thesis or main idea.
>
> - When you summarize the main idea of a passage, provide a complete description but stay within the boundaries of the text.

EXERCISE

DIRECTIONS: This exercise consists of passages followed by questions. Read each passage and answer the questions based upon what is stated or implied in the passage. Answers are on page 752.

Passage 1

Peanut was four years old when we adopted him. The name "Peanut" just seemed to fit. We had a quarter horse and a thoroughbred, and he seemed so small next to them. Peanut is a Kiger mustang. When he was four years old, he had zebra legs, a dark mane, and a dorsal stripe down his back. He is now 14 years old and
5   stands 13 hands. He is a little overweight right now, but very sturdy. I have never been around any horse as smart and mischievous. Looking back, we should have named him Pest. If it is possible to get out of a stall, he will find a way. We had him boarded for a while at a facility that had plastic fencing. After a couple of months, he figured out he could hook his leg over a railing, pop it out and be out of the
10 pasture. He was put right back in another pasture and within 15 minutes, he popped out another railing and was free. He wants to know what everything is about. He is such a curious mustang. He loves jumping, running, and leading on a trail ride. He is such a wonderful horse.

322 • READING KEY IDEAS AND DETAILS

1. The writer is primarily interested in explaining:

   A. what Peanut does on a typical day.
   B. how to feed and train a horse.
   C. where Kiger mustangs come from.
   D. why Peanut is a wonderful horse.

2. Which of the following would be the best title for the paragraph?

   F. Peanut: A Really Nice Horse
   G. Peanut Escapes from the Pasture
   H. Procedures for Adopting a Horse
   J. How to Choose a Name for a Horse

3. Which of the following could the writer add to the paragraph to help the reader understand why the horse should have been called Pest?

   A. The name and address of the farm where Peanut lives
   B. A story of how Peanut dumped his water bucket every time it was filled
   C. Information about the number of horses adopted each year
   D. A description of the origin of Kiger mustangs

Passage 2

Composting can provide you with homemade, all natural fertilizer. All you really need to compost are three basic ingredients: browns, greens, and water. Browns are materials such as pieces of cardboard, loosely balled paper, dead leaves, small branches, and twigs. Greens include grass clippings, uncooked vegetable
5   peelings, green leaves, fruit scraps, and coffee grounds. The ideal compost pile contains equal amounts of browns and greens. The browns supply the carbon for your compost, the greens provide nitrogen, and the water provides the moisture needed to break down the organic matter. Do not add glass, tin, plastic, or cooked food to your compost pile. You'll also need a big container to hold your compost. You
10 can buy a compost bin at the home supply store or just build a big box yourself from plywood. Keep adding browns, greens, and water on the top of the pile. In 10 weeks or so, you can start shoveling out rich compost from the bottom of the pile.

4. The writer is mainly interested in explaining to the reader how to:

   F. conserve resources by using less.
   G. compost at home to make fertilizer.
   H. build a large box to hold compost material.
   J. apply fertilizer to a vegetable garden.

5. Which of the following would be the best title for the paragraph?

   A. How to Plant a Garden
   B. How to Conserve Natural Resources
   C. How to Make a Compost Pile
   D. How to Recycle Glass, Tin, and Plastic

6. The writer wants to add some detail to the paragraph. Which of the following would be most helpful to the reader in understanding the paragraph?

   F. The name of the home supply store where the writer shops
   G. Information about how plants use fertilizer
   H. The amount of water to add to browns and greens
   J. The types of vegetables to plant in a garden

Passage 3

I've got to tell you what happened to my dad! On Saturday, my mom cooked a chicken at noon, and we all ate lunch. We rushed out of the house for baseball practice, and Mom forgot to put the cooked chicken in the refrigerator. When my dad came home, the chicken was still out on the kitchen table. Dad was hungry, so he
5 made a sandwich with the leftover chicken. That night, my dad was throwing up, had stomach cramps, and went to the bathroom a lot. The next day, we drove him to the doctor. My dad told the doctor about the cooked chicken he ate that was left on the table. The doctor said he probably got sick from the food. The doctor told my mom, "The problem was caused by dangerous bacteria that grow very fast on food
10 that is left out of the refrigerator for more than two hours. You cannot tell if food is still safe to eat just by looking at it because you can't see, smell, or taste harmful bacteria." How can you avoid this problem? Refrigerate chicken within two hours after cooking it.

7. The writer mainly wants to tell:

   A. what she and her mom ate for lunch.
   B. what happened at baseball practice.
   C. why her dad got sick Saturday night.
   D. what her dad did Saturday morning.

8. The writer wants the reader to learn:

   F. how to cook chicken so that it is safe to eat.
   G. why it is important to refrigerate food.
   H. when to go to the doctor with a stomach illness.
   J. what doctors do for someone who is ill.

9. The writer wants to add information to the paragraph. Which of the following additional facts would help the writer make her main point?

   A. Her father is a police officer who often works on Saturday.
   B. Her baseball team was practicing for a championship game.
   C. The doctor's office was only 30 minutes from her home.
   D. Her father came home at 5:00 p.m. and ate the chicken sandwich.

Unit 1 | Main Idea • 325

Passage 4

Paper money is very durable, but it does eventually wear out. Worn-out notes are destroyed. The destroyed notes are replaced by new currency made by the Bureau of Engraving and Printing. The note most frequently replaced is the $1 bill. Larger bills are handled less, so they last longer. There are over four billion $1 bills in circulation, and the life expectancy of each one is about 18 months.

5

10. The main point of the paragraph is that:

    F. paper money wears out and must be replaced.
    G. dollar bills last longer than larger bills.
    H. money comes from the Bureau of Engraving and Printing.
    J. four billion $1 bills are now in circulation.

11. Which of the following would be the best title for the paragraph?

    A. A History of US Currency
    B. How Money is Printed
    C. The Life Cycle of Paper Money
    D. Detecting Counterfeit Bills

12. The writer is thinking of adding some more information to the paragraph. Which of the following details would be most helpful to the reader in understanding the paragraph?

    F. The metallic content of US coins
    G. The life expectancy of larger bills
    H. The location of the Bureau of Engraving and Printing
    J. The cost of printing a new $1 bill

Passage 5

Pirates in cartoons and movies seem to be likable characters. They dress in pirate clothes and say "Aaarrr!" But real piracy is very dangerous. Pirates have been attacking ships in the Indian Ocean off the coast of Somalia. These real pirates use speedboats. A group of three or four boats will surround a slow-moving commercial
5 tanker or a fishing vessel. They attack with automatic weapons and rocket-propelled grenade launchers and try to board the vessels. Unlike pirates of old, who were after gold and silver, these modern pirates don't want cargo. Instead, they want the ship and its crew, whom they hold hostage for ransom. The ship's owner will usually pay to save the crew and get back a valuable ship. In recent years, these real pirates have
10 been paid over $100 million.

13. The writer is primarily discussing the:

    A. danger posed by modern pirates.
    B. cartoon and movie characters.
    C. people of India and Somalia.
    D. pirates who lived many years ago.

14. Which of the following would be the best title for the paragraph?

    F. The History of Piracy
    G. The Problem of Modern Piracy
    H. Popular Images of Pirates
    J. Sailing the Indian Ocean

15. The writer is considering adding more information to the paragraph. Which of the following would most help the reader understand the main point the writer wants to make?

    A. The number of pirate attacks in recent years
    B. The titles of movies with pirate characters
    C. The names of famous pirates from sailing times
    D. The type of clothes worn by modern-day pirates

Passage 6

The Arizona Highway Department is worried that some squirrels could become roadkill. These squirrels are not ordinary squirrels. They are rare red squirrels. For years, the squirrels were thought to be extinct, but in 1970 a new population was discovered. There is only one road in the area where the squirrels live, and about
5 five squirrels are killed by cars and trucks every year. All told, there are only about 250 of the squirrels left. The state will build rope bridges over the road in the area to help the squirrels cross safely. That sounds like a good idea, but the bridges will cost $1.25 million. That works out to $250,000 for each squirrel saved. Those are expensive squirrels.

16. The writer mainly discusses:

F. the amount of money the Arizona Highway Department spends every year.
G. a plan to spend $1.25 million to build rope bridges for squirrels.
H. the different species of squirrels that live in Arizona.
J. various ways of protecting wildlife from vehicle traffic.

17. The writer's main point is that:

A. squirrels once thought extinct were discovered in Arizona.
B. the squirrel's habitat is crossed by only a single road.
C. the plan to build squirrel bridges will cost a lot of money.
D. every year five endangered squirrels are killed by cars and trucks.

18. Which of the following titles best describes the paragraph?

F. Nearly Extinct Red Squirrels Found in Arizona
G. Car and Truck Accidents in the United States
H. Arizona Residents Rally to Save Squirrels
J. Rare Squirrels to Get Expensive Bridges

Passage 7

Many coins have images of former presidents. Lincoln is on the penny. Jefferson is on the nickel. Washington is on the quarter. Kennedy is on the half dollar. But there is no link between the president and the value of the coin.

The exception to this rule is the dime. It features Franklin Delano Roosevelt, the 32nd president. When Roosevelt was almost 40, he developed polio. He was paralyzed from the waist down. He learned to walk short distances with canes, and he could stand in public with assistance. He never let his disability prevent him from pursuing his goals.

In 1937, President Roosevelt announced the founding of the National Foundation for Infantile Paralysis to fight polio. The Foundation became known as the March of Dimes. Roosevelt died in 1945. In 1946, a new dime featuring his likeness was introduced just in time for the annual March of Dimes.

19. The writer mainly discusses:

A. the connection between Roosevelt and the dime.
B. the search for a cure for polio.
C. a list of presidents of the United States.
D. the death of President Roosevelt in 1946.

20. The passage helps to answer which of the following questions?

F. How does polio cause paralysis?
G. Why is Washington on the quarter?
H. What presidents are on the paper money?
J. Why is Roosevelt on the dime?

21. The writer is thinking about adding some more detail to the passage. Which of the following would be most helpful to the reader in understanding the main point of the passage?

A. A list of the non-presidents who appear on US money
B. An explanation of why the Foundation is associated with dimes
C. A description of the reverse side of the Roosevelt dime
D. A discussion of the important decisions made by President Roosevelt

Passage 8

The movies usually show US Marshals chasing criminals or protecting witnesses, but US Marshals have also helped to make history. In 1961, James Meredith decided that he would become the first black person to attend the University of Mississippi. Several times the university turned down his application
5   on technicalities. Finally, the university had no choice but to accept him after court rulings. He enrolled on October 1, 1962, under the protection of 128 US Marshals. Those marshals faced off against a much larger crowd of armed protesters opposed to Meredith's enrollment. The marshals carried handguns under their suit jackets but were ordered not to shoot. Over the next two days, two people were killed in
10 riots, and 28 US Marshals were wounded by gunfire. Meredith graduated two years later, but during that time he was constantly harassed and intimidated. At all times, he was accompanied by a team of marshals who were subjected to the same harassment and intimidation but kept Meredith safe.

22. The writer mainly discusses:

    F. how US Marshals protected the first black student at the University of Mississippi.

    G. movies that show US Marshals in pursuit of fugitives or protecting witnesses.

    H. why the University of Mississippi at first refused to accept James Meredith as a student.

    J. the history of the US Marshals and some of the famous people who have served as marshals.

23. The writer is thinking of adding more detail to the passage. Which of the following would help develop the theme of the paragraph?

    A. A brief account of what James Meredith did after he graduated

    B. A discussion of the training program that US Marshals must undergo

    C. An explanation of why James Meredith wanted to attend the University of Mississippi

    D. A description of the procedures the marshals used to protect Meredith

24. The writer's main point is that:

F. James Meredith was the first black person to attend the University of Mississippi.
G. federal marshals helped to make history when James Meredith entered the University of Mississippi.
H. the University of Mississippi did not have any black students prior to 1962.
J. James Meredith graduated from the University of Mississippi two years after he first enrolled.

Passage 9

The 2010 Soccer World Cup used a new soccer ball called Jabulani, the Zulu word for "celebration." This was not the first time the soccer ball was redesigned. The original design had 32 hexagons of synthetic leather.

In 2006, the soccer ball was changed so that it had 14 thermally fused panels and no internal stitching. The manufacturer said this smoother, rounder ball was the most accurate soccer ball ever made. But players complained that the new ball wobbled in flight. This made the goalie's job of blocking the ball more difficult.

In 2010, the Jabulani manufacturer reduced the number of panels to eight and added ridges. But NASA scientists who tested the 2010 ball in a wind tunnel found a knuckle ball effect. When a smooth ball with seams flies through the air without much spin, the seams produce an uneven air flow around the ball. This creates side forces that can suddenly push the ball in one direction. So, the ball swerves and swoops.

Wind tunnel studies show that the Jabulani ball knuckles at 45 to 50 miles per hour. That's the speed of the ball during a free-kick around the goal area. Also, a lot of stadiums are located at high altitudes. The thin air affects the ball as well. At high altitudes, the ball will tend to fly faster and swerve less.

So, just as they criticized the 2006 ball design, players complained about the 2010 ball. The design will probably be changed again in 2014, but it doesn't seem like the knuckle ball effect will be completely eliminated.

25. The writer is primarily discussing:

    A. techniques for kicking a soccer ball.
    B. new rules of soccer for the World Cup.
    C. changes in the design of the soccer ball.
    D. plans for the 2014 Soccer World Cup.

26. The writer is thinking of adding additional details to the passage. Which of the following would be most helpful to the reader in understanding the author's main point?

    F. The name given by the manufacturer to the 2006 World Cup soccer ball
    G. The names of some of the top players in the 2006 World Cup finals
    H. A description of the wind tunnel used by NASA scientists to test the soccer ball
    J. A report on any other unpredictable movements by the soccer ball seen by players

27. The main focus of the passage is on:

    A. how changes in the design of the soccer ball affect play.
    B. why the World Cup is played every four years.
    C. when the design for the 2014 soccer ball will be available.
    D. how stadiums are chosen to host World Cup soccer matches.

Passage 10

Butterflies fill gardens with excitement, joy, and life—and much more. When gardening for butterflies, we are creating healthy garden ecosystems that supply food and safe havens for other pollinators as well, including hummingbirds, which are attracted to many of the same flowers as butterflies. While producing sources of nectar, our gardens will support green lacewings, ladybugs, and other good insects. And as more people plant these gardens, we will be creating corridors for migrating butterflies and hummingbirds.

Remember, butterflies go through metamorphosis. To have butterflies, we must have caterpillars. Butterflies go through four life-cycle stages: egg, larva, pupa (chrysalis), and adult. Fortunately, only a few butterfly caterpillars are considered serious pests, and some caterpillars are as colorful and fun to watch as the butterflies themselves. Plants that are eaten by caterpillars are called "host plants." Probably the most well-known host plant is the milkweed. Monarch butterflies lay their eggs only on milkweed, and the caterpillars that emerge will only eat milkweed leaves.

Growing host plants in your garden provides food for the caterpillars. By growing a wide variety, you will be supporting the larval stage of many types of butterflies, as well as supplying fruit, nuts, and shelter for birds or other wildlife. Place the host plants in areas where the leaf damage caused by the feeding caterpillars won't be so visible. And above all, avoid pesticides.

Your butterfly garden needs to be located in full sun. Most nectar plants require at least six hours of full sun. In addition, butterflies need sunshine to help them regulate their body temperature because they cannot fly if their bodies are too cold. You can often see them, wings outstretched, soaking up the morning sun in preparation for a day of searching for nectar.

Plant brightly colored, fragrant flowers with abundant nectar. Many butterflies are attracted to red (as are hummingbirds), and some have a preference for yellow flowers. In addition, butterflies are usually attracted to blue, hot pink, purple, and orange flowers. Composites (flowers in the aster family) are particularly favored as they supply a relatively flat "landing pad" with lots of tiny flowers in the center to supply nectar.

If you don't have room for a garden, you can attract butterflies by planting in containers on a patio or in window boxes.

Finally, have a good field guide to butterflies handy. That way, you'll be able to identify the visitors to your garden.

28. The writer is mainly interested in answering which of the following questions?

   F. What kinds of flowers thrive in direct sunlight?
   G. What are the life stages of butterflies?
   H. How do you create a butterfly garden?
   J. What are the most common species of butterflies?

29. Assume that the writer was given an assignment to write an essay on planting a garden to produce fresh vegetables for eating. Does this essay follow the instructions of the assignment?

   A. Yes, because the writer talks about planting a garden.
   B. Yes, because almost everyone likes to watch butterflies.
   C. No, because the writer doesn't discuss the use of fertilizer.
   D. No, because the writer discusses planting a flower garden.

30. The author is primarily interested in explaining how to:

   F. plant a flower garden that will attract butterflies.
   G. identify different species of commonly seen butterflies.
   H. plant a garden that will take advantage of available sunlight.
   J. explain the ecological importance of butterflies and other insects.

Reading **Key Ideas and Details**

Unit 2 | **Specific Details**

INSIDE THIS UNIT:
– The Basic Facts – – Read the Passage Carefully – – Read the Questions Carefully – – Exercise –

Non-Negotiable Skill:

Identify details stated in a passage such as names, dates, and events.

The Basic Facts

It's an old rule of newspaper reporters that the important questions are, "Who? What? When? Where? Why?" These are also five basic questions in Reading Comprehension. In this unit, we will deal with the first four. In Unit 4, we'll discuss the "Why?"

Every reading passage tells a story. Obviously, a "What I Did on My Vacation" essay is a story and so are "Describe an Important Event" essays. Essays on history tell stories and so do reports on current events.

It may not seem obvious, but science passages also tell stories such as "How Volcanoes Are Formed" and "What Happens When a Rocket Takes Off." For example, the events that unfold when a rocket takes off—the ignition of the fuel, the lift-off, the acceleration, the separation of the stages, the point of no return—together make an exciting story.

Even odd bits of writing like "How to Fix a Bicycle Tire" tell a story: the tire is flat, the wheel is removed, the tire is removed, the tube is patched, the wheel is reassembled, and the tire is filled with air. Maybe the story of the flat tire won't be made into a movie, but it is a series of events.

So for any passage that you are likely to encounter, the basic elements will be the "Who, What, When, and Where?" Not every element will figure prominently in every story. For example, in the "How to Fix a Bicycle Tire" story, the "Who?" is not important because it is understood that the "Who" is you.

So as you read, try to find the answers to the "Who? What? When? Where?" questions.

Read the Passage Carefully

A good reader is a careful reader, and getting the facts right depends on reading carefully. Imagine the results that might follow from incorrectly reading the following sentences:

Statement: Add two cups of sugar and stir the cake batter thoroughly.

Misread: Add two cups of salt and stir the cake batter thoroughly.

Outcome?

Statement: It will be dark when you get there.
The house is on the left; the lake is on the right.

Misread: It will be dark when you get there.
The house is on the right; the lake is on the left.

Outcome?

Statement: First, find a match or a lighter. Then, turn the gas on.

Misread: First, turn the gas on. Then, find a match or a lighter.

Outcome?

Read the Questions Carefully

You might not think so, but reading the questions on a test is just as important as reading the passages. If you read the question incorrectly, then you might pick a choice that is a fact mentioned in the passage—but a fact that doesn't answer the question asked.

Summary

- As you read, think about answering the following questions: "Who? What? When? Where?"

- Read carefully. Make sure that you get your facts straight.

- Read the questions carefully. Make sure you answer the question that is asked. Pay extra attention to words like "NOT" and "EXCEPT."

EXERCISE

DIRECTIONS: This exercise consists of passages followed by questions. Read each passage and answer the questions based upon what is stated or implied in the passage. Answers are on page 752.

Passage 1

Barack H. Obama is the 44th president of the United States.

Obama's father was from Kenya, and his mother was from Kansas. Obama was born in Hawaii on August 4, 1961. He was raised with help from his grandfather, Stanley Dunham, and his grandmother, Madelyn. His grandmother worked her way up from the secretarial pool to middle management at a bank.

President Obama worked his way through college with the help of scholarships and student loans. After graduating from Columbia University in 1983, President Obama moved to Chicago. In Chicago, he worked with a group of churches to help rebuild neighborhoods hurt by the closing of steel mills.

In the fall of 1988, he enrolled in law school at Harvard University. As a student there, he was honored by being selected as president of the prestigious *Harvard Law Review*. He was the first African-American to receive that honor. Upon graduation, he returned to Chicago to help lead a voter registration drive. He also taught constitutional law at the University of Chicago.

As a member of the Illinois State Senate, he cut taxes for working families and expanded health care for children and their parents. As a United States senator, he worked on plans to control dangerous weapons.

He was elected the 44th president of the United States on November 4, 2008, and sworn in on January 20, 2009. He and his wife, Michelle, have two daughters, Malia and Sasha.

340 • READING KEY IDEAS AND DETAILS

1. According to the passage, President Obama's wife is:

A. Michelle.
B. Sasha.
C. Malia.
D. Madelyn.

2. According to the passage, Stanley Dunham was Obama's:

F. father.
G. stepfather.
H. grandfather.
J. brother.

3. According to the passage, Obama's grandmother worked as a:

A. lawyer.
B. senator.
C. teacher.
D. bank manager.

4. According to the passage, while he was a student in law school, Obama was honored by being:

F. chosen president of the *Harvard Law Review.*
G. voted the 44th president of the United States.
H. elected to the United States Senate.
J. appointed to teach law school.

5. According to the passage, Obama assumed the duties of president of the United States:

A. on August 4, 1961.
B. in the fall of 1988.
C. on November 4, 2008.
D. on January 20, 2009.

6. According to the passage, Obama graduated from college in:

F. 1961.
G. 1983.
H. 1988.
J. 2008.

7. According to the passage, Obama taught law at:

A. Harvard University.
B. University of Chicago.
C. Kenya University.
D. University of Illinois.

8. According to the passage, President Obama was born in:

F. Kenya.
G. Chicago.
H. Hawaii.
J. Kansas.

Passage 2

Sometimes pennies can be more trouble than they're worth. In 1909, a penny could send a postcard or buy some eggs. Starting in 2009, a penny would not even buy itself. The US Mint spends about 1.4 cents to make a penny.

Despite the decline in the penny's buying power, it is still the most popular
5 coin. In 2008, 5.4 billion pennies were produced. That's more than twice the number of Washington quarters and five times as many Roosevelt dimes. The Lincoln penny accounts for roughly half of all coins minted within a year. About 1,000 pennies are made per second.

Pennies are so expensive to make, compared to their value of one cent, because
10 they are made from copper. Copper also has many other uses such as electrical wiring. Since there are other, better uses for copper, this has led to the suggestion that pennies be made from tin, plastic, or even paper.

While most pennies are almost worthless, some pennies are extremely valuable. The 1943 copper cent is the most valuable Lincoln penny of all. During
15 World War II, copper was used to make shell casings for ammunition, and pennies were made from steel. One day, someone at the mint accidentally used some leftover copper blanks, and about 40 copper pennies were minted bearing the date 1943. Last year, one of these unusual pennies sold for nearly $2 million.

Counterfeiters often make fake 1943 copper cents by coating steel cents with
20 copper. Think you might have a 1943 copper penny? Use a magnet. If the penny sticks, it's not copper. Better luck next time.

9. According to the passage, who is likely to make a fake 1943 cent?

    A. The US mint
    B. Counterfeiters
    C. Collectors
    D. The post office

10. According to the passage, whose likeness is on the dime?

    F. Lincoln
    G. Washington
    H. Roosevelt
    J. Jefferson

11. According to the passage, in 1943, pennies were supposed to be made from:

   A. copper.
   B. steel.
   C. tin.
   D. plastic.

12. The passage mentions which of the following as a use of copper?

   F. Medical devices
   G. Writing implements
   H. Magnets
   J. Electrical wiring

13. According to the passage, what is the cost of making a penny?

   A. 1 cent
   B. 1.4 cents
   C. 10 cents
   D. 25 cents

14. According to the passage, the most valuable Lincoln penny was minted in the year:

   F. 1909.
   G. 1943.
   H. 2008.
   J. 2009.

15. According to the passage, approximately how many pennies are made per second?

   A. $\frac{1}{2}$
   B. 1.4
   C. 1,000
   D. 5.4 billion

16. According to the passage, about how many copper pennies were minted in 1943?

   F. 40
   G. 1,000
   H. 2 million
   J. 5.4 billion

17. According to the information in the passage, during World War II copper was used to manufacture:

   A. plumbing fixtures.
   B. armor plates.
   C. airplanes.
   D. shell casings.

18. According to the author, if a penny sticks to a magnet, then it is:

   F. not made of copper.
   G. not made of steel.
   H. made of plastic.
   J. made of tin.

Passage 3

Modern synthetic rubber is made by mixing petroleum byproducts with soapsuds to produce milky liquid latex. The liquid is then coagulated into chunks. The chunks are melted down and poured into molds to create various products.

The process for making synthetic rubber was developed during World War II
5   when the United States was not able to get natural rubber. Today more than three-quarters of all rubber products are made from synthetic rubber.

Even today, however, one product is usually made from natural rubber: the rubber band. You probably have at least one rubber band in your locker or desk or a drawer at home. It's a short length of rubber formed in the shape of a loop. The
10   rubber band was invented in England in 1845 by Stephen Perry.

Natural rubber is used because it is more elastic or "stretchable" than synthetic rubber. Rubber bands are made by extruding natural rubber into a long tube, curing the rubber tube with heat, and then slicing little circular strips called bands.

Natural rubber is made from latex. Latex comes from the sap in the bark layers
15   of the rubber tree and is obtained by tapping the trees. Rubber trees grow in warm, tropical areas near the equator. So most natural latex is produced in the Southeast Asian countries of Malaysia, Thailand and Indonesia.

Temperature affects the elasticity of a rubber band in an unusual way. Heating causes the rubber band to contract, and cooling causes expansion. If you stretch a
20   rubber band, it produces heat. When you stretch it and then release it, it becomes cooler. You can prove this with a little experiment. Just stretch a rubber band, and then hold it to your lips. Then release it, and test the temperature again with your lips.

19. According to the passage, when you stretch a rubber band it becomes:

A. hotter.
B. cooler.
C. stiffer.
D. shorter.

20. According to the passage, natural latex comes from:

F. petroleum.
G. soapsuds.
H. sap.
J. bark.

21. According to the passage, when a rubber band is heated, it:

A. forms a tube.
B. contracts.
C. cools.
D. stretches.

22. The passage mentions all of the following as steps in manufacturing rubber bands EXCEPT:

F. extruding.
G. curing.
H. slicing.
J. tapping.

23. Which of the following is NOT mentioned in the passage as a producer of natural latex?

A. Malaysia
B. Thailand
C. United States
D. Indonesia

Passage 4

The first time I began to sneeze, a friend told me to go and bathe my feet in hot water and go to bed. I did so. Shortly afterward, another friend advised me to get up and take a cold shower. I did that also. Within the hour, another friend assured me that it was policy to "feed a cold and starve a fever." I had both. So I thought it best to
5   fill myself up for the cold, and then let the fever starve awhile.

I encountered another friend, who told me that a quart of salt water, taken warm, would come as near to curing a cold as anything in the world. I tried it, and I believe I threw up my immortal soul. If I had another cold, and there was no course left me but to take either an earthquake or a quart of warm salt water, I would take
10 my chances on the earthquake.

I came across a lady who said she had lived in a part of the country where doctors were scarce and had from necessity acquired considerable skill in the treatment of simple "family complaints." I knew she must have had much experience, for she appeared to be a hundred and fifty years old. She mixed a
15 concoction composed of molasses, *aqua fortis*, turpentine, and various other drugs, and instructed me to take a glass full of it every fifteen minutes. I took one dose; that was enough. It nearly killed me.

Another friend said to travel for my health. I went to Lake Bigler with my comrade, Wilson. A sheet-bath was recommended. I determined to take a sheet-
20 bath, notwithstanding the fact that I had no idea what it was. It was administered at midnight, and the weather was very frosty. My chest and back were bared, and a sheet soaked in ice-water was wound around me. It froze the marrow in my bones and stopped the beating of my heart. I thought my time had come. My advice: never take a sheet-bath—never.

25 A lady friend recommended the application of a mustard plaster to my chest. I believe that would have cured me, if it had not been for young Wilson. When I went to bed, I put my mustard plaster where I could reach it when I was ready for it. But young Wilson got hungry in the night, and ate it.

I went to Steamboat Springs, and beside the steam baths, I took a lot of the
30 vilest medicines that were ever concocted.

I offer the various courses of treatment I have lately gone through for anyone who gets a cold. Try them; if they don't cure you, you'll be grateful that they kill you.

346 • READING KEY IDEAS AND DETAILS

24. The concoction mixed by the lady who had lived in an area without doctors included all of the following EXCEPT:

F. salt.
G. turpentine.
H. *aqua fortis*.
J. molasses.

25. During the course of experimenting with various treatments, the author tries all of the following EXCEPT:

A. a sheet-bath.
B. drinking warm salt water.
C. a hot shower.
D. a cold shower.

26. According to the author, a sheet-bath consists of:

F. covering the patient with warm sheets on a cold night.
G. having the patient drink large amounts of ice water.
H. soaking the patient in a tub filled with ice water.
J. wrapping the patient in sheets drenched with ice water.

27. The advice given in the passage to someone suffering from fever is to:

A. go without food.
B. drink liquids.
C. stay in bed.
D. take a steam bath.

28. During the course of the treatments described, the author experiences all of the following EXCEPT:

F. chills.
G. back pain.
H. sneezing.
J. fever.

Reading **Key Ideas and Details**

Unit 3 | **Practice**

INSIDE THIS UNIT:
– Exercise –

EXERCISE

DIRECTIONS: This exercise consists of passages followed by questions. Read each passage and answer the questions based upon what is stated or implied in the passage. Answers are on page 752.

Passage 1

The ancient Greek scientist Aristotle thought earthquakes were caused by weather. He thought winds were trapped in underground caves. Small tremors were caused by air pushing on the cave roofs, and large ones were caused by the air breaking through to the surface. So, he believed hot, calm weather caused
5 earthquakes. However, earthquakes are really the result of movement deep within the earth. They originate miles underground. Wind, rain, and temperature affect only the surface of the earth. So, there is no way that weather causes earthquakes.

1. The writer's main point is that:

   A. scientists think earthquakes are caused by weather.
   B. earthquakes are not caused by weather.
   C. weather affects the surface of the earth.
   D. ancient scientists studied the weather.

2. The writer is thinking of adding additional detail to the paragraph. Which of the following facts would be most appropriate?

   F. Aristotle thought the world was made of earth, wind, fire, and water.
   G. Primitive people believed illness was caused by evil spirits.
   H. Earthquakes are energy released by sudden shifts of the earth's crust.
   J. Weather-related damage from hurricanes, tornadoes, and other storms can be serious.

3. The author is primarily writing about:

   A. daily life in ancient Greece.
   B. damage caused by earthquakes.
   C. a false scientific theory.
   D. exploring caves and caverns.

Passage 2

Electric cars have several advantages. Electric motors convert 75 percent of the chemical energy from the batteries to power. Gasoline-powered engines only convert 20 percent. Electric cars don't emit tailpipe pollutants, and electric motors are quiet. They are powered by rechargeable batteries. Best of all, electricity is a
5 domestic energy source. Gasoline-powered cars can go 200 to 400 miles on a single tank of gas. However, electric cars can only go about 100 to 200 miles before recharging, and battery recharging can take four to eight hours. Researchers are working on improving batteries to increase driving range and reduce charging time. Ultimately, electric cars will be the vehicles of the future.

4. The paragraph is mainly about:

   F.   electric motors.
   G.   electric cars.
   H.   rechargeable batteries.
   J.   gasoline-powered engines.

5. In the passage, the author mainly:

   A.   compares electric cars to gasoline-powered cars.
   B.   states that electric cars are battery powered.
   C.   mentions that electric motors are quiet.
   D.   notes that researchers are improving electric cars.

6. Which of the following titles best describes the content of the paragraph?

   F.   Gasoline-Powered Engines: Proven Technology
   G.   Electric Cars: The Vehicles of the Future
   H.   Rechargeable Batteries: A New Invention
   J.   Tailpipe Emissions: A Cause of Air Pollution

Passage 3

The seal of the US Military Academy includes a sword: a universal symbol of war. It also includes the helmet of Athena, the Greek goddess of war. Athena was also the goddess of wisdom and learning. The emblem is attached to a shield. On the shield's crest is a bald eagle. The eagle holds 13 arrows, representing the 13 original
5 states, and olive branches, the traditional symbols of peace. The eagle is grasping a scroll with the motto "Duty, Honor, Country." "Honor" forms the keystone of the arch of the three ideals on which West Point is founded.

7. The writer wants to add more detail to the paragraph. Given the topic, which of the following would be most appropriate?

    A. The names of the 13 original states
    B. The motto of the US Naval Academy
    C. The names of other Greek gods and goddesses
    D. The year that the seal was adopted

8. The writer primarily describes the Academy's:

    F. seal.
    G. history.
    H. function.
    J. campus.

9. Which of the following titles best describes the paragraph?

    A. The Seal of the US Military Academy
    B. Military Symbols and Decorations
    C. The United States Armed Forces
    D. Greek Gods and Goddesses

UNIT 3 | PRACTICE • 351

Passage 4

Diplomats deal with both friends and enemies. They negotiate treaties with our allies and give aid to friendly countries. Diplomats also work out problems with enemies. Sports are also a kind of diplomacy, with athletes as diplomats. Athletes represent our country on the world stage. They make contacts with people from
5   other countries. They increase goodwill and communication, and athletes often help to ease international tensions. Successful athletes promote our country's image and ideals. At times, a boycott of a sporting event has been a peaceful way to oppose another country's actions. In all these ways, athletes and the sports they play are a part of our country's diplomacy.

10. The main point of the paragraph is that:

F.   sports are a kind of war.
G.   a boycott is like war.
H.   athletes are like diplomats.
J.   countries are like enemies.

11. The writer is thinking of adding an example to the paragraph. Which of the following would best illustrate the main point of the paragraph?

A.   A war between two neighboring countries
B.   A peaceful relationship between neighboring countries
C.   A track meet at which two runners from the same country tied
D.   A friendship between athletes from enemy countries

12. In the paragraph, the author primarily describes:

F.   the popularity of sporting events.
G.   the difficulties of being a diplomat.
H.   the role of athletes and sports in diplomacy.
J.   the process of becoming a diplomat.

Passage 5

For many years, canoeing has provided people with both a pleasant outdoor hobby and a mode of transportation. Canoes generally seat two to four people comfortably and are propelled by paddles. Unlike oars, which are attached to the boat, paddles are independent and can be used on either side and from either end.

5   Paddles also become rudders when boaters need to steer the canoe in a particular direction. Typically, the person in the rear of the boat does most of the steering by turning the paddle in the desired direction. The canoe can also be turned by paddling on the side opposite the direction the canoe should go.

When steering around large objects in tight spaces, it is always best to lean
10 into the object. Although this is the opposite of what most people would think, it helps to balance the weight of the canoe.

Basic safety procedures recommend closed-toe shoes in case a passenger falls from the canoe and needs to walk over rocks to shore. Passengers are also required to wear a life jacket. Even proficient swimmers can be swept away in a rapid
15 current. A person caught in a rapidly moving current should always try to float downstream feet first so that the feet, rather than the head, hit any rocks or debris.

Once a canoeist is aware of the necessary safety precautions and steering procedures, canoeing offers a valuable form of exercise and the potential for many wonderful adventures.

13. According to the passage, a canoe is usually designed for how many people?

  A. One to two
  B. Two to four
  C. Four to six
  D. Six to eight

14. According to the passage, the person with primary responsibility for steering sits:

  F. in the front of the canoe.
  G. in the middle of the canoe.
  H. in the rear of the canoe.
  J. on the opposite side of the canoe.

15. According to the passage, most people incorrectly think that the correct way to steer a canoe around a large object in a tight space is to:

  A. lean away from the object while paddling.
  B. lean toward the object while paddling.
  C. remain centered in the canoe while paddling.
  D. move to the rear of the canoe while paddling.

16. The passage mentions all of the following suggestions for safe canoeing EXCEPT:

   F. wearing closed-toe shoes.
   G. wearing a life jacket.
   H. protecting one's head from rocks.
   J. securing oneself to the canoe.

17. According to the passage, all of the following are true of paddles EXCEPT:

   A. They are used to propel the canoe.
   B. They are used to steer the canoe.
   C. They are permanently attached to the canoe.
   D. They can be used from either end of the canoe.

Passage 6

   Basketball was invented by Dr. James Naismith in 1891. Naismith, who was born in Canada, was working at a YMCA in Springfield, Massachusetts, when he decided to come up with a game that could be played indoors during the cold winter months. Naismith based the sport on a childhood game called "duck on a rock" in
5 which participants try to knock down a stone guarded by the opposing team by tossing small rocks at the goal.

   Because there was no budget for the development of sports, Naismith's original game used a soccer ball and two peach baskets that he nailed to the walls of the gym. He came up with 13 rules for play. Although many of the original rules are
10 still used today, others were discarded long ago. For example, in the original rules, players were not allowed to bounce the ball, but today dribbling is a major part of the sport. The game was originally designed for 18 players with nine on each team. Today, five players form a team, and specific positions such as center, forward, and guard define each player's role in the game.

15   In the early part of the twentieth century, college leagues developed. Professional teams soon followed. The first Olympic basketball tournament took place during the Berlin games of 1936, although a demonstration of the sport was a part of the Olympics in 1904. Women's basketball was not introduced into the Olympics until 1976 when the games were held in Canada, where the inventor of
20 basketball was born. The United States won the gold medal in men's basketball at that Olympics.

18. According to the passage, in what year was basketball invented?

    F. 1891
    G. 1904
    H. 1936
    J. 1976

19. According to the passage, the 1904 Olympics included:

    A. both men's and women's basketball.
    B. women's basketball only.
    C. basketball as a demonstration sport.
    D. medals for the sport of basketball.

20. According to the passage, the game of basketball was originally played with a total of:

    F. 3 players.
    G. 5 players.
    H. 13 players.
    J. 18 players.

21. The author states that the 1976 Olympic Games were significant for all of the following reasons EXCEPT:

    A. That year, the rules of basketball were changed to increase the number of players on a team.
    B. The games that year were held in Canada, the country of the inventor's birth.
    C. Women's basketball was first played in the Olympic Games of 1976.
    D. The United States won the gold medal for men's basketball in that year's Olympic Games.

22. The author mentions all of the following as features of basketball that have been changed since the game's invention EXCEPT:

    F. Bouncing the basketball is now permitted.
    G. Player positions presently include guard, forward, and center.
    H. A basketball team now consists of five players.
    J. Women were not permitted to play on basketball teams.

Passage 7

Benjamin Franklin was one of the founders of the United States. He was also a writer, a publisher, a public official, a political theorist, an ambassador, and a scientist. His influence was so great that he is often considered the "First American."

Franklin was born in Boston, Massachusetts, in 1706. At the age of 12, he was
5 apprenticed to his brother James, a printer. Three years later, James started the *New-England Courant*, the first truly independent newspaper in the colonies. Young Franklin wrote a series of letters to the newspaper under the assumed name of Mrs. Silence Dogood, supposedly a middle-aged widow. The letters were quite influential, but James was not happy when he learned that his brother was the writer. So
10 Franklin left his apprenticeship and moved to Philadelphia.

In 1733, Franklin wrote and published *Poor Richard's Almanac* under the assumed name of Richard Saunders. The publication included numerous sayings that eventually became famous for their wit. Some of his sayings were practical such as "a stitch in time saves nine," while others were meant to be funny, including, "fish
15 and visitors stink in three days' time."

Franklin helped to write the Declaration of Independence and the Constitution and argued forcefully for the political ideas in both. When others hesitated to sign the Declaration of Independence, Franklin said boldly, "We must all hang together, or most assuredly we shall all hang separately," referring to the fact
20 that if they were convicted of treason they would be executed.

Later, Franklin served as ambassador to France and lived in Paris for many years. In between his other duties, Franklin pursued his scientific interests. He studied electricity and is credited with the invention of the lightning rod. He created practical devices such as the Franklin stove and bifocal glasses. He also charted the
25 flow of the Gulf Stream in the Atlantic Ocean, describing sea routes in *Sundry Maritime Observations* that allowed ships' captains to avoid sailing against the current. Franklin died in 1790 at the age of 84.

23. According to the passage, Benjamin Franklin was credited with all of the following inventions EXCEPT:

   A. the printing press.
   B. bifocal glasses.
   C. the lightning rod.
   D. the Franklin stove.

24. According to the passage, Franklin included "fish and visitors stink in three days' time" in *Poor Richard's Almanac* as:

   F. serious advice.
   G. a humorous saying.
   H. a political idea.
   J. a scientific discovery.

25. According to the passage, which of the following documents was written by Benjamin Franklin under an assumed name?

   A. The Declaration of Independence
   B. *Poor Richard's Almanac*
   C. *The New-England Courant*
   D. *Sundry Maritime Observations*

Reading **Key Ideas and Details**

Unit 4 | **Events and Relationships**

INSIDE THIS UNIT:
– When? – – Why? – – Exercise –

Non-Negotiable Skill:

Be alert to the sequence of events to determine
when (or if) an event occurred in a passage.

In Unit 2, we postponed our discussion of the "Why?" of the "Who? What? Where? When? Why?" In this unit, we will take up the "Why?" in reading, and we will also refine our thinking about "When?"

When?

In Unit 2, we concentrated on basic facts, and "When?" was answered by a time or day or year. Now we will look at questions that ask about "When?" in relation to other events. These questions ask whether an event occurred before, after, or at the same time as another event or where the event occurred in a sequence of events. A question may also ask whether an event occurred at all.

This variation on the "When?" question is another reading skill. Writers often tell their stories using a sequence of events.

Example:

Juanita got up early that morning and ate a very small breakfast. After she got dressed, she walked to the bus stop. She caught the B70 bus and rode it all the way to the museum. There she met her friend Alicia. They spent the rest of the morning in the modern art exhibit. Then they went to lunch. In the afternoon, 5 they went to the movies. Juanita caught the bus and was home by dinner.

In this brief story, there are no dates, but there is a sequence of events. The "when" facts are still there, but they are described in "before" and "after" terms:

1. What did Juanita do just after she got to the museum?

   A. Walked to the bus
   B. Ate breakfast
   C. Went to the movies
   D. Met her friend

2. When did Juanita return home?

   F. By dinner
   G. Before lunch
   H. In the afternoon
   J. Late at night

3. Did Juanita and Alicia go to the movies in the morning?

   A. No, they spent the morning at the library.
   B. No, they spent the morning in the museum.
   C. Yes, they went to the movies before lunch.
   D. Yes, they went to the movies from the bus stop.

   With "When?" questions of this sort, you must make sure that you understand the sequence of events.

Summary

- As you read, think about answering the question "When?" by paying attention to the sequence of events.

Non-Negotiable Skill:

Identify the cause-effect relationships within a passage.

Why?

A similar type of reading question asks about cause-effect relationships. In a cause-effect relationship, the events are also ordered in time, that is, one event follows the other. But there is something more: the first event causes the occurrence of the second event. The cause-effect connection answers the "Why?" question:

Why did the ice turn to water? The sun melted it.

Why did the rabbit run away? The noise frightened it.

Why did the car stop? The fuel tank was empty.

Why did the balloon pop? Too much air was forced into it.

If you look carefully at each of these examples, you see both the element of sequence and the element of cause: the noise happened, then the rabbit ran away.

Closely related to this type of connection is the explanation for behavior:

Why did you give Allen a gift? Because I like him.

Why did you close the window? Because I felt cold.

Why did the teacher reprimand Cliff? Because he was misbehaving.

Why did the doctor prescribe the medicine? Because the patient was ill.

Why doesn't Kendra quit her job? Because she needs the money.

Here the cause-effect answer to the "Why?" question mentions a reason or a motive: because I was cold, I closed the window.

Many questions of this sort mention both the cause and effect in the same sentence, making it fairly easy to answer the "Why?" question.

UNIT 4 | EVENTS AND RELATIONSHIPS • 361

Example:

We were all sitting in the cafeteria eating lunch when Doodnauth sat down. He said he was late because he wanted to talk to our science teacher, Dr. Engels, about a science fair project. Doodnauth wanted to build a rocket powered by compressed air, but he needed the school's permission to test the rocket on the
5   school grounds. Dr. Engels said he would grant permission for a rocket test under faculty supervision. Dr. Engels explained that faculty supervision was required because the school could be liable for any injuries caused by the rocket test. Doodnauth and Dr. Engels agreed to do the test on the ball field in the middle of the morning when no other students would be around. Doodnauth
10   said that he asked whether some friends could attend, but Dr. Engels said that for the initial test, only the two of them could be present. Dr. Engels did say, however, that for the official flight as part of the science fair, other spectators would be welcome, provided that they were positioned far enough away to avoid any injury. Doodnauth is very excited about his science fair project and
15   thinks he has a good chance of winning. In any event, he is looking forward to showing off his rocket to everyone because he thinks it will reach a height of perhaps 300 feet. So for the rest of the lunch period, Doodnauth answered our questions about how to build a rocket and how it will work.

1. Doodnauth was late for lunch because he:

   A. was accepting an award for winning the science fair.
   B. was explaining to friends how to build a compressed air rocket.
   C. tested a rocket powered by compressed air on school grounds.
   D. talked with Dr. Engels about a science fair project.

2. Why was the initial test of the rocket scheduled for midmorning?

   F. Only spectators would be present on the ball field at that time.
   G. No other students would be present at the test site at that time.
   H. Doodnauth's friends would not be in the cafeteria until the lunch period.
   J. Doodnauth would be in Dr. Engels' regular class at that time.

3. Why is it necessary for the initial rocket test to take place under faculty supervision?

   A. Only faculty members have the authority to approve a science fair project.
   B. The school could be liable in the event that the rocket test causes injuries.
   C. Dr. Engels does not believe that the rocket will actually work as planned.
   D. A faculty member must certify to the science fair that the test has been successful.

Summary

- The cause-effect connection answers the "Why?" question.
- In a cause-effect relationship, the first event causes the occurrence of the second event.

EXERCISE

DIRECTIONS: This exercise consists of passages followed by questions. Read each passage and answer the questions based upon what is stated or implied in the passage. Answers are on page 753.

Passage 1

It was dark when we reached the landing place on the river, and we had just enough time to get our baggage on to the dock before we heard the distant ringing of the steamboat bell, which was soon followed by the noise of her wheels splashing in the water and the hissing of the steam. Then the boat herself came in sight, pouring
5   forth smoke and fire. It was the first steamer I had ever seen. The dim outline of her huge form was partially illuminated by the lights on her deck. As she floated past on the dark surface of the river, my mind was full of ideas about her size and shape.

As I stood staring at her, a small boat suddenly darted up to the dock with lightning speed. Two men jumped on to the dock and began to throw the baggage
10 into the boat. One by one, my companions in travel all disappeared into the boat. I was completely bewildered and at a loss what to do with myself.

"Lend a hand," cried a gruff voice from the boat, "or you'll be left."

"Get in, boss," said one of the men on the dock.

Without more ado, somebody gave me a push, and I tumbled headlong into the
15 boat. Fortunately, I landed upon a heap of bags, and although I was not much hurt, I was most terribly frightened. The boat went with amazing speed through the water, and we were very soon alongside of the steamer.

The passengers scrambled on board. I recovered my senses sufficiently to notice a beautiful fellow traveler sitting in the stern of the boat; I resolved to show
20 my gallantry, so asked her if I should have the pleasure of assisting her out of the boat. She thanked me very sweetly and took hold of my extended hand. As I stepped back, my foot slipped, and I fell flat in the bottom of the boat. When I got to my feet, she was gone.

I hobbled on board the steamer, but I did not see her. Then I saw that I had
25 caught her pocket handkerchief in my fall, and as I could not find her to return it, I put it into my pocket to keep in remembrance of her.

1. The narrator first hears the steamboat just:

   A. after arriving at the dock.
   B. after boarding the small boat.
   C. before helping the traveler.
   D. before climbing aboard the steamboat.

2. The narrator notices the handkerchief:

   F. while standing on the dock.
   G. after boarding the steamer.
   H. during the ride in the small boat.
   J. before offering to help the traveler.

3. The narrator arrives at the dock:

   A. in the morning.
   B. at noon.
   C. in the afternoon.
   D. after dark.

4. The first indication that the narrator has that the steamboat is approaching is the:

   F. ringing of the bell.
   G. splashing of the wheels.
   H. hissing of the steam.
   J. lights on the deck.

5. As the group of travelers gets into the small boat, the narrator boards:

   A. first.
   B. immediately before the beautiful traveler.
   C. immediately before the man with the gruff voice.
   D. last.

Passage 2

It was cold and gusty, and the wind howled about the old mansion. The breeze was damp and chilly as if from a dungeon. My uncle threw a quantity of wood on the fire, which soon sent up a flame in the great wide-mouthed chimney that lit up the whole room and made the shadow of the tongs on the opposite wall look like a long-legged giant. My uncle climbed into the bed, which stood in a deep recess, then tucked himself snugly in, burying himself up to the chin in the bedclothes. He lay looking at the fire and listening to the wind.

He had not slept long when he was awakened by the clock, which struck midnight. It was just such an old clock as ghosts are fond of. It had a deep, dismal tone and struck slowly and tediously. He counted and counted until he was confident he counted twelve, and then it stopped.

The fire was burning down, and the blaze was almost out. Only small blue flames remained. My uncle had just fallen asleep again, when he was suddenly aroused by the sound of footsteps that seemed to be slowly pacing along the corridor. My uncle supposed that this might be some other guest on his way to bed. The footsteps, however, approached his door; the door gently opened; and a figure all in white glided in.

It was a female, tall and stately in person, and of a most commanding air. Her dress was of an ancient fashion. She walked up to the fireplace without looking at my uncle, who was staring at her. She remained for some time standing by the fire. Her face was ghastly pale, and perhaps rendered still more so by the bluish light of the fire. It possessed beauty, but its beauty was saddened by care and anxiety.

The figure remained for some time by the fire, putting out first one hand, then the other, then each foot alternately, as if warming itself. Ghosts, if it really was a ghost, are apt to be cold. My uncle also observed that it wore old fashioned, high-heeled shoes with diamond buckles that sparkled as though they were alive. At length the figure turned gently round, casting a glassy look about the room, which, as it passed over my uncle, made his blood run cold, and chilled the very marrow in his bones. It then stretched its arms toward heaven, clasped its hands, and wringing them in a supplicating manner, glided slowly out of the room.

6. Before the narrator's uncle got into bed, he:

   F. saw a figure in his room.
   G. heard footsteps in the hall.
   H. counted the chimes of the clock.
   J. put more wood on the fire.

7. The narrator's uncle was first awakened by the sound of:

   A. the wind.
   B. the clock.
   C. footsteps.
   D. the fire.

8. After the figure stretches its arms upward and wrings its hands, it:

   F. looks carefully around the room.
   G. speaks to the narrator's uncle.
   H. slowly leaves the uncle's room.
   J. warms itself by the fireplace.

9. In the narrative, the narrator's uncle falls asleep:

   A. once.
   B. twice.
   C. three times.
   D. four times.

10. The narrator's uncle first sees the mysterious figure when she:

    F. enters the room through the door.
    G. warms herself by the fire.
    H. glances around the room.
    J. stretches her arms above her.

Passage 3

Born in 1898, Paul Robeson was raised by his father, an escaped slave turned minister, in predominantly white middle-class New Jersey. He was valedictorian of the Rutgers class of 1919, winner of the school's oratory award for four straight years, and an All-American football player. He was a lawyer briefly, but quit the firm
5 after the secretaries refused to work for him and the partners relegated him to pushing papers.

He became an actor. It was the Harlem Renaissance, and the New Negro movement was in full swing. Robeson was a commanding figure of that time. He toured in the United States and abroad. In 1930 he became the first black man in
10 fifty years to play *Othello* in England. During the 1930s, he commanded a salary of more than $1,000 a concert and hobnobbed in international society.

He returned to the United States as World War II was breaking out, and his "Ballad for Americans" was broadcast across the country. He performed in New York in 1943 in *Othello*.

15 At the end of the war, Robeson helped found the Progressive Party and campaigned for Henry Wallace for president in 1948. He gave speeches against racism, against colonialism, for socialism, and in defense of the Soviet Union.

It was in 1949, however, at the Congress of the World Partisans of Peace in Paris that Robeson alienated mainstream America. He was misquoted as stating that
20 "American Negroes would not fight for the United States against the Soviet Union." The reaction was virulent and immediate. Violence erupted at a Robeson benefit concert for the Harlem chapter of the Civil Rights Congress on August 27, 1949. The concert was rescheduled, but shortly after the performance ended, rioting began.

After that, life was bleak for Robeson. His albums were burned, his concerts
25 were canceled, his name was erased from the published lists of All-Americans, and as a final insult in 1950, his passport was revoked. In 1952, he was stopped while attempting to cross the Washington-Canadian border for a concert. Robeson remained under constant surveillance by the FBI. He was unable to travel and was called before the House Committee on Un-American Activities. He suffered an
30 emotional breakdown in March of 1956.

In 1958, after lawsuits filed by Robeson and others, the United States Supreme Court ruled that it was unconstitutional to require a loyalty oath to travel freely. Despite the Supreme Court's decision, the damage to his career and to the man himself was already done. After a whirlwind return to the international stage,
35 Robeson suffered another breakdown a year later in Moscow. Depression plagued him the rest of his life. He kept apart from the public arena, even the rising Civil

368 • READING KEY IDEAS AND DETAILS

Rights Movement. He died on January 23, 1976—remembered by some as a great artist, by some as an activist for the oppressed, and by others as a Communist.

11. According to the passage, Robeson became a lawyer after:

- A. graduating college at Rutgers.
- B. studying acting in New York City.
- C. traveling to Canada for a concert.
- D. filing a suit with the Supreme Court.

12. According to the passage, Robeson helped found the Progressive Party:

- F. while he was a student at Rutgers.
- G. after his passport was canceled.
- H. at the end of World War II.
- J. after testifying before a House Committee.

13. According to the passage, after the benefit concert for the Harlem chapter of the Civil Rights Congress on August 27, 1949, was canceled:

- A. the concert was rescheduled.
- B. the concert was moved to Europe.
- C. Robeson permanently retired.
- D. Robeson and others filed a lawsuit.

14. According to the passage, mainstream Americans were alienated by remarks made by Robeson:

- F. during a performance of *Othello*.
- G. in support of Henry Wallace for president.
- H. at a conference in Paris.
- J. before the Supreme Court.

15. According to the passage, when did Robeson become involved in the rising Civil Rights Movement?

- A. While he was a student at Rutgers
- B. During his travels in Europe
- C. Following his mental breakdown
- D. Robeson remained apart from the Civil Rights Movement.

Passage 4

We had delightful Sunday breakfasts together at Lena's. At the back of her long workroom was a bay window, large enough to hold a box couch and a reading table. We breakfasted in this recess, after drawing the curtains to shut out the part of the room with cutting tables and wire women and sheet-draped garments on the walls. The sunlight poured in, making everything on the table shine and glitter and the flame of the alcohol lamp disappear altogether. Lena's curly black water spaniel, Prince, breakfasted with us. He sat beside her on the couch and behaved very well until the Polish violin teacher across the hall began to practice, when Prince would growl and sniff the air with disgust. Lena's landlord had given her the dog, and at first she was not pleased because she had spent too much of her life taking care of animals. But eventually she grew fond of him. After breakfast, I made him do his lessons: play dead dog, shake hands, stand up like a soldier. We used to put my cadet cap on his head—I had to take military drill at the University—and give him a yard measure to hold with his front leg. His gravity made us laugh immoderately.

16. According to the narrator, Prince would growl when:

F. the narrator would make him do tricks.
G. the neighbor would play the violin.
H. no more food was available for breakfast.
J. Lena would draw the curtains in her room.

17. According to the narrator, the objects on the table shone and glittered because:

A. the sunlight was bright.
B. the lamp illuminated them.
C. Lena had polished them.
D. Lena used them in her work.

18. The narrator states that dressing the dog up in a cadet cap caused the group to be:

F. angry.
G. hungry.
H. entertained.
J. annoyed.

19. The narrator says that she had a cadet cap because:

A. she bought it for the dog.
B. military drill was required at school.
C. Lena made the cap for her.
D. Lena wore the cap while she worked.

20. The narrator states that before breakfast the group would draw the curtains to:

F. block the light from the window.
G. shut out the view of the work area.
H. dampen the noise of the violin-playing.
J. keep the dog from growling and sniffing.

Passage 5

There was so long a pause, and Mrs. Todd still looked so absentminded, that I was afraid she and the cat were growing drowsy together before the fire, and I should have no reminiscences at all. The wind struck the house again, so that we both started in our chairs, and Mrs. Todd gave a curious, startled look at me. The cat
5 lifted her head and listened too, in the silence that followed, while after the wind sank we were more conscious than ever of the awful roar of the sea. The house jarred now and then, in a strange, disturbing way.

"Who was Mrs. Captain Tolland?" I asked eagerly.

"Cap'n John Tolland was the leastest smartest of any of 'em, but he was full
10 smart though, an' commanded a good brig. He was away fittin' out, but came home to see his wife and say farewell. He was lost with his ship in the Straits of Malacca, and she lived there alone in the old house a few months longer till she died. He left her well off; 'twas said he left his money about the house and she knew where 'twas. Oh, I expect you've heard that story over an' over twenty times since you moved
15 here."

"Never one word," I insisted.

"That's not surprising because it was a good while ago," explained Mrs. Todd with reassurance. "Yes, it all happened a great while ago."

UNIT 4 | EVENTS AND RELATIONSHIPS • 371

21. The narrator and Mrs. Todd become more aware of the ocean because:

    A. Mrs. Todd's story concerns a ship.
    B. the house is jarred from time to time.
    C. the wind has died down somewhat.
    D. the cat has become restless and uneasy.

22. The narrator is worried that Mrs. Todd will not share a story with her because:

    F. the cat is distracting Mrs. Todd.
    G. the storm is increasing in intensity.
    H. Mrs. Todd doesn't remember the event.
    J. Mrs. Todd seems to be falling asleep.

23. Mrs. Todd and the narrator are both startled by the:

    A. sound of the ocean.
    B. movement of the cat.
    C. blowing of the wind.
    D. warmth of the fire.

24. According to the passage, Mrs. Todd believes that the narrator has not heard her story before because the:

    F. narrator has not been paying attention.
    G. story is not very interesting.
    H. narrator is new to the area.
    J. events happened a long time ago.

25. Mrs. Todd explains that Cap'n Tolland returned home before leaving with his ship in order to:

    A. hide his money in the house.
    B. say good-bye to his wife.
    C. retrieve his money to take it with him.
    D. wait until the storm had passed.

Passage 6

The vast majority of the moon's craters are formed by the impact of meteoroids, asteroids, and comets. The shape of craters varies with their size. Small craters with diameters of less than 6 miles have relatively simple bowl shapes. Slightly larger craters cannot maintain a bowl shape because the crater wall is too
5 steep and material falls inward from the wall to the floor. As a result, the walls become scalloped and the floor becomes flat. Still larger craters have terraced walls and central peaks.

Surrounding each crater is rough, mountainous material—crushed and broken rocks that were ripped out of the crater cavity by shock pressure. This material,
10 called the crater ejecta blanket, can extend about 60 miles from the crater.

Farther out are patches of debris and, in many cases, irregular secondary craters. Those craters come in a range of shapes and sizes, and they are often clustered in groups or aligned in rows. Secondary craters are formed when material thrown out of the original crater strikes the surface. This material consists of large
15 blocks, clumps of loosely joined rocks, and fine sprays of ground-up rock. The material may travel thousands of miles.

Crater rays are light, wispy deposits of powder that can extend thousands of miles from the crater. Rays slowly vanish as micrometeoroid bombardment mixes the powder into the upper surface layer. Thus, craters that still have visible rays
20 must be among the youngest craters on the moon.

26. According to the passage, the shape of a crater is determined by its:

F. location.
G. age.
H. size.
J. color.

27. According to the passage, most of the moon's craters are formed by:

A. volcanic activity.
B. weathering forces.
C. atmospheric pressure.
D. objects from space.

28. According to the passage, secondary craters are created by:

   F. collisions with extra-lunar objects.
   G. material ejected from a primary crater.
   H. collapsed walls of primary craters.
   J. micrometeroid bombardment.

29. According to the passage, medium-sized craters have scalloped walls and flat floors because the:

   A. walls are so steep material falls into the crater.
   B. crater is located many miles away from the initial impact.
   C. crater is surrounded by light, wispy deposits of powder.
   D. craters are clustered in groups or aligned in rows.

30. According to the passage, crater rays eventually disappear because the powder deposits:

   F. mix into the surface of the moon.
   G. can extend thousands of miles.
   H. collapse into the bowl of the crater.
   J. are ejected from the crater.

Reading Craft and Structure

Unit 5 | Vocabulary

INSIDE THIS UNIT:
– An Experiment – – Be a Word Detective – – Common Clues – – Exercise –

Non-Negotiable Skill:

Use context clues to determine the meaning of unfamiliar words and phrases.

Vocabulary is obviously an important element of reading. The better your vocabulary is, the better reader you'll be. Plus, the better your vocabulary is, the easier reading will be for you.

Much of your vocabulary you've learned from your reading. You learn vocabulary as you read because you encounter new words in a context that helps you to understand the meaning of the words.

An Experiment

Try a little experiment to prove just how important context is to learning a new word. Here is a sentence with a word that will be unfamiliar to you. Yet, you will be able to figure out the meaning of the word by just studying the verbal clues that you find within the sentence.

Example:

Even though no one was injured, the automobile wreck left Clarence very *phragimellic*; he was sitting on the curb shaking, sweating, and unable to speak.

In the sentence above, the word *phragimellic* most likely means:

A. calm.
B hopeful.
C. upset.
D. welcome.

How would you feel after an accident? How would you describe someone who was sitting at the accident scene shaking, sweating, and unable to speak? Calm? Hopeful? Welcome? Or upset?

"Upset" is the correct answer. Or at least that's the procedure you follow for figuring out the meaning of a new vocabulary word in context. In this case, "phragimellic" isn't really a word. It's a made-up word that was placed in the sentence just to prove to you that you can figure out the meaning of a completely new vocabulary word that you cannot possibly have seen before just by studying it in context.

What would be a real word that could be used in place of the made-up "phragimellic"? You might think of "distressed" or "shocked."

Be a Word Detective

In a mystery movie, how does the detective find the solution to the crime? By looking for and studying clues that have been left behind. In the case of vocabulary in context, the clues have not been left accidentally. Instead, they create a map that can lead you to the meaning of an unfamiliar word.

Example:

Before the game, the referee *admonished* the players in a stern voice to play by the rules, adding that the rules would be strictly enforced.

In the context of the sentence, the word *admonished* means the referee is giving the players:

F. a hint.
G a scolding.
H. praise.
J. a warning.

> The correct answer is (J). One clue is the word "stern." The referee doesn't just announce that the players should abide by the rules. Rather, the referee makes the statement with authority. A second clue is "strictly enforced." So the referee announces that there will be consequences to rules violations. The referee is also talking to the players before the game and before any rules have been broken, so the best description of this scenario is "warning."

Example:

With a *whimsical* friend like Carlos, I never know what I'm going to be doing on the weekend. He might suggest that we see a movie, watch the cook at Mario's make pizzas, or even ride the subway from one end to the other and back without ever getting off the train.

In the context above, the word *whimsical* means:

A. dreary.
B unpredictable.
C. familiar.
D. generous.

The correct answer is (B). The second sentence lists some activities that Carlos might suggest, and the activities range from the ordinary to the very unusual. The speaker also says that it's not possible to know what Carlos will want to do. Thus, "whimsical" means "unpredictable."

Common Clues

"Same as" Clues

Writers usually describe persons, situations, and events in some detail. If the description includes a word that is unknown to you, you may be able to figure out its meaning by treating the other details as "same as" clues.

Example:

Harvey's intense *antipathy* to killing animals for either food or clothing led him to be a strict vegetarian who avoided dishes containing meat, fish, or poultry.

In the context of the sentence above, *antipathy* means:

F. support for.
G ignorance of.
H. opposition to.
J. attraction to.

The correct answer is (H). The details of the sentence tell us that Harvey avoids eating animals. How would such a person feel about killing animals for food? Such a person would be opposed to the practice. So "antipathy" must mean "opposition to."

Example:

Tabitha witnessed the accident but did not want to become involved, so she *feigned* ignorance when the officer asked her if she knew what had happened.

In the context of the sentence above, *feigned* means:

A. proved.
B pretended.
C. welcomed.
D. denied.

> The correct answer is (B). Tabitha saw the accident, but she did not want to say so. So she gave the false impression that she hadn't seen it. She "pretended" to be ignorant.

Example:

After his last novel received very bad reviews, Barry became a *recluse*, living alone in a cabin in the mountains, going to the nearest town only once a month to buy groceries, and never receiving visitors.

In the context of the sentence above, *recluse* means:

F. hermit.
G. traveler.
H. farmer.
J. librarian.

> The correct answer is (F). The writer gives us several details about Barry. He lives alone in an isolated area, and he doesn't socialize. So he lives like a "hermit." And "recluse" means "hermit."

"Opposite of" Clues

The clues in the previous examples were "same as" clues. The details provided by the writer reinforced the key word. Writers also provide details that contrast with other points, helping those points to stand out in black and white. These contrasting details are "opposite of" clues.

Example:

My horse was quite well behaved and responded easily to a gentle pulling of the reins, but Chris's mount was *fractious* and nearly bucked her off.

In the context of the sentence above, *fractious* means:

A. uncooperative.
B. well trained.
C. easily frightened.
D. eager to please.

The correct answer is (A). The "but" sets up an "opposite of" structure. The speaker's horse is well behaved, *but* Chris's horse is not. So "fractious" must mean the opposite of "well behaved."

Example:

As the time for the start of the race approached, the champion was confidently stretching her leg muscles, while the challenger was *apprehensively* pacing about worrying that even with all of the preparation she would not be up to the task.

In the context of the sentence above, *apprehensively* means:

F. securely.
G fearfully.
H. spontaneously.
J. victoriously.

The correct answer is (G). The "while" sets up an "opposite of" structure. The champion is confident, while the challenger is not. So "apprehensively" must mean "fearfully."

Example:

Though the playwright originally envisioned the drama as being performed on an *austere* stage, the director was experimenting with an elaborate production that included flashing lights, moving sets, and even a flock of live birds.

In the context of the sentence above, *austere* means:

A. comfortable.
B. outdoor.
C. fancy.
D. simple.

> The correct answer is (D). The "though" sets up an "opposite of" structure. The first clause contrasts with the second. Since the second clause describes an elaborate, ornate staging, the first clause describes a simple staging. And "austere" means "simple" or without decoration.

Summary

- "Same as" words are important clues and signal that the unknown word or phrase is similar in meaning to the words and phrases that surround it.

- "Opposite of" words are important clues and signal that the unknown word or phrase is opposite in meaning to the words or phrases that surround it.

EXERCISE

> **DIRECTIONS:** Each of the following items is a sentence with a word that has been italicized. You are to choose the answer that has the meaning that is <u>most like</u> that of the italicized word. Answers are on page 753.

1. The *blustery* wind broke off tree limbs, flattened utility poles, and even blew the roofs off buildings.

    In the context of the sentence above, *blustery* means:

    A. gentle.
    B. powerful.
    C. invisible.
    D. ordinary.

2. When the ambulance arrived at the hospital, the emergency room doctor worked quickly to *arrest* the bleeding before the victim lost even more blood and died.

    In the context of the sentence above, *arrest* means:

    F. detain.
    G. stop.
    H. increase.
    J. accept.

3. Mr. Garner was an *exacting* teacher who insisted that every homework assignment be completed, be neatly written, and be submitted on time, and any violation of his rules resulted in a failing grade.

    In the context of the sentence above, *exacting* means:

    A. understanding.
    B. relaxed.
    C. demanding.
    D. ordinary.

4. The evil warlord gave a *sinister* look at the hero, promising that the hero would soon get a chance to see the castle's dungeon.

    In the context of the sentence above, *sinister* means:

    F. beneficial.
    G. helpful.
    H. inviting.
    J. menacing.

5. After he hit his head on the pavement, Clint babbled *incoherently* for twenty minutes about needing a pink rabbit wearing blue sandals to lead the way into the candy forest.

   In the context of the sentence above, *incoherently* means:

   A. illogically.
   B. persuasively.
   C. generously.
   D. realistically.

6. The most *eloquent* speaker at the graduation ceremony was Caren, who received a standing ovation for her speech entitled "A Call to Action" in which she encouraged the new graduates to dedicate themselves to making the world a better place for everyone.

   In the context of the sentence above, *eloquent* means:

   F. monotonous.
   G. articulate.
   H. ill-prepared.
   J. cautious.

7. The scientists found the increase in temperature in the test tube *paradoxical* because many other repetitions of the same experiment showed that the temperature in the test tube decreased as predicted by the laws of chemistry.

   In the context of the sentence above, *paradoxical* means:

   A. well documented.
   B. reassuring.
   C. productive.
   D. puzzling.

8. After the blizzard *abated*, we dug ourselves out of the cabin and watched the last few flakes drifting down onto the deep piles of snow.

   In the context of the sentence above, *abated* means:

   F. began.
   G. continued.
   H. lessened.
   J. increased.

9. In the comic strip "Dennis the Menace," Dennis' *irascible* neighbor Mr. Wilson is constantly scowling in disapproval and complaining about everything that Dennis does.

In the context of the sentence above, *irascible* means:

A. open-minded.
B. irritable.
C. affectionate.
D. insensitive.

10. The newspaper won a journalistic prize for its *poignant* story on the family dog who ultimately died from injuries sustained in a house fire while rescuing three kittens.

In the context of the sentence above, *poignant* means:

F. touching.
G. lengthy.
H. informative.
J. unstable.

11. Crop rotation and similar practices, which ensure that different plants are grown on the same land, offer the best guarantee of soil conservation and sustainability, while *monoculture* quickly exhausts the soil by using up the limited supply of plant nutrients.

In the context of the sentence above, *monoculture* means:

A. growing one crop.
B. growing many crops.
C. not growing crops.
D. not harvesting mature crops.

12. The laboratory rats treated with the vitamin supplements had *prodigious* energy and were extremely active, but those that did not receive supplements were tired and refused to exercise even when tempted with food.

In the context of the sentence above, *prodigious* means:

F. unruly.
G. preplanned.
H. enormous.
J. experimental.

13. The side of the mountain range closest to the sea is luxuriously green with dense foliage fed by the rains that fall as the moist air rises, but the side away from the sea is *arid*.

    In the context of the sentence above, *arid* means:

    A. moist.
    B. fertile.
    C. frigid.
    D. dry.

14. Washington County seemed anxious to *facilitate* the opening of new businesses by relaxing rules and regulations, while Warren County seemed to use strict enforcement of its laws to discourage new business.

    In the context of the sentence above, *facilitate* means to:

    F. outlaw.
    G. confuse.
    H. make easier.
    J. transgress.

15. The heroine of the story really never lived and the events related did not actually happen, but her journey can be understood as an *allegorical* account of growing from childhood into adulthood.

    In the context of the sentence above, the word *allegorical* means:

    A. symbolic.
    B. fateful.
    C. individual.
    D. recorded.

16. The training program for new recruits was difficult and challenging, but those few who were chosen for the *elite* Red Beret Corps were put through an even more rigorous regimen.

    In the context of the sentence above, the word *elite* means:

    F. highly selective.
    G. prematurely finished.
    H. mainly inactive.
    J. more experienced.

17. Even though he had been dancing anonymously in the chorus line of out-of-town productions for over three years, Amari *aspired* to be a featured dancer in a big Broadway production and see his name in lights.

In the context of the sentence above, the word *aspired* means:

A. gave up.
B. feared.
C. denounced.
D. hoped.

18. The racecar fitted with extra-wide tires hugged the track and followed a straight course to the finish line, but the car with ordinary tires *careened* on the curves.

In the context of the sentence above, *careened* means:

F. sped up quickly.
G. stopped completely.
H. lost control.
J. maintained a course.

19. The professor's lecture on the Law of Motion was long and involved, but at the end of the hour, she *recapitulated* her lecture in a few brief points in just a couple of minutes.

In the context of the sentence above, *recapitulated* means:

A. continued.
B. summarized.
C. contradicted.
D. translated.

20. As a commander, the general preferred to monitor a situation and think out a careful plan rather than to act *precipitously* without all the information needed.

In the context of the sentence above, *precipitously* means:

F. rashly.
G. alone.
H. repeatedly.
J. silently.

21. Because the royal family and the Church of England opposed his relationship, in 1936 King Edward VIII decided to voluntarily *abdicate* his royal title so he could marry an American woman, Wallis Simpson.

In the context of the sentence above, *abdicate* means:

A. accept.
B. give up.
C. destroy.
D. cherish.

22. Carissa's parents always taught her to be *tactful*, but their lessons didn't seem to have an impact on her; her behavior could typically be described as crude, thoughtless, and obnoxious.

In the context of the sentence above, *tactful* means:

F. meek.
G. rude.
H. polite.
J. unkind.

23. When Ivy arrived in her new dorm room, she realized that movies depicting college students with *capacious* living spaces are inaccurate; she found her dorm to be tiny and cramped.

In the context of the sentence above, *capacious* means:

A. comfortable.
B. small.
C. dirty.
D. spacious.

24. The man who had been wrongly accused of murder was finally *vindicated* when new evidence led to the arrest of the actual criminal.

In the context of the sentence above, *vindicated* means:

F. sentenced for a crime.
G. arrested.
H. questioned.
J. freed from blame.

25. Gautama Buddha, the founder of Buddhism, abandoned his life in society and lived a *reclusive* life because he believed he needed to be alone to achieve full spiritual enlightenment.

    In the context of the sentence above, *reclusive* means:

    A. depressing.
    B. independent.
    C. withdrawn.
    D. sociable.

26. The relationship between Romeo and Juliet was disapproved of by their families, the Montagues and Capulets, because the families felt strong *animosity* toward each other.

    In the context of the sentence above, *animosity* means:

    F. discomfort.
    G. hatred.
    H. confusion.
    J. love.

27. More than 300 *lobbyists* picketed outside of the state capitol building in an attempt to persuade the governor to increase school funding.

    In the context of the sentence above, *lobbyists* means:

    A. activists.
    B. criminals.
    C. foreigners.
    D. officers.

28. Anderson was worried that he would fail his driver's test for not pausing long enough at the stop sign, but his mistake turned out to be *inconsequential*; he passed anyway.

    In the context of the sentence above, *inconsequential* means:

    F. devastating.
    G. unimportant.
    H. severe.
    J. dangerous.

29. Though Mrs. Juarez prefers to keep her house *pristine*, Mr. Juarez has a horrible habit of leaving his wet towels, dirty dishes, and muddy shoes all over the house.

In the context of the sentence above, *pristine* means:

A. empty.
B. white.
C. sloppy.
D. clean.

30. Annette's eccentric aunt claims to be *clairvoyant*; she is constantly trying to read people's auras and predict their deaths.

In the context of the sentence above, *clairvoyant* means:

F. psychic.
G. intelligent.
H. spiritual.
J. predictable.

Reading **Craft and Structure**

Unit 6 | **Practice**

INSIDE THIS UNIT:
– Exercise –

EXERCISE

> **DIRECTIONS:** The first part of this exercise (Questions 1–15) consists of passages followed by questions. Read each passage and answer the questions based upon what is stated or implied in the passage. Answers are on page 753.

Passage 1

Every hour, hundreds of commercial aircraft push back from their departure gates and begin flights that follow a common flight profile. The flight begins with the Preflight Phase. During this phase, the pilot performs the various preflight checks, gets the most recent weather information, and files a flight plan. After getting the departure clearance from the tower, the aircraft pushes back from the gate and receives instructions from the Ground Controller in the airport's control tower regarding the appropriate taxiways to take toward the takeoff runway.

The Takeoff Phase begins when the aircraft is cleared for departure (or takeoff) by the Local Tower Controller and starts its takeoff roll down the runway.

Once the plane has lifted off from the ground, it is in the Departure Phase. The pilot is instructed to change radio frequency and contact the Departure Controller working in the Terminal Radar Approach Control (TRACON). The pilot is given a preferred, predetermined route that will take the plane up and away from the airport to its route. The pilot is given any additional heading and altitude instructions and then the plane is tracked by radar until it reaches the boundary of the TRACON airspace. There the pilot is handed off to a Center Controller and told to make contact on a given radio frequency.

The En Route Phase of the flight begins when the Center Controller takes charge of the aircraft's heading and altitude. The En Route Phase may last several hours during which time the plane will be passed from one Center Controller to the next as it moves toward its destination. If the flight is a short one, only one Center Controller will be involved.

Once the aircraft is within approximately 150 miles of its destination airport, it enters the Descent Phase of the flight. The pilot contacts Approach Control on a designated radio frequency and receives instructions regarding heading, altitude, and rate of descent. Approximately 50 miles from the airport, the aircraft starts the Approach Phase. It is handed off to the TRACON Approach Controller, and the descent continues as the Approach Controller choreographs a line of approaching aircraft all heading for the same runway.

30   The flight is then handed off for the Landing Phase from the controller in the TRACON to the Local Controller who is stationed at the destination airport's control tower. The Local Controller issues landing clearance. The aircraft lands and is handed off electronically to the Ground Controller (also in the airport's control tower) who directs the pilot across the taxiways to the destination gate.

1. According to the passage, the En Route Phase is followed immediately by the:

    A. Takeoff Phase.
    B. Approach Phase.
    C. Descent Phase.
    D. Landing Phase.

2. According to the passage, the final phase of the flight is the:

    F. Departure Phase.
    G. En Route Phase.
    H. Descent Phase.
    J. Landing Phase.

3. According to the passage, the Approach Phase begins approximately:

    A. 150 miles from the departure airport.
    B. 150 miles from the destination airport.
    C. 50 miles from the destination airport.
    D. upon touching down.

4. According to the passage, the Takeoff Phase is when the aircraft is told it:

    F. may push back from the gate.
    G. should ascend to a pre-determined altitude.
    H. must file a flight plan.
    J. is cleared for departure on the runway.

5. According to the passage, when a departing aircraft reaches the boundary of the TRACON airspace, it:

    A. is cleared for landing at its destination.
    B. is handed off to a Center Controller.
    C. begins its descent to its destination.
    D. is told to contact the Local Controller.

Passage 2

Global warming is an increase in the average temperature of Earth's surface. Since the late 1800s, the global average temperature has increased about 0.7 to 1.4 degrees Fahrenheit. A majority of climatologists have concluded that human activities are responsible for most of the warming. Human activities contribute to global warming by intensifying Earth's natural greenhouse effect. The greenhouse effect warms Earth's surface through a complex process involving sunlight, gases, and particles in the atmosphere. The gases that trap heat in the atmosphere are known as greenhouse gases.

The main human activities that contribute to global warming are the burning of fossil fuels such as coal, oil, and natural gas and the clearing of land. Most of the burning occurs in automobiles, in factories, and in electric power plants that provide energy for houses and office buildings. The burning of fossil fuels creates carbon dioxide. Carbon dioxide is a greenhouse gas that slows the escape of heat into space. Trees and other plants remove carbon dioxide from the air during photosynthesis, the process they use to produce food. The clearing of land contributes to the buildup of carbon dioxide by reducing the rate at which the gas is removed from the atmosphere or by the decomposition of dead vegetation.

Widespread shifts might occur in the natural habitats of animals and plants if global warming continues. Through global warming, the surface waters of the oceans could become warmer, increasing the stress on ocean ecosystems, such as coral reefs. High water temperatures can cause a damaging process called coral bleaching. When corals bleach, they expel the algae that give them their color and nourishment. The corals turn white and, unless the water temperature cools, they die. Many flowering plants on land also will not bloom without a sufficient period of winter cold.

Due to global warming, extreme weather conditions might become more frequent and therefore more damaging. Changes in rainfall patterns could increase both flooding and drought in some areas. More hurricanes and other tropical storms might occur, and they could become more powerful. Longer-lasting and more intense heat waves could cause the spread of tropical diseases such as malaria into other regions.

Although global warming is still a hypothesis, many scientists believe that it is correct. Thus, policymakers are looking for ways to avoid the long-term damage that global warming could cause.

6. According to the passage, without a sufficient period of cold winter weather, many plants:

   F. would grow out of control.
   G. would not flower.
   H. would trap heat in the atmosphere.
   J. would spread various diseases.

7. According to the passage, most scientists have concluded that a primary cause of global warming is:

   A. burning fossil fuels.
   B. coral bleaching.
   C. photosynthesis.
   D. extreme weather.

8. According to the passage, during photosynthesis plants:

   F. emit excess carbon dioxide into the air.
   G. decompose into various harmless chemicals.
   H. consume large amounts of stored energy.
   J. remove carbon dioxide from the air.

9. According to the passage, carbon dioxide in the atmosphere:

   A. blocks the ability of diseases to spread around the world.
   B. provides a protective layer that blocks the sun's rays.
   C. decreases the rate at which plants convert energy to food.
   D. slows the escape of heat from the earth back into space.

10. According to the passage, clearing land contributes to global warming by:

    F. emitting carbon dioxide that slows the retransmission of heat into space.
    G. reducing the rate at which carbon dioxide is removed from the air.
    H. adding to the carbon dioxide in the atmosphere through the burning of fuel.
    J. absorbing flood waters that would otherwise lower ocean temperatures.

Passage 3

General George Washington's victory over Hessian forces—or German regiments hired by the British—at the Battle of Trenton on December 26, 1776, ranks as an occasion where intelligence properly gathered and utilized secured a major Patriot victory. The Battle of Trenton and the war might have turned out completely different without the help of a willing double agent: John Honeyman.

The Battle of Trenton marked the first major American victory in the Revolutionary War. Prior to this time, Patriot forces had endured nearly constant defeat as the British pushed them from New York and into Pennsylvania. The Continental Congress pleaded for a victory to save the cause. In response, Washington decided to attack the exposed Hessian garrison at Trenton, comprised of roughly 1,400 men in three regiments under the command of Col. Johann Rall. Washington's plan depended on surprise and on intelligence provided by John Honeyman.

Born in Ireland, Honeyman was the son of a poor farmer. Although he had little formal education, he learned several trades and taught himself to read and write. At age 29, he enlisted in the British Army and served with distinction in the French and Indian War. Honeyman moved to Philadelphia in 1775 and met George Washington while he was there to attend meetings of the Continental Congress. Although he had served the British, Honeyman was sympathetic to the Americans and offered his services to Washington.

Posing as a Loyalist, Honeyman moved to Griggstown, New Jersey, where he practiced his trades as a butcher and weaver. As a recognized wartime hero, he moved freely within the town and gathered intelligence about British and Hessian forces. Honeyman then arranged his capture by Continental forces and met with Washington, providing details on the strength, location, morale, and security arrangements of the Hessian troops. With Washington's help, Honeyman escaped and returned to Trenton where he told Colonel Rall of his capture and feigned escape. He reported that the Continental Army was in such a low state of morale that they could not attack, so Rall let down his defenses, making the garrison vulnerable to attack.

On Christmas night, Washington crossed the swollen Delaware River with 2,400 soldiers and made the long, cold march over muddy roads to Trenton. When Continental forces attacked after dawn, 300 surprised Hessians surrendered immediately, as the remainder struggled to mount a defense. When the brief battle had ended, the Americans counted a handful of casualties, while the Hessians lost more than 1,000 men, including 918 prisoners. All four Hessian colonels, including

Rall, were killed. By noon, Continental forces had moved safely back across the Delaware, giving the Patriot cause new confidence and hope.

11. According to the passage, the Hessian garrison was vulnerable because:

   A. Colonel Rall believed the Patriots were too weak to attack.
   B. Colonel Rall did not know the location of Washington's troops.
   C. Hessian soldiers were inexperienced and not effective fighters.
   D. Washington had informed Colonel Rall that the Patriots would not attack.

12. According to the passage, one effect of the victory at Trenton was to:

   F. force the British to withdraw from North America.
   G. give Patriot forces new hope and confidence.
   H. drive the British back across the Delaware River.
   J. prompt the Hessian forces to return to Germany.

13. According to the passage, Honeyman was able to gather intelligence about British and Hessian forces as a double agent because he:

   A. had been a war hero in the British army.
   B. escaped after being captured by Washington.
   C. had served at the Hessian garrison in Trenton.
   D. crossed the Delaware River with Washington's troops.

14. According to the passage, following the victory, the Patriot troops:

   F. occupied the Hessian garrison at Trenton.
   G. pursued the Hessian forces for several days.
   H. crossed back over the Delaware River to safety.
   J. held the four Hessian colonels as prisoners of war.

15. According to the passage, the Battle of Trenton was:

   A. the final Patriot victory in the Revolutionary War.
   B. the first major Patriot victory in the Revolutionary War.
   C. the first Patriot defeat in the Revolutionary War.
   D. the final Patriot defeat in the Revolutionary War.

DIRECTIONS: Each of the following items (Questions 16–30) is a sentence with a word that has been italicized. You are to choose the answer that has the meaning that is <u>most</u> <u>like</u> that of the italicized word. Answers are on page 754.

16. The poor people in eighteenth-century France, who could barely afford to feed themselves, became resentful of Marie Antoinette's *opulent* lifestyle.

   In the context of the sentence above, *opulent* means:

   F. strict.
   G. wealthy.
   H. immoral.
   J. selfish.

17. Churchgoers maintain a solemn attitude during services in order to show their *reverence* for the rituals they are practicing.

   In the context of the sentence above, *reverence* means:

   A. confusion.
   B. thoughtfulness.
   C. indifference.
   D. respect.

18. Many golfers try to improve their own swing by studying and *emulating* the form of famous golfers such as Phil Mickelson.

    In the context of the sentence above, *emulating* means:

    F. changing.
    G. following.
    H. criticizing.
    J. imitating.

19. Though the pressures of society cause many people to *conform*, Transcendentalist writers such as Ralph Waldo Emerson encourage us to embrace our individuality.

    In the context of the sentence above, *conform* means:

    A. behave strangely.
    B. behave independently.
    C. follow the majority.
    D. think differently.

20. Jonathan Edwards, a Puritan preacher from the 1700s, wrote powerful sermons that moved his congregation to hysterics in spite of the fact that his monotonous, drawn-out speeches meant he was not an interesting *orator*.

    In the context of the sentence above, *orator* means:

    F. writer.
    G. speaker.
    H. believer.
    J. researcher.

21. Alexa's *jubilation* at her engagement was contagious; soon, all her friends and family members were jumping up and down and hugging her.

    In the context of the sentence above, *jubilation* means:

    A. happiness.
    B. anxiety.
    C. disappointment.
    D. indifference.

400 • READING CRAFT AND STRUCTURE

22. Years ago, women were expected to be *submissive* to their husbands, but today, partners tend to assume more equal roles in their marriages.

In the context of the sentence above, *submissive* means:

F. overbearing.
G. polite.
H. meek.
J. loving.

23. Though the McMurrays were obviously proud of their massive new house, I felt the gold-threaded curtains, stone gargoyles, and marble fountains were *ostentatious*.

In the context of the sentence above, *ostentatious* means:

A. showy.
B. unattractive.
C. cheap.
D. beautiful.

24. The author's so-called autobiography was well received by critics until members of his family *discredited* his stories; later he admitted that many details from his book were fictional.

In the context of the sentence above, *discredited* means:

F. disproved.
G. praised.
H. disliked.
J. believed.

25. Edna's grandchildren were shocked to learn from her will that, after years of *frugal* habits, the librarian was able to save her small salary so that when she died, she had nearly a million dollars in her savings account!

In the context of the sentence above, *frugal* means:

A. careless.
B. thrifty.
C. lavish.
D. smart.

26. Though Quasimodo, from the story *The Hunchback of Notre Dame*, lives most of his life as a *pariah* due to his deformed figure, he eventually becomes more willing to join society, even if that means risking rejection.

    In the context of the sentence above, *pariah* means:

    F. hero.
    G. villain.
    H. outcast.
    J. cripple.

27. All superheroes must fight against a *malefactor* who commits atrocious crimes against humanity; Spiderman fights the Green Goblin, Superman goes against Lex Luthor, and Batman must take on the Joker.

    In the context of the sentence above, *malefactor* means:

    A. opposite.
    B. murderer.
    C. evildoer.
    D. friend.

28. Bradley gasped when he accidentally slid the sharp knife across his hand, but luckily he was not injured because his hand did not rub against the *serrated* side of the blade.

    In the context of the sentence above, *serrated* means:

    F. smooth.
    G. rusty.
    H. metal.
    J. jagged.

29. For his science project, Charlie attempted to build a jetpack that would allow him to go to the moon; he thought it was completely possible, but his teacher, who did not believe it was quite so *feasible*, gave him a D for the assignment.

    In the context of the sentence above, *feasible* means:

    A. possible.
    B. impressive.
    C. interesting.
    D. technological.

30. Though my nephew was supposed to come over to water my plants each day, when I returned from my vacation and saw my *parched* flowers, I knew he didn't follow through with his job.

In the context of this sentence, *parched* means:

F. dried up.
G. healthy.
H. watery.
J. unhealthy.

Reading Craft and Structure

Unit 7 | Implied Ideas and Conclusions

INSIDE THIS UNIT:
– What Is an Inference? – – Exercise –

Non-Negotiable Skill:

Draw conclusions about the people or events in straightforward narratives.

What Is an Inference?

One skill practiced by good readers is drawing additional conclusions from the text. That is, they *read between the lines*. Sometimes they find clues that the author has left that help them to better understand the people and events described. But readers should be careful or they may deduce conclusions that even the author was not aware of or did not intend to communicate.

The trick to drawing further conclusions is to know when an inference is strongly supported by the text and when an inference is too far-fetched to be justified. Read the following story called "The Lady or the Tiger" to see the difference illustrated.

Example:

In olden times, there lived a king. When a subject was accused of a crime of sufficient importance to interest the king, public notice was given that, on an appointed day, the fate of the accused person would be decided in the king's arena. When all the people had assembled in the galleries, and the king,

5 surrounded by his court, sat high up on his throne, he gave a signal, a door beneath him opened, and the accused subject stepped out into the amphitheater. Directly opposite him were two doors, exactly alike and side by side. It was the duty and the privilege of the person on trial to walk directly to these doors and open one of them.

10 He could open either door. If he opened the one, there came out of it a hungry tiger, the fiercest and most cruel that could be found, which immediately sprang upon him and tore him to pieces as a punishment for his guilt. But, if the accused person opened the other door, there came forth from it a lady, the most suitable to his years and station that could be selected from among the king's

15 subjects, and to this lady he was immediately married as a reward of his innocence.

This was the king's method of administering justice. On some occasions the tiger came out of one door, and on some out of the other. The decisions of this tribunal were not only the outcome of impartial chance, they were positively

UNIT 7 | IMPLIED IDEAS AND CONCLUSIONS • 405

20 final: the accused person was instantly punished if he found himself guilty, and, if innocent, he was rewarded on the spot, whether he liked it or not. There was no escape from the judgments of the king's arena.

This king had a daughter, the apple of his eye, and the king loved her above all else. Among the king's courtiers was a young man, handsome and brave to a
25 degree unsurpassed in all the kingdom. The princess loved him passionately. One day the king discovered the relationship. The youth was immediately cast into prison, and a day was appointed for his trial in the king's arena. This, of course, was an especially important occasion; never before had a subject dared to love the daughter of the king.

30 The kingdom was searched for the most savage tiger for the arena, and the ranks of maiden youth and beauty throughout the land were carefully surveyed by competent judges in order that the young man might have a fitting bride. Of course, everybody knew that the deed with which the accused was charged had been done. He had loved the princess, and neither he, she, nor anyone else,
35 thought of denying the fact; but the king would not think of allowing any fact of this kind to interfere with the workings of the tribunal. No matter how the relationship turned out, the course of events would determine whether or not the young man had done wrong in allowing himself to love the princess.

The appointed day arrived. From far and near the people gathered, and
40 thronged the great galleries of the arena, and crowds, unable to gain admittance, massed outside the walls. The king and his court were in their places, opposite the twin doors, those fateful portals, so terrible in their similarity.

Everything was ready. The signal was given. A door beneath the royal party opened, and the young man walked into the arena. Tall, beautiful, fair, his
45 appearance was greeted with a low hum of admiration and anxiety. Most of the audience had never before seen such a handsome youth. No wonder the princess loved him! What a terrible thing for him to be there!

As the youth advanced into the arena he turned, according to custom, to bow to the king, but his eyes were fixed upon the princess, who sat to the right
50 of her father. From the moment that the decree had gone forth that the young man should decide his fate in the king's arena, she had thought of nothing else, night or day, but this great event and the various subjects connected with it. Possessed of more power, influence, and character than any one who had ever before been interested in such a case, she had done what no other person had
55 done: she had obtained the secret of the doors. She knew behind which of the doors stood the cage of the tiger and behind which waited the lady. Through these thick doors, heavily curtained with animal skins on the inside, it was impossible that any noise or suggestion should come from within to the person

406 • READING CRAFT AND STRUCTURE

60 who should approach to raise the latch of one of them. But gold, and the power of a woman's will, had brought the secret to the princess.

Not only did she know in which room stood the lady ready to emerge, all blushing and radiant, should her door be opened, but she knew who the lady was, one of the fairest and loveliest of the damsels of the court, and her rival. The princess hated the woman who blushed and trembled behind that silent
65 door and who would become the wife of the man she loved if he picked that door.

When the young man turned and looked at her, he saw in her eyes that she knew behind which door crouched the tiger and behind which stood the lady. Indeed, he had expected her to know it. The moment he looked upon her, he saw
70 she had succeeded, as in his soul he knew she would succeed.

Then it was that his quick and anxious glance asked the question: "Which?" It was as plain to her as if he shouted it from where he stood. There was not an instant to be lost. The question was asked in a flash; it must be answered in another.

75 Her right arm lay on the cushioned railing in front of her. She raised her hand, and made a slight, quick movement toward the right. No one but the young man saw her. Every eye but his was fixed on the man in the arena.

He turned, and with a firm and rapid step, he walked across the empty space. Every heart stopped beating, every breath was held, and every eye was
80 fixed immovably upon that man. Without the slightest hesitation, he went to the door on the right, and opened it.

UNIT 7 | IMPLIED IDEAS AND CONCLUSIONS • 407

1. Which of the following statements can be inferred from the passage?

A. The princess told the young man to open the door behind which waited the lady.
B. The princess was not sure which door held the tiger and which held the lady.
C. The princess told the young man to open the door behind which waited the tiger.
D. The accused knew beforehand whether the tiger or the lady was waiting behind the door he opened.

2. It can be inferred that most people in the kingdom:

F. did not believe that the accused was guilty of loving the princess.
G. were not aware that someone had been accused of loving the princess.
H. did not discuss the accusations made against the young man who loved the princess.
J. accepted the fact that the princess and the young man were really in love with each other.

3. It can be inferred that animal skins on the doors were used to:

A. suppress any noises.
B. keep the tiger warm.
C. decorate the doors.
D. keep the door locked.

4. Which of the following conclusions about the appearance of the doors is most justified?

F. The doors had features that would allow a clever accused to figure out which concealed the lady and which the tiger.
G. The doors were identical because the king liked the design so much that all arena doors used the design.
H. The doors differed in some small details, and prisoners sometimes used these to help them choose a door.
J. The doors were identical so that an accused had to pick at random rather than by using some feature of a door.

5. It can be inferred that a special effort was made to find a particularly ferocious tiger because:

A. the case was especially important to the king.
B. the people found a ferocious tiger more entertaining.
C. the king expected the accused to choose the door with the tiger.
D. the princess planned to save the life of the young man.

"The Lady or the Tiger" is a literary classic. In fact, the phrase "lady or the tiger" often refers to any situation in which someone must choose between two options.

"The Lady or the Tiger" is an unusual story just because it presents the central question of the story in such a way that it is impossible to answer with certainty. Most often, however, questions about what else can be inferred from the passage can be confidently answered—if you read between the lines.

Example:

Carter Harden glanced at his watch. His 3:30 appointment was due in five minutes. He got up from his desk and took his Armani suit coat from the rack where it had been hanging while he wrote his client report for the Duchess of Camden-on-Avonshire, explaining he had recovered her diamond brooch from a
5   pawn broker to whom the piece had been pledged by her husband, the Duke, a man who liked slow horses. Carter wore only Armani because the fabrics were the best, the cut suited his lean frame, and the workmanship was truly world-class.

He slipped on the pewter-grey coat and adjusted it to conceal the .44
10   Magnum revolver that he was licensed to carry in his shoulder holster. In his opinion, the .44 Magnum—the gun, not the Japanese heavy metal band, the music of which he detested—was the best handgun for someone in his line of work. The .44 wasn't a true .44 caliber weapon. He'd once measured the inside of the weapon's barrel using a Vernia caliper. The diameter was .425 inches
15   from one land (rifled groove) to the other. The cartridges were .429 inches. So the bullet actually expanded to the .44 size on exiting the muzzle. This was very

effective, but not the most powerful handgun in the world. That honor went to the .454 Casull Magnum, a custom-made revolver. The .44 Magnum was a production model. Technically speaking, Carter liked to point out, Dirty Harry

20 should have said, "This is the most powerful double-action production revolver in the world," but he agreed that the more exact statement didn't have the same dramatic effect as Clint Eastwood's actual warning in the movie.

Carter checked his watch again, 3:29. If he could conclude his appointment by 4:15, he could take off the rest of the afternoon and be at the arena in time

25 for the 7:30 face-off of tonight's semi-final hockey match. The local arts council had protested long and loud when the city informed it that a gala benefit by the New Town Ballet and a performance by the City Orchestra would be canceled, but the hockey franchise had first dibs on the arena. And, Carter reflected, he hated Balanchine and Mahler even more than heavy metal.

30 At precisely 3:30, a knock on the office door announced the arrival of the client.

"S'open," Carter growled.

The door swung wide framing a tall woman, perhaps 6'1" or 6'2", made four inches taller by the shoes she wore, her figure backlit by the fluorescent

35 tubes in the hallway. The charcoal grey, pinstriped suit was clearly a custom-made number, strictly one-of-a-kind, and had been hemmed a fashionable 2 1/4 inches above the knees. She wore a white silk blouse, barely open at the neck, with a single strand of natural, not cultured, pearls. Carter quickly calculated the value of the outfit at $8,000 with another $75,000 for the hardware around her

40 neck.

She spoke first and in a tone that said she was used to being in charge. "I'm Monica del Monaco, President of Associated Consolidated Metalworking and Electronics," she said, producing a business card from her jacket pocket in a fluid motion that would have done credit to any magician.

45 Carter recognized her from newspapers and television. ACME was the largest manufacturer of heavy arms in the West and supplied not only the US military but most of its allies. According to a recent profile in the business weekly *Fortune* magazine, Ms. del Monaco had attended Wellesley, then earned a Masters in Business Administration at Harvard, and went on for a PhD in

50 electrical engineering at Cal Tech, all completed by the age of 25. She was an acknowledged martial artist who competed at top international levels. It was rumored that she trained with the Navy SEALS and Mossad. It was also said that she had her own reserved parking space at CIA headquarters in Langley, Virginia.

410 • READING **CRAFT AND STRUCTURE**

55   Before Carter could speak, she seated herself in the chair opposite his and began.

   "ACME's security has been compromised, and the top-secret plans for a Doomsday weapon have been stolen. We need your help in locating and recovering those plans. We'll pay $10,000 a day plus all reasonable expenses.
60 Can you come with me right now to our factory?"

   Stunned and awed by the terms of the offer, and unwilling to trust his voice, Carter nodded a silent "yes." He had forgotten all about the hockey semifinals.

6. It can be inferred that Carter's profession is a:

 F. hockey player.
 G. corporate executive.
 H. private detective.
 J. military officer.

7. Which of the following statements can be inferred about Carter Harden?

 A. He is knowledgeable about handguns.
 B. He was a member of the Navy SEALS.
 C. He is a long-time employee of ACME.
 D. He is punctual and on time for meetings.

8. It can be inferred that Monica del Monaco:

 F. is a well-known and powerful business leader.
 G. is currently an engineering student at Cal Tech.
 H. has driven to Harden's office in her expensive car.
 J. likes to attend the ballet and orchestra concerts.

9. It can be inferred that Carter:

 A. refused Monica del Monaco's offer.
 B. accepted Monica del Monaco's offer.
 C. asked Monica del Monaco for more details about the offer.
 D. did not understand Monica del Monaco's offer.

10. It can be inferred that Carter Harden likes:

 F. orchestra performances.
 G. the ballet.
 H. sports.
 J. rock concerts.

Example:

"Do?" said an ominous, yet familiar voice outside their berth. "There is nothing you can *do*, kiddoes. In exactly forty-seven ticks of the clock, this train will come to the final bridge, and I do mean *final!*"

"Boppo?" Joe and Nancy said in unison and stuck their heads out between 5 the curtains to see the face they thought they'd left far behind. "What are you doing on this train?"

Boppo laughed. It was an evil sound that sent shivers down their spines.

"Did you think you could run away so easily? But, no time to chat. I have to de-train before de train de-molishes." And with that Boppo raced away in the 10 direction of the caboose.

"Pull the emergency cord, Nancy!" cried Joe as he leapt from the berth and gave chase. Nancy yanked the red handle above the berth. Almost immediately the great train shuddered and squawked to a stop. In the distance she could hear a gigantic explosion. She pushed her way down the aisle that was quickly 15 filling with passengers, furious at being so rudely awakened. She found Joe staring off the back of the train. Boppo was long gone.

"Nancy, we've got to get off this train. Now. While it's stopped."

"And not warn the police about Boppo?" Nancy was horrified. "No," she said, "first we need to make an anonymous tip. If only we had a cell phone."

20 "There are lots of people milling around," said Joe. "I'll pickpocket a phone." Joe had learned a lot of useful tricks working in and around a circus.

"That's dishonest," said Nancy, "but I guess it's better than letting a potential killer get away."

Joe pulled a cell phone from the jacket pocket of a nearby passenger and 25 called the authorities. The twins left the borrowed phone on the rear platform, climbed off the train, and with a clear conscience walked forward past the stalled engine. Ahead in the moonlight they could see the twisted metal remains of the bridge their train had been scheduled to cross.

"Now what?" said Joe, peering down into the deep gorge. "It would take us 30 hours in broad daylight to hike down and up this chasm, and we'd never be able to swim that roaring river at the bottom anyway."

"Fortunately, the moon is bright," said Nancy, "and having been raised in a circus, we are expert tightrope walkers. We will walk across the surviving bridge."

35 "Without a net?"

"Naturally," said Nancy. "Take off your shoes. We'll do it sock-footed."

Joe wasn't exactly afraid, but he was a better pickpocket than acrobat. Still, by humming a cheery tune and never, ever once looking down through the gaps between the ties into the abyss or to the side at the mangled wreckage of the destroyed bridge, he managed to follow his sister across the treacherous rail.

"Well," said Joe, "that wasn't so bad. Now all we have to do is follow the clues and rescue our parents."

"Look at the birthday card again," said Nancy. "See if it gives us any clue to begin with."

"I left it on the train!" cried Joe. "I've lost our only clue!"

"Perhaps I can help, dearies." Coming toward them out of the night shadows was a sight so frightening it was almost enough to make them turn and race back across the ominous gorge.

"Boppo!" they exclaimed in unison.

11. It can be inferred that Nancy and Joe are:

A. pleased to see Boppo.
B. not acquainted with Boppo.
C. afraid of Boppo.
D. long-time friends of Boppo.

12. It can be inferred that Boppo:

F. was not aware that the bridge would be destroyed.
G. intended for the train to wreck at the bridge.
H. had worked for many years in and around circuses.
J. tried to prevent the train from crashing at the bridge.

13. It can be inferred that the time of day in the story is:

A. early morning.
B. midday.
C. late afternoon.
D. late night.

14. It can be inferred from Nancy and Joe's reactions as they look through the curtains of their berths that they:

F. are expecting Boppo.
G. recognize Boppo's voice.
H. have been sleeping.
J. have been eating.

15. It can be inferred that Nancy and Joe are:

A. sister and brother.
B. married to each other.
C. orphans.
D. unrelated friends.

UNIT 7 | IMPLIED IDEAS AND CONCLUSIONS • 413

16. It can be inferred that Boppo crossed the bridge:

   F. before it was demolished by the explosion.
   G. before the train made the emergency stop.
   H. after the train crossed the bridge.
   J. before Nancy and Joe crossed the bridge.

17. It can be inferred that Joe and Nancy take off their shoes before crossing the bridge in order to:

   A. avoid getting their shoes dirty.
   B. sneak up quietly on Boppo.
   C. be more sure-footed as they cross.
   D. keep from leaving shoe prints.

18. It can be inferred that Joe:

   F. is a convicted criminal.
   G. dislikes riding on trains.
   H. does not like heights.
   J. is a relative of Boppo's.

19. It can be inferred that Nancy believes that Boppo:

   A. has been driving the train.
   B. could murder someone.
   C. knows where the clue is hidden.
   D. owns a traveling circus.

20. Which of the following best describes Nancy and Joe?

   F. They are honest people who understand that circumstances may require them to do things they would prefer not to do.
   G. They are impractical people who are not able to make good decisions when they are in an emergency situation.
   H. They are immature people who are likely to make decisions without thinking through the consequences of their choices.
   J. They are insincere people who lie to other people in order to get others to give them things or to do things for them.

Summary

- Read between the lines to draw conclusions about the people or events in a text.
- Be careful not to draw a conclusion that is not supported by the text.

EXERCISE

DIRECTIONS: This exercise consists of passages followed by questions. Read each passage and answer the questions based upon what is stated or implied in the passage. Answers are on page 754.

Passage 1

Sylvia sat in the sunshine with an expression on her face half mirthful, half melancholy, as she looked backward to the girlhood just ended, and forward to the womanhood just beginning, for on that midsummer day, she was eighteen. Voices roused her from her reverie, and, looking up, she saw her brother approaching with
5   two friends, their neighbor Geoffrey Moor and his guest Adam Warwick. Her first impulse was to throw down her work and run to meet them, her second to remember her new dignity and sit still, awaiting them.

They rowed briskly across the bay, and Sylvia met them with a look that gave a heartier welcome than her words. She greeted the neighbor cordially, the stranger
10   courteously, and began to gather up her work when they seated themselves in the bamboo chairs.

"You need not disturb yourself," said Mark. "Can you tell me where my knapsack is?"

"Are you going away again so soon, Mark?"

15   "Only a two days' trip up the river with these mates of mine. No, Sylvia, it can't be done."

"I didn't say anything."

"Not in words, but you looked a 'Can't I go?' and I answered it. You even hate picnics, and this trip will be a long and rough one."

20   "I'd like to go as a birthday present. We used to have such happy times together before we were grown up. I don't like to be so separated now. But if it is not best, I'm sorry that I even looked a wish."

Sylvia tried to keep the disappointment out of her voice as she spoke, but there was an unconscious reproach in her last words, a mute appeal in the wistful eyes
25   that looked across the glittering bay to the green hills beyond. Mark was both fond and proud of his younger sister, who, while he was studying art abroad, had studied nature at home. He remembered her devotion to him, his late neglect of her, and longed to make atonement. With elevated eyebrows and inquiring glances, he turned from one friend to another.

UNIT 7 | IMPLIED IDEAS AND CONCLUSIONS • 415

30   Moor nodded and smiled, Warwick nodded and sighed privately, and having taken the sense of the group by a vote, Mark suddenly announced, "You can go if you like, Sylvia."

     "What!" cried his sister, starting up with a characteristic enthusiasm that sent her basket tumbling down the steps, and covered her dozing cat with the shawl that
35 she'd been wearing.

1. It can be reasonably inferred that Sylvia regards her older brother with:

    A. resentment.
    B. affection.
    C. reverence.
    D. jealousy.

2. It can most reasonably be inferred that Mark agrees that his younger sister can go on the trip because:

    F. he needs her special knowledge about nature.
    G. he has not paid enough attention to her recently.
    H. his friends asked that she be allowed to come.
    J. Sylvia is not able to stay alone at home.

3. It can be inferred that Sylvia's reaction to the invitation to go on the trip is:

    A. indifference.
    B. annoyance.
    C. excitement.
    D. uncertainty.

4. It can be inferred that Sylvia thinks that, as a young woman, she should:

    F. no longer listen to her brother's opinions.
    G. not make requests of her older brother.
    H. keep the home while her brother travels.
    J. exercise greater control over her emotions.

5. It can be inferred that Mark silently consults his friends in order to:

    A. determine whether they are aware that it is Sylvia's eighteenth birthday.
    B. ask whether either of them has recently seen his missing knapsack.
    C. determine whether they would object to Sylvia's presence on the trip.
    D. propose that they sit with Sylvia while she continues to do her work.

Passage 2

Mr. Pontellier lit a cigar and began to smoke, letting the paper drag idly from his hand. He fixed his gaze upon a white sunshade that was advancing at a snail's pace from the beach. The gulf looked far away, melting hazily into the blue of the horizon. The sunshade continued to approach slowly. Beneath its shelter were his
5   wife, Mrs. Pontellier, and young Robert Lebrun. When they reached the cottage, the two seated themselves with some appearance of fatigue upon the step of the porch, each leaning against a post.

"What folly to swim at such an hour in such heat!" exclaimed Mr. Pontellier. He himself had taken a dip at daylight. "You are sunburned."

10 His wife held up her hands and surveyed them critically. Looking at them reminded her of her rings, which she had given to her husband before leaving for the beach. She silently reached out to him, and he, understanding, took the rings from his pocket and dropped them into her open palm. She slipped them upon her fingers, looked at Robert, and began to laugh.

15 "What is it?" asked Mr. Pontellier. It was some nonsense out there in the water, and they both tried to relate it at once. It did not seem half so amusing when told. They realized this, and so did Mr. Pontellier. He yawned and stretched himself. Then he got up, saying he had half a mind to go over to Klein's hotel and play a game of billiards.

20 "Come along, Lebrun," he proposed to Robert, but Robert admitted that he preferred to stay and talk to Mrs. Pontellier.

"Well, send him about his business when he bores you, Edna," instructed her husband as he prepared to leave.

"Here, take the umbrella," she said, holding it out to him. He accepted the
25 sunshade and lifted it over his head as he descended the steps.

"Coming back to dinner?" his wife called after him. He shrugged his shoulders. He felt in his pocket; there was a ten-dollar bill there. Perhaps he would return for the early dinner and perhaps he would not. It all depended on the company he found over at Klein's and the size of the game. He did not say this, but she understood it,
30 laughed, and nodded good-bye.

6. Which of the following conclusions about the relationship between Mrs. Pontellier and her husband can be inferred?

   F. They dislike each other intensely.
   G. They understand each other very well.
   H. They are rarely separated from each other.
   J. They are indifferent to each other's well-being.

7. It can be inferred that Robert:

   A. is younger than Mr. Pontellier.
   B. does not like Mrs. Pontellier.
   C. is a close friend of Mr. Pontellier.
   D. enjoys playing billiards with Mr. Pontellier.

8. It can be inferred that the event that Mrs. Pontellier and Robert tell about:

   F. did not actually occur.
   G. was a secret shared only by the two of them.
   H. involved the umbrella carried by Mrs. Pontellier.
   J. was interesting only to them.

9. Which of the following conclusions can be inferred about Mr. Pontellier?

   A. He prefers to be alone.
   B. He does not like physical activity.
   C. He is an uneducated man.
   D. He enjoys gambling occasionally.

10. It can be inferred that at the time Mr. Pontellier says good-bye to his wife he:

    F. has not yet decided whether to return for the early dinner.
    G. has already determined that he will remain at Klein's past dinner.
    H. plans to go visit friends after he has played billiards.
    J. is going to walk to the beach, take a swim, and sit under the umbrella.

Passage 3

Well, the Fourth of July is over. The people are all gone, and I am tired out. John thought it might do me good to see a little company, so we had mother and Nellie and the children down for a week. It tired me out. Of course, I didn't do a thing. Jennie sees to everything now. But it tired me out all the same.

5 John said if I don't pick up faster, he'll send me to a specialist in the fall. But I don't want to go.

I don't feel as if it is worthwhile to turn my hand over for anything, and I'm getting dreadfully fretful and quarrelsome. I cry at nothing, and I cry most of the time. Of course, I don't when John is here or anybody else, but when I am alone. And
10 I am alone a lot. John is kept in town often with serious cases, and Jennie lets me alone when I want her to. So I walk a little in the garden or down the lovely lane, sit on the porch under the roses, and lie down a great deal in my room.

I'm getting really fond of the room in spite of the yellow wallpaper. Perhaps because of the wallpaper. It occupies my mind.

15 I lie here on this great immovable bed—it is nailed down, I believe—and follow the pattern by the hour. I start at the bottom down in the corner where it has not been touched, and I determine for the thousandth time that I will follow that pointless pattern to some sort of a conclusion. But it makes me tired, so I take a nap.

11. It can be inferred from the passage that the narrator is tired because she:

    A. has been working hard.
    B. was entertaining company.
    C. cares for several children.
    D. is suffering from an illness.

12. It can be inferred that the narrator studies the pattern of the wallpaper because:

    F. she is an artist.
    G. the pattern distracts her.
    H. it contains a secret message.
    J. yellow is her favorite color.

13. What is the narrator's attitude toward the wallpaper?

    A. She has mixed emotions about the wallpaper.
    B. She wants to paint over the wallpaper.
    C. She chose the wallpaper and likes it.
    D. She pays no attention to the wallpaper.

UNIT 7 | IMPLIED IDEAS AND CONCLUSIONS • 419

14. It can be inferred that the narrator believes that she is:

F. recovering rapidly.
G. not really ill.
H. getting worse.
J. likely to die soon.

15. It can be inferred that the narrator's attempts to understand the pattern have been:

A. unsuccessful.
B. half-hearted.
C. frequently interrupted.
D. ridiculed by others.

Passage 4

Calliope Catesby began to drink. At nine the next morning, crisscrossed with cartridge belts, decorated with revolvers, and copiously drunk, he poured into Quicksand's main street. He fired two shots from his forty-five to test his aim. A citizen carrying a bottle of kerosene ran, still grasping the neck of the shattered
5   bottle. The weathercock on Judge Riley's house flapped in the breeze.

Down the street went Calliope, shooting right and left. In his office, Buck Patterson, with his bright "City Marshal" badge on the breast of his blue flannel shirt, gave his posse instructions. "Shoot as soon as you can. Keep behind cover and bring him down. Remember what Calliope shoots at, he hits."

10   The first volley from the posse broke the lock of one of Calliope's guns, cut a neat underbit in his right ear, and exploded a cartridge in his crossbelt, scorching his ribs as it burst. Calliope returned the fire and then made a bold move for the railroad station, reaching it safely. The city marshal started for Calliope's fort, slowly pushing a hand truck loaded with freight before him for protection. Buck, his gun
15   ready, dashed into the station. The members of the posse heard one shot fired inside, and then there was silence.

At length the wounded man opened his eyes. A tall man wearing a badge with "City Marshal" engraved upon it stood over him. A little old woman in black was holding a wet handkerchief against one of his temples. The old woman began to talk.

20   "There now! That bullet jest skeeted along the side of your head and sort of paralyzed ye for a spell. I come in on that train from Alabama to see my son. This is my son, sir."

The old woman looked up at the standing man, her worn face lighting with a proud and wonderful smile. "I ain't seen my son," she continued, "in eight years.
25   That little boy of mine has got to be a officer—a city marshal of a whole town! He didn't say nothin' about it in his letters."

"Yes, yes, you'll be all right," said the old woman. "Son told me about you, sir, while you was layin' senseless on the floor. And you mustn't hold no grudge for havin' to shoot at ye. It's his duty."

30 "Lawsy!" exclaimed the old woman, in a sudden flutter, "I clear forget that trunk of mine!" Away she trotted. Then Calliope Catesby spoke out to Buck Patterson:

"I just couldn't help it, Buck. I seen her through the window. I didn't have the nerve to let her know I was a worthless cuss bein' hunted down. There you was lyin'
35 where my shot laid you, like you was dead. I just took your badge off and fastened it onto myself. I told her I was the marshal and you was a holy terror. You can take your badge back now, Buck."

With shaking fingers Calliope began to unfasten the disc of metal from his shirt.

"Easy there!" said Buck Patterson. "You keep that badge right where it is,
40 Calliope Catesby. Don't you take it off till the day your mother leaves this town."

16. It can be inferred that the old woman believes:

F. Buck Patterson is her son.
G. Calliope Catesby is the city marshal.
H. the man hunted by the posse escaped.
J. Calliope Catesby is not her son.

17. It can be inferred that Buck Patterson tells Calliope to keep his badge because he:

A. no longer wants to be the city marshal of Quicksand.
B. mistakenly believes that Calliope is really the city marshal.
C. does not want the old woman to learn the truth about her son.
D. is afraid that Calliope will attempt a second time to shoot him.

UNIT 7 | IMPLIED IDEAS AND CONCLUSIONS • 421

18. All of the following can be inferred about Calliope Catesby EXCEPT:

F. When he drinks to excess, he becomes violent.
G. He does not want his mother to think badly of him.
H. He is an excellent shot with his firearms.
J. He works at the railroad station as a baggage handler.

19. Which of the following statements is most strongly supported by the passage?

A. Buck Patterson is a strong but compassionate person.
B. Buck Patterson is an impatient and uncaring person.
C. Buck Patterson insists on enforcing the letter of the law.
D. Buck Patterson is not an effective city marshal.

20. It can be inferred that the old woman's attitude toward Calliope Catesby is one of:

F. parental disappointment.
G. superficial curiosity.
H. calculated indifference.
J. motherly pride.

Reading **Craft and Structure**

Unit 8 | **Purpose of Sentences**

INSIDE THIS UNIT:
– The Craft of Writing –   – Exercise –

Non-Negotiable Skill:

Analyze how one or more sentences in passages relate to other parts of the passage when the function of those sentences is explicitly stated or clearly indicated.

The Craft of Writing

According to Wikipedia, a craft is a "pastime or profession that requires some particular kind of skilled work." Thus, we refer to weaving, woodworking, metal-working, cabinetry, and other skilled undertakings as crafts. And it is also not uncommon to hear writing referred to as a craft.

The application of the term "craft" to writing is appropriate. Just as a woodworker builds an object, say a cabinet, an author builds an essay, a novel, or some other written product. The analogy is not perfect, but it is helpful. When you examine a cabinet, you can understand the structure and how the various elements—the legs, the braces, the brackets, and so on—work together. If you are especially knowledgeable about cabinets, you can even identify subtle features such as the types of woods used, the method of joining corners, and the style of the decorative elements.

Writing is similar. When we read, we can assess the author's creation: we notice a clever choice of words, see how the author found the best place for this idea, observe how the author creates a smooth transition between this notion and that one. Good writers think about the structure they are building for the reader. They don't just dump a bunch of sentences together, shake them up, and pull them out at random. A good piece of writing has a structure with pieces that fit together. And good readers can analyze and understand—and even appreciate, admire, and enjoy—the structure.

Example:

[1] Most people think of the North Pole as a remote and isolated place covered by snow and ice. [2] Every day, however, we are directly affected by the North Pole in many important ways. [3] The Arctic cold helps to moderate the global climate. [4] Polar sea ice and snow reflect solar radiation back into space, helping to cool the planet. [5] The magnetosphere created by the North and South magnetic poles shields us from solar radiation. [6] Boreal forests and

permafrost underlying the taiga and tundra are major storehouses of carbon that, if released, could accelerate global warming. [7] In short, life on earth might not exist without the North Pole.

1. The function of sentences 3–6 is to:

   A. illustrate ways in which the North Pole affects us daily.
   B. provide evidence that that the magnetic poles are disappearing.
   C. show that carbon storage causes global warming.
   D. suggest ways that the reader can help to save the planet.

2. Sentence 7 of the passage functions primarily as a(n):

   F. restatement of the first sentence.
   G. overview of a plan to save life on earth.
   H. dramatic conclusion for the paragraph.
   J. warning about the effects of solar radiation.

3. Which of the following best describes the relationship between the first two sentences?

   A. The first sentence describes an inaccurate opinion, and the second sentence corrects that error.
   B. The first sentence reveals a surprising fact, and the second sentence explains its significance.
   C. The first sentence presents the writer's opinion, and the second sentence provides proof of the opinion.
   D. The first sentence describes a scientific point of view, and the second summarizes the unscientific opinion of most people.

Let's examine the structure of the paragraph. The author begins with a statement about the common opinion of the North Pole, and the second sentence contradicts this false opinion. Then the author provides four specific examples of the ways in which the northern region affects our lives:

- Cold moderates climate.
- Ice and snow reflect solar radiation, cooling the planet.
- The magnetosphere protects us.
- Trees and ground store carbon.

The final sentence dramatically underscores the importance of the North Pole: life depends on it.

The correct answer to first question is (A). The sentences mentioned are the examples given in the paragraph.

The correct answer to the second item is (H). The final sentence, which is introduced by "in short," is a conclusion summarizing the importance of the North Pole—and a very dramatic conclusion in fact.

The correct answer to the third item is (A). The author begins by stating that a certain opinion about the North Pole is wrong. We can infer that the author believes that many readers will hold this incorrect belief, namely, that the North Pole is a cold, faraway place that doesn't have much to do with us. The second sentence contradicts this opinion.

Example:

[1] Every day, 32 people die in motor vehicle crashes caused by drunk drivers. [2] This amounts to one death every 45 minutes. [3] One of the most effective tools for reducing drunk driving is the sobriety checkpoint. [4] A sobriety checkpoint is a traffic stop where law enforcement officers systematically select drivers to assess their level of alcohol impairment. [5] Studies show that sobriety checkpoints reduce alcohol-related crashes by about 20 percent. [6] The checkpoints work by increasing the risk of arrest. [7] When drivers think that they are more likely to be arrested, they are less likely to drive while impaired. [8] Unlike some other approaches, checkpoints don't become less effective over time. [9] In fact, they may become more effective because drivers know that a checkpoint is always waiting for them.

4. The author's purpose for including sentence 2 is to:

   F. dramatize the significance of a problem.
   G. provide a specific example of behavior.
   H. announce the topic of the paragraph.
   J. suggest a solution to a problem.

5. Sentence 4 primarily provides the reader with:

   A. statistics
   B. an informal definition
   C. an expert opinion
   D. examples

6. Sentence 6 and 7 are used by the writer to show:

   F. how the checkpoint system reduces drunk driving.
   G. why people sometimes drink excessively before driving.
   H. which drunk drivers are likely to be detected by checkpoints.
   J. when checkpoints should be set up to be most effective.

7. Sentences 8 and 9 are intended to introduce:

   A. a weakness in the check point system.
   B. an advantage of the checkpoint system.
   C. an alternative to checkpoint system.
   D. an improvement to the checkpoint system.

The opening sentence of the paragraph identifies the topic, and the second sentence dramatically emphasizes the significance of the problem identified: one death every 45 minutes, day in and day out. Thus, the answer to the fourth item is (F).

The third sentence introduces the reader to the checkpoint system. And the fourth sentence describes how the system works. Thus, the correct answer to the fifth item is (B).

The fifth sentence states in simple terms the result of implementing the system, and the sixth and seventh sentences explain how the system works:

drivers are afraid they will be arrested, so they stay sober. Thus, the correct answer to the sixth item is (F).

The eighth and ninth sentences explain that the checkpoint system doesn't lose effectiveness over time. Drivers know that a checkpoint is waiting, so the deterrence value is reinforced. Thus, the correct answer to the seventh item is (B).

Example:

[1]

[1] The Red Death had long devastated the country. [2] No plague before had been so hideous. [3] Blood was its Avatar and its seal. [4] There were sharp pains and sudden dizziness and then profuse bleedings at the pores. [5] The scarlet stains upon the body and especially upon the face of the victims were the pest-ban that shut the victims out from the comfort of fellow humans. [6] And the whole seizure, progress, and termination of the disease lasted only half an hour.

[2]

[1] But Prince Prospero was happy. [2] While his dominions were half-depopulated, he summoned a thousand friends from the knights and dames of his court, and with these retreated to the deep seclusion of his castle. [3] A strong and lofty wall girdled it. [4] The wall had gates of iron. [5] The guests, having entered, brought furnace and massive hammers and welded the bolts, locking out the rest of the world.

[3]

[1] The castle was amply provisioned, and the prince provided all pleasures. [2] There were buffoons, improvisations, ballet dancers, and musicians. [3] There were cards and wine. [4] Plus, there was security within.

[4]

It was towards the close of the fifth or sixth months of seclusion, while the pestilence raged most furious outside, that Prince Prospero entertained his thousand friends at a masked ball of the most unusual magnitude. The revel went whirling on, until at length was sounded the twelfth hour upon the clock. Then the music ceased, and the evolutions of the waltzers were quieted. Now there were twelve strokes to be sounded by the bell of the clock.

[5]

Before the last echoes of the last chime had sunk into silence, many revelers became aware of a masked figure. The figure was tall and gaunt and shrouded from heat to foot. The mask was made to resemble the countenance of a stiffened corpse. And the mummer had gone so far as to assume the type of the Red Death. His vesture was dabbled in blood, and his face sprinkled with the scarlet horror.

[6]

[1] When the eyes of Prince Prospero fell on this spectral image, he was convulsed with a strong shudder of terror. [2] Then his brow reddened with rage, and he demanded "Who dares to make a mockery of our woes?"

[7]

The figure passed unimpeded and by measured step from the room. Prince Prospero, maddening with rage, rushed after and bore aloft a dagger and approached to within three or four feet of the retreating figure, who turned to confront his pursuer. There was a sharp cry, and the dagger fell upon the carpet upon which instantly afterwards fell Prince Prospero, prostrate in death, the Red Death.

[8]

Other revelers grasped the vestures and tore off the mask of the figure only to find the robes empty of any tangible form. And now was acknowledged the presence of the Red Death. He had come like a thief in the night. One by one he dropped the revelers in the blood-bedewed halls of the revel, and each died in the despairing posture of his fall.

[9]

The life of the ebony clock went out, and the torch flames expired. And Darkness and Decay and the Red Death held illimitable dominion over all.

8. Paragraph 1, sentences 3, 4, and 5 describe:

    F. typical conditions in the castle.
    G. life outside of the castle before the plague.
    H. the appearance of the masked stranger.
    J. the symptoms of the plague.

9. The author uses the ideas in paragraph 3 to create:

   A. tension between Prince Prospero and his invited guests.
   B. a contrast between life inside the castle and outside of it.
   C. a parallel between routine conditions inside the castle and the masked ball.
   D. the sense that something bad is about to befall the residents of the castle.

10. Prince Prospero's question in paragraph 6, sentence 2 is ironic because:

    F. the stranger is actually death.
    G. the people outside the castle have woes.
    H. only Prince Prospero is not a guest.
    J. the party ended at midnight.

And now we look at the structure of the story. The author begins by describing a plague, and sentences 3–5 detail the symptoms of the disease. So the correct answer to the eighth item is (J).

Then the author recounts how the Prince and his invited guests shut themselves up in the castle to protect themselves from the plague. The third paragraph describes the comfortable conditions inside, so the correct answer to the ninth item is (B).

In the fourth paragraph, the author describes a magnificent party, a masked ball or what we might call a costume party. Suddenly, in paragraph five, the plot takes a distinct turn: one guest has had the poor taste to come costumed as the plague. In paragraph six, the Prince challenges the guest with a question laden with irony: How dare you mock our woes? Of course, the Prince and his guests inside the castle don't really have any woes (at least not yet) as they have locked themselves away from the rest of the world and the plague. So the correct answer to the final item is (G).

And from there to the end, the plot thickens. It turns out that the masked guest is really Death in the form of the scarlet plague. The plague has infiltrated the castle's defense and kills the Prince and all of the guests.

Summary

- Writing is a craft requiring skilled work.
- Good writing requires good structure.

EXERCISE

> **DIRECTIONS:** This exercise consists of passages followed by questions. Read each passage and answer the questions based upon what is stated or implied in the passage. Answers are on page 754.

Passage 1

[1] When a vaccine enters the body, the immune system responds the same way it would to any germ. [2] The vaccine is easier to fight than the illness you're being vaccinated against, and it won't make you sick while your immune system fights it. [3] Once the immune system figures out how to fight and defeat the antigens, it remembers what works against them. [4] Should such an enemy enter your body again, your body will move to attack it before it has a chance to implement its plans to make you sick. [5] Sometimes, your immune system needs a refresher course, which is why you get booster doses of some vaccines. [6] Some antigens are especially tricky and change over time, like flu viruses. [7] That's why people need to get flu shots every year to make sure they're ready to take on the latest version.

1. The function of sentence 4 in the context of the passage is to provide:

   A. an introduction to the later discussion of booster vaccinations.
   B. an example of disease for which there is no effective vaccine.
   C. a transition between the discussion of ineffective and effective vaccines.
   D. the conclusion of the explanation of how a vaccination usually works.

2. The purpose of sentence 5 in the context of the passage is to:

   F. explain how the body's immune system can weaken as a person ages.
   G. introduce the idea that some vaccines lose their effectiveness.
   H. summarize the discussion of how vaccines normally protect the body.
   J. provide specific examples of vaccines that require boosters.

Passage 2

[1] Three-fourths of the world's flowering plants and about 35 percent of the world's food crops depend on animal pollinators to reproduce. [2] Put another way, one out of every three bites of food we eat exists because of animal pollinators. [3] These include bees, butterflies, moths, beetles, and other insects. [4] Pollinators visit flowers in their search for food (nectar and pollen). [5] During a flower visit, a pollinator may accidentally brush against the flower's reproductive parts, unknowingly depositing pollen from a different flower. [6] The plant then uses the pollen to produce a fruit or seed. [7] Many plants cannot reproduce without pollen carried to them by foraging pollinators.

3. The purpose of sentence 2 is to:

A. propose a system for addressing world hunger.
B. explain how plants reproduce by distributing pollinated seeds.
C. help the reader understand the importance of insect pollinators.
D. describe different methods of plant pollination.

4. The function of sentence 3 is to:

F. explain in detail the process of plant pollination.
G. provide examples of insects that pollinate plants.
H. list various plants that require insect pollination.
J. describe the mechanical process by which pollination occurs.

Passage 3

[1] If you like recreational activities that involve wheels on concrete, asphalt, or dirt, such as skateboarding or biking, then protect your brain by wearing a helmet. [2] Your helmet should sit flat on your head—make sure it is level and is not tilted backward or forward. [3] The front of the helmet should sit low—about two finger widths above your eyebrows to protect your forehead. [4] The straps on each side of your head should form a "Y" over your ears, with one part of the strap in front of your ear and one behind, just below your earlobes. [5] If the helmet leans forward, adjust the rear straps. If it tilts backward, tighten the front straps. [6] Buckle the chinstrap securely at your throat so that the helmet feels snug on your head and does not move up and down or from side to side.

5. Sentence 1 primarily:

  A. lists many activities for which a protective helmet should be worn.
  B. details the risk of head injuries entailed in engaging in certain activities.
  C. explains the importance of wearing properly fitting headgear.
  D. provides examples of the dangers posed by certain recreational activities.

6. Sentences 2–6 of the passage:

  F. explain the dangers of riding a bicycle without protective headgear.
  G. describe the series of steps to be followed in putting on a bicycle helmet.
  H. discuss the advantages of wearing protective headgear for various activities.
  J. try to persuade the reader that a helmet should be worn for certain activities.

Passage 4

Jarndyce versus Jarndyce drones on. This scarecrow of a suit has, in course of time, become so complicated that no man alive knows what it means. There are not three Jarndyces left upon the earth, but Jarndyce versus Jarndyce still drags its dreary length before the court, perennially hopeless.

Jarndyce versus Jarndyce has become a joke. That is the only good that has ever come of it. The last Lord Chancellor handled it neatly, when, correcting Mr. Blowers, who said that a certain thing might happen "when the sky rains potatoes," he observed, "or when we get through Jarndyce versus Jarndyce, Mr. Blowers."

At the heart of the fog sits the Lord High Chancellor in his High Court of Chancery.

"Mr. Tangle," says the Lord High Chancellor.

"Mlud,"* says Mr. Tangle. Mr. Tangle knows more of Jarndyce and Jarndyce than anybody. He is famous for it—supposed never to have worked on anything else since he left law school.

"Have you nearly concluded your argument?"

"Mlud, no—variety of points—feel it my duty tsubmit—ludship," is the reply that slides out of Mr. Tangle.

"Several members of the bar are still to be heard, I believe?" says the Chancellor with a slight smile.

Eighteen of Mr. Tangle's learned friends, each armed with a little summary of eighteen hundred sheets, bob up like eighteen hammers in a piano, make eighteen bows, and drop into their eighteen places of obscurity.

"We will proceed with the hearing on Wednesday," says the Chancellor. For the question at issue is only a question of costs, a mere bud on the forest tree of the parent suit, and really will come to a settlement one of these days.

"In reference," proceeds the Chancellor, still on Jarndyce versus Jarndyce, "to the young girl—"

"Begludship's pardon—boy," says Mr. Tangle prematurely. "In reference," proceeds the Chancellor with extra distinctness, "to the young girl and boy, the two young people"—Mr. Tangle crushed—"whom I directed to be in attendance today and who are now in my private room, I will see them and satisfy myself as to the expediency of making the order for their residing with their uncle."

Mr. Tangle on his legs again. "Begludship's pardon—dead."

"With their"—Chancellor looking through his double eye-glass at the papers on his desk—"grandfather."

"Begludship's pardon—victim of rash action—brains."

Suddenly a very diminutive lawyer with a terrific bass voice arises, fully inflated, in the back settlements of the fog, and says, "Will your lordship allow me? I appear for a family member. He is a cousin, several times removed. I am not at the moment prepared to inform the court in what exact remove he is a cousin, but he IS a cousin."

But the Chancellor has dexterously vanished. Everybody else quickly vanishes too. A battery of blue bags is loaded with papers and carried off by clerks; the empty court is locked up. If all the injustice it has committed and all the misery it has caused could only be locked up with it, and the whole burnt away in a great funeral pyre—why so much the better for the parties in Jarndyce versus Jarndyce!

*"My Lord," addressing the judge.

Adapted from *Bleak House* (1852) by Charles Dickens

7. The exchange between Mr. Tangle and the Lord High Chancellor is a(n):

   A. lengthy debate over an important point of law.
   B. example of the many insignificant details of the case.
   C. illustration of the jokes inspired by the case.
   D. heated argument over the final verdict in the case.

8. The statement by the diminutive lawyer that he does not know "in what exact remove" his client is a cousin (line 40) helps to emphasize that:

   F. the lawyer is intimately familiar with the details of the case.
   G. the cousin is only remotely connected with the case.
   H. the Chancellor is anxious to resolve the issue presented.
   J. other lawyers in the courtroom are still waiting to speak.

9. The description of the eighteen lawyers in line 20 helps to reinforce the point that:

   A. even Mr. Tangle can on occasion be mistaken about details of the case.
   B. none of the eighteen lawyers has new information this is very important.
   C. the children in the judge's private room are important to the case.
   D. the outcome of the case will depend on the arguments of the eighteen lawyers.

10. The mentions of the dead uncle (lines 32–33), the incapacitated grandfather (lines 35–36), and the distant cousin (lines 39–40) are intended by the author to show:

    F. how complicated the case of Jarndyce versus Jarndyce has become.
    G. the careful treatment of minors given by the court.
    H. the court's familiarity with the details of the Jarndyce case.
    J. a typical example of good lawyerly trial tactics.

Passage 5

[1] One of the toughest and most nerve-racking things for new moms is figuring out when to call the doctor. [2] If a parent suspects something is not right, she should always call the doctor. [3] Even small changes in eating, sleeping, and crying can be signs of serious problems for newborns. [4] Parents should call immediately if their baby has trouble breathing or is running a temperature above 100.4°F or below 97.8°F. [5] Parents should monitor their baby carefully if the baby doesn't want to eat, vomits, or has diarrhea. [6] Parents should call if these symptoms do not disappear in a day or so. [7] And as a general rule of thumb, moms and dads should trust their instincts. [8] If a baby is crying more than usual, something serious may be wrong. [9] In general, parents should call because it's better to be safe than sorry.

11. The purpose of Sentence 1 is to:

    A. anticipate an answer to a question raised later in the passage.
    B. pose a problem that the rest of the passage will help to solve.
    C. hint at a possible solution to a puzzle the author will discuss.
    D. reassure the reader that medical problems rarely occur.

12. Sentence 4 describes symptoms that:

    F. can safely be ignored.
    G. rarely require a doctor's attention.
    H. could develop into a more serious condition.
    J. require immediate medical attention.

Passage 6

[1] Bioenergy is made from biomass. [2] Biomass comes from plants. [3] Plants use sunlight to turn water and carbon dioxide into sugar by a process called photosynthesis. [4] Some plants, like sugar cane and sugar beets, store energy as simple sugars. [5] These plants are mostly used for food. Other plants store energy as starch. [6] These plants include grains like corn and are also used for food. [7] A third type of plant is specifically used for bioethanol. [8] This includes energy crops like fast-growing trees and grasses. [9] Biomass also includes leftover material such as the stalks, leaves, and husks of corn plants and other organic waste that began as plants. [10] So, bioenergy is not only renewable, it is also sustainable.

13. The author mentions sugar cane and sugar beets as examples of plants that:

    A. are fast-growing and are usually used to make bioethanol.
    B. store energy as simple sugars and are usually used for food.
    C. store energy as simple sugars and are used for bioethanol.
    D. store energy as starch and are usually used for food.

14. Sentence 10 primarily provides:

    F. a conclusion for the passage.
    G. a question that is remains to be answered.
    H. an exception to a general rule.
    J. a point that contradicts the author's position.

Passage 7

[1] Many people wonder why hunting migratory waterfowl is permitted in wildlife refuges. [2] After all, the purpose of the refuge is to provide a safe habitat for the birds. [3] Here are some of the reasons why hunting is allowed. [4] Hunting is a traditional American recreational activity. [5] The taxes on hunting equipment and the fees for hunting licenses raise money to manage wildlife refuges. [6] Duck stamps, for example, are required for hunting waterfowl. [7] Duck stamps have raised $650 million that was used to buy 5 million acres of habitat for waterfowl. [8] This habitat is now a part of the National Wildlife Refuge System. [9] Also, hunting helps to control the size of flocks. [10] This ensures that the bird population remains robust and healthy. [11] So, there is nothing inconsistent with allowing hunting in an area that is set aside to help waterfowl survive.

15. The purpose of sentences 1 and 2 is to:

A. point out a seeming inconsistency.
B. refute a commonly held opinion.
C. provide an extended definition.
D. introduce an interest story.

16. The purpose of sentences 3–10 is to:

F. resolve the apparent contradiction set forth at the beginning of the passage.
G. invite the reader to form a response to a question raised earlier.
H. show that the difficulty noted earlier is more serious than common thought.
J. introduce a note of humor into an otherwise serious discussion.

Passage 8

[1]

A cloudy day: what is that like in a town of iron-works? The sky sinks down before dawn, muddy, flat, immovable. The air is thick, clammy with the breath of crowded human beings. It stifles me. I open the window, and, looking out, can scarcely see through the rain the grocer's shop opposite, where a drunken crowd
5   are puffing cheap tobacco in their pipes. I can detect the scent through all the foul smells ranging loose in the air.

[2]

The idiosyncrasy of this town is smoke from the mills. It rolls sullenly in slow folds from the great chimneys of the iron-foundries, and settles down in black, slimy pools on the muddy streets. Smoke on the wharves, smoke on the dingy boats, on
10   the yellow river, clinging in a coating of greasy soot to the house-front, the two faded poplars, the faces of the passers-by. The long train of mules, dragging masses of pig-iron through the narrow street, have a foul vapor hanging to their reeking sides. Here, inside, is a little broken figure of an angel pointing upward from the mantel-shelf; but even its wings are covered with smoke, clotted and black. Smoke
15   everywhere! A dirty canary chirps desolately in a cage beside me. Its dream of green fields and sunshine is a very old dream—almost worn out, I think.

[3]

I will only tell my story. It will, perhaps, seem to you as foul and dark as this thick vapor about us, and as pregnant with death; but if your eyes are free as mine are to look deeper, no perfume-tinted dawn will be so fair with promise of the day
20   that shall surely come.

Adapted from "Life in the Iron-Mills" (1861) by Rebecca Harding Davis

17. The question that the author raises in the opening sentence of the passage is:

    A. answered in the first paragraph.
    B. answered in the second paragraph.
    C. answered in the third paragraph.
    D. not answered in the passage.

18. The figure of the angel on the mantel-shelf in paragraph two is mentioned by the author as a(n):

    F. product of the factory operating in the mill town.
    G. example of the effects of the smoke from the iron mills.
    H. feature of a cloudy day in the iron mill town.
    J. key to the story the author will tell.

19. In the final paragraph, the "thick vapor" refers to the:

    A. clouds mentioned in paragraph one.
    B. pipe smoke mentioned in paragraph one.
    C. angel mentioned in paragraph two.
    D. smoke from the mills mentioned in paragraph two.

20. The "perfume-tinted dawn" of the final sentence of the passage is intended by the author to:

    F. contrast with the disagreeable odors and darkness of the mill town.
    G. refer to the starry evening that follows a cloudless day.
    H. describe the conditions of the interior of the homes of the mill workers.
    J. reinforce the idea that the lives of the mill workers will never improve.

Reading **Craft and Structure**

Unit 9 | **Practice**

INSIDE THIS UNIT:
– Exercise –

EXERCISE

DIRECTIONS: This exercise consists of passages followed by questions. Read each passage and answer the questions based upon what is stated or implied in the passage. Answers are on page 754.

Passage 1

She had intended to take the Elevated train, and naturally she looked in her purse to make certain she had the fare, and was pleased to find forty cents in the coin envelope. She was going to pay her own fare, even if Camilo did have the habit of seeing her up the steps and dropping a nickel in the machine before he gave the
5   turnstile a little push and sent her through it with a bow. Camilo, by a series of compromises, had managed to make effective a fairly complete set of smaller courtesies, ignoring the larger and more troublesome ones. She had walked with him to the station in a pouring rain, because she knew he was almost as poor as she was, and when he insisted on a taxi, she was firm and said, "You know it simply will
10 not do." He was wearing a new hat of a pretty biscuit shade, for it never occurred to him to buy anything of a practical color; he had put it on for the first time and the rain was spoiling it. She kept thinking, "But this is dreadful, where will he get another?" She compared it with Eddie's hats that always seemed to be precisely seven years old and as if they had been quite purposely left out in the rain, and yet
15 they sat with a careless and incidental rightness on Eddie. But Camilo was far different; if he wore a shabby hat it would be merely shabby on him, and he would lose his spirits over it. If she had not feared Camilo would take it badly, for he insisted on the practice of his little ceremonies up to the point he had fixed for them, she would have said to him as they left Thora's house, "Do go home. I can surely
20 reach the station by myself."

"It is written that we must be rained upon tonight," said Camilo, "so let it be together."

At the foot of the platform stairway she said, "At least, Camilo, do not climb these stairs, since for you it is only a matter of coming down again at once."

25 He made three quick bows, he was Spanish, and leaped off through the rainy darkness. She stood watching him, for he was a very graceful young man, thinking that tomorrow morning he would gaze soberly at his spoiled hat and soggy shoes and possibly associate her with his misery. As she watched, he stopped at the far corner and took off his hat and hid it under his overcoat.

1. It can be inferred that the narrator:

    A. is a wealthy woman.
    B. has more money than Camilo.
    C. does not have a lot of money.
    D. does not have the fare for the train.

2. It can be inferred from the passage that Camilo:

    F. is not aware that it is raining.
    G. does not like the color of his hat.
    H. realizes that the rain will ruin his hat.
    J. is wearing a hat to keep his head dry.

3. It can be inferred from the passage that the narrator and Camilo have come from:

    A. a ride on the Elevated train.
    B. an evening at Thora's home.
    C. traveling abroad in Spain.
    D. a trip to the clothing store.

4. It can be inferred that Camilo's behavior toward the narrator is:

    F. courteous and gallant.
    G. rude and insulting.
    H. calloused and uncaring.
    J. insincere and mocking.

5. It can be inferred that Camilo and the narrator:

    A. share an apartment.
    B. live in the same building.
    C. live together with Thora.
    D. live in different neighborhoods.

Passage 2

There was a full moon that night. About nine o'clock Louisa strolled down the road a little way and sat on a low stone wall near the road. She was just thinking of rising, when she heard footsteps and low voices, and remained quiet. Just before they reached her, the voices and footsteps ceased. She realized that their owners had found seats on a stone wall. She was wondering if she could not steal away unobserved, when a voice broke the stillness. It was Joe Dagget's. She sat still and listened.

The voice was announced by a loud sigh, which was as familiar as itself. "Well," said Dagget, "you've made up your mind, then, I suppose?"

"Yes," returned another voice; "I'm going day after tomorrow."

"That's Lily Dyer," thought Louisa to herself. The voice embodied itself in her mind. She saw a girl tall and full-figured, with a firm, fair face, looking fairer and firmer in the moonlight, her strong yellow hair braided in a close knot. Lily Dyer was a favorite with the village folk; she had just the qualities to arouse admiration.

"Well," said Joe Dagget, "I ain't got a word to say."

"I don't know what you could say," returned Lily Dyer.

"Not a word to say," repeated Joe, drawing out the words heavily. Then there was silence. "I ain't sorry," he began at last, "that that happened yesterday—that we kind of let on how we felt to each other. I guess it's just as well we knew. Of course, I can't do anything different. I'm going right on an' get married next week. I ain't going back on a woman that's waited for me fourteen years, an' break her heart."

"If you should jilt her tomorrow, I wouldn't have you," spoke up the girl with sudden vehemence.

"Well, I ain't going to give you the chance," said he, "but I don't believe you would, either."

Lily spoke again—the voice sounded as if she had risen. "This must be put to a stop," said she. "We've stayed here long enough. I'm going home."

Louisa sat there in a daze. After a while she got up and went home. The next day she did her housework methodically, but she did not sew on her wedding dress. In the evening Joe came.

She never mentioned Lily Dyer. She simply said while she had no cause of complaint against him, she had lived so long in one way that she could not make a change. Louisa, all alone by herself that night, wept a little. She hardly knew why. The next morning, on waking, she felt like a queen who, after fearing her domain would be taken from her, sees it firmly in her own possession.

6. It can be inferred that the woman Joe Dagget refers to in his conversation with Lily Dyer is:

   F. Louisa.
   G. Lily herself.
   H. an unnamed person of the village.
   J. Joe's wife of fourteen years.

7. Which of the following best describes Louisa's feelings about her broken engagement?

   A. She is distraught over having learned that her fiancé is going to marry someone else.
   B. She is relieved that she will be able to continue to live her life as she has.
   C. She is hopeful that Joe will change his mind and proceed with the wedding as they had planned.
   D. She is planning to take revenge on the woman who broke up her engagement to Joe.

8. It can be inferred that Joe and Lily:

   F. have been deeply in love with one another for a long time.
   G. have recently learned of their affection for each other.
   H. are planning to get divorced so that Joe can remarry.
   J. have only met within the past day or two.

9. It can be inferred that Joe and Lily:

   A. are aware that Louisa is nearby and are talking softly to avoid being heard.
   B. are not aware that anyone is nearby and listening to their private conversation.
   C. have invited Louisa to meet them at the stone wall and are waiting for her to arrive.
   D. are concerned that Louisa has not arrived and are worried about her safety in the dark.

10. It can be inferred that Joe believes that if he asked Lily to marry him, Lily would:

    F. accept his proposal.
    G. refuse to marry him.
    H. seek Louisa's approval.
    J. tell the townspeople

Passage 3

Old Man Anderson lived seven or eight miles out in the country from Eatonville. He raised feed corn and cassava, and went to market with it two or three times a year. He bought all of his food wholesale so he wouldn't have to come to town for several months more.

5   He was different from city-bred folks. He had never seen a train. Everybody laughed at him, for even the smallest child in Eatonville had either been to Maitland or Orlando and had watched a train go by. On Sunday afternoons all of the young people of the village would go over to Maitland, a mile away, to see Number 35 whizz southward on its way to Tampa and to wave at the passengers. So we looked
10   down on him a little. Even we children felt superior in the presence of a person so lacking in worldly knowledge.

    The grown-ups kept telling him he ought to go see a train. He always said he didn't have time to wait so long. Only two trains a day passed through Maitland. But patronage and ridicule finally had its effect and Old Man Anderson drove in one
15   morning early. Number 78 went north to Jacksonville at 10:20. He drove his light wagon over in the woods behind the railroad below Maitland, and sat down to wait. He began to fear that his horse would get frightened and run away with the wagon. So he took him out and led him deeper into the grove and tied him securely. Then he returned to his wagon and waited some more. Then he remembered that some of
20   the train-wise villagers had said the engine belched fire and smoke. He had better move his wagon out of danger. It might catch fire. He climbed down from the seat and placed himself between the shafts to draw it away. Just then 78 came thundering over the trestle spouting smoke, and suddenly began blowing for Maitland. Old Man Anderson became so frightened he ran away with the wagon
25   through the woods and tore it up worse than the horse ever could have done. He doesn't know still what a train looks like, and says he doesn't care.

11. It can be inferred that at the time of the story the narrator was a:

    A. railroad worker.
    B. train passenger.
    C. storekeeper.
    D. child.

12. It can be inferred that the narrator lived in:

    F. Orlando.
    G. Maitland.
    H. Eatonville.
    J. Tampa.

13. It can be inferred from the passage that the narrator's attitude toward Mr. Anderson was one of:

    A. curiosity and amusement.
    B. admiration and fear.
    C. concern and caring.
    D. mistrust and dislike.

14. It can be inferred from the narrative that after the incident Mr. Anderson:

    F. planned to return to Maitland frequently to watch trains.
    G. had no intention of going back to Maitland to see a train.
    H. hoped that the railroad would build a track near his farm.
    J. sold his farm and moved to the nearby town.

15. It can be inferred from the passage that Mr. Anderson was:

    A. sophisticated.
    B. naïve.
    C. ill-mannered.
    D. well educated.

Passage 4

[1]

Miss Morstan entered the room with a firm step and an outward composure of manner. "I have come to you, Mr. Holmes," she said, "because you once enabled my employer to unravel a little domestic complication."

[2]

5 Holmes leaned forward in his chair with an expression of extraordinary concentration. "State your case," said he, in brisk, business tones.

[3]

I felt that my position was an embarrassing one. "You will, I am sure, excuse me," I said, rising from my chair. To my surprise, the young lady held up her gloved hand to detain me. "If your friend," she said, "would be good enough to stay, he might be of inestimable service to me." I sat back down in my chair.

[4]

10 "Briefly," she said, "the facts are these. My father, a widower, was an officer in an Indian regiment who sent me home to England when I was a small child. I was placed in a comfortable boarding establishment at Edinburgh, and there I remained until I was seventeen years of age. In the year 1878 my father obtained leave and came home. He telegraphed to me from London that he had arrived safely, and directed me to come
15 down at once, giving the Langham Hotel as his address. On reaching London I drove to the Langham, and was informed that Captain Morstan was staying there, but that he had gone out the night before and had not yet returned. I waited all day without news of him. That night, on the advice of the manager of the hotel, I communicated with the police, and next morning we advertised in all the papers. From that day to this no word has ever
20 been heard of my unfortunate father.

[5]

"The date?" asked Holmes, opening his notebook.

[6]

"He disappeared upon the 3rd of December, 1878, nearly ten years ago."

[7]

"His luggage?"

[8]

"Remained at the hotel. There was nothing in it to suggest a clue."

[9]

25 "Had he any friends in town?"

[10]

"Only one that we know of, Major Sholto, of his own regiment."

[11]

"A singular case," remarked Holmes.

16. The exchange described in Paragraph 3:

   F. provides the reader with information not available to the characters.

   G. ensures that the narrator is present to give the account that follows.

   H. reveals to the reader the clue that will enable Holmes to solve the case.

   J. shares with the reader the inner thoughts of Holmes.

17. The remarks of Miss Marston in lines 10 through 26 provide details:

   A. known to the narrator but not known to the reader.

   B. not known to Holmes but already known by the narrator.

   C. known by Holmes and Miss Marston but not by the reader.

   D. not yet known to Holmes and the narrator nor to the reader.

18. Holmes' characterization of the case as "singular" signals to the reader the story will:

   F. end abruptly.

   G. continue.

   H. be interrupted.

   J. be uninteresting.

19. What is the significance of the phrase "opening his notebook?"

   A. It introduces a theory about the mystery for the benefit of the reader.

   B. It allows Holmes to elicit details of the mystery.

   C. It provides a reason for the narrator to summarize information known to the characters but not the reader.

   D. It permits the author to foreshadow the ultimate outcome of the mystery.

Passage 5

    Yesterday, W. W. Goelet, physician, man of the world, and graduate of Columbia College, was arrested as a desperate burglar and tonight charged with half a dozen bold crimes. Up until a few days ago, Goelet had been dividing his time between his practice as physician with an active social life and that of burglar. Goelet had been a
5 guest at the fashionable North Gate Apartments for two days and while there had been known as W. H. Wythe, a man of style and fine presence, entirely beyond suspicion as a marauding housebreaker.

    Goelet's part in the crimes first came to light a week ago when Mrs. Goelet, his bride of only four months, went to the Chief of Police Vollmer and, in great distress,
10 declared that her husband was a criminal. A trap was set for the gentleman crook. Yesterday evening, by prearrangement, Goelet and his wife took an automobile ride, leaving San Francisco for Oakland. In another auto were Berkeley officers. The arrest was made on the ferry boat where there would be no chance for the burglar to escape the law.

15   Mr. Goelet's dual life had nearly come to an end two weeks earlier when he barely escaped a posse of students who pursued him across the University of California campus after he had been surprised rifling the rooms of Miss Fannie Brewster at the North Gate Apartments.

20. The final paragraph describes an incident that occurred:

    F. after Mr. Goelet's wife visited the police.
    G. while Goelet was not yet known to be a burglar.
    H. before the Goelets' recent wedding.
    J. as the Goelets were boarding the ferry in San Francisco.

21. In the first paragraph, the passage contrasts:

    A. Mr. Goelet the sophisticated doctor and Mr. Goelet the criminal.
    B. Mr. Goelet the bachelor and Mr. Goelet the married man.
    C. Mr. Goelet the man about town and Mr. Goelet the physician.
    D. Mr. Goelet the student and Mr. Goelet the professional.

UNIT 9 | PRACTICE • 453

Passage 6

In the summer of 1941, sixteen-year-old Glenn Frazier, distraught because the girl he loved confessed her devotion to someone else, ran away from his home in Alabama. He lied to Army recruiters about his age and signed up to serve in the Philippines, thinking he would be safe from the war raging in Europe. After the
5 December 7 attack on Pearl Harbor, Frazier became one of 31,000 men under the command of General Douglas MacArthur, fighting the war in the Pacific theater.

The Americans were soon overwhelmed by the more than 50,000 Japanese troops converging on Manila. MacArthur ordered a retreat to the Bataan Peninsula, a mountainous, malarial place. Short on supplies, the Americans fought off one
10 Japanese attack after another, waiting for the reinforcements MacArthur said were on the way. The help never came.

After four months, Frazier and the other surviving Americans were captured. They endured brutal treatment at the hands of their captors, beginning with a forced march through the jungle that came to be known as the Bataan Death March.
15 Frazier survived the march but spent the remainder of the war in slave labor camps. One day, before being relocated to Japan and while on burial detail above a mass grave, he threw his dog tags into the pit. He was certain he would die shortly. Confident that the tags would be found after the war, he wanted to relieve his family of uncertainty about his fate.

20 When the Allies retook the Philippines, they discovered the mass grave with Frazier's dog tags in it. The Army believed that Frazier was dead and notified his family.

Miraculously, Frazier survived his internment. When he returned to the United States at the end of the war, he called home. His mother answered the phone and
25 fainted upon hearing the voice of the son she had been told was dead.

22. The events in the passage are narrated primarily in:

    F. chronological order.
    G. reverse order of occurrence.
    H. order of importance.
    J. no particular order.

23. The sentence "The help never came," line 11, indicates that:

    A. Frazier's plan failed.
    B. Frazier's plan succeeded.
    C. McArthur's plan failed.
    D. McArthur's plan succeeded.

24. The phrase "one day" (line 16) is used to indicate:

F. the specific date in history of be beginning of war.
G. the day that the Philippines surrendered to Japanese forces.
H. a time after Frazier's capture but before his transfer to Japan.
J. a time after Frazier's release from captivity before he returned home.

Passage 7

My father was impulsive, and it was his impulsiveness that led him to volunteer to serve four years in the Confederate army—trying years for my mother, with seven children to feed, clothe, and house. Toward the end of the war, Sherman's army passed through our county and destroyed almost everything in its path.

5 Our stock consisted of two yoke of oxen and three cows. There was a wild, several-hundred-acre canebrake in which the cattle fed about a mile from our little farm, and it was necessary to bell the cattle in order to locate them when wanted. But the cows were in the habit of coming up to be milked, and a soldier can hear a bell as well as anyone. I was a lad of eight at the time, and while my two older
10 brothers worked our few fields, I was sent into the canebrake to herd the cattle. We had removed the bells from the oxen and cows, but one ox was belled after darkness each evening, to be unbelled again at daybreak after we had located the cattle. I always carried the bell with me, stuffed with grass to muffle the clapper.

My vigil was trying for one so young—the days seemed like weeks—but the
15 importance of hiding our cattle from the soldiers was thoroughly impressed on my mind. Food was secretly brought to me, and under cover of darkness my mother and eldest brother would come and milk the cows. Then we would all return home together. The next day before daybreak we would be in the cane listening for the first tinkle, in order to find the cattle and remove the bell. And my day's work began
20 again.

About the middle of the third day I grew very hungry, and I crept to the edge of the canebrake to see if my dinner was coming. Soldiers were in sight, which explained why dinner was late. Suddenly a squad of five or six rode within fifty feet of me. I stood like a stone statue. After they had passed, I took a step forward, the better to watch them as they rode away, when the grass dropped out of the bell and it clattered. A soldier heard the tinkle and rode back. I grasped the clapper and lay flat on the ground, my heart beating like a trip-hammer. He rode within twenty feet of me, peering into the thicket, and not seeing anything unusual, turned and galloped away. The day my mother taught me the lesson of being "faithful over a few things" filled my thoughts.

25. The sentence "Suddenly a squad...of me" (lines 23–24) is intended by the author to:

    A. introduce an element of drama.
    B. announce the climax of the story.
    C. provide background about farm life.
    D. develop the character of the narrator.

26. The phrase "faithful over a few things" (lines 29–30) functions as a(n):

    F. flashback
    G. foreshadowing
    H. aside
    J. recap

Passage 8

[1]

Large flocks of blackbirds congregate in the northern Great Plains from August to October in preparation for the migration to southern wintering areas. The birds acquire food energy for the migration by eating agricultural crops, especially sunflowers. Red-winged blackbirds, common grackles, and yellow-headed blackbirds cause the most damage.

[2]

A new farming technique has been introduced to help protect commercial sunflower crops from these birds: lure crops. The lure crop is a small field, about 20 acres, that is planted with an early maturing variety oilseed sunflower to draw blackbirds away from nearby commercial sunflower fields. The commercial sunflower crop is much more valuable than the lure crop.

[3]

Farmers continue to spray registered repellents on the commercial fields and to harass the birds in order to drive them from the commercial fields. The lure crop does not receive insecticide treatment or protection from bird damage. Instead, the goal is to keep the birds in the lure crop field as long as possible, thereby reducing the time they spend feeding on the commercial sunflower fields.

[4]

Each seed eaten in the lure crop field is one less seed eaten in the commercial field. An additional, unexpected benefit of the lure crop is that other, desirable bird species feed there. These species include goldfinch, clay-colored sparrows, mourning doves, and Savannah sparrows.

27. The first paragraph of the passage explains why:

A. the birds migrate from the Northern Great Plains in late summer and fall.
B. a new farming technique was needed to protect the sunflower crop.
C. agricultural crops are the primary source of food energy for the birds.
D. sunflowers are a valuable commercial crop in the northern Great Plains.

28. In Paragraph 1, Sentence 3 the author provides examples of birds that:

F. feed on wild seeds and not on crop seeds.
G. remain on the northern Great Plains year-round.
H. do not store energy for their annual migration.
J. are especially damaging to the sunflower crop.

29. In Paragraph 3, the author mentions repellents and harassment as techniques that are:

A. employed to discourage the birds from eating the lure crop.
B. more effective when used without a lure crop because it attracts birds.
C. no longer effective since the introduction of lure crops.
D. used in addition to the lure crop to protect the agricultural crop.

30. In the final sentence of Paragraph 4, the author provides:

F. examples of bird species that are destructive because they eat the lure crop.
G. illustrations of good bird species that feed on the lure crop.
H. counter-examples to the general rule that birds are desirable wildlife.
J. a rule by which to distinguish whether a bird belongs to a desirable species.

Reading

Unit 10 | **Practice**

INSIDE THIS UNIT:
– Exercise –

460 • READING

EXERCISE

DIRECTIONS: This exercise consists of passages followed by questions. Read each passage and answer the questions based upon what is stated or implied in the passage. Answers are on page 754.

Passage 1

The Rotunda is the heart of the U.S. Capitol building. Hanging in the Rotunda are four giant canvases painted by John Trumbull, an aide-de-camp to General Washington, who painted scenes of the American Revolution. Paintings by four other artists depict events associated with the exploration and settlement of the
5   United States. On the canopy, 180 feet above the Rotunda floor, the Italian-American artist Constantino Brumidi painted *The Apotheosis of Washington*. It shows George Washington surrounded by symbols of American democracy and technological progress. Brumidi painted and decorated many of the rooms and corridors of the Capitol, and he was painting the frieze that rings the Rotunda when he died. His
10 work, which illustrates major events in the nation's history, was completed by other artists.

1. The paragraph primarily discusses:

    A. John Trumbull.
    B. the Capitol Rotunda.
    C. *The Apotheosis of Washington*.
    D. Constantino Brumidi.

2. The writer is primarily concerned with:

    F. listing the artists who have painted George Washington.
    G. describing the artwork and decoration of the Rotunda.
    H. explaining the function of the U.S. Capitol.
    J. discussing the architecture of the U.S. Capitol.

3. The writer is thinking of adding more detail to the paragraph. Which of the following would best fit with the main theme of the paragraph?

    A. Details of Constantino Brumidi's life
    B. Information about other buildings near the U.S. Capitol
    C. Important dates in the history of the United States
    D. A description of the symbols in *The Apotheosis of Washington*

Passage 2

If you are ever evacuated from your home because of a natural disaster, you'll be anxious to get back when officials say that the area is safe. Even though the area may be safe, there may be hidden dangers inside your home. When you go inside, enter carefully and check for damage. Watch out for loose boards and slippery
5 floors. If you smell gas or hear a hissing or blowing sound, open a window and leave immediately. Turn off the main gas valve from the outside, if you can. Call the gas company from a neighbor's residence. If possible, turn off the electricity at the main circuit breaker. However, do not touch any electrical switches, boxes, or fixtures if you are wet or standing in water. If you see structural damage to the walls, the roof,
10 the floors, or the foundation, leave immediately. Once you are sure that you will not be injured, you can begin the task of cleaning up.

4. The writer is primarily describing steps to take when:

   F. preparing for a natural disaster.
   G. the odor of gas is in the air.
   H. returning home after an evacuation.
   J. making repairs to a damaged home.

5. Which of the following titles best describes the content of the paragraph?

   A. Early Warning Systems for Natural Disasters
   B. Home Repairs Following a Natural Disaster
   C. Maintaining Your Home in a Safe Condition
   D. Returning Home after a Natural Disaster

6. The writer is thinking of adding more detail to the passage. Which of the following would be most useful in helping the reader to understand the main point of the paragraph?

   F. The most likely location for the main circuit breaker
   G. A list of steps to be followed when cleaning up
   H. Procedures to be followed when ordered to evacuate
   J. How to repair structural damage to a building's foundation

Passage 3

Some historians theorize that nursery rhymes commemorate actual events in history. For example, the children's game, "Ring around the Rosies," seems to make reference to the Bubonic Plague, which struck London in 1665. One symptom of the disease is a red rash in the shape of a ring. Additionally, the line "ashes, ashes, all fall
5 down" is sometimes sung, "a-choo, a-choo, all fall down." During the plague, people infected with disease would develop respiratory problems and die soon after.

"London Bridge is Falling Down" almost surely refers to a series of bridges that spanned the Thames River, which flows through London. One theory of origin is that the rhyme relates to destruction of London Bridge by Vikings led by King Olaf II of
10 Norway in 1014. The nineteenth century translation of the Norse saga the *Heimskringle*, published by Samuel Laing in 1844, included a verse by Óttarr Svarti that looks very similar to the nursery rhyme:

London Bridge is broken down.
Gold is won, and bright renown.

15 However, modern research makes it clear that Laing was using the nursery rhyme as a model for his very free translation, and the reference to London Bridge does not appear at the start of the verse. So it is unlikely that this is an earlier version of the nursery rhyme. Additionally, many historians doubt that the attack ever took place.

20 In the nursery rhyme "Old Doctor Foster," the character is said to go to Gloucester where he steps in a puddle and refuses to go back to the city ever again. Doctor Foster has been identified with Edward I of England who, traveling to Gloucester, fell off his horse into a puddle and, because of the embarrassment to his royal personage, refused to return to the city. The problem with this interpretation
25 is that Edward I ruled England from 1272 to 1307, but the rhyme is first recorded in the mid-1800s.

The nursery rhyme "Jack and Jill" is sometimes said to have its roots in France. There, in the aftermath of the French Revolution of 1789, King Louis XVI was beheaded, or in other words, "lost his crown." His queen, Marie Antoinette, was
30 beheaded a short time later. That is to say that she, like Jill, "came tumbling after." However, the beheadings took place in 1793, and the first versions of the rhyme were published before that date.

Still, these tales were probably passed down by word of mouth for hundreds of years before finally being published in books in the 1800s. So it is possible that
35 historical events were grafted on to an already existing rhyme. For example, even though "Jack and Jill" predates the French Revolution, people may later have noticed

the similarity between Jack and the king and Jill and the queen and sung the ditty to commemorate the royal execution.

7. Which of the nursery rhymes mentioned in the passage is thought to have been associated with historical events that took place in France?

   A. "London Bridge is Falling Down"
   B. "Old Doctor Foster"
   C. "Jack and Jill"
   D. "Ring around the Rosies"

8. According to the passage, the historical event that may have been associated by people with "Jack and Jill" took place in:

   F. 1014.
   G. 1272.
   H. 1789.
   J. 1793.

9. According to the author, what is the evidence that "Ring around the Rosies" may be descriptive of events in London in 1665?

   A. Medical symptoms of the Bubonic Plague
   B. A Norse saga entitled *Heimskringle*
   C. A version of the verse published in the 1800s
   D. The reference to ashes which are the residue of fire

10. The passage mentions all of the following as suggesting that Old Doctor Foster refers to King Edward I EXCEPT:

    F. Both travel to the city of Gloucester.
    G. Both get wet in a puddle of water.
    H. Both refuse to return to Gloucester.
    J. Both lived in England at the same time.

11. All of the following are mentioned in the passage as being characters associated by some people with the events of a nursery rhyme EXCEPT:

    A. King Olaf II of Norway.
    B. Samuel Laing.
    C. Edward I of England.
    D. Marie Antoinette.

Passage 4

Ahead of us was a waterless stretch of forty miles. But after grazing, by watering the herd about the middle of one morning, we could get to water again the following evening. During the afternoon of the second day's dry drive, we finally scaled the last divide, and there, below us in the valley of the South Platte, nestled
5   Ogallala. It was the Gomorrah of the cattle trail, for among its half hundred buildings, no church spire pointed upward, but instead three fourths of its business houses were dance halls, gambling houses, and saloons.

It was there that Joel Collins and his outfit rendezvoused when they robbed the Union Pacific train in October, '77. Collins had driven a herd of cattle for his father
10 and brother, and after selling them in the Black Hills, gambled away the proceeds. Some five or six of his outfit returned to Ogallala with him, and being moneyless, concluded to recoup their losses at the expense of the railway company. Going eighteen miles up the river to Big Springs, seven of them robbed the express and passengers, the former yielding sixty thousand dollars in gold. The next morning
15 they were in Ogallala, paying debts, and getting their horses shod. In Collins's outfit was Sam Bass, and under his leadership, until he met his death the following spring at the hands of Texas Rangers, the course of the outfit southward was marked by a series of daring bank and train robberies.

We reached the river late that evening, and after watering, grazed until dark
20 and camped for the night. After the herd had been bedded, with the exception of the first guard, we rode across the river.

Flood had gone ahead to get cash. His letter of credit was good anywhere on the trail, and on reaching town, he took us into a general outfitting store and paid us twenty-five dollars apiece. After warning us to be on hand at the wagon to stand our
25 watches, he left us, and we scattered like lost sheep in that sinful place.

12. According to the passage, before driving the cattle over the waterless forty-mile stretch, the narrator and the others:

   F. went ahead into Ogallala to commit a robbery.
   G. crossed the river into Ogallala to get money.
   H. grazed the cattle and then watered them.
   J. rendezvoused at the general outfitting store.

13. According to the passage, after robbing the Union Pacific train, Joel Collins and his outfit:

   A. returned to Ogallala to draw money on a line of credit.
   B. recouped their losses at the gambling tables in Ogallala.
   C. traveled to the Black Hills to hide from the authorities.
   D. went back to Ogallala to pay debts and have their horses shod.

14. According to the passage, Flood went to Ogallala ahead of the others in order to:

   F. get cash for the group.
   G. find someone to buy the cattle.
   H. meet up with Joel Collins.
   J. located the group's lost sheep.

15. According to the passage, the robbery spree of the Joel Collins gang ended when:

   A. the gang reached Big Springs.
   B. Joel Collins was killed by authorities.
   C. the gang sold its cattle.
   D. Texas Rangers killed Sam Bass.

16. According to the passage, the narrator arrived in Ogallala:

   F. in the evening.
   G. late at night.
   H. early in the morning.
   J. at around noon.

Passage 5

The leaves were so still that even Bibi thought it was going to rain. Bibinôt, who was accustomed to converse on terms of perfect equality with his little son, called the child's attention to certain somber clouds that were rolling with sinister intention from the west, accompanied by a sullen threatening roar. They were at
5 Friedheimer's store and decided to remain there till the storm had passed. They sat within the door on two empty kegs. Bibi was four years old and looked very wise.

"Mama'll be 'fraid, yes," he suggested with blinking eyes.

"She'll shut the house. Maybe she got Sylvie helpin' her this evenin'," Bibinôt responded reassuringly.

10 "No, she ent got Sylvie. Sylvie was helpin' her yistiday," piped Bibi.

Bibinôt rose and, going across to the counter, purchased a can of shrimps of which Calixta was very fond. Then he returned to his perch on the keg and sat stolidly holding the can while the storm burst. It shook the wooden store and seemed to be ripping furrows in the distant field. Bibi laid his little hand on his
15 father's knee and was not afraid.

Calixta, at home, felt no uneasiness for their safety. She sat at a side window sewing furiously on a sewing machine. She was greatly occupied and did not notice the approaching storm. She felt warm and often stopped to mop her face on which the perspiration gathered in beads. She unfastened her white sacque at her throat. It
20 began to grow dark, and suddenly realizing the situation she got up hurriedly and went about closing windows and doors.

Out on the small front gallery she had hung Bibinôt's Sunday clothes to dry and she hastened out to gather them before the rain fell. As she stepped outside, Alcée Laballière rode in at the gate. She had not seen him very often since her marriage,
25 and never alone. She stood there with Bibinôt's coat in her hands, and the big rain drops began to fall. Alcée rode his horse under the shelter of a side projection where the chickens had huddled and there were plows and a harrow piled up in the corner.

"May I come and wait on your gallery till the storm is over, Calixta?" he asked.

"Come 'long in, Mister Laballière."

17. It can be inferred that Bibi's mother is:

    A. Sylvie.
    B. Freidheimer.
    C. Bibi.
    D. Calixta.

18. It can be inferred that Bibinôt purchases the can of shrimp for his:

    F. son.
    G. wife.
    H. visitor.
    J. father.

19. It can be inferred that the storm makes Bibi concerned for:

    A. his own safety.
    B. his father's safety.
    C. his mother's safety.
    D. Friedheimer's safety.

20. It can be inferred that as the storm first approaches Calixta is:

    F. preoccupied with her work.
    G. worried about her family.
    H. expecting a visit from Alcée.
    J. conversing with Bibi.

21. It can be inferred that Calixta addresses Alcée as "Mr. Laballière" because:

    A. they have never been properly introduced.
    B. he was first to speak in a formal manner.
    C. she wants to remind him that she is married.
    D. the storm has made it difficult to be heard.

468 • READING

> **DIRECTIONS:** Each of the following items is a sentence with a word that has been italicized. You are to choose the answer that has the meaning that is <u>most</u> <u>like</u> that of the italicized word. Answers are on page 755.

22. Churchgoers maintain a solemn attitude during services in order to show their *reverence* for the rituals they are practicing.

In the context of the sentence above, *reverence* means:

F. confusion.
G. thoughtfulness.
H. indifference.
J. respect.

23. The poor people in eighteenth-century France, who could barely afford to feed themselves, became resentful of Marie Antoinette's *opulent* lifestyle.

In the context of the sentence above, *opulent* means:

A. strict.
B. wealthy.
C. immoral.
D. selfish.

24. Though the pressures of society cause many people to *conform*, Transcendentalist writers such as Ralph Waldo Emerson encourage us to embrace our individuality.

In the context of the sentence above, *conform* means:

F. behave strangely.
G. behave independently.
H. follow the majority.
J. think differently.

25. Many golfers try to improve their own swing by studying and *emulating* the form of famous golfers such as Phil Mickelson.

In the context of the sentence above, *emulating* means:

A. changing.
B. imitating.
C. criticizing.
D. following.

26. Alexa's *jubilation* at her engagement was contagious; soon, all her friends and family members were jumping up and down and hugging her.

    In the context of the sentence above, *jubilation* means:

    F. happiness.
    G. anxiety.
    H. disappointment.
    J. indifference.

27. Jonathan Edwards, a Puritan preacher from the 1700s, wrote powerful sermons that moved his congregation to hysterics in spite of the fact that his monotone, drawn-out speeches meant he was not an interesting *orator*.

    In the context of the sentence above, *orator* means:

    A. writer.
    B. speaker.
    C. preacher.
    D. researcher.

28. Though the McMurrays were obviously proud of their massive new house, I felt the gold-threaded curtains, stone gargoyles, and marble fountains were *ostentatious*.

    In the context of the sentence above, *ostentatious* means:

    F. tacky.
    G. unattractive.
    H. cheap.
    J. beautiful.

29. Years ago, women were expected to be *submissive* to their husbands, but today, partners tend to assume more equal roles in their marriages.

    In the context of the sentence above, *submissive* means:

    A. overbearing.
    B. polite.
    C. meek.
    D. loving.

30. Edna's grandchildren were shocked to learn from her will that, after years of *frugal* habits, the librarian was able to save her small salary so that when she died, she had nearly a million dollars in her savings account!

In the context of the sentence above, *frugal* means:

F. careless.
G. thrifty.
H. lavish.
J. smart.

Reading

Unit 11 | **Practice**

INSIDE THIS UNIT:
– Exercise –

EXERCISE

DIRECTIONS: This exercise consists of passages followed by questions. Read each passage and answer the questions based upon what is stated or implied in the passage. Answers are on page 754.

Passage 1

The Oval Office is in the West Wing of the White House. It is the office of the president of the United States. The office is named for its oval shape. There are three large windows behind the president's desk. The ceiling has an elaborate molding around the edge with elements of the presidential seal. Each president chooses new furniture, new drapes, and carpet. The president often uses the Oval Office for televised addresses. It is the symbol of the power and prestige of the presidency in the minds of Americans and people around the world. Many foreign leaders have met with presidents in this office.

1. The writer primarily discusses:

   A. presidential elections.
   B. the Oval Office.
   C. foreign leaders.
   D. the president's desk.

2. Which of the following titles best describes the paragraph?

   F. The Oval Office: A Symbol of Power
   G. The Oval Office: An Impressive Ceiling
   H. The White House: The President's Home
   J. The West Wing: Presidential Business

3. The writer is thinking of adding more detail to the paragraph. Which of the following facts would be most helpful to the reader in understanding the main theme of the paragraph?

   A. The name of the architect who designed the Oval Office
   B. The name of the interior decorator who provides the furnishings
   C. The names of some foreign leaders and their reasons for visiting the Oval Office
   D. The names of some of the presidents who lived in the White House

Passage 2

Soft drinks, fruit juices, pickles, fresh fruit, and yogurt are acidic. Frequently eating acidic foods can lead to dental erosion. Dental erosion is the breakdown of tooth structure caused by the effect of acid on the teeth. Dental enamel is the thin, outer layer of hard tissue that helps maintain the tooth's structure and shape while
5   protecting it from decay. When you consume acidic food or drink, the enamel softens for a short amount of time. Normally this is temporary because saliva restores the natural balance of the acid in the mouth. If you consume foods high in acid on an excessive basis, your mouth can't recover and there is a greater chance for dental erosion. Of course, regular brushing is the best way to clean the mouth.
10   You can also chew sugar-free gum to stimulate saliva flow, and you can rinse with water for 30 seconds.

4. The writer is primarily discussing the:

   F. dental erosion caused by eating acidic foods.
   G. importance of seeing a dentist on a regular basis.
   H. function of saliva in cleansing the mouth of food.
   J. need to chew sugar-free gum on a regular basis.

5. The writer primarily wants the reader to learn how to:

   A. avoid dental erosion caused by eating too many acidic foods.
   B. identify highly acidic foods that may cause dental erosion.
   C. eat a diet that combines many healthful foods.
   D. brush properly to avoid the decay caused by dental erosion.

6. The writer is thinking of adding more detail to the paragraph. Which of the following additional pieces of information would most help the reader understand the main point of the paragraph?

   F. A list of foods that are not high in acid
   G. An explanation of how much acidic food is too much
   H. A description of good techniques for brushing the teeth
   J. A discussion of various other problems leading to tooth decay

Passage 3

To tell the story of the tango is to relate a cultural, economic, and political as well as musical history. Tango is a dance, poetry, and music that originated in Buenos Aires at the end of the nineteenth century. Immigrants from every European country mixed with earlier generations of settlers of all races from other South
5   American countries. They brought their native music and dances with them. Traditional polkas, mazurkas, and waltzes mixed with the *habanera*, a popular dance from Cuba. The new dance form and its music were called *milonga*.

Perhaps the most important element of *milonga* was the influence of African cultures including dances such as the *candombe*, which contributed the *cortes,* or
10   pauses, that are a central feature of tango. The African population also provided the name *tango*. It is a word from the Gulf of Guinea, the Congo, and southern Sudan that simply means a place for dancing.

In the early 1900s, Buenos Aires was a very poor city. Of the nearly two million immigrants, many were single men, hoping to make enough money to return to
15   Europe and live comfortably or to bring their future wives and families from Europe. So many young men and so few young women was a recipe for crime—and the tango. The tango dance originated from the *compadritos*, or minor tough guys.

Gradually, the dance and music were popularized and adopted by wealthier young men. By 1910 the rich sons of Argentina were making their way to Paris,
20   center of the cultural world. They introduced the tango into a society eager for innovation and not entirely opposed to the risqué nature of this import, especially as taught by the dashing, rich Latin boys who brought it.

By 1920, the tango had spread from Europe back to Argentina. The Argentine upper classes who had shunned the tango now accepted it because it was
25   fashionable in Paris. In Hollywood, handsome film star Rudolph Valentino danced the tango on camera. The tango lost much of its outlaw association. It became a mass entertainment, danced by thousands of respectable citizens in the clubs of prospering cities. The dance was refined to the slick and elegant salon style, and lyrics became generic love songs for the mass market.

30   By 1930, tango was out of fashion in Europe, and a military coup in Argentina suppressed and censored it for ten years. Out of this censorship came the Golden Age of Tango. Indeed, it was championed by the nationalist political movement of Juan and Eva Perón in 1946. The Golden Age lasted through the 40s and early 50s, and this is the period of the tango's greatest development and expression. At the end
35   of the 1950s tango eventually went out of fashion again, this time crushed, like many other dances, by the arrival of American rock and roll. It was also repressed by the

post-Peronist nationalist government. From the 1960s to the 1980s it was only danced and played by a few of the older generation and enthusiasts.

40   Today, the tango is enjoying yet another revival. Through the ebb and flow of popularity, tango has always remained a unique expression of what it means to be Argentine.

7. According to the author, tango originated in:

    A. Paris.
    B. Buenos Aires.
    C. Cuba.
    D. Hollywood.

8. According to the passage, the Golden Age of the Tango lasted from:

    F. 1890 to 1910.
    G. 1910 to 1930.
    H. 1940 to 1960.
    J. 1960 to 1980.

9. According to the passage, the word "tango" comes from:

    A. Argentinean Spanish.
    B. Parisian French.
    C. African languages.
    D. American English.

10. According to the passage, in Argentina in the 1950s American rock and roll:

    F. was suppressed by the post-Peronist government.
    G. replaced the tango as a popular form of dance and music.
    H. was dismissed by the sophisticated upper classes of Argentina.
    J. contributed to the development of the tango during the Golden Age.

11. All of the following are mentioned in the passage as being forms of dance EXCEPT:

    A. *compadritos.*
    B. *habanera.*
    C. *milonga.*
    D. *candombe.*

Passage 4

In December 1606, three ships carrying an expedition from England sailed for Virginia. The crossing, which should have been completed in a month, turned into a five-month ordeal. When the expedition docked at the Canary Islands to take on provisions, Captain John Smith was put in chains and charged with plotting to make himself king of Virginia. In reality, Smith, a commoner with strong opinions, had quarreled with Edward Maria Wingfield, a gentleman and one of the lead investors in the expedition. When Smith refused to submit to Wingfield's superior social rank, Wingfield put him in chains, where he remained for the final thirteen weeks of the voyage to Virginia.

The colonists spotted the coast of Virginia on April 26, 1607; and on May 13, 1607, they founded Jamestown. Food was a problem. The long voyage had depleted most of the colony's stocks, and the colonists had arrived too late in the year to plant crops. Smith refused to let the colony starve. He explored the region for additional food sources.

In December 1607, while mapping the Chickahominy River and hunting for deer, Smith and his party were ambushed by a band of Powhatan Indians. They captured Smith and brought him to Wahunsunacock, the Powhatan chief. Accounts differ on what happened next. One has Pocahontas, the chief's young daughter, placing herself between Smith and his intended executioner. The other suggests that Wahunsunacock, impressed with Smith's bravery, adopted him into the tribe. Whatever happened that fateful day, a friendship between Smith and Pocahontas developed and that bond kept the Jamestown colony from starving.

In September 1608, Smith was elected colony president. He used his practical experience from his years as a farmer and a soldier to put the colony on solid footing. Under his direction, tar, pitch, and soap ash were made, a well was dug, houses were built, fishing parties sent out regularly, and acres of crops were planted.

In September 1609, Smith was injured when his powder bag exploded. The injury forced his return to London, but even had it not occurred, Smith likely would have left anyway. The company's shareholders in London instituted a reorganization of the colony's leadership, and the new appointees had little regard for Smith. By the time Smith died in 1631, Jamestown colony was thriving, having discovered tobacco farming.

12. According to the passage, John Smith was placed in chains aboard the ship:

    F. while the ship took on supplies at the Canary Islands.
    G. before the ship had reached the Canary Islands.
    H. just off the coast of Virginia.
    J. after the founding of the colony at Jamestown.

13. According to the passage, Smith returned to London from Jamestown because he:

    A. was injured when a powder bag exploded.
    B. was disliked by Wingfield and other members of society.
    C. hoped to raise additional funds for the colonists.
    D. had been summoned to England by the investors.

14. According to the passage, Smith was spared by Wahunsunacock because:

    F. Smith was not a member of the English upper class.
    G. Pocohantas intervened or Wahunsunacock admired Smith's bravery.
    H. Pocohantas asked Wahunsunacock to allow her to marry Smith.
    J. Wahunsunacock regarded Smith as a long-time friend and ally.

15. According to the passage, when Smith died, the Jamestown colony was successful because:

    A. Smith was no longer in charge.
    B. new settlers moved in.
    C. the colony grew tobacco.
    D. the colonists learned to grow food.

16. According to the passage, Smith was elected president of the colony:

    F. the year the colony was founded.
    G. before being captured by Wahunsunacock.
    H. the year before he returned to England.
    J. when he returned from England to the colony.

478 • READING

> **DIRECTIONS:** Each of the following items is a sentence with a word that has been italicized. You are to choose the answer that has the meaning that is <u>most</u> <u>like</u> that of the italicized word. Answers are on page 754.

17. All superheroes must fight against a *malefactor* who commits atrocious crimes against humanity; Spiderman fights the Green Goblin, Superman goes against Lex Luther, and Batman must take on the Joker.

In the context of the sentence above, *malefactor* means:

A. opposite.
B. murderer.
C. evildoer.
D. friend.

18. Though Quasimodo, from the story *The Hunchback of Notre Dame*, lives most of his life as a *pariah* due to his deformed figure, he eventually becomes more willing to join society, even if that means risking rejection.

In the context of the sentence above, *pariah* means:

F. hero.
G. villain.
H. outcast.
J. disabled person.

19. For his science project, Charlie attempted to build a jetpack that would allow him to go to the moon; he thought it was completely possible, but his teacher, who did not believe it was quite so *feasible*, gave him a D for the assignment.

In the context of the sentence above, *feasible* means:

A. possible.
B. impressive.
C. interesting.
D. technological.

20. Bradley gasped when he accidentally slid the sharp knife across his hand, but luckily he was not injured because his hand did not rub against the *serrated* side of the blade.

In the context of the sentence above, *serrated* means:

F. smooth.
G. rusty.
H. metal.
J. jagged.

21. Though my nephew was supposed to come over to water my plants each day, when I returned from my vacation and saw my *parched* flowers, I knew he didn't follow through with his job.

    In the context of this sentence, *parched* means:

    A. dried up.
    B. healthy.
    C. watery.
    D. unhealthy.

22. In order to attain a relationship with God and nature, Orthodox Christian monks choose to live in secluded, *serene* communities far from the bustle and craziness of cities.

    In the context of this sentence, *serene* means:

    F. rare.
    G. boring.
    H. strange.
    J. peaceful.

23. Marguerite enjoys going to flea markets so that she can get good deals; for example, last week she got an antique table at a cheap price because the surface of the table was *marred* and one of the legs was wobbly.

    In the context of this sentence, *marred* means:

    A. damaged.
    B. old.
    C. rotten.
    D. weak.

24. The *uproarious* movie had most of the audience in hysterics, but Johanna, who found the film offensive, was not laughing.

    In the context of this sentence, *uproarious* means:

    F. crude.
    G. hilarious.
    H. discriminatory.
    J. loud.

25. In the famous fable, the tortoise wins the race because of his consistent hard work while the hare's *indolence*, seen in his numerous naps and breaks, costs him the race.

In the context of this sentence, *indolence* means:

A. sleepiness.
B. distraction.
C. slowness.
D. laziness.

DIRECTIONS: This exercise consists of passages followed by questions. Read each passage and answer the questions based upon what is stated or implied in the passage. Answers are on page 754.

Passage 5

"Have you been to that old castle?" asked the young girl, pointing her parasol to the far-gleaming walls of the Château de Chillon.

"Yes, more than once," said Winterbourne. "You too, I suppose, have seen it?"

"No, we haven't been there. I want to go there dreadfully. Of course I mean to go there. I wouldn't go away from here without having seen that old castle."

"It's a very pretty excursion," said Winterbourne, "and very easy to make. You can drive, you know, or you can go by the little steamer."

"You can go in the cars," said Miss Miller.

"Yes; you can go in the cars," Winterbourne assented.

"Our guide says they take you right up to the castle," the young girl continued. "We were going last week, but my mother gave out. She said she couldn't go. Randolph wouldn't go either; he says he doesn't think much of old castles. But I guess we'll go this week, if we can get Randolph."

"You brother is not interested in ancient monuments?" Winterbourne inquired, smiling.

UNIT 11 | PRACTICE • 481

"He says he doesn't care much about old castles. He's only nine. He wants to stay at the hotel. Mother's afraid to leave him alone."

"I think it might be arranged," said Winterbourne. "Couldn't you get someone to stay—for the afternoon—with Randolph?"

20   Miss Miller looked at him a moment; and then, very placidly, "I wish you would stay with him!" she said.

Winterbourne hesitated a moment. "I would much rather go to Chillon with you."

"With me?" asked the young girl.

25   She didn't rise, blushing, as a young girl at Geneva would have done; and yet Winterbourne, conscious that he had been very bold, thought it possible she was offended. "With your mother," he answered very respectfully.

But it seemed that both his audacity and his respect were lost upon Miss Miller. "I guess my mother won't go, after all," she said. "She doesn't like to ride around in 30 the afternoon. But did you really mean what you said just now; that you would like to go up there?"

"Most earnestly," Winterbourne declared.

"Then we may arrange it. If Mother won't stay with Randolph, I guess Eugenio will."

35   "Eugenio?" the young man inquired.

"Eugenio's our guide. He doesn't like to stay with Randolph, but I'll guess he'll stay with Randolph if Mother does, and then we can go to the castle."

26. It can be inferred that Randolph is Miss Miller's:

F. guide.
G. acquaintance.
H. brother.
J. father.

27. The author implies that who will be going to the castle?

A. Miss Miller only
B. Miss Miller and Winterbourne only
C. Miss Miller and Eugenio only
D. Miss Miller, Winterbourne, and Eugenio only

28. It can be inferred that Miss Miller:

    F. has visited the castle several times in the past.

    G. has not yet paid a visit to the castle.

    H. does not want to visit the Château de Chillon.

    J. prefers to remain at the hotel with her mother.

29. It can be inferred from the passage that Miss Miller is older than:

    A. Randolph.

    B. Eugenio.

    C. Winterbourne.

    D. the young girl.

30. It can be inferred from the information in the passage that Miss Miller and her family:

    F. are tourists.

    G. travel on business.

    H. work as tour guides.

    J. have servants.

Reading Integration of Knowledge and Ideas

Unit 12 | Analyzing Arguments

INSIDE THIS UNIT:
– The Structure of Logical Arguments – – Exercise –

Non-Negotiable Skill:

Analyze how one or more sentences in passages support a claim when a relationship is clearly indicated.

The Structure of Logical Arguments

Your life is filled with arguments. We're not talking about bickering and quarrels; we mean logical arguments. They are everywhere: newspaper and magazine articles, political speeches and advertising, debates and discussions, and even ordinary conversations.

Example:

> The Red Sox are playing the Yankees today, and their traditional rivalry should make it a great game. The best pitchers for both teams are scheduled to be on the mound. And the weather is supposed to be great. We can go to the movies some afternoon when it's raining. Plus, they're giving away Red Sox bumper stickers, and hot dogs are half-price. So let's go to Fenway Park this afternoon.

Though you may not think of it as such, this is an argument. It is a reasoned presentation for going to the ballpark.

Every argument has a main point or conclusion. It is also sometimes called a claim. This is the point the author or speaker hopes to prove. In the argument above, the conclusion is "Let's go to the game."

Often the conclusion of an argument is the very last sentence of the speech or passage. This makes sense because it is the point that the author or speaker is leading up to. Of course, the conclusion doesn't have to be the last sentence. You could move the last sentence of the paragraph above to the top of the paragraph, and it would still make sense. In this example the placement of that sentence is a matter of preference.

The conclusion of an argument is signaled by a word or phrase such as "therefore," "hence," "thus," "so," "consequently," "it follows," "as a result," or even "this proves." This list is by no means exhaustive; there many other words and phrases that would

Unit 12 | Analyzing Arguments • 485

do just as well. While a transition to signal the conclusion is not required as a matter of logic, it can help the reader understand the development of the argument.

So far we've discussed the conclusion of an argument. What is the rest of the information in the presentation? Logically speaking, everything else is a reason given to prove the conclusion. These supporting reasons are sometimes called "evidence," "supporting points," or "justifications," or any number of other terms. What makes "evidence" evidence is not what you call it, but how it functions in the presentation.

In the Red Sox example, the speaker offers reasons for the conclusion:

> It'll be a great game.
>
> Good pitchers are scheduled.
>
> The weather will be good.
>
> There are giveaways.

All of these are reasons for the conclusion.

When you analyze an argument, you need to pay attention to several things. First, you usually want to begin by identifying the conclusion of the argument because everything else is logically connected to it. Also, you want to pay careful attention to the exact wording of the conclusion. You want to make sure you understand what the author or speaker is trying to prove. Then everything else in the presentation is a reason for or that conclusion.

When you are asked to demonstrate these skills on a multiple-choice, standardized test, you will be asked questions such as:

> What is the point the author hopes to prove?
>
> What is the main point of the selection?
>
> The author's main purpose is to show . . .
>
> How does sentence (#) function in the passage?
>
> What is the logical connection between sentence (#) and sentence (#)?

These are the questions that a logical thinker asks about arguments.

Example:

> Who was the greatest hitter of all time? No question, it was Ted Williams. Slugging and on-base averages are the best measures of hitting, and Williams

led the American League in both in the same season eight times, once for six consecutive years. He also won six batting titles and four home run crowns, as well as two MVPs and two Triple Crowns.

The biggest difference between Williams and everyone else is that Williams was always a dominant hitter. Yes, in 1959 he hit only .254, but that was because of a neck injury. At age 20, as a rookie, Williams batted .327 and led the league with 145 runs batted in. Then at age 39, he hit .388 to win the batting title again. In his final season, he batted .316 and had 29 home runs.

Williams was the last major league hitter to bat .400. On the final day of the 1941 season, though he was statistically guaranteed to finish the season better than .400, he elected to play a double-header in Philadelphia. He went six-for-eight and finished the season at .406.

1. Which of the following best states the central claim of the passage?

   A. Slugging and on-base averages are good measures of hitting.
   B. Ted Williams won the batting title when he was 39 years old.
   C. The last major league player to bat .400 was Ted Williams.
   D. By different measures, Ted Williams is the greatest hitter.

   The conclusion of the argument is in response to the question that introduces the passage: Ted Williams was the greatest hitter of all time, (D). Everything else in the passage is supporting evidence for that claim.

2. The author mentions that Williams played with a neck injury in 1959 in order to:

   F. show that even a great player like Williams could have an off season.
   G. explain why the season was not representative of Williams' abilities.
   H. specify what measures should be used to identify the "greatest hitter."
   J. prove that a great hitter can come back from a single disappointing season.

   In the second paragraph, the author provides evidence to show that Williams was a "dominant hitter," a point that supports the conclusion set forth in the beginning that Williams was the greatest hitter of all time. But there is a potential problem with Williams' dominance. His performance in 1959 was weak. In order to put that into perspective, the author points out that Williams played with an injury. The fairly obvious implicit conclusion of this sub-argument is that the 1959 season doesn't count, (G).

Example:

[1] Last year, locomotives emitted 46.9 million metric tons of greenhouse gases (GHGs). [2] Although this is less than 1% of total U.S. GHG emissions, GHG emissions from railroads increased by 20% over the past 20 years, more than five times the rate of increase for total U.S. emissions. [3] In addition, locomotives emit substantial amounts of black carbon (soot), which has significant global warming potential through its ability to absorb solar radiation. [4] According to a report from NASA's Goddard Institute for Space Studies, black soot may be responsible for 25% of observed global warming over the past century. [5] Therefore, it is important that the government set standards for both GHG emissions and for black carbon emissions of locomotives.

3. Which of the sentences states the conclusion of the argument in the paragraph above?

   A. 2
   B. 3
   C. 4
   D. 5

   Sentence 5 includes the transition "therefore," and it states the author's main point, (D).

4. What is the logical relationship between sentences 1 and 3?

   F. Sentence 3 is intended to contradict sentence 1.
   G. Sentence 3 is intended to support sentence 1.
   H. Sentence 3 supports the conclusion while sentence 1 does not.
   J. The sentences give independent reasons to support the conclusion.

   Sentences 1 and 3 provide different reasons for the conclusion, (J).

5. In sentence 4 the author cites a statistic in order to prove that:

   A. soot contributes significantly to global warming.
   B. global warming will have serious consequences.
   C. locomotives produce GHGs and black carbon.
   D. the United States produces significant amounts of GHGs.

   The purpose of sentence 4 is to show that soot, some of which is produced by locomotives, is a serious pollution problem, (A).

Summary

- Arguments are reasoned presentations with conclusions and supporting points.
- When analyzing an argument, begin by identifying the conclusion.

EXERCISE

DIRECTIONS: This exercise consists of paragraphs or passages followed by questions. Read each paragraph or passage and answer the questions based upon what is stated or implied in the paragraph or passage. Answers are on page 755.

American Pharaoh, now retired to stud, was the first Triple Crown winner in 37 years. He banked over $8.6 million in winnings, and he lost only two of eleven career races. Plus, he won the Breeder's Cup Classic, the championship of thoroughbred racing. Those accomplishments clearly prove that American Pharaoh was a superior racehorse.

1. Which of the following statements best expresses the conclusion of the paragraph?

    A. American Pharaoh won the Triple Crown.
    B. American Pharaoh won the Breeder's Cup Classic.
    C. American Pharaoh lost two races.
    D. American Pharaoh was a superior racehorse.

Some people argue that it is important to minimize the effects of wildfires since they release carbon dioxide and contribute to global warming. But wildfires are a natural phenomenon. In pre-industrial America, 200 to 500 years ago, wildfires burned nearly 10 times as many acres and as much biomass as has been burned in recent years. Additionally, lightning makes wildfires all but inevitable; therefore, there is no reason to try to control them.

2. The conclusion of the argument above is that:

    F. Wildfires release carbon dioxide and increase global warming.
    G. Wildfires are natural occurences and are in any event unavoidable.
    H. It is unnecessary to make attempts to control wildfires.
    J. More wildfires occurred hundreds of years ago than today.

[1] The combined efforts of the food industry and government regulatory agencies work together to make the U.S. food supply among the safest in the world. [2] Nonetheless, public health officials have estimated that each year in the United States, many millions of people become sick, and thousands die from foodborne illnesses. [3] For example, in 2006 more than 200 confirmed illnesses and three deaths were linked to bagged fresh spinach grown in California and contaminated with E. coli. [4] In 2008, more than 1,300 persons were infected with Salmonella Saintpaul traced to a farm in Mexico. [5] In late 2008 and early 2009, a multi-state outbreak of Salmonella Typhimurium was linked to a well-known brand of peanut butter.

3. Which of the following BEST explains the function of sentences 3–5?

   A. They restate and amplify the main point of the paragraph.
   B. They provide examples to prove the conclusion of paragraph.
   C. They contradict and refute the claims of sentences 1 and 2.
   D. They set forth additional conclusions to be drawn from sentence 1.

[1] Because Asian carp compete with Great Lakes fish for food, the carp pose a serious danger to native species in the Great Lakes. [2] It is not possible to provide an estimate of the potential economic harm. [3] Nonetheless, the Great Lakes fisheries generate economic activity of approximately $7 billion annually. [4] Therefore, even though it is not possible to predict the effect of the spread of Asian carp on a lake-by-lake or species-by-species basis, it is certain that the Asian carp has the potential to cause considerable economic harm.

4. The conclusion of the paragraph is set forth in sentence:

   F. 1
   G. 2
   H. 3
   J. 4

[1] The potential for terrorist attacks against agricultural targets (agroterrorism) is a grave national security threat because agricultural production is geographically disbursed in unsecured environments. [2] Livestock are frequently concentrated in confined locations and then transported and commingled with other herds, making it easy for agroterrorists to quickly reach large numbers of animals. [3] Since pest and disease outbreaks can quickly halt economically important exports, this sort of attack would have an immediate negative effect on the US economy. [4] Furthermore, many veterinarians lack experience with foreign animal diseases that are resilient and endemic in foreign countries. [5] Each of these factors makes agroterrorism a very serious threat to the United States.

5. Which of the sentences in the paragraph is the main claim of the author?

   A. 1
   B. 2
   C. 3
   D. 5

Today's farming systems perpetuate practices that harm animals. Large numbers of livestock or poultry are kept in close confinement with little or no room for natural movement and activity. Surgeries such as docking hog tails, dehorning cattle, and trimming poultry beaks are needed to ensure that confined animals do not injure each other. Regulations still permit the commercial transport of disabled livestock ("downers"). Poultry and other livestock are often not fully stunned prior to slaughter. Whether or not you think that animals are suitable for human consumption, you have to agree that these and similar practices are inhumane.

6. The author proves the claim of the paragraph by:

   F. providing examples of inhumane treatment of animals.
   G. citing statistics to document the inhumane treatment of animals.
   H. defining carefully the terms "harmful" and "inhumane."
   J. showing that the practices cited are immoral.

Homegrown violent jihadists usually lack in-depth knowledge of specialized tradecraft, such as bomb making, that characterizes international terrorists. Additionally, they do not have the financing or training camps available to international organizations. These shortcomings tend to keep homegrown violent jihadists from independently engaging in large-scale suicide strikes. Nonetheless, the shortcomings pose a challenge for law enforcement because it is much more difficult to detect smaller conspiracies that can develop quickly. When compared to international terrorist networks, homegrown violent jihadists are more prone to acts not requiring elaborate preparation, such as individual assaults using firearms.

7. The author believes that the lack of access to financing and training helps to explain why homegrown violent jihadists:

   A. lack a sophisticated understanding of bomb-making techniques.

   B. are prone to terrorist acts such as assaults using firearms.

   C. easily escape the notice of law enforcement agencies.

   D. are not usually recruited by international terrorist organizations.

Questions 8–10

[1]

China is the world's most populous country with over 1.3 billion people. It has experienced tremendous economic growth over the last three decades with an annual average increase in gross domestic product of 9.8% during that period. This has led to an increasing demand for energy, spurring China to add an average of 53 gigawatts (GW) of electric capacity each year over the last ten years to its power generation capabilities.

[2]

China essentially functions as a "command and control" economy. The national government owns many of the country's industries and enterprises and sets goals for economic development. China's industries and enterprises, whether government or privately owned, are expected to comply with the goals set in the national government's economic plan.

[3]

China has set ambitious targets for developing its non-hydropower renewable energy resources. The wind power sector is illustrative of China's accomplishments. Installed wind power capacity has gone from 0.567 GW in 2003 to 12.2 GW. Plans already exist to grow China's wind power capacity to 100 GW by 2020. A similar goal exists for the solar photovoltaic power sector which China intends to

35 increase from 0.14 GW of generating capacity as of 2009 to over 1.8 GW by 2020.

[4]

China recognizes that given the growing demand for energy at home, 40 developing its domestic renewable energy industry and building manufacturing capacity can lead to advantages in future export markets. Energy efficiency and conservation are 45 officially China's top energy priority. These are considered the easiest ways to reduce energy use and cut demand. In China, energy conservation investment projects have priority over 50 energy development projects.

8. The author mentions the 9.8% growth in gross domestic product (lines 6–7) in order to prove that China:

F. is the most populous country in the world.
G. has increased its energy capacity over the last ten years.
H. experienced tremendous economic growth for the past 30 years.
J. hopes to become energy self-sufficient by the year 2020.

9. The author's statement in paragraph 2 that the national government owns many industries helps to prove that China:

A. gives priority to energy conservation over energy development.
B. has a "command and control" economy directed by the government.
C. intends to increase its energy capacity dramatically in the future.
D. hopes to meet its increased energy demands by conservation.

10. Which of the following BEST describes the logical structure of paragraph 3?

F. conclusion supported by two examples
G. general claim without any proof
H. counter-example to a general claim
J. generalization based on one example

Reading Integration of Knowledge and Ideas

Unit 13 | Analyzing Paired Passages

INSIDE THIS UNIT:
– Relationships between Passages – – Exercise –

Non-Negotiable Skill:

Make simple comparisons between two passages.

Relationships between Passages

Thus far, we have worked on stand-alone passages. Now we'll take a look at some exercises that require you to discuss the relationship between two passages on the same general topic. Double passages, as these are often called, are not necessarily twice as hard as stand-alone passages. On standardized tests, double passages usually include quite a few questions about each passage alone, just as though there were two stand-alone passages. A few questions, however, will ask you about the relationship between the two passages. The types of questions that are typically asked include the following:

Do the authors agree or disagree?

What is the most significant point of disagreement?

How might one author respond to the other author?

What is the most important difference between the two passages?

Example:

Passage 1

Many households use a woodstove as a supplementary heating source or even the primary heating appliance. Unfortunately, smoke from wood burning stoves can be a significant source of air pollution.

Fine particulate matter, the very small particles that make up smoke and soot, is the most dangerous component of wood smoke pollution. The most harmful particles are those ten microns or less in diameter (a human hair is approximately 70 microns in diameter). These particles can easily be inhaled deep into the lungs, collecting in the tiny air sacs (called alveoli) where oxygen enters the blood, causing breathing difficulties and sometimes permanent lung damage. Inhalation of fine particulate matter can increase cardiovascular problems, irritate lungs and eyes, and worsen respiratory diseases such as asthma, emphysema, and bronchitis.

Pollution from woodstoves is a problem especially when temperature inversions occur. During a temperature inversion, a layer of colder air near the
15 surface of the Earth is covered by warmer, less-dense air, effectively creating a bubble that traps everything below it. Pollutants are concentrated near the ground.

In addition to its potential health hazards, wood smoke creates the unpleasant brown haze that we see on winter mornings. Computer models show
20 that 80 percent of the particulate matter in the air in some areas is attributable to woodstoves.

1. The main point of the passage is that:

   A. wood is used as a heating fuel for many households.
   B. heating with fire wood produces dangerous air pollution.
   C. people with respiratory diseases may be affected by wood smoke.
   D. temperature inversions increase the danger of wood smoke pollution.

   (B) nicely summarizes the development of the passage. The author begins by stating that wood is a fuel that is used by many. In the second paragraph, the author describes the dangers of wood smoke pollution. And in the final paragraph, the author discusses the environmental impact of wood smoke and its particulates in the air. (A) is a point made in the first paragraph but is not a good summary of the overall development. Nor is (C), though (C) is an important part of paragraph two. Similarly, (D) is a good summary of paragraph three—but not the whole passage. Therefore (B) is the correct answer.

2. The author states that small particles in wood smoke are dangerous because they:

   F. create haze that obscures visibility.
   G. collect in aveoli and block oxygen.
   H. cause temperature inversions on cold days.
   J. are widely dispersed in the atmosphere.

   This is a cause-and-effect question. In the second paragraph, the author explains the mechanism by which the small particles in wood smoke pollution cause harmful effects: they collect in the air sacs and interfere with oxygen transfer, (G).

3. The author compares small wood smoke particles to human hair (lines 6–7) in order to:

   A. illustrate the dangers posed by air pollution.
   B. establish that air pollution is caused by humans.
   C. clarify the meaning of "very small particles."
   D. invite a debate on the causes of wood smoke.

   The author inserts the parenthetical information about human hair in order to give the reader a better idea of what is meant by "very small particles," those that are 10 microns or less in diameter, (C). With this information, the reader can appreciate that the harmful particles are no larger than 1/7 the width of a human hair.

Example:

Passage 2

Smoke from woodstoves is generated primarily by incomplete combustion, which can be caused by burning the wrong fuel. The best wood to use in wood burning stoves is air-dried hardwood (oak, beech, maple, elm, ash), seasoned for six to eight months prior to burning and stored under cover for protection from
5 the weather. Wet or freshly cut ("green") wood is not energy efficient because the heat produced is used to evaporate water rather than heat the home. The water content of a tree or freshly-cut firewood can be as high as 50 percent, compared with 15–20 percent in dry, well-seasoned wood.

Burning dry wood also produces a more even burn and helps prevent the
10 formation of creosote, a highly-flammable crusty deposit that sticks to the inside walls of the chimney. Creosote deposits can lead to a chimney fire.

The use of properly sized wood pieces is also important. Wood should be split to a maximum thickness of four to six inches, depending on stove size. This size increases the surface area exposed to flame, resulting in higher burn
15 efficiency. A fire that is burning brightly without visible smoke is a sign of good combustion. Smoldering fires are the worst polluters because they burn at a temperature too low for efficient combustion. The result is more smoke, which is unburned wood going up the chimney, wasted. This means more air pollution.

4. Which of the following best characterizes the relationship of Passage 2 to Passage 1?

   F. Passage 2 provides information that could help reduce the severity of the problem highlighted in Passage 1.
   G. It reinforces the main point of Passage 1 by identifying one of the causes of wood smoke pollution.
   H. It contradicts the main point of Passage 1 by suggesting that pollution from wood smoke is not serious.
   J. It identifies additional problems associated with emissions produced by heating with wood.

   The main thing the author of Passage 2 is describing is the proper way of using a woodstove to avoid producing excess pollution, (F). Since the author of Passage 2 doesn't deny that woodstoves cause pollution, (H) is incorrect. Nor does the author argue that Passage 1 understates the case against woodstoves, (G). The purpose of Passage 2 is to show that the problem can be mitigated. And (J) is wrong because Passage 2 doesn't mention any other problems associated with smoke pollution.

5. Compared to Passage 1, Passage 2 provides more information about the:

   A. dangers of wood smoke.
   B. history of wood heating.
   C. functioning of woodstoves.
   D. purchase cost of woodstoves.

   Passage 1 talks about the dangers of wood smoke but doesn't really provide any information about how the devices work (or why they might be pollutants). Passage 2 specifically talks about the best practices for operating a woodstove: use the right kind of wood for fuel. Thus, (C) is correct.

Summary

- On standardized tests, double passages include some of the same types of questions that are asked about single passages.

- Reading double passages also provides an opportunity to consider whether the authors agree or disagree and how their arguments compare.

EXERCISE

DIRECTIONS: This exercise consists of passages and related questions. Read each passage and answer the questions based upon what is stated or implied in the passage. Answers are on page 755.

Questions 1–10

Passage 1

By the end of World War I, music was big business, but the industry in the United States was controlled by three phonograph giants: Victor, Columbia, and Edison. These companies issued thousands of titles in dozens of foreign languages to cultivate consumers in immigrant communities; yet, they all but refused to release records by African-American performers and ignored African-American consumers.

Then court decisions and the expiration of some crucial patents essential to the manufacturing of records loosened the grip of the three giants, making it possible for independent record companies to enter the market. Music publisher Harry Pace launched Black Swan in 1921. The company issued records by African Americans in all genres—not just the popular styles such as blues, ragtime, and comic songs, but opera, spirituals, and classical music as well. Also, the company was a model of small-business development, inspiring and instructing African Americans in capital accumulation and the potential for economic self-determination.

The first Black Swan record appeared in May 1921, and the company issued its last records in the summer of 1923. Its premature end was precipitated by a perfect storm of ill-timed expansion, increased competition in the blues and jazz fields, and the expansion of radio, which destabilized even the largest, most secure phonograph companies.

Despite its rapid rise and fall, many of the goals of Black Swan were achieved. Black Swan issued more than 180 recordings in a wide range of styles, sold hundreds of thousands of discs, and distributed them around the United States and abroad. The label appealed to a wide audience, far beyond African-American consumers. Black Swan launched the recording careers of Fletcher Henderson, Ethel Waters, Trixie Smith, and Alberta Hunter, and put out records by a host of talented musicians unlikely to have found other recording opportunities. Meanwhile, the company emerged as a prominent and influential black-owned business, and, as a manufacturer, distinguished itself even from other black-owned companies by retaining control of its own economic destiny.

Passage 2

The Detroit, Michigan record company Motown was founded in 1959 by Berry Gordy, Jr. as Tamla Records and incorporated as Motown Record Corporation in 1960. At that time, Detroit was the center of US auto manufacturing, and the name Motown is a portmanteau of motor and town. During the 1960s, Motown achieved spectacular success for a small record company with 79 records in the Top Ten of the Billboard Hot 100 chart between 1960 and 1969.

Many of Motown's executives and performers grew up within blocks of one another in post-World War II Detroit. Berry Gordy got his start as a songwriter for local Detroit acts such as Jackie Wilson and the Matadors. Wilson's single "Lonely Teardrops," written by Gordy, became a huge success; but Gordy did not feel he made as much money as he deserved from this and other singles he wrote for Wilson. He realized that the more lucrative end of the business was in producing records and owning the publishing. He started Tamla Records with an $800 loan from his family.

In 1956, Bobby Rogers was a Detroit teenager whose hobby was singing doo-wop harmonies with his friends in the park. His first group, the Matadors, was joined by Smokey Robinson, who kept a school notebook with songs and musical ideas. The group added Claudette Rogers (later Claudette Robinson), Bobby's cousin, who brought sex appeal as well as vocal ability, and the Miracles were born.

Paradoxically, the Miracles flopped in their first audition before Jackie Wilson for his record label, but they attracted the interest of Gordy. Gordy began an artistic collaboration with Robinson that laid the foundation for Motown and sustained the streak of successes that would span two decades.

In 1967, Norman Whitfield became the company's top producer, turning out hits for The Temptations, Marvin Gaye, Gladys Knight & the Pips, and Rare Earth. In the meantime, Gordy established Motown Productions, a television subsidiary which produced TV specials for the Motown artists, including Diana Ross & the Supremes and the Temptations. For a total of $61 million, Berry Gordy sold his share of ownership in Motown in 1988 and his share of ownership in Motown Productions TV/film operations in 1989. In 1998, Motown was bought out by Universal Music Group.

Motown specialized in a type of soul music using percussion to accent the back beat, prominent and often melodic electric bass-guitar lines, distinctive chord structures, and a call-and-response singing style that originated in gospel music. Every song produced on the Motown label had a distinctly recognizable sound. Additionally, the artists voiced a hopeful, positive message that reflected the aspirations of the civil rights era. The Motown sound established itself with mainstream audiences, and concerts by Motown groups saw the unprecedented spectacle of racially mixed fans joining each other on the dance floor. As an African-American-owned record label, Motown played an important role in the racial integration of popular music.

1. Passage 1 implies that without Black Swan, performers such as Ethel Waters and Alberta Hunter would not have:

   A. been able to record music.
   B. had performance careers.
   C. opened music businesses.
   D. learned to be musicians.

2. Passage 1 states that an important change that permitted Black Swan to enter the phonograph business was the:

   F. expiration of patents on important manufacturing processes.
   G. increased competition from music recorded by immigrants.
   H. peaceful conditions following the end of World War I.
   J. discovery by big companies of a demand for African-American artists.

3. Passage 1 mentions all of the following as factors that caused Black Swan to go out of business EXCEPT:

   A. an increase in business competition.
   B. the growth of radio as a music source.
   C. a risky decision to expand business.
   D. a court order to stop selling recordings.

4. According to Passage 1, at the end of World War I very little music performed by African Americans was recorded because:

F. the large companies controlling the industry were not interested in recording African-American performers or distributing to their audience.
G. the demand for music by African-American performers was much stronger in Europe than it was in the United States.
H. very few African-American controlled recording labels existed at the end of World War I to record African-American performers.
J. the large recording companies were primarily interested in recording and distributing the music of immigrant groups to specific ethnic populations.

5. According to Passage 1, Black Swan was unusual in that it was a:

A. black-owned business that made its own business decisions.
B. record-producing company that recording a variety of music.
C. business that was founded after the end of World War I.
D. music publishing company that eventually became a record company.

6. In context, *portmanteau* (line 32) refers to a:

F. style of music.
G. business transaction.
H. geographical location.
J. blending of words

7. The primary purpose of Passage 2 is to:

A. describe a style of music popular in the 1960s and 1970s.
B. explain how music contributed to the civil rights movement.
C. present a history of the black-owned Motown business.
D. identify the most important musical artists of the 1960s and 1970s.

504 • READING INTEGRATION OF KNOWLEDGE AND IDEAS

8. Which of the following is an important difference between the Black Swan and the Motown labels?

F. Black Swan recorded many different types of music, while Motown specialized in a particular sound.
G. Motown is still in existence as a Black-owned company, while Black Swan went out of business in the 1920s.
H. Motown recruited and employed its own musical artists, but Black Swan relied on artists under contract to other companies.
J. Motown promoted the names of individual artists to sell records, but the artists used by Black Swan remain anonymous.

9. Based on the information provided in both passages, it can be inferred that:

A. Motown was more successful as a business than Black Swan.
B. Motown sound was musically superior to the Black Swan releases.
C. artists on the Black Swan label influenced those who performed for Motown.
D. Black Swan records would have sold more records had it been based in Detroit.

10. The two passages are alike in that they both:

F. provide a history of an African-American owned record company.
G. debate the merits of various musical styles popular at the time.
H. discuss the foundations of American music in the 20th century.
J. offer information on steps to be taken to open a small business.

Questions 11–20

Passage 1

"We come from Mr. Rivet," the lady finally said. She was as tall and straight as her companion, and with ten years less to carry. She was sad as a woman could look whose face was not charged with expression. That is, her tinted oval mask showed waste as an exposed surface shows friction. The hand of time had played over her
5   freely. She was slim and stiff, and so well-dressed, in dark blue cloth, that it was clear that she employed the same tailor as her husband. The couple had an indefinable air of prosperous thrift—they evidently got a good deal of luxury for their money. If I was to be one of their luxuries it would benefit me to consider my terms.

10   "Ah, Claude Rivet recommended me?" I echoed, and I added that it was very kind of him, though I could reflect that, as he only painted landscapes, this wasn't a sacrifice.

The lady looked very hard at the gentleman, and the gentleman looked around the room. Then staring at the floor a moment and stroking his moustache, he rested
15   his pleasant eyes on me with the remark: "He said you were the right one."

"I try to be, when people want to sit."

"Yes, we should like to," said the lady anxiously.

"Do you mean together?"

My visitors exchanged a glance. "If you could do anything with *me* I suppose it
20   would be double," the gentleman stammered.

"O yes, there's naturally a higher charge for two figures than for one."

"We should like to make it pay," the husband confessed.

"That's very good of you," I said, for I supposed he meant pay the artist.

A sense of strangeness seemed to dawn on the lady.

25   "We mean for the illustrations—Mr. Rivet said you might put one in."

"Put in—an illustration?" I was equally confused.

"Sketch her off, you know, you know," said the gentleman, coloring.

It was only then that I understood the service Claude Rivet had rendered me; he had told them how I worked in black-and-white, for magazines, for storybooks,
30   for sketches of contemporary life, and consequently had a lot of jobs for models. These things were true, but it was not less true that I could not get the honors, to say nothing of the monetary rewards, of a great painter of portraits out of my head.

"So you're—you're—a—?" I began as soon as I'd overcome my surprise. I could hardly bring myself to say the word "models," as it seemed so little to fit their case.

Passage 2

There were two possessions of the James Dillingham Youngs in which they both took a mighty pride. One was Jim's gold watch that had been his father's and his grandfather's. The other was Della's hair, which ripped and shone like a cascade of waters, reaching below her knee.

Della did her hair up nervously and quickly. Once, she faltered and stood while a tear splashed on the worn red carpet. Then, she fluttered out the door and down the stairs to the street.

The sign read: "Mme. Sofronie. Hair Goods of All Kinds." One flight up Della ran.

"Will you buy my hair?" asked Della.

"Twenty dollars," said Madame.

"Give it to me quick," said Della.

The next two hours she ransacked the stores for Jim's present. She found it at last. It was a platinum fob chain simple and chaste in design, properly proclaiming its value by substance alone and not by meretricious ornamentation—as all good things should do. It was even worthy of The Watch.

Twenty-one dollars they took from her for it, and she hurried home. With that chain on his watch Jim might be properly anxious about the time in any company. Grand as the watch was, he sometimes looked at it on the sly on account of the old leather strap that he used in place of a chain.

She went to work repairing the ravages made by generosity added to love. Within forty minutes her head was covered with tiny, close-lying curls that made her look wonderfully like a truant schoolboy.

Jim was never late. She heard his step on the stair. The door opened and Jim stepped in. He looked thin and very serious. Poor fellow, he needed a new overcoat and he was without gloves.

His eyes were fixed upon Della, and there was an expression in them that she could not read. It was not anger, nor surprise, nor disapproval. He simply stared at her fixedly with that peculiar expression on his face.

"Jim, darling," she cried, "don't look at me that way. I had my hair cut off and sold because I couldn't have lived through Christmas without giving you a present. It'll grow out again."

Unit 13 | ANALYZING PAIRED PASSAGES • 507

"You've cut off your hair?" asked Jim, laboriously, as if he had not arrived at that patent fact yet even after the hardest mental labor.

Jim drew a package from his overcoat pocket and threw it upon the table.

"Don't make any mistake, Dell," he said. "I don't think there's anything that
70 could make me like my girl any less. But if you'll unwrap that package you may see why you had me going."

White fingers tore at the string and paper. There lay the Combs—the set of combs that Della had worshipped long in a Broadway window. Beautiful combs, pure tortoise shell, with jeweled rims—just the shade to wear in the beautiful
75 vanished hair. They were expensive combs, she knew, and her heart had simply craved them without the least hope of possession. And now, they were hers, but the tresses that should have adorned the coveted adornments were gone.

Jim had not yet seen his beautiful present. She held it out to him eagerly upon her open palm. Jim tumbled down on the couch and put his hands under the back of
80 his head and smiled. "Dell," said he, "I sold the watch to buy your combs."

11. It can be inferred that the couple who come to see the narrator in Passage 1 are:

 A. looking for an artist to paint a family portrait.
 B. hoping to find work modeling for an artist.
 C. art students who wish to learn from an established painter.
 D. friends of Claude Rivet who have come to pay a social call.

12. It can be inferred that the narrator in Passage 1 thinks that Claude Rivet:

 F. was very generous to refer the couple to him.
 G. gave up nothing by referring the couple to him.
 H. expected the narrator to return the favor of the referral.
 J. doesn't have as much artistic talent as the narrator.

13. It can be inferred that the woman in Passage 1:

 A. is better dressed than her husband.
 B. is older than her husband.
 C. looks older than she really is.
 D. is extremely attractive.

14. It can be inferred that the narrator in Passage 1:

   F. hopes to one day be a famous painter of portraits.
   G. is studying to become an illustrator.
   H. is a well-known painter of landscapes.
   J. is a wealthy magazine and book illustrator.

15. In Passage 1, it can be inferred that Claude Rivet is:

   A. a publisher who sometimes employs the narrator.
   B. an artist who primarily paints landscape pictures.
   C. a relative of the couple who call on the narrator.
   D. a close friend and business partner of the narrator.

16. In context, *meretricious* (line 48) means:

   F. expensive.
   G. worthless.
   H. accurate.
   J. unfathomable.

17. It can be inferred that the combs mentioned in Passage 2 are:

   A. used for grooming purposes.
   B. intended only for store display.
   C. worn ornamentally in the hair.
   D. more valuable than the watch fob.

18. In Passage 2, it can be inferred that Jim stares at Della because he:

   F. realizes that his gift is no longer useful.
   G. is angry that Della has cut all her hair off.
   H. hopes that Della will let her hair grow back.
   J. fails to recognize Della as his wife.

19. The couples in Passages 1 and 2 are alike in that both are:

   A. married with children.
   B. looking for employment.
   C. young and recently married.
   D. in need of money.

20. The two narratives are both characterized by:

   F. extensive use of metaphor.
   G. ironic endings.
   H. conflict between good and evil.
   J. flashbacks and foreshadowing.

READING MASTERY TEST 1

DIRECTIONS: Read each passage and answer the questions based upon what is stated or implied in the passage. Answers are on page 755.

Passage 1

In India, about 40 percent of elected officials in the villages are women. More than a million women have been elected at the local level. This is the highest percentage of women leaders for any democracy. Their success in politics has often been called a silent revolution. Women-led local governments have provided public
5 services such as wells and roads. They have also worked to improve sanitation and education. The large number of women in local government has inspired self-confidence, and it has led to a greater role for women in their households and in the community.

1. The writer is primarily discussing the:

   A. women in politics around the world.
   B. impact of women on local politics in India.
   C. need for improving government services in India.
   D. importance of providing good role models.

2. Suppose that the writer had been given an assignment to write a paragraph about the role of women in politics in one country. This paragraph fulfills the assignment because it discusses:

   F. women-led local governments in India.
   G. the services that government provides.
   H. the advantages of democratic government.
   J. a large country with a large population.

3. The writer would like to add more detail to the paragraph. Which of the following would be most appropriate to add?

   A. The names of one or two women who have been elected to positions in village government

   B. A description of a sanitary improvement project made by a women-led local government

   C. A list of repairs needed to the school of a particular local village

   D. Statistical information about the number of people who live in villages

4. The passage mentions that women in local government have worked to provide all of the following services EXCEPT:

   F. sanitation.
   G. wells.
   H. police.
   J. education.

5. According to the passage, the large number of women in local government has led to:

   A. more self-confidence.
   B. violent revolution.
   C. increased democracy.
   D. population migration.

Passage 2

In the Romance languages, which include Spanish and French, and are derived from Latin, the modern names for the days of the week come from the names of the first seven planets, which were named for Roman deities. The early Romans used Saturday, named for Saturn, the Roman god of justice, as the first day
5 of the week, but as sun worship became increasingly accepted, the sun's day became the first day of the week. In French, the modern name for Sunday, *dimanche*, comes from the Latin *Dominica*, which means "Lord's day." In Spanish, Sunday is *domingo*.

The second day was named for that other prominent celestial feature, the moon. The Spanish *lunes* and the French *lundi* closely resemble the Latin word *luna*,
10 which means *moon*, the day of the week honoring the goddess of the moon.

Tuesday, which is *martes* in Spanish and *mardi* in French, was named for Mars, the god of war. Wednesday is *miércoles* and *mercredi* and is named for Mercury. *Jueves* and *jeudi* or Thursday is named for Jove or Jupiter, the chief Roman god; and *viernes* and *vendredi* or Friday is named for Venus, the goddess of love.

15 Later, for English, the Anglo-Saxons assigned their words for sun and moon to create *Sunnandæg* for Sunday and *Mónandæg* for Monday. They also substituted the names of the Norse gods for the original Roman deities. Tuesday is Týr's day. Týr is

the one-armed Norse god of combat and the son of Odin. Wednesday is the day of Odin, the head god in Norse mythology, who is also called Wotan. Thursday is

20   named for Thor, the god famous for his powerful hammer and ability to control the weather. Friday is Fríge's day. Fríge is Odin's wife and the Norse goddess of love.

In English, Saturday is the only day which still carries the name of a Roman god. The other days have been given Anglo-Saxon names or bear the names of gods from Teutonic mythology.

6. The author states that Sunday became the first day of the week because of:

    F. the importance of justice.
    G. a greater acceptance of Norse mythology.
    H. a decline in the influence of the Romans.
    J. an increase in sun worship.

7. The passage primarily discusses the origins of the names of the:

    A. first seven planets.
    B. days of the week.
    C. Teutonic deities.
    D. Roman gods and goddesses.

8. According to the passage, the modern English name for Thursday was originally given to that day by the:

    F. Anglo-Saxons.
    G. Norse.
    H. French.
    J. Romans.

9. According to the passage, the Romans originally used what day as the first day of the week?

    A. Saturday
    B. Sunday
    C. Monday
    D. Friday

10. According to the passage, the wife of the Norse god Odin is also the goddess of:

    F. war.
    G. weather.
    H. love.
    J. the moon.

11. According to the passage, in Spanish and French, the modern name for Wednesday comes from the god:

    A. Odin.
    B. Wotan.
    C. Mercury.
    D. Jupiter.

12. According to the passage, in Norse mythology which of the following gods is Odin's son?

F. Týr
G. Mercury
H. Fríge
J. Saturn

Passage 3

Heavier-than-air flight was only eleven years old in August 1914, when the fragile airplane was pressed into military service during World War I. The great weapon of that war was artillery, and the airplane contributed to the carnage by providing aerial reconnaissance, which greatly increased artillery's effectiveness.

5 Observation aircraft photographed and mapped trenches and military positions, reported transient targets, and provided direct control for artillery batteries. Further, aircraft photographs and reports enabled commanders to identify the enemy's position, determine its strength, surmise the enemy's intentions, and organize their response.

10 The need to protect one's own observation aircraft or deny the air to the enemy quickly led to a quest for control of the air. In 1915, an asynchronization or "interrupter" mechanism allowed machine guns to fire through a spinning propeller, enabling the pilot to aim the entire airplane. This ability gave birth to the "pursuit," or fighter. To gain superiority in the air, the airplane now hunted other airplanes.

15 Over time, this new role demanded more sophisticated machines and combat techniques, and the men who flew the machines, as well as the machines themselves, became famous, dramatic symbols of knightly combat.

Soon, the airplane was also used as a bomber. Initially, pilots simply tossed small, handheld bombs or even darts from the cockpit. But the potential of

20 destruction from the air quickly led to larger, more powerful, often multi-engine airplanes designed specifically for bombing. With airplanes able to carry heavier loads, the size of the bombs themselves grew rapidly. The development of mechanical bomb sights enabled aircraft to hit targets more accurately and from higher altitudes. Most aerial bombardment targeted enemy troops and facilities

25 along the front, but the airplane also allowed the war to be carried to manufacturing and population centers far behind the lines.

In 1915, Germany began Zeppelin raids against England. The Zeppelins—large, slow, rigid airships filled with explosive hydrogen gas—ultimately proved

vulnerable to aerial defenses and were gradually replaced by giant multi-engine
30 strategic bombers, the vanguard of future war.

By the end of the war, commanders had explored almost every role that the airplane would play in the future except global air transport. Although the airplane was not the decisive weapon of World War I, it had demonstrated its potential to change the way wars were fought.

13. The author mentions that aircraft were used in all of the following capacities during World War I EXCEPT:

A. directing artillery fire against the enemy.
B. gathering information about enemy positions.
C. dropping bombs on manufacturing centers.
D. transporting troops and equipment.

14. According to the passage, the first use of the airplane during World War I was for:

F. dropping bombs on enemy manufacturing and population centers.
G. gathering information and directing artillery fire.
H. attacking other airplanes in air-to-air combat.
J. defending against the attacks of Zeppelins.

15. Which of the following best describes the main point of the passage?

A. The airplane was used in World War I to photograph and map enemies' positions and direct artillery fire.
B. At the time that World War I began, the airplane was still an untested machine that had not yet been used in combat.
C. Military leaders during World War I found many uses for the airplane even though the technology was still relatively new.
D. During World War I, the pilots of military aircraft regarded themselves as modern knights who did battle in the air with other knights.

16. The passage primarily discusses the:

F. invention of the airplane.
G. shortcomings of World War I planes.
H. use of aircraft throughout military history.
J. role of early aircraft in combat.

514 • READING

17. According to the passage, the most destructive weapon used in World War I was:

    A. the Zeppelin.
    B. the machine gun.
    C. air bombardment.
    D. artillery.

18. According to the passage, the interrupter mechanism made it possible to:

    F. track the movement of transient enemy targets.
    G. fire a machine gun through a spinning propeller.
    H. drop bombs from the cockpit of an airplane.
    J. attack manufacturing centers far behind enemy lines.

19. According to the passage, mechanical bombsites had the effect of:

    A. enabling pilots to drop darts from the cockpit.
    B. making it possible to bomb from higher altitudes.
    C. introducing the concept of air-to-air combat.
    D. encouraging the use of Zeppelins to deliver bombs.

20. According to the passage, the size of aerial bombs increased dramatically once:

    F. pilots learned how to throw bombs from the cockpit.
    G. a device was developed that permitted the airplane to be aimed.
    H. airplanes became powerful enough to carry the added weight.
    J. commanders realized that planes could be used for global transport.

DIRECTIONS: Each of the following items (Questions 21–30) is a sentence with a word that has been italicized. You are to choose the answer that has the meaning that is <u>most</u> <u>like</u> that of the italicized word. Answers are on page 755.

21. According to Alfred Nobel, the Nobel Prize in literature is an *accolade* reserved for only "the most outstanding work" written by the best authors.

In the context of the sentence above, *accolade* means:

A. honor.
B. payment.
C. publication.
D. celebration.

22. Disney World guests who ride the Twilight Zone Tower of Terror ride an elevator to the top of a tall building then quickly *plummet* in free fall all the way to the bottom in a terrifying drop.

In the context of the sentence above, *plummet* means:

F. rise.
G. swing.
H. drop.
J. fly.

23. Though Kiana just got engaged yesterday, she and her fiancé have already set a *tentative* date for their wedding, provided that the reception hall is available on that day and other details can be worked out.

In the context of the sentence above, *tentative* means:

A. definite and irrevocable.
B. permanent and unchanging.
C. uncertain but improbable.
D. definite but changeable.

24. After Diana of Wales died in 1997, thousands of people lined the streets outside her funeral to *lament* the loss of their beloved princess.

In the context of the sentence above, *lament* means:

F. discuss.
G. celebrate.
H. mourn.
J. share.

25. My dog typically *heeds* my directions, but today he is completely ignoring all of my commands!

In the context of the sentence above, *heeds* means:

A. ignores.
B. obeys.
C. misunderstands.
D. hears.

26. As an astrophysicist, Brenda had a vast theoretical knowledge of the stars, their movements, their evolution, and their eventual fiery end, but she could not remember the most *mundane* details of her daily existence, such as her zip code or her cell phone password.

In the context of the sentence above, *mundane* means:

F. important.
G. ordinary.
H. innocent.
J. biased.

27. The solos played by the jazz musician seemed to be *improvised* on the stage, but they were actually carefully thought out and well rehearsed.

In the context of the sentence above, *improvised* means:

A. copied from elsewhere.
B. played as a group.
C. planned in advance.
D. invented on the spot.

28. During the first week of our vacation, the bright sun, balmy temperatures, and gentle breezes were ideal for swimming, hiking, and tennis; but the *inclement* weather of the final three days left us stuck in our hotel room with nothing to do but watch the same television reruns we could have seen at home.

In the context of the sentence above, *inclement* means:

F. abundant.
G. predictable.
H. calm.
J. stormy.

29. The audience came to the studio recital expecting to hear an amateur cellist perform an easy piece or two, but what they heard was a *virtuoso* performance by a well-trained musician of three of the most difficult pieces in the cello repertory.

In the context of the sentence above, *virtuoso* means:

A. masterful.
B. clumsy.
C. uninspiring.
D. foolhardy.

30. The occupants of the overcrowded life boat carefully secured the water and food to the seats so that the containers would not be lost as the boat pitched wildly, but they *jettisoned* their personal belongings in order to make the boat lighter.

In the context of the sentence above, *jettisoned* means:

F. dumped.
G. consumed.
H. conserved.
J. retained.

READING MASTERY TEST 2

> **DIRECTIONS:** Read each passage and answer the questions based upon what is stated or implied in the passage. Answers are on page 755.

Passage 1

The stranger came one wintry day, through a driving snow, walking from the railway station. He was wrapped from head to foot, and the brim of his soft felt hat hid his face. He staggered into the Coach and Horses and called, "I need a room!" He shook the snow from off himself and followed Mrs. Hall into her guest parlor.

5 Mrs. Hall lit a fire and went to prepare him a meal. A guest in the wintertime was a piece of luck. She carried a place setting into the parlor and laid it on the table. She was surprised to see that her visitor still wore his hat and coat. The snow from his shoulders was melting in the warm room, and it dripped upon her new carpet. "Can I take your hat and coat, sir," she said, "and dry them in the kitchen?"

10 "No," he said. He looked at her over his shoulder. "I prefer to keep them on." She noticed that he wore sunglasses and had his coat-collar turned up so that it completely hid his cheeks and face.

"As you like," she said. "The room seems quite warm to me."

He made no answer and turned away as Mrs. Hall whisked out of the room.
15 When she returned, he was still standing in the same place, his dripping hat-brim turned down, hiding his face and ears completely. She put down the eggs and bacon. The stranger sat down at the table with eager quickness.

As she went toward the kitchen, she heard a spoon being rapidly whisked round a bowl. "That girl!" she said. "I clean forgot it, and she's taking so long!" Mrs.
20 Hall finished mixing the mustard herself, giving Millie a few verbal jabs for her excessive slowness. She had cooked the ham and eggs, laid the table, and done everything, while Millie had only succeeded in delaying the mustard. And him a new guest wanting to stay! Then Mrs. Hall filled the mustard pot, put it with a certain stateliness upon a gold and black tea-tray, and carried it into the parlor.

25 She rapped upon the door and entered promptly. As she did, her visitor quickly picked something up from the floor. She slammed down the mustard pot on the table, and then she noticed the overcoat and hat had been taken off and put over one of her good chairs. She went to these things resolutely. "I suppose I may have them to dry now," she said firmly.

520 • READING

30 "Leave the hat," said her visitor, in a muffled voice. For a moment she was too surprised to speak. He held a white cloth over the lower part of his face, so that his mouth and jaws were completely hidden, and all of his forehead above his sunglasses was covered by a white bandage. He wore a dark-brown velvet jacket with a high, black, linen-lined collar turned up about his neck. She couldn't see any
35 part of his face.

She went quite softly to the kitchen and was too preoccupied to ask Millie what she was messing about with now when she got there.

The visitor resumed his meal. He took a mouthful, glanced suspiciously at the window, took another mouthful, then rose and, taking the napkin in his hand,
40 walked across the room and pulled the blind down. This done, he returned with an easier air to the table and his meal.

"The poor soul's had an accident or an op'ration or somethin'," thought Mrs. Hall. "Ain't you done with them taters yet, Millie?"

When Mrs. Hall went to clear away the stranger's lunch, he was smoking a pipe,
45 and he never loosened the silk muffler wrapped round the lower part of his face to put the mouthpiece to his lips. "I have some luggage at the station," he said, and he asked her when he could have it sent.

"Tomorrow?" he said. "There is no speedier delivery?"

"It's a steep road," she said; and then, snatching at an opening, added, "It was
50 there a carriage was upsettled, a year ago. A gentleman killed, besides his coachman. Accidents, sir, happen in a moment, don't they?"

But the visitor was not to be drawn so easily. "They do," he said through his muffler, eyeing her quietly through his impenetrable glasses.

"But they take long enough to get well, don't they? There was my sister's son,
55 Tom, jest cut his arm with a scythe. He was badly hurt."

"Was he?" he said. "Will you get me some matches? My pipe is out."

She went for the matches.

"Thanks," he said concisely, as she put them down, and turned his shoulder upon her and stared at the blind covering the window. Evidently he was sensitive on
60 the topic of injuries.

The visitor remained in the parlor until four o'clock, without explaining why he had come. For the most part, he sat in the growing darkness smoking his pipe in the firelight—perhaps dozing. Once or twice, there was audible pacing in the room. He seemed to be talking to himself. Then the armchair creaked as he sat down again.

READING MASTERY TEST 2 • 521

1. It can be inferred that Mrs. Hall:

   A. is the proprietor of the Coach and Horses.
   B. stayed as a guest at the Coach and Horses.
   C. was stranded at the Coach and Horses by the weather.
   D. is in charge of transportation from the inn to the station.

2. It can be inferred that Millie is:

   F. the owner of the Coach and Horses.
   G. Mrs. Hall's employee.
   H. the companion of the stranger.
   J. a guest at the inn.

3. Mrs. Hall mentions the accident of her sister's son, Tom, because she:

   A. hopes that the guest will provide information about the injuries she supposes him to have.
   B. wants to reassure the guest that he is welcome at the Coach and Horses for as long as he wishes.
   C. expects the stranger to need medical attention during his stay at the Coach and Horses.
   D. needs to explain that it will not be possible to retrieve luggage from the station until the weather clears.

4. It can be inferred that the stranger wears the bandages:

   F. because he has been injured.
   G. because he has had an operation.
   H. in order to hide his face.
   J. in order to warm his head.

5. Mrs. Hall's behavior toward the guest indicates that she is:

   A. indifferent to his presence at the Coach and Horses.
   B. anxious to please him so that he will remain.
   C. unconcerned with the quality of service that she provides.
   D. preoccupied with the other guests at the Coach and Horses.

6. It can be inferred that the stranger sits down at the table quickly because he is:

   F. fatigued.
   G. hungry.
   H. cold.
   J. angry.

Passage 2

It was after Bourbaki's defeat in the east of France. The army, broken up, decimated, and worn out, had been obliged to retreat into Switzerland. Hunger, the terrible cold, and forced marches caused us the greatest suffering. Of our little band that had numbered twelve hundred men on the first of January, there remained only
5   twenty-two pale, thin, ragged wretches. But we were safe and could rest. We gained fresh life. We actually had something to eat every day and could sleep every night.

Meanwhile, the war continued in the east of France. It was disgraceful and irritating to know that within two or three miles the Prussians were victorious and insolent. Our captain had a plan. A man in that part of the country was going to lend
10 him a cart and suits of peasants' clothes. We could hide under some straw at the bottom of the wagon, which would be loaded with Gruyere cheese, which he was supposed to be going to sell in France.

At the border, a Swiss officer walked around the wagon, touching this and that wheel or board in a knowing manner, but that was in order to impress his soldiers.
15 Our captain spoke to him in German, and the officer, who understood not a word, nodded solemnly and waved us through.

"Get up," the captain said to the horses, as he cracked his whip, while the three guards quietly smoked their pipes. I was half suffocated in my box, which only admitted the air through holes in front, and at the same time I was nearly frozen, for
20 it was terribly cold. The wagon loaded with Gruyere cheese entered our own country.

We arrived at a small village at nightfall. While three of us hid in a cellar, the captain continued the journey as far as Besançon with the empty wagon and one man. They crossed the plateau until they were within about ten miles of the city
25 walls. Then they left the wagon at Omans, among the Germans, and escaped at night on foot, so as to gain the heights which border the River Doubs. The next day they entered Besançon, where there were plenty of rifles. There were nearly forty thousand of them left in the arsenal, and General Roland, a brave marine, laughed at the captain's daring project, but let him have six rifles and wished him good luck.
30 Going was nothing in comparison to returning. They were obliged to travel by night, so as to avoid meeting anybody, as the possession of six rifles would have made them liable to suspicion. But, in spite of everything, a week after leaving us, the captain and our comrade-in-arms were back with us again. The campaign was about to begin.

7. It can be inferred that the narrator and his companions are:

   A. French.
   B. Swiss.
   C. German.
   D. Prussian.

8. It can be inferred that the mission originates in:

   F. Switzerland.
   G. Prussia.
   H. Germany.
   J. France.

9. It can be inferred that the "campaign" mentioned in line 33 refers to:

   A. the trip back to where the group started.
   B. a military action against the enemy.
   C. a secret mission planned by General Roland.
   D. the continuing convalescence of the soldiers.

10. The narrator implies that the Swiss officer who inspects the wagon:

    F. suspects that the men are hidden beneath the straw but lets them pass.
    G. knows the man who lent the group the cart and their clothing.
    H. wants his men to believe that he is in control of the situation.
    J. plans to join the group after it has made its way to Besançon.

Passage 3

A newly married pair boarded the train in San Antonio and took seats in the coach. The man's face was reddened from many days in the wind and sun, and he wore new black clothes. He sat stiffly with a hand on each knee. He was constantly moving his hands in a self-conscious manner, and he glanced furtively and shyly at
5   the other passengers.

The bride wore a dress of blue cashmere with bits of velvet here and there. She continually twisted her head to look at her puff sleeves as though they embarrassed her.

They were evidently very happy. "Ever been on a train before?" he asked,
10   smiling with delight.

"No," she answered. "I never was. It's fine, ain't it?"

"Great! And then after a while we'll go forward to the diner and get a big lay-out. Finest meal in the world. Charge a dollar."

"Oh, do they?" cried the bride. "Charge a dollar? Why, that's too much—for
15   us—ain't it, Jack?"

"Not this trip," he answered bravely. "We're going to do the whole thing."

He explained to her about trains. "You see, it's a thousand miles from one end of Texas to the other, and this train runs right across it and never stops but four times." He pointed out the dazzling fittings of the coach, and her eyes opened wide
20   as she contemplated the sea-green figured velvet, the shining brass, silver and glass, the wood that gleamed as darkly brilliant as the surface of a pool of oil.

"We are due in Yellow Sky at 3:42," he said, looking tenderly into her eyes.

"Oh, are we?" she said, as if she had not been aware of it. To show surprise at her husband's statement was part of her wifely amiability. She took out a little silver
25   watch and stared at it with a frown of concentration. The new husband's face beamed proudly.

"I bought it in San Anton' from a friend of mine," he told her gleefully.

"It's seventeen minutes past twelve," she said, looking up at him with a shy and clumsy flirtation.

30   A passenger, noting this interplay, winked cynically at his reflection in the window. After a while, the couple got up and went to the dining car.

11. It can be inferred that the passenger who winked at his reflection regarded the couple with:

    A. amusement.
    B. admiration.
    C. jealousy.
    D. indifference.

12. It can be inferred that the husband explains the train to his new bride in order to:

    F. make her feel self-conscious.
    G. ensure that she is not afraid.
    H. impress her with his knowledge.
    J. show other passengers they are married.

13. It can be inferred that the husband:

    A. travels frequently by train.
    B. spends a lot of time outdoors.
    C. has been married before.
    D. is older than his new wife.

14. It can be inferred that the wife's watch:

    F. does not keep time accurately.
    G. was a gift from her new husband.
    H. is a family heirloom.
    J. was made in Yellow Sky.

15. Which of the following statements about the newly married couple is best supported by the passage?

    A. The man and the woman are a little uncomfortable in their new roles as husband and wife.
    B. The man and woman are sophisticated world travelers enjoying a train trip as their honeymoon.
    C. The man and the woman are very outgoing and eager to engage other passengers in conversation.
    D. The man and the woman have been married for several months and are relaxed in each other's company.

Passage 4

Dr. Seuss's real name was Theodor Geisel. Geisel liked to say that he adopted the pen name "Seuss" because he was saving his real name for the Great American Novel he would one day write. That's not really true. The real story is that in the spring of 1925, Geisel was editor of *Jack-o-Lantern*, the humor magazine at
5 Dartmouth College. Geisel and nine friends were caught drinking gin in his room. The dean put them all on probation for violating school rules regarding alcohol. During his probation, Geisel was not permitted to contribute to the magazine, so he published cartoons under various assumed names including "T. Seuss" and "Seuss."

"Seuss" was his mother's maiden name and his middle name. Many aspects of
10 Seuss' writings were based on his own life and other real events. The inspiration for the character of the Grinch in *How the Grinch Stole Christmas!* was Dr. Seuss himself. He was brushing his teeth the morning of one December 26th and noticed a very Grinch-like character in the mirror. He sensed that something had gone wrong with his feelings about the holiday season and wrote the story in an attempt to recapture
15 those feelings. As anyone familiar with the story knows, the Grinch tries to prevent Christmas by stealing the presents, decorations, and other trappings of the holiday. But in the end, Christmas comes to the Whos all the same, and the Grinch learns that Christmas is not just about presents and decorations.

Dr. Suess himself was once a part of the business world, and his first job after
20 graduating from college was writing ad slogans and jingles. In 1927, he created "Quick, Henry, the Flit!," the ad slogan for a bug spray. The ad campaign that centered around the slogan ran for 27 years and made Dr. Seuss both famous and wealthy.

Many of Dr. Seuss' stories had distinct political messages. In 1954, he published
25 the tale of individualism titled *Horton Hears a Who!*; in 1961, the anti-discrimination fable *The Sneetches*; in 1958, the anti-Fascist parable *Yertle the Turtle*; and in 1984, the anti–arms-race story *The Butter Battle Book*. Dr. Seuss has sold more children's books than any other author, but his political messages are often overlooked because they are delivered in language and settings suitable for very young children.

16. In the first paragraph, when the author writes "That's not really true," the author is referring to the:

   F. belief that Dr. Seuss was the real name of the author of *Horton Hears a Who!*
   G. theory that Theodor Geisel was the creator of the "Quick, Henry, the Flit" slogan.
   H. opinion held by many readers that *Jack-o-Lantern* was a book written by Theodor Geisel.
   J. suggestion by Theodor Geisel that he would use his real name as the author of a novel he hoped to write.

17. The author cites *Horton Hears a Who!*, *The Sneetches*, and *Yertle the Turtle* as:

   A. proof that Theodor Geisel is the real name of "Seuss."
   B. evidence that Theodor Geisel was not a real person.
   C. biographical details of the life of Theodor Geisel.
   D. examples of children's books with political messages.

18. The author describes the incident involving alcohol leading to probation in order to:

   F. explore the origins of Geisel's political views.
   G. explain how Seuss became Geisel's pen name.
   H. disprove the idea that authors are model citizens.
   J. show that authors should use pen names for their writing.

Passage 5

We hear a lot about the "rough-and-tumble of politics," but today's political skirmishes are civilized compared to the pre-election battles of the mid-nineteenth century. Baltimore, in particular, was so unruly that it was known as Mobtown and was home to political clubs with names like Plug Uglies, American Rattlers, and
5 Blood Tubs.

Between 1830 and 1860, immigration pushed Baltimore's population from 80,000 to 212,000, and nearly 25 percent of the city was foreign-born. Local political bosses, especially Democrats, sought immigrant support through the promise of jobs and other preferences. On the other side, native-born residents felt threatened
10 by the increasing population of immigrants and flocked to the Know Nothings, so called because of their stock response to questions about clandestine activities.

Baltimore's patchwork of neighborhoods provided the setting for confrontations between natives and newcomers. Riots often followed baseball games and holiday parades. But election season—municipal elections in September, city council polling in October, and the presidential vote in November—provided numerous excuses for "raw heads and bloody bones."

Because the party that ruled the streets also controlled the polls, partisans regularly marched through opposing wards. They also infiltrated opposition rallies and jabbed bystanders with ice picks. At the polls, the Plug Uglies surrounded opposition voters and forced them to retreat.

A favorite election strategy was "cooping." Days before an election, immigrants would be abducted and held in cellars or sheds called "coops." Then on election day, they were transported to the polls in small groups to vote for the kidnappers' candidates, and vote again, and again. A single "coop" might hold a hundred captives, each of whom would vote a dozen times.

Often the political clashes were pitched battles fought with picks and axes, pistols and muskets, and occasionally even cannons. In 1858, mayoral candidate Colonel Schutt, fearful of the violence, made what is perhaps the earliest concession speech in American history, bowing out of the race at noon on Election Day with several hours left to vote.

19. The author intends for the names of political clubs mentioned in lines 4–5 to suggest the:

A. importance of a peaceful democratic process.
B. violence that characterized Baltimore politics.
C. melting pot quality of Baltimore's population.
D. risk associated with being a recent immigrant.

20. In Paragraph 2, the author draws a contrast between:

F. Democrats and the Know Nothings.
G. Democrats and recent immigrants.
H. political bosses and native-born residents.
J. native-born residents and Know Nothings.

Level 1
SCIENCE

INTERPRETATION OF DATA

Unit 1 | Tables...........531
What Is the Purpose of Data Tables? 532
Organizing Data.................533
Exercise.................537

Unit 2 | Tables Practice.................545
Exercise 1.................546
Exercise 2.................551

Unit 3 | Bar Graphs 557
How to Interpret Bar Graphs 558
Exercise.................563

Unit 4 | Bar Graphs Practice 571
Exercise 1.................572
Exercise 2.................577

Unit 5 | Line Graphs 583
How to Interpret Line Graphs.................584
Exercise 589

Unit 6 | Line Graphs Practice 597
Exercise 1.................598
Exercise 2.................603

Unit 7 | Practice.................609
Exercise 1.................610
Exercise 2.................617

SCIENTIFIC INVESTIGATION

Unit 8 | Describing Experiments 623
Introducing Simple Scientific Investigations
and Experiments 624
Extracting Information from Simple Experiments.................631
Exercise.................637

Unit 9 | Describing Experiments Practice 641
Exercise.................642

Unit 10 | Experimental Tools and Methods 651
Understanding Tools and Their Functions 652
Exercise.................662

Unit 11 | Experimental Tools and Methods Practice.................669
Exercise.................670

EVALUATION OF MODELS, INFERENCES, AND EXPERIMENTAL RESULTS

Unit 12 | Understanding Models 681
Extracting Information from Text Describing
Conceptual Models 682
Exercise.................689

Unit 13 | Understanding Models Practice 695
Exercise.................696

MASTERY TESTS

Science Mastery Test 1 707
Science Mastery Test 2 725

Science Interpretation of Data

Unit 1 | Tables

INSIDE THIS UNIT:
– What Is the Purpose of Data Tables? – – Organizing Data – – Exercise –

532 • SCIENCE INTERPRETATION OF DATA

Non-Negotiable Skill:

Recognize a table's features and use a table
to select a single piece of data.

What Is the Purpose of Data Tables?

The most basic method of organizing data is to present it in table form. Just as
scientists use tables, we also use tables in everyday life. For example:

TRAIN SCHEDULE (Bayville to Hightop)							
Train Name	Leaves Bayville	Arrives Clearview	Arrives Dalton	Arrives Easton	Arrives Fremont	Arrives Glendale	Arrives Hightop
Meteor	9:00 a.m.	9:44 a.m.	10:01 a.m.	10:15 a.m.	10:55 a.m.	11:17 a.m.	11:21 a.m.
Streak	9:20 a.m.	10:00 a.m.	10:20 a.m.	11:39 a.m.	12:30 p.m.	12:50 p.m.	12:59 p.m.
Comet	1:05 p.m.	1:45 p.m.	2:10 p.m.	2:31 p.m.	3:20 p.m.	3:45 p.m.	3:55 p.m.
Flash	4:30 p.m.	5:10 p.m.	5:34 p.m.	6:04 p.m.	6:35 p.m.	7:00 p.m.	7:08 p.m.

There is no real mystery to reading this table. You read presentations like it all the
time. You can surely answer the following questions:

- What time does the Meteor get to Fremont?

- What train leaves Bayville at 1:05 p.m.?

- Which train makes the trip from Bayville to Hightop in the shortest time?

When we talk about a table we call the horizontal lines the **rows** and the vertical
lines the **columns**. The rows intersect the columns to create **cells** with data in them.
Thus, the first row (Meteor) and the last column (Hightop) intersect at the cell
containing the time that the Meteor train arrives at the Hightop station: 11:21 a.m.

If you can read the train schedule (and you can), then you can read many of the
tables used in science. Some will be larger and more complicated than the train
schedule, but the procedure is always the same.

Organizing Data

Tables help to make data easier to understand. To illustrate this, let's look at the following experiment.

A group of students conducted an experiment to determine which liquid—rainwater, distilled water, sparkling water, or diet soda—produced the greatest plant growth. They planted germinated pea seeds in individual pots of identical soil and watered each of them with the same amount of one of the four liquids. The students measured the height of the plants every five days for 25 days using a ruler and recorded the data.

The plant that was watered with diet soda reached a final height of 15.0 centimeters, while the plant watered with distilled water reached a final height of 18.0 centimeters. The tallest plant on Day 20 was the one watered with rainwater at 17.7 centimeters. The plant watered with sparkling water was 16.2 centimeters on Day 20. On Day 5, the rainwater plant was 3.0 centimeters tall, and the sparkling water plant was 1.2 centimeters tall. The plant watered with distilled water grew from 9.5 centimeters on Day 10 to 15.8 centimeters on Day 15. One plant was 12.2 centimeters tall on Day 15, and that was the plant watered with diet soda. On Day 20, the plant watered with distilled water was 16.5 centimeters, while the sparkling water plant was 14.5 centimeters on Day 15. The shortest plant on Day 10, at 8.4 centimeters, was the one watered with diet soda, and on Day 10 the rainwater plant measured 10.2 centimeters. The plant watered with diet soda grew from 1.5 centimeters on Day 5 to 13.6 centimeters on Day 20. On Day 25, the sparkling water plant was 17.0 centimeters while the rainwater plant was 19.0 centimeters. The sparkling water plant was 11.5 centimeters on Day 10, while the rainwater plant was 13.8 centimeters on Day 15. On Day 5, the plant watered with distilled water was only 2.0 centimeters tall.

Now let's look at some questions based upon the data:

1. On Day 25, the tallest plant was the one watered with:

   A. rainwater.
   B. distilled water.
   C. sparkling water.
   D. diet soda.

2. On Day 10, the shortest plant was the one watered with:

   F. rainwater.
   G. distilled water.
   H. sparkling water.
   J. diet soda.

3. On Day 20, the second tallest plant was the one watered with:

   A. rainwater.
   B. distilled water.
   C. sparkling water.
   D. diet soda.

4. On Day 10, the plant watered with sparkling water measured:

   F. 8.4 centimeters.
   G. 9.5 centimeters.
   H. 11.5 centimeters.
   J. 14.5 centimeters.

5. On Day 15, which of the plants measured 13.8 centimeters?

   A. The one watered with rainwater
   B. The one watered with distilled water
   C. The one watered with sparkling water
   D. The one watered with diet soda

The answers are pretty difficult to find, but not because the questions themselves are difficult. In fact, the questions are easy. They ask things like "What's the tallest?" and "What's the shortest?" What makes them difficult is the fact that the data are all jumbled up. If the data were better organized, the questions would be much easier. And that is the purpose of a table.

TABLE 1.1						
Height of Plants (centimeters)						
	Day					
	1	5	10	15	20	25
Rainwater	0	3.0	10.2	13.8	17.7	19.0
Distilled Water	0	2.0	9.5	15.8	16.5	18.0
Sparkling Water	0	1.2	11.5	14.5	16.2	17.0
Diet Soda	0	1.5	8.4	12.2	13.6	15.0

Now you can see the experimental results at a glance. The plant watered with rainwater measured 3.0 centimeters on Day 5, 10.2 centimeters on Day 10, 13.8 centimeters on Day 15, and so on. Following the rows from left to right, we can see how fast the four plants grew during the experiment.

Then if we look at the columns—the days—we can see how the plants ranked on the given days. On Day 10, the tallest plant was the one watered with sparkling water (11.5 centimeters), and shortest was the one watered with diet soda (8.4 centimeters). Or you can see in the last column that at the end of the experiment, the tallest plant was the one watered with rainwater, the second tallest plant was the one watered with distilled water, the third tallest plant was the one watered with sparkling water, and the shortest plant was the one watered with diet soda.

Now let's look at the questions again:

5. On Day 15, the rainwater plant measured 13.8 centimeters.

1. On Day 25, the rainwater plant was the tallest at 19 centimeters.

TABLE 1.1						
Height of Plants						
	Day					
	1	5	10	15	20	25
Rainwater	0	3.0	10.2	13.8	17.7	19.0
Distilled Water	0	2.0	9.5	15.8	16.5	18.0
Sparkling Water	0	1.2	11.5	14.5	16.2	17.0
Diet Soda	0	1.5	8.4	12.2	13.6	15.0

4. On Day 10, the sparkling water plant was 11.5 centimeters.

2. On Day 10, the shortest plant was the one watered with diet soda at 8.4 centimeters.

3. On Day 20, the second tallest plant was 16.5 centimeters and was watered with distilled water.

536 • SCIENCE INTERPRETATION OF DATA

1. On Day 25, the tallest plant was the one watered with:

   A. rainwater.
   B. distilled water.
   C. sparkling water.
   D. diet soda.

2. On Day 10, the shortest plant was the one watered with:

   F. rainwater.
   G. distilled water.
   H. sparkling water.
   J. diet soda.

3. On Day 20, the second tallest plant was the one watered with:

   A. rainwater.
   B. distilled water.
   C. sparkling water.
   D. diet soda.

4. On Day 10, the plant watered with sparkling water measured:

   F. 8.4 centimeters.
   G. 9.5 centimeters.
   H. 11.5 centimeters.
   J. 14.5 centimeters.

5. On Day 15, which of the plants measured 13.8 centimeters?

   A. The one watered with rainwater
   B. The one watered with distilled water
   C. The one watered with sparkling water
   D. The one watered with diet soda

Tables can be used to present information about anything from the amounts of various nutrients in food to toxic chemicals in industrial waste. But no matter what the *content* of the table, the *form* of the table is the same. The table is always made up of rows and columns that create cells to be filled with data. Tables may also summarize data generated by experiments. The following in-class practice passages further illustrate the use of tables.

Summary

- A table consists of (horizontal) rows and (vertical) columns.

- The cells formed by the intersection of the rows and columns contain data.

- The table always includes the units of the data.

EXERCISE

DIRECTIONS: Each passage below is followed by questions based on its content. Answer the questions on the basis of what is stated or implied in the corresponding passage. Answers are on page 755.

Passage 1

A student was assigned to do a report on the nutritional content in peanut butter. The student collected information about the fat content of peanut butter. The results are summarized in Table 1.2.

TABLE 1.2		
PEANUT BUTTER FAT CONTENT (grams)[1]		
	Chunky	Smooth
Saturated Fat	20.8	27.1
Polyunsaturated Fat	38.2	36.5
Monounsaturated Fat	63.4	63.4
Other Fat	6.4	3.0
Total Fat	128.8	130.0

[1]Per cup (8 ounces)

1. In Table 1.2, the amounts of fat are given in measurements of:

   A. cups.
   B. grams per ounce.
   C. grams per cup.
   D. ounces.

2. According to Table 1.2, smooth peanut butter contains how many grams of polyunsaturated fat?

   F. 27.1
   G. 38.2
   H. 36.5
   J. 63.4

3. According to Table 1.2, chunky peanut butter has the most of which kind of fat?

   A. Saturated
   B. Polyunsaturated
   C. Monounsaturated
   D. Other

4. According to Table 1.2, smooth peanut butter contains how many more total grams of fat than chunky peanut butter?

   F. 0.2
   G. 1.2
   H. 1.8
   J. 3.4

5. According to Table 1.2, smooth and chunky peanut butter contain equal amounts of which type of fat?

   A. Saturated
   B. Polyunsaturated
   C. Monounsaturated
   D. Other

Passage 2

A newspaper company wanted to determine the benefit of having consumers recycle newspapers rather than dispose of them in a landfill. A scientist calculated the amounts of certain metals found in the paper and ink of the newspaper in both the daily edition and the Sunday edition. Using information provided by the company, the scientist compiled a table to show how much metallic waste ended up in the landfill each year.

TABLE 1.3
METALLIC WASTE (pounds per year)

	Daily Editions	Sunday Edition	Total
Barium	2,800	2,380	5,180
Chromium	136	132	268
Copper	980	1,820	2,800
Iron	1,420	6,160	7,580
Lead	86	252	338
Manganese	7,600	7,000	14,600
Zinc	560	1,540	2,100
Total	13,582	19,284	32,866

540 • SCIENCE INTERPRETATION OF DATA

6. In Table 1.3, the amounts of metallic waste are given in measurements of:

   F. pounds per edition.
   G. pounds per day.
   H. pounds per week.
   J. pounds per year.

7. According to Table 1.3, how many pounds of manganese ended up in the landfill each year from the Sunday edition?

   A. 7,000
   B. 7,600
   C. 14,600
   D. 19,284

8. According to Table 1.3, for which of the following types of metallic waste was the amount generated by the Sunday edition greater than the amount generated by the daily editions?

   F. Barium
   G. Chromium
   H. Copper
   J. Manganese

9. According to Table 1.3, the amount of metallic waste contributed to the landfill by daily editions and the Sunday edition combined was greatest for:

   A. barium.
   B. copper.
   C. iron.
   D. manganese.

10. According to Table 1.3, how many pounds of metallic waste from daily editions ended up in the landfill each year?

   F. 5,180
   G. 13,582
   H. 19,284
   J. 32,866

Passage 3

True north is the direction along the earth's surface toward the geographic North Pole. For practical purposes, this is the position of Polaris or the North Star. A compass does not necessarily point to true north. This is because the earth's magnetic field does not exactly align with the geographic poles. For this reason, depending on location, a compass may point to the west or to the east of true north. The difference is called magnetic declination: the declination is positive when the magnetic north is east of true north. The declination is negative when the magnetic north is west of true north. Magnetic declination is illustrated in Figure 1.1. Table 4.2 summarizes the magnetic declination for selected cities around the world.

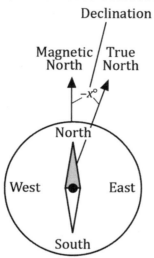

The declination in the figure is negative because magnetic north is west of true north.

Figure 1.1

TABLE 1.4	
City	Magnetic Declination (degrees)
Anchorage (USA)	20E
Buenos Aires (Argentina)	10W
Los Angeles (USA)	3E
Montreal (Canada)	9W
Perth (Australia)	9E
Rio de Janeiro (Brazil)	10W
St. Petersburg (Russia)	12W
Sydney (Australia)	13E

542 • SCIENCE INTERPRETATION OF DATA

11. In Table 1.4, the magnetic declination is given in measurements of:

A. degrees.
B. latitudes.
C. longitudes.
D. miles.

12. According to Table 1.4, the magnetic declination for Perth, Australia is:

F. 9E.
G. 13E.
H. 10W.
J. 12W.

13. According to Table 1.4, the magnetic declination is 9W for which of the following cities?

A. Buenos Aires, Argentina
B. Montreal, Canada
C. Perth, Australia
D. St. Petersburg, Russia

14. According to Table 1.4, the city with the greatest declination west is:

F. Montreal, Canada.
G. Anchorage, USA.
H. Rio de Janeiro, Brazil.
J. St. Petersburg, Russia.

15. According to Table 1.4, the city with the smallest declination east is:

A. Anchorage, USA.
B. Los Angeles, USA.
C. Perth, Australia.
D. Sydney, Australia.

Passage 4

Wastewater treatment plants produce approximately seven million tons of dry biosolids each year. These biosolids are used as fertilizers by farmers, landscapers, and homeowners. Because various household chemicals have been found in wastewater, researchers asked whether these same chemicals are present in the biosolids. Researchers analyzed biosolids for chemicals found in cleaners, personal care products, and other products. Table 1.5 summarizes the findings, giving the amounts of the chemicals in micrograms of the chemical per kilogram of biosolid.

TABLE 1.5		
Chemicals Found in Waste Water Treatment Plant Biosolids		
Chemical	Usage	Concentration (micrograms/kilogram)
d-limonene	fragrance	630
tonalide	fragrance	11,600
galazolide	fragrance	3,900
indole	fragrance	19,600
4-tert-octylphenol	detergent	4,030
para-nonylphenol	detergent	261,000
bisphenol A	plastics	4,690
phenol	disinfectant	2,180
triclosan	disinfectant	10,200
diethylhexyl phthalate	plasticizer	10,500
para-cresol	preservative	4,400

544 • SCIENCE INTERPRETATION OF DATA

16. In Table 1.5, the concentrations of chemicals in the biosolids are given in measurements of:

F. kilograms.
G. micrograms.
H. micrograms per kilogram.
J. tons.

17. According to Table 1.5, bisphenol A is used in:

A. plastics.
B. fragrances.
C. detergents.
D. disinfectants.

18. According to Table 1.5, the concentration of phenol in the biosolids was:

F. 2,180 micrograms/kilogram.
G. 3,900 micrograms/kilogram.
H. 4,400 micrograms/kilogram.
J. 4,690 micrograms/kilogram.

19. According to Table 1.5, which of the following chemicals had the highest concentration in the biosolids?

A. 4-tert-octylphenol
B. d-limonene
C. para-nonylphenol
D. Tonalide

20. According to Table 1.5, how many of the chemicals found in the biosolids are used as fragrances?

F. One
G. Two
H. Three
J. Four

Science **Interpretation of Data**

Unit 2 | **Tables Practice**

INSIDE THIS UNIT:
– Exercise 1 – – Exercise 2 –

EXERCISE 1

DIRECTIONS: Each passage below is followed by questions based on its content. Answer the questions on the basis of what is stated or implied in the corresponding passage. Answers are on page 756.

Passage 1

The federal government keeps statistics on the amount of energy consumed by various sectors of the economy. In the transportation sector, statistics are collected on energy used by vehicle type. The data for a recent year are presented in Table 2.1.

TABLE 2.1	
Percent of Energy Consumption by Vehicle Type	
Agriculture and Construction	4%
Aircraft	9%
Automobiles	32%
Trains and Buses	3%
Trucks (Light)	28%
Trucks (Other)	16%
Watercraft	5%
Other Vehicles	3%

1. In Table 2.1, the data are presented in terms of:

   A. gallons of fuel used.
   B. number of vehicles by type.
   C. percent of energy consumption.
   D. percent per gallon.

2. According to Table 2.1, the percent of energy consumed by trucks (other) was:

   F. 3%.
   G. 16%.
   H. 28%.
   J. 44%.

UNIT 2 | TABLES PRACTICE • 547

3. According to Table 2.1, which of the following vehicle types consumed 9% of the energy?

   A. Agriculture and construction
   B. Aircraft
   C. Light trucks
   D. Watercraft

4. According to Table 2.1, which of the following vehicle types consumed the greatest percent of the energy?

   F. Automobiles
   G. Trains and buses
   H. Light trucks
   J. Other trucks

5. According to Table 2.1, which of the following vehicle types consumed the smallest percent of the energy?

   A. Aircraft
   B. Automobiles
   C. Light trucks
   D. Watercraft

Passage 2

After crude oil is removed from the ground, it is sent to a refinery. Different parts of the crude oil are separated into useable petroleum products. A barrel produces almost 45 gallons of refined petroleum products. Table 2.2 shows the amounts of the different products obtained from one barrel of crude oil.

TABLE 2.2	
Refined Products from One Barrel of Crude Oil	
Product	Amount (gallons)
Diesel	10.31
Heating Oil	1.38
Jet Fuel	4.07
Heavy Fuel Oil	1.68
LP Gases	1.72
Gasoline	18.56
Other	7.01
Total	44.73

548 • SCIENCE INTERPRETATION OF DATA

6. In Table 2.2, the amounts of the different products obtained from the refining process are given in measurements of:

   F. barrels.
   G. gallons.
   H. quarts.
   J. barrel-gallons.

7. According to Table 2.2, the total amount of refined products obtained from one barrel of crude oil is:

   A. 3.00 gallons.
   B. 7.01 gallons.
   C. 42.00 gallons.
   D. 44.73 gallons.

8. According to Table 2.2, the amount of heating oil obtained from one barrel of crude oil is:

   F. 1.38 gallons.
   G. 1.68 gallons.
   H. 1.72 gallons.
   J. 7.01 gallons.

9. According to Table 2.2, one barrel of crude oil produces 4.07 gallons of:

   A. diesel.
   B. jet fuel.
   C. LP gases
   D. gasoline.

10. According to Table 2.2, one barrel of crude oil produces the greatest amount of which of the following products?

    F. Gasoline
    G. Jet fuel
    H. Heavy fuel oil
    J. Diesel

Passage 3

Using data gathered by bird-banders, scientists have discovered that 22 species of passerines—members of the most common order of birds, Passeriformes—are carriers of avian influenza. The greatest number of cases has been identified in the Plains region of the United States. Table 2.3 gives the estimated number of cases of avian influenza in each state of the Plains region.

TABLE 2.3	
Estimated Cases of Avian Influenza in Passerines (Plains Region)	
Iowa	196
Kansas	132
Minnesota	250
Missouri	112
Nebraska	135
North Dakota	90
South Dakota	97
Total	1,012

11. In Table 2.3, the data describe the number of:

    A. passerine species.
    B. estimated cases of avian influenza.
    C. birds living in various states.
    D. bird-banders assisting in the study.

12. According to Table 2.3, the number of cases of avian influenza in passerines in Missouri was:

    F. 90.
    G. 97.
    H. 112.
    J. 250.

13. According to Table 2.3, which of the following states had 132 cases of avian influenza in passerines?

    A. Iowa
    B. Kansas
    C. Nebraska
    D. South Dakota

14. According to Table 2.3, which of the following states had the greatest number of cases of avian influenza in passerines?

    F. Minnesota
    G. Iowa
    H. Nebraska
    J. North Dakota

15. According to Table 2.3, the number of cases of avian influenza in passerines estimated in the Plains region was:

    A. 7.
    B. 196.
    C. 250.
    D. 1,012.

EXERCISE 2

DIRECTIONS: Each passage below is followed by questions based on its content. Answer the questions on the basis of what is stated or implied in the corresponding passage. Answers are on page 756.

Passage 1

A moon is a celestial body that orbits a planet. The Earth has one moon. Other planets in our solar system have more than one moon. Some planets in our solar system have no moons. Table 2.4 lists the number of officially confirmed moons for each planet of the solar system, based on 2014 data.

TABLE 2.4		
Planet Name	Position from Sun	Number of Officially Confirmed Moons
Mercury	1	0
Venus	2	0
Earth	3	1
Mars	4	2
Jupiter	5	67
Saturn	6	62
Uranus	7	27
Neptune	8	14

552 • SCIENCE INTERPRETATION OF DATA

1. According to Table 2.4, Venus occupies which position from the Sun?

   A. 0
   B. 1
   C. 2
   D. 3

2. According to Table 2.4 which planet is the fifth planet from the Sun?

   F. Earth
   G. Mars
   H. Jupiter
   J. Saturn

3. According to Table 2.4, how many moons does Saturn have?

   A. 2
   B. 27
   C. 62
   D. 67

4. According to Table 2.4, which of the following planets has 27 moons?

   F. Mars
   G. Mercury
   H. Jupiter
   J. Uranus

5. According to Table 2.4, which of the following planets has the greatest number of moons?

   A. Mercury
   B. Neptune
   C. Jupiter
   D. Saturn

Passage 2

A student conducted a research project on the health benefits of exercise. One of the benefits of exercise is that it burns calories. The data gathered by the student on the energy expended for different types of physical activity are summarized in Table 2.5.

TABLE 2.5		
Calories Burned (per 10 minutes of exercise)		
	180 pound adult	155 pound adult
Light Activities: Cleaning, Baseball, Golf	61	53
Moderate Activities: Brisk Walk, Leisure Biking, Dancing	75	65
Strenuous Activities: Jogging, Football, Swimming	123	106
Very Strenuous Activities: Running, Racquetball, Cross-Country Skiing	150	129

6. In Table 2.5, the data are given in units of Calories burned per:

F. 10 minutes.
G. minute.
H. pound.
J. hour.

7. According to Table 2.5, approximately how many Calories will a 180 pound adult burn during 10 minutes of jogging?

A. 12
B. 106
C. 123
D. 1,230

8. According to Table 2.5, approximately how many Calories will a 155 pound adult burn during 10 minutes of swimming?

F. 53
G. 65
H. 75
J. 106

9. According to Table 2.5, approximately how many Calories will a 180 pound adult burn during 10 minutes of brisk walking?

A. 61
B. 65
C. 75
D. 123

10. According to Table 2.5, which of the following activities burns Calories at the fastest rate?

F. Racquetball
G. Jogging
H. Football
J. Dancing

Passage 3

According to data gathered by conservationists, lightning starts about half of all woodland and range fires. Table 2.6 provides data reported by the National Interagency Fire Center on the number of lightning fires in 2009 and the number of acres destroyed.

TABLE 2.6					
Lightning Fires and Acres Destroyed in 2009 (by region)					
	Northwest	Southwest	East	South	Total
Fires	1,843	1,546	62	557	4,008
Acres Destroyed	148,238	475,436	427	64,155	688,256

11. According to Table 2.6, the total number of lightning fires in 2009 was:

    A. 1,843.
    B. 4,008.
    C. 64,155.
    D. 688,256.

12. According to Table 2.6, the number of acres destroyed by lightning fires in 2009 in the Southwest was:

    F. 1,546.
    G. 64,155.
    H. 475,436.
    J. 688,256.

13. According to Table 2.6, which of the following regions had the fewest number of lightning fires in 2009?

    A. Northwest
    B. Southwest
    C. East
    D. South

14. According to Table 2.6, which of the following regions had the greatest number of acres destroyed by lightning fires in 2009?

    F. Southwest
    G. Northwest
    H. East
    J. South

15. According to Table 2.6, the total number of acres destroyed by lightning fires in 2009 was:

    A. 4,008.
    B. 64,155.
    C. 475,436.
    D. 688,256.

Science Interpretation of Data

Unit 3 | Bar Graphs

INSIDE THIS UNIT:
– How to Interpret Bar Graphs – – Exercise –

Non-Negotiable Skill:

Recognize a graph's features and use a graph
to select a single piece of data.

How to Interpret Bar Graphs

The first science skills unit concentrated on data tables. In this science lesson, you will see data presentations that are "pictures" of the data. You'll find that in many ways these data pictures are easier than tables.

Here is the table summarizing the growth of the pea plants that you saw in the first unit. The row labeled "Rainwater" is now highlighted:

TABLE 1.1					
Height of Plants (centimeters)					
	Day				
	1	5	10	15	20	25
Rainwater	0	3.0	10.2	13.8	17.7	19.0
Distilled Water	0	2.0	9.5	15.8	16.5	18.0
Sparkling Water	0	1.2	11.5	14.5	16.2	17.0
Diet Soda	0	1.5	8.4	12.2	13.6	15.0

Instead of a table, the data in this row can be displayed as a picture by using a grid:

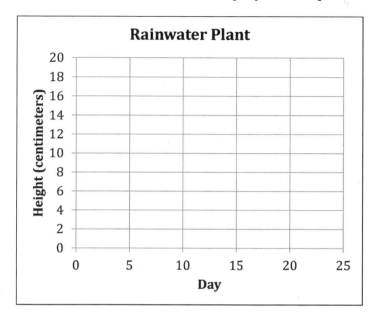

The data values are plotted on the grid:

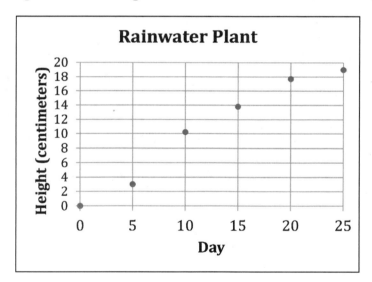

Now it's easy to draw conclusions such as:

- The plant grows between every measurement.
- The plant is about 19 centimeters tall on Day 25.
- The plant didn't grow very much from Day 20 to Day 25.
- The plant grew a lot from Day 5 to Day 10.
- The plant was about 14 centimeters tall on Day 15.

The points might be a little difficult to read, but this is easily corrected. Usually, the graph-maker will fill in beneath the points and clean up the grid:

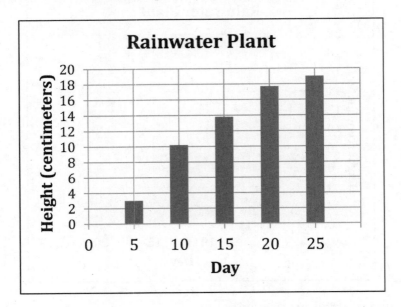

Notice that the bars are arranged vertically, like the columns on a building. This kind of presentation is often called a **column graph**:

A column graph looks like the columns of a building.

The table we started with had four rows—one for each plant. And we can add those other rows to the graph:

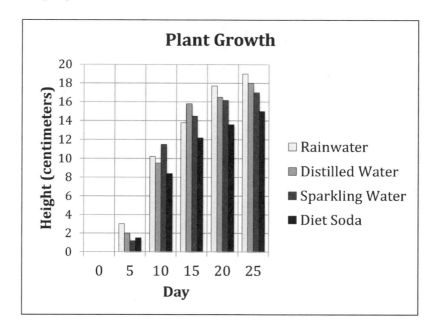

This graph really is a data picture. It contains the same data that is in the table, but now the information is available visually. The following questions are the same questions that accompanied the "Height of Plants" table in Unit 1. Since the data haven't changed, the answers will be the same, but answer them now based on the bar graph.

1. On Day 25, the tallest plant was the one watered with:

   A. rainwater.
   B. distilled water.
   C. sparkling water.
   D. diet soda.

2. On Day 10, the shortest plant was the one watered with:

   F. rainwater.
   G. distilled water.
   H. sparkling water.
   J. diet soda.

3. On Day 20, the second tallest plant was the one watered with:

   A. rainwater.
   B. distilled water.
   C. sparkling water.
   D. diet soda.

4. On Day 10, the plant watered with sparkling water measured:

   F. 8.4 centimeters.
   G. 9.5 centimeters.
   H. 11.5 centimeters.
   J. 14.5 centimeters.

5. On Day 15, which of the plants measured 13.8 centimeters?

   A. The one watered with rainwater
   B. The one watered with distilled water
   C. The one watered with sparkling water
   D. The one watered with diet soda

> **Summary**
> - Graphs present data "pictures" that may be easier to read than tables.
> - A bar graph is so named because data are represented by bars.
> - A bar graph typically presents data arranged vertically, similar to columns on a building. A bar graph can also present data horizontally.
> - Bar graphs may include several types of data, represented by different types of bars.

EXERCISE

DIRECTIONS: Each passage below is followed by questions based on its content. Answer the questions on the basis of what is stated or implied in the corresponding passage. Answers are on page 756.

Passage 1

Ground-water is vitally important in supplying water for everyday needs. Ground-water is used to irrigate crops and supply homes, businesses, and industries with water. Figure 3.1 shows the amount of fresh groundwater withdrawn for all uses from aquifers in the United States in selected years.

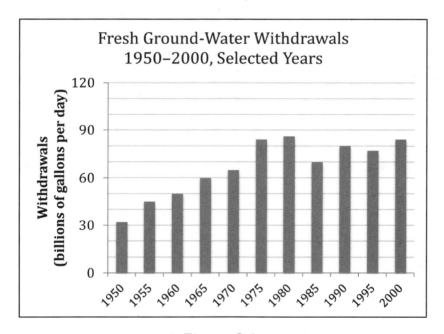

Figure 3.1

564 • SCIENCE INTERPRETATION OF DATA

1. In Figure 3.1, the fresh ground-water withdrawals are given in measurements of:

   A. days.
   B. gallons.
   C. gallons per day.
   D. billion gallons per day.

2. According to Figure 3.1, fresh ground-water withdrawals in 1965 were approximately:

   F. 45 billon gallons.
   G. 45 billon gallons per day.
   H. 60 billon gallons.
   J. 60 billon gallons per day.

3. According to Figure 3.1, in which year were fresh ground-water withdrawals the greatest?

   A. 1950
   B. 1980
   C. 1990
   D. 2000

4. According to Figure 3.1, from 1980 to 1985, fresh ground-water withdrawals:

   F. increased by about 10 billion gallons per day.
   G. decreased by about 15 gallons per day.
   H. decreased by about 15 billion gallons per day.
   J. decreased by about 70 billion gallons per day.

5. According to Figure 3.1, in which year were fresh ground-water withdrawals the least?

   A. 1950
   B. 1955
   C. 1960
   D. 1965

Passage 2

Although most energy in the United States is produced by fossil fuel and nuclear power plants, hydroelectricity is still important. About 7% of total power is produced by hydroelectric plants. Hydropower doesn't burn fuel, so it generates minimal pollution. Water to run the power plant is provided free by nature and is renewable: rainfall refills a reservoir or river with water that falls over a dam or turns turbines powered by tidal currents. Figure 3.2 shows how much hydroelectric power is generated by the United States and several other countries.

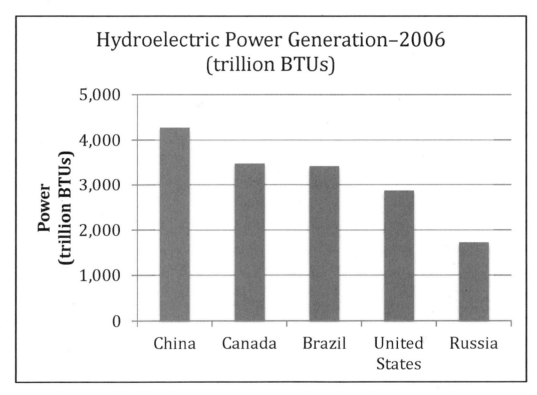

Figure 3.2

6. The amount of energy generated is measured in:

F. BTUs.
G. megawatts.
H. watts.
J. trillion BTUs.

7. According to Figure 3.2, which of the following countries produced the greatest amount of hydroelectric power in 2006?

A. Brazil
B. Canada
C. China
D. United States

8. According to Figure 3.2, which of the following countries produced the least amount of hydroelectric power in 2006?

F. Brazil
G. Canada
H. United States
J. Russia

9. According to Figure 3.2, the United States produced approximately how many trillion BTUs of hydroelectric power in 2006?

A. 1,750
B. 2,800
C. 3,500
D. 4,250

10. According to Figure 3.2, which of the following two countries produced approximately the same amount of hydroelectric power in 2006?

F. China and Canada
G. Canada and Brazil
H. Brazil and the United States
J. Russia and China

Passage 3

The specific gravity of a gas is the ratio of the density of the gas to the density of air. (Density is mass per unit volume.) The specific gravity of natural gas varies according to the mixture of different hydrocarbons that are found in methane, which is the primary component of natural gas. An engineer took samples of natural gas from a group of wells and determined the specific gravity of each sample. Figure 3.3 summarizes the results of the testing.

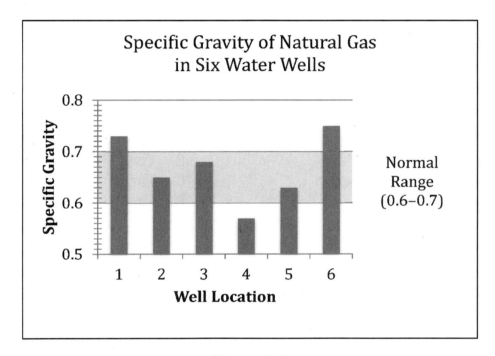

Figure 3.3

568 • SCIENCE INTERPRETATION OF DATA

11. According to Figure 3.3, the specific gravity of the natural gas in Well Location 3 was approximately:

    A. 0.5.
    B. 0.68.
    C. 0.74.
    D. 7.0.

12. According to Figure 3.3, the specific gravity of the natural gas in Well Location 5 was:

    F. less than 0.5.
    G. more than 0.5 but less than 0.6.
    H. more than 0.6 but less than 0.7.
    J. more than 0.7.

13. According to Figure 3.3, the well location with natural gas of the lowest specific gravity was:

    A. Well Location 1.
    B. Well Location 2.
    C. Well Location 4.
    D. Well Location 6.

14. According to Figure 3.3, how many of the well locations had natural gas with a specific gravity greater than the normal range?

    F. One
    G. Two
    H. Three
    J. Four

15. According to Figure 3.3, how many of the well locations had natural gas with a specific gravity within the normal range?

    A. One
    B. Two
    C. Three
    D. Four

Passage 4

A staple food is one that can be easily stored for year-round use. Rice is the most important staple food for a large part of the world's population. Rice provides more than one-fifth of the calories consumed worldwide by humans. Figure 3.4 shows the rice production and consumption of several rice-producing countries in Year X.

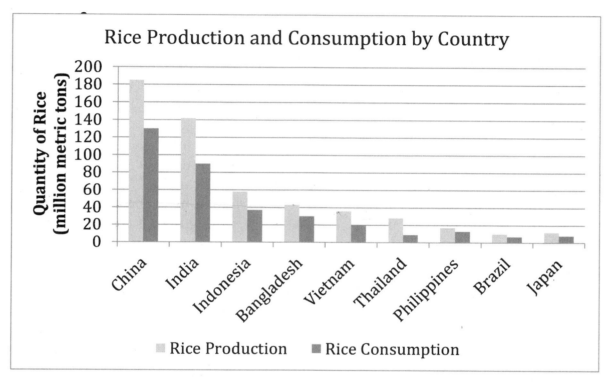

Figure 3.4

16. In Figure 3.4, the amount of rice production and consumption by country is given in measurements of:

   F. tons.
   G. metric tons.
   H. million tons.
   J. million metric tons.

17. According to Figure 3.4, Vietnam produces approximately how much rice?

   A. 35 metric tons
   B. 20,000 metric tons
   C. 35,000,000 metric tons
   D. 42,000,000 metric tons

18. According to Figure 3.4, which of the following countries produces the most rice?

   F. China
   G. India
   H. Vietnam
   J. Japan

19. According to Figure 3.4, which of the following countries consumes the most rice?

   A. China
   B. Bangladesh
   C. Vietnam
   D. Thailand

20. According to Figure 3.4, which of the following countries consumes more rice than it produces?

   F. China
   G. Indonesia
   H. Brazil
   J. None of the countries in Figure 3.4 consumes more rice than it produces.

Science **Interpretation of Data**

Unit 4 | **Bar Graphs Practice**

INSIDE THIS UNIT:
– Exercise 1 – – Exercise 2 –

EXERCISE 1

DIRECTIONS: Each passage below is followed by questions based on its content. Answer the questions on the basis of what is stated or implied in the corresponding passage. Answers are on page 756.

Passage 1

The Space Shuttle Program was used by NASA to launch astronauts into low Earth orbit for nearly 30 years. The first test flights of the program took place in 1977. Manned, orbital flights of space shuttles began in 1981 and ended in 2011.

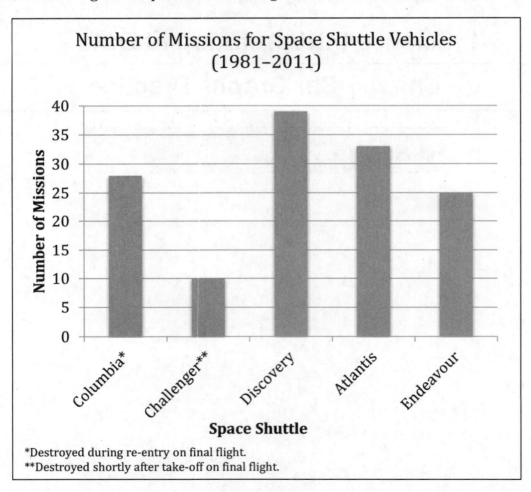

Figure 4.1

1. According to Figure 4.1, the space shuttle that flew the most missions is:

   A. Atlantis.
   B. Challenger.
   C. Discovery.
   D. Columbia

2. According to Figure 4.1, the space shuttle that flew the fewest missions is:

   F. Columbia.
   G. Challenger.
   H. Discovery.
   J. Atlantis.

3. According to Figure 4.1, which of the following space shuttles flew more than 30 but fewer than 35 missions?

   A. Columbia
   B. Challenger
   C. Discovery
   D. Atlantis

4. According to Figure 4.1, which of the following space shuttles flew a total of 10 missions?

   F. Columbia
   G. Challenger
   H. Discovery
   J. Atlantis

5. According to Figure 4.1, which space shuttle(s) was(were) destroyed during a mission?

   A. Columbia
   B. Challenger
   C. Columbia and Challenger
   D. Columbia, Challenger, and Discovery

Passage 2

A group of students studied the effect of five different activities on heart rates. They engaged in each of the selected physical activities for an extended period of time and measured their heart rates at regular intervals. They then averaged the results. The results of the experiment are summarized in Figure 4.2.

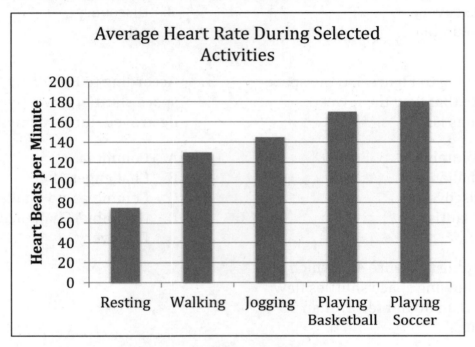

Figure 4.2

6. In Figure 4.2, average heart rate is given in measurements of:

   F. heart beats.
   G. heart beats per minute.
   H. minutes.
   J. five minutes.

7. According to Figure 4.2, the average heart rate of the students while playing soccer was approximately:

   A. 130 beats per minute.
   B. 145 beats per minute.
   C. 160 beats per minute.
   D. 180 beats per minute.

8. According to Figure 4.2, the average heart rate of the students while jogging was:

   F. between 80 and 100 beats per minute.
   G. between 100 and 120 beats per minute.
   H. between 120 and 140 beats per minute.
   J. between 140 and 160 beats per minute.

9. According to Figure 4.2, the average heart rate of the students was lowest while:

   A. resting.
   B. walking.
   C. jogging.
   D. playing basketball.

10. According to Figure 4.2, the average heart rate of the students was greatest while:

    F. playing soccer.
    G. playing basketball.
    H. jogging.
    J. walking.

Passage 3

Federal law requires 10 hours of rest for every 11 hours that long-haul truck drivers are on the road. The Truck-Stop Electrification Program was established so that, when resting, drivers are able to operate the heater, air conditioner, television, and other appliances in their trucks without running the engines. Parking spaces that provide electricity for semi-trucks save fuel and reduce air pollution and engine wear. Figure 4.3 shows the number of electrified parking spaces that were added each year at truck stops in the United States from 2006 to 2010.

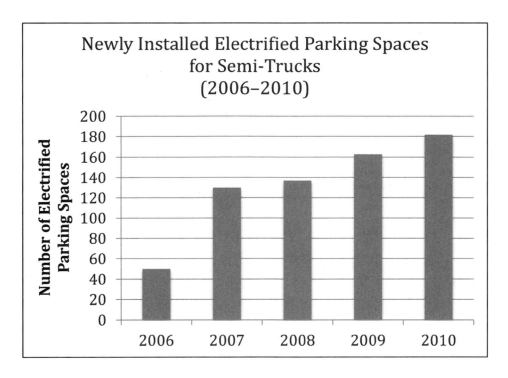

Figure 4.3

576 • SCIENCE INTERPRETATION OF DATA

11. Figure 4.3 shows the:

    A. number of newly installed electrified parking spaces from 2006 to 2010.

    B. number of trucks using truck-stops from 2006 to 2010.

    C. amount of electricity used by trucks at rest stops from 2006 to 2010.

    D. number of truck-stops available to truckers from 2006 to 2010.

12. According to Figure 4.3, the number of electrified parking spaces added in 2010 was approximately:

    F. 45.

    G. 125.

    H. 138.

    J. 180.

13. According to Figure 4.3, the number of electrified parking spaces added in 2007 was:

    A. more than 100 but fewer than 120.

    B. more than 120 but fewer than 140.

    C. more than 140 but fewer than 160.

    D. more than 160 but fewer than 180.

14. According to Figure 4.3, approximately how many more electrified parking spaces were added in 2010 than in 2009?

    F. 20

    G. 160

    H. 180

    J. 340

15. According to Figure 4.3, how many electrified parking spaces were added in 2006 and 2007 combined?

    A. Fewer than 40

    B. More than 40 but fewer than 60

    C. More than 120 but fewer than 140

    D. More than 160 but fewer than 200

EXERCISE 2

DIRECTIONS: Each passage below is followed by questions based on its content. Answer the questions on the basis of what is stated or implied in the corresponding passage. Answers are on page 756.

Passage 1

Wattage refers to the amount of energy needed to light a bulb. The luminous flux (measured in lumens) is a measure of the amount of light (or brightness) actually produced by the bulb. Figure 4.4 shows the relationship between wattage and lumens for incandescent light bulbs.

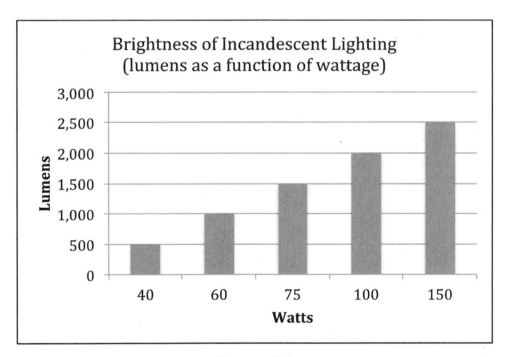

Figure 4.4

1. In Figure 4.4, the brightness of the bulbs is given in measurements of:

   A. lumens.
   B. watts.
   C. wavelengths.
   D. number of bulbs.

2. According to Figure 4.4, a 75-watt incandescent bulb will produce approximately how many lumens?

   F. 40
   G. 75
   H. 800
   J. 1,500

3. According to Figure 4.4, if 2,500 lumens of incandescent light are needed, the required wattage is:

   A. 60.
   B. 75.
   C. 100.
   D. 150.

4. According to Figure 4.4, a 40-watt bulb will produce approximately:

   F. 500 lumens.
   G. 800 lumens.
   H. 1,050 lumens.
   J. 1,600 lumens.

5. According to Figure 4.4, which of the following incandescent bulbs produces approximately 1,500 lumens?

   A. 40-watt bulb
   B. 60-watt bulb
   C. 75-watt bulb
   D. 100-watt bulb

Passage 2

Individuals who commute to work or school by bicycle help the environment by reducing their carbon footprint. A survey was conducted to assess attitudes about bicycle use. Of the 1,000 people surveyed, 359 said that they do commute by bicycle, 370 said that they bicycle recreationally but do not commute by bicycle, and 271 said that they do not bicycle recreationally or commute by bicycle. The reasons recreational cyclists gave for not commuting by bicycle and the number of responses are summarized in Figure 4.5.

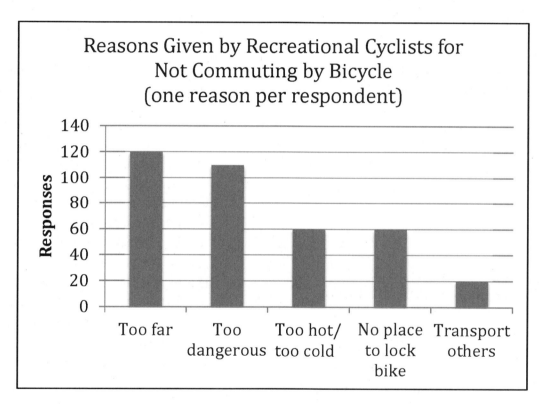

Figure 4.5

580 • SCIENCE INTERPRETATION OF DATA

6. Figure 4.5 provides information about the:

    F. number of people surveyed.
    G. number of people who commute by bicycle.
    H. number of responses per reason for not commuting by bicycle.
    J. number of people who do not commute by bicycle.

7. According to Figure 4.5, how many people answered that they do not commute by bicycle because it is too far?

    A. 20
    B. 60
    C. 110
    D. 120

8. According to Figure 4.5, 20 people gave as their reason for not commuting by bicycle that they:

    F. thought it too dangerous.
    G. found it too hot or too cold.
    H. had to transport others.
    J. had no place to lock a bicycle.

9. According to Figure 4.5, the most frequently given reason for not commuting by bicycle was that:

    A. the commute was too far.
    B. the commute was too dangerous.
    C. the conditions were too hot or too cold.
    D. there was not place to lock a bike.

10. According to Figure 4.5, which of the following statements is true?

    F. More people found the conditions of the commute to be too hot or too cold than thought it was too dangerous.
    G. More people found the conditions of the commute too hot or too cold than had to transport others.
    H. More people had no place to lock a bike than found the conditions of the commute too hot or too cold.
    J. More people thought the commute to be too dangerous than thought it to be too far.

Passage 3

Automobiles make a significant contribution to levels of atmospheric carbon dioxide and other air pollutants. Statistics on automobile ownership provide important information for policy makers wishing to address this problem. Figure 4.6 provides data on the number of automobiles owned per person for eight countries in Year X.

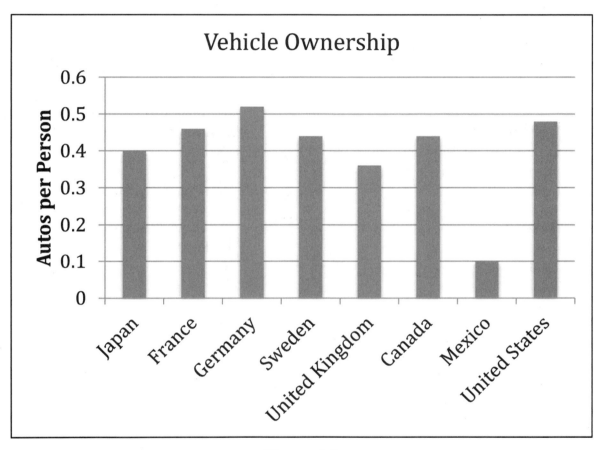

Figure 4.6

582 • SCIENCE INTERPRETATION OF DATA

11. Figure 4.6 provides information about the:

   A. number of autos in various countries.
   B. number of autos per person in various countries.
   C. tons of air pollution in various countries.
   D. miles driven in various countries.

12. According to Figure 4.6, which country has the highest per person rate of vehicle ownership?

   F. Japan
   G. Germany
   H. Canada
   J. United States

13. According to Figure 4.6, which country has the lowest per person rate of vehicle ownership?

   A. France
   B. Sweden
   C. Mexico
   D. United Kingdom

14. According to Figure 4.6, the number of autos per person in Japan is:

   F. 0.1.
   G. 0.2.
   H. 0.4.
   J. 0.6.

15. According to Figure 4.6, for how many of the listed countries was the number of autos per person greater than 0.4 but less than 0.5?

   A. One
   B. Two
   C. Three
   D. Four

Science **Interpretation of Data**

Unit 5 | **Line Graphs**

INSIDE THIS UNIT:
– How to Interpret Line Graphs – – Exercise –

Non-Negotiable Skill:

Recognize a line graph's features and use a line graph to select a single piece of data.

How to Interpret Line Graphs

Thus far, you've seen that data can be presented using a table or a bar (column) graph. In this unit, you'll study a third type of visual presentation: the line graph, in which the data are represented by a line.

You probably see examples of line graphs every day. For example, weather reports often show temperatures in line graph form:

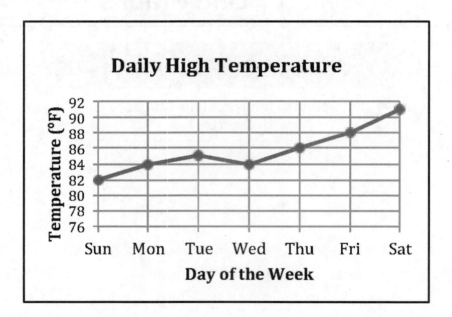

Many line graphs represent time on the horizontal axis—days, hours, minutes, seconds, years, and so on. The line graph above shows how temperature changed over time—from day to day—so it is easy to see which days the temperature increased or decreased and by how much. For example, the high temperature decreased from Tuesday to Wednesday; every other day the high temperature increased. The high temperature increased more from Sunday to Monday than from Monday to Tuesday. The high temperature on Thursday was 86°F, and the hottest day was Saturday. All of this information and more is available at a glance.

Here's another example:

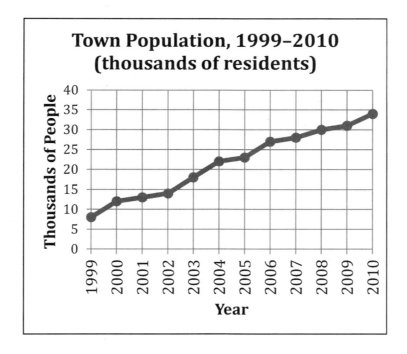

In this line graph, the time axis (horizontal scale) is presented in years—1999 through 2010. You can see at a glance that the population increased from about 8,000 people in 1999 to about 34,000 people in 2010. You can see years in which the population grew rapidly (1999 to 2000 and 2002 to 2004) and years in which the population grew more slowly (2001 to 2002 and 2004 to 2005).

The data on the growth of the plants that appeared in both Units 1 and 2 can also be presented using a line graph. You will remember that the data was first presented in a table:

TABLE 1.1						
Height of Plants (in centimeters)						
	Day					
	1	5	10	15	20	25
Rainwater	**0**	**3.0**	**10.2**	**13.8**	**17.7**	**19.0**
Distilled Water	0	2.0	9.5	15.8	16.5	18.0
Sparkling Water	0	1.2	11.5	14.5	16.2	17.0
Diet Soda	0	1.5	8.4	12.2	13.6	15.0

The highlighted row shows the growth of the plant watered with rainwater. Then in Unit 2, this same data was presented in bar graph form.

The data values were plotted on the grid:

And the columns added:

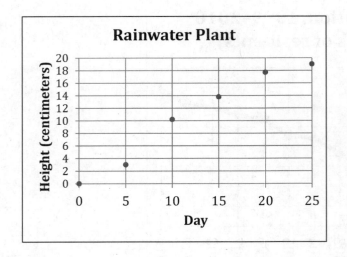
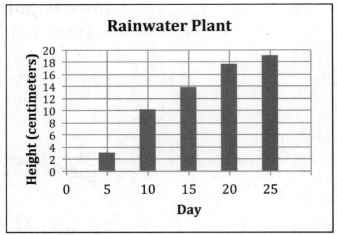

But instead of the columns, the graph-maker could have joined the data points with a line:

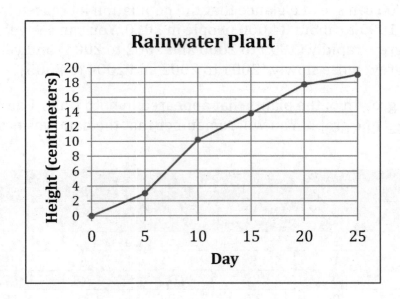

Not only is it easy to see that the plant grew from Day 0 through Day 25, but the graph shows how quickly the plant grew between measurements. The growth between Day 5 and Day 10 was very rapid, while the growth between Day 10 and Day 15 was slower.

The table has four rows—one for each plant. We can add those other rows of data to the bar graph from the previous page:

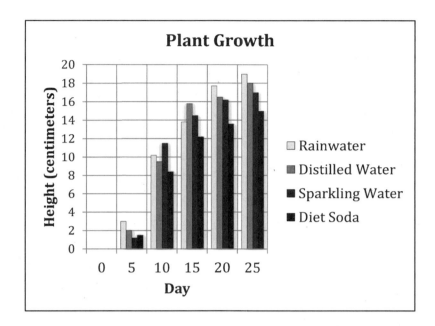

And eliminate the columns:

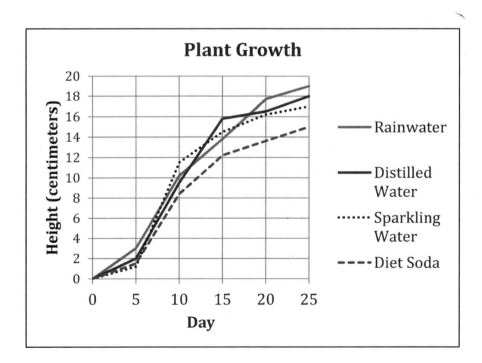

Remember that this is the same data that you saw in Science Unit 1 and again in Science Unit 2. Here are the same questions. You should get the same answers:

588 • SCIENCE INTERPRETATION OF DATA

1. On Day 25, the tallest plant was the one watered with:

   A. rainwater.
   B. distilled water.
   C. sparkling water.
   D. diet soda.

2. On Day 10, the shortest plant was the one watered with:

   F. rainwater.
   G. distilled water.
   H. sparkling water.
   J. diet soda.

3. On Day 20, the second tallest plant was the one watered with:

   A. rainwater.
   B. distilled water.
   C. sparkling water.
   D. diet soda.

4. On Day 10, the plant watered with sparkling water measured:

   F. 8.4 centimeters.
   G. 9.5 centimeters.
   H. 11.5 centimeters.
   J. 14.5 centimeters.

5. On Day 15, which of the plants measured 13.8 centimeters?

   A. The one watered with rain water
   B. The one watered with distilled water
   C. The one watered with sparkling water
   D. The one watered with diet soda

Although line graphs frequently are used to show change over time, they are also used to show the relationship between other measurements. Several variations are shown in the exercise that follows.

Summary

- A line graph is so named because data are represented by a line.
- Line graphs often present units of time as the horizontal axis.
- Line graphs may include several types of data, represented by different types of lines.

EXERCISE

DIRECTIONS: Each passage below is followed by questions based on its content. Answer the questions on the basis of what is stated or implied in the corresponding passage. Answers are on page 756.

Passage 1

Ozone is a molecule that contains three atoms of oxygen (O_3). Close to the earth's surface, in the layer of the atmosphere called the troposphere, ozone is one of the components of smog. In high concentrations, ozone can cause severe damage to plants and animals, as well as contribute to greenhouse warming. But ozone in the stratosphere, the layer of the atmosphere above the troposphere, absorbs harmful ultraviolet radiation from the sun. Researchers use helium-filled balloons to carry equipment into the atmosphere to measure the partial pressure that ozone contributes to the overall atmospheric pressure at different altitudes.

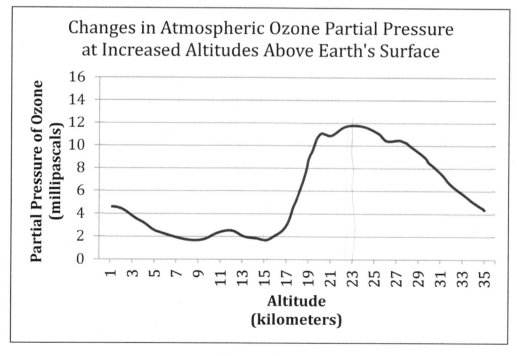

Figure 5.1

1. In Figure 5.1, the partial pressure of ozone is given in measurements of:

   A. miles.
   B. millipascals.
   C. millipascals per kilogram.
   D. kilometers.

2. In Figure 5.1, altitude is presented in intervals of:

   F. 1 millipascal.
   G. 1 kilometer.
   H. 2 millipascals.
   J. 2 kilometers.

3. According to Figure 5.1, the highest ozone partial pressure occurs at an altitude of approximately:

   A. 14 kilometers.
   B. 19 kilometers.
   C. 23 kilometers.
   D. 35 kilometers.

4. According to Figure 5.1, the ozone partial pressure at an altitude of 15 kilometers is:

   F. less than 2 millipascals.
   G. more than 2 but less than 4 millipascals.
   H. more than 4 but less than 6 millipascals.
   J. more than 6 but less than 8 millipascals.

5. According to Figure 5.1, the greatest change in ozone partial pressure occurs in the altitude range of:

   A. 1 to 15 kilometers.
   B. 15 to 20 kilometers.
   C. 20 to 25 kilometers.
   D. 25 to 30 kilometers.

Passage 2

Figure 5.2 shows the speed of sound in air at various temperatures.

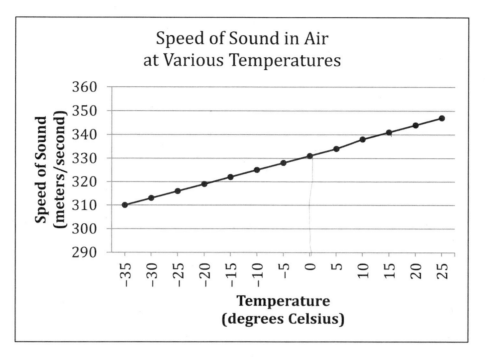

Figure 5.2

6. In Figure 5.2, air temperature is given in measurements of:

    F. meters.
    G. degrees Kelvin.
    H. degrees Celsius.
    J. meters per second.

7. In Figure 5.2, speed of sound is presented in intervals of:

    A. 1 meter.
    B. 10 meters.
    C. 1 meter per second.
    D. 10 meters per second.

8. According to Figure 5.2, the speed of sound in air at 0°C is:

    F. more than 300 but less than 320 meters per second.
    G. more than 310 but less than 320 meters per second.
    H. more than 320 but less than 330 meters per second.
    J. more than 330 but less than 340 meters per second.

9. According to Figure 5.2, sound travels in air at 344 meters per second when the air temperature is:

   A. −35°C.
   B. −20°C.
   C. 15°C.
   D. 20°C.

10. According to Figure 5.2, as the temperature of the air increases, the speed of sound:

    F. increases.
    G. decreases.
    H. increases, then decreases.
    J. decreases, then increases.

Passage 3

In the wild, there is a predator-prey relationship between foxes and rabbits. Figure 5.3 shows an idealized model of this relationship, in which predator and prey populations are in equilibrium. As the fox population grows, the foxes eat more rabbits, forcing the rabbit population to decline. Then, because the foxes' food supply (rabbits) is less plentiful, the number of foxes begins to decline. With fewer fox predators, the rabbit population increases again, leading the fox population to also increase, and the cycle starts over.

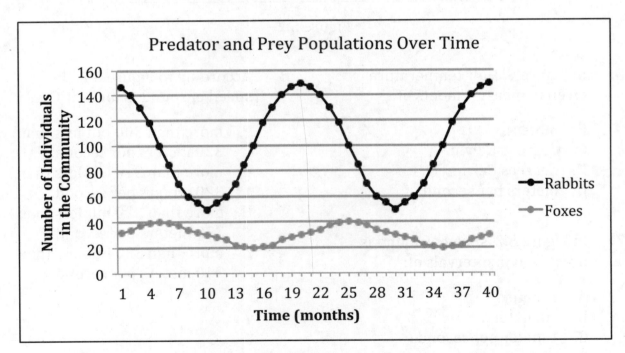

Figure 5.3

11. According to Figure 5.3, one complete cycle of the predator-prey model takes how long to complete?

   A. 5 months
   B. 10 months
   C. 20 months
   D. 40 months

12. According to Figure 5.3, the number of foxes in the community is smallest in which of the following months?

   F. Months 1 and 40
   G. Months 5 and 25
   H. Months 10 and 30
   J. Months 15 and 35

13. According to Figure 5.3, the number of rabbits in the community is greatest in which of the following months?

   A. Months 5 and 25
   B. Months 10 and 30
   C. Months 15 and 30
   D. Months 20 and 40

14. According to Figure 5.3, from Month 10 to Month 20 of the predator-prey cycle, the number of rabbits in the community:

   F. decreases.
   G. increases.
   H. decreases, then increases.
   J. increases, then decreases.

15. According to Figure 5.3, during the time that the number of rabbits in the community increases, the number of foxes in the community:

   A. decreases, then increases.
   B. increases, then decreases.
   C. decreases.
   D. increases.

Passage 4

Biologists concerned about bald eagle survival rates have found high concentrations of various contaminants in bald eagle eggs of nesting eagle pairs in Maine. The biologists theorize that the contaminants were discharged into waterways where they have entered the food chain, ultimately being absorbed by fish that are the main food of the bald eagle. Figure 5.4 shows the levels of these contaminants in the eggs of Maine bald eagles over a 10-year period.

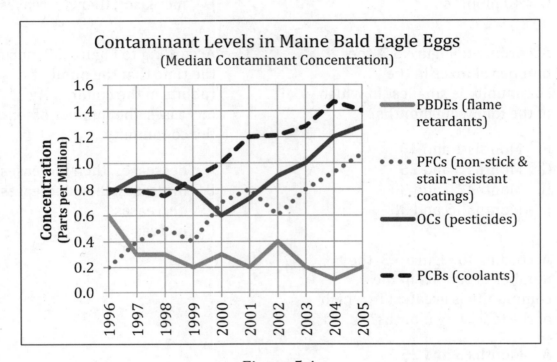

Figure 5.4

16. Figure 5.4 provides information about:

   F. the median concentration of contaminants in four waterways.
   G. the median concentration of four contaminants in bald eagle eggs.
   H. the number of eagles that have ingested contaminated fish.
   J. the age of the bald eagles that have hatched from contaminated eggs.

17. In Figure 5.4, the values on the vertical scale range from:

   A. 0 parts to 1.6 parts.
   B. 0 parts to 1,600,000 parts.
   C. 0 parts per million to 1.6 parts per million.
   D. 1996 parts to 2005 parts.

18. According to Figure 5.4, which of the following years had the lowest concentration of OCs?

   F. 2000
   G. 2002
   H. 2004
   J. 2005

19. According to Figure 5.4, the highest concentration of PCBs recorded was:

   A. less than 0.2 parts per million.
   B. more than 0.4 parts per million but less than 0.6 parts per million.
   C. more than 0.8 parts per million but less than 1.0 parts per million.
   D. more than 1.4 parts per million but less than 1.6 parts per million.

20. According to Figure 5.4, for which of the following contaminants was the concentration in 2005 less than it was in 1996?

   F. PCBs
   G. OCs
   H. PFCs
   J. PBDEs

Science **Interpretation of Data**

Unit 6 | **Line Graphs Practice**

INSIDE THIS UNIT:
– Exercise 1 – – Exercise 2 –

EXERCISE 1

DIRECTIONS: Each passage below is followed by questions based on its content. Answer the questions on the basis of what is stated or implied in the corresponding passage. Answers are on page 757.

Passage 1

Municipal Solid Waste (MSW), also known as trash or garbage, consists of everyday items such as product packaging, grass clippings, furniture, clothing, bottles, food scraps, newspapers, appliances, paint, and batteries. U.S. residents, businesses, and institutions produce about 4.5 pounds of waste per person per day. Several MSW management practices, such as source reduction, recycling, and composting, prevent or divert materials from the waste stream. Figure 6.1 shows total Municipal Solid Waste in the United States by year.

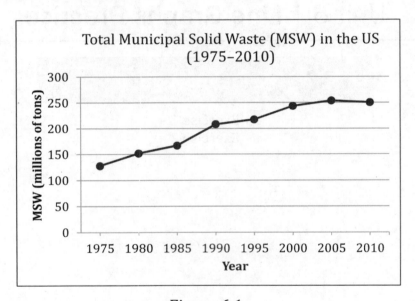

Figure 6.1

1. In Figure 6.1, total Municipal Solid Waste is given in measurements of:

    A. tons.
    B. years.
    C. millions of tons.
    D. pounds.

2. In Figure 6.1, time is presented in intervals of:

    F. 1 year.
    G. 5 years.
    H. 35 years.
    J. 50 years.

UNIT 6 | LINE GRAPHS PRACTICE • 599

3. According to Figure 6.1, total Municipal Solid Waste in 1975 was:

   A. less than 50 million tons.
   B. more than 50 million tons but less than 100 million tons.
   C. more than 100 million tons but less than 150 million tons.
   D. more than 150 million tons.

4. According to Figure 6.1, in which of the following years was the greatest weight of Municipal Solid Waste produced?

   F. 1975
   G. 2000
   H. 2005
   J. 2010

5. According to Figure 6.1, in which of the following years did the total Municipal Solid Waste first exceed 200 million tons?

   A. 1980
   B. 1985
   C. 1990
   D. 2000

Passage 2

Commercial fertilizers are applied to agricultural crops to increase crop yields. Prior to the 1950s, most farming occurred on small family farms with limited use of chemicals. The shift since then to larger corporate farms has coincided with the use of chemical fertilizers in modern agricultural practices. The three major types of commercial fertilizer used in the U.S. are nitrogen, phosphate, and potash. Phosphorus runoff can lead to nuisance algae and plant growth, often in freshwater streams, lakes, and estuaries. Government scientists monitor many streams, rivers, and lakes to track phosphate runoff. Figure 6.2 shows the amount of phosphorous (measured in milligrams of phosphorous per liter of water) in water samples taken from two streams during an 8-month period.

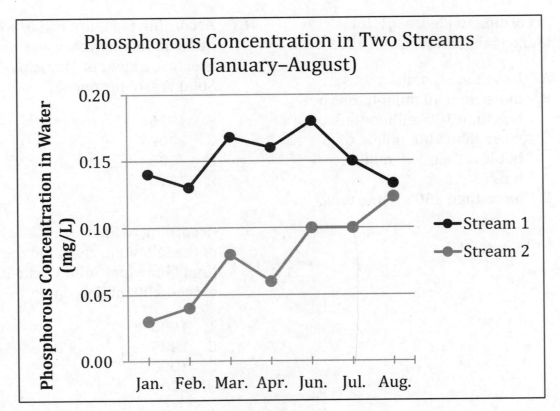

Figure 6.2

6. In Figure 6.2, the two lines represent:

   F. phosphorous concentrations from two different streams.
   G. readings of concentrations of two different chemicals.
   H. phosphorous concentrations from two different years.
   J. phosphorous concentrations using two different measuring systems.

7. In Figure 6.2, phosphorous concentrations are given in measurements of:

   A. grams.
   B. grams per liter.
   C. milligrams per liter.
   D. grams per milliliter.

8. According to Figure 6.2, the Stream 2 sample taken in July had a phosphorous concentration of:

   F. 0.05 mg/L.
   G. 0.10 mg/L.
   H. 0.15 mg/L.
   J. 0.20 mg/L.

9. According to Figure 6.2, in which of the following months did the Stream 1 sample have a phosphorous concentration of 0.15 mg/L?

A. March
B. June
C. July
D. August

10. According to Figure 6.2, the Stream 1 sample taken in February had a phosphorous concentration of:

F. less than 0.05 mg/L.
G. more than 0.05 mg/L but less than 0.10 mg/L.
H. more than 0.10 mg/L but less than 0.15 mg/L.
J. more than 0.15 mg/L.

Passage 3

Like human beings, race horses have running styles. Some horses like to set the pace (be in the lead); others like to follow the leader; still others like to close late in the race. In a 1-mile race between three horses, the times each horse passed the quarter-mile markers were recorded. Figure 6.3 summarizes the elapsed running times of the three horses in the 1-mile race.

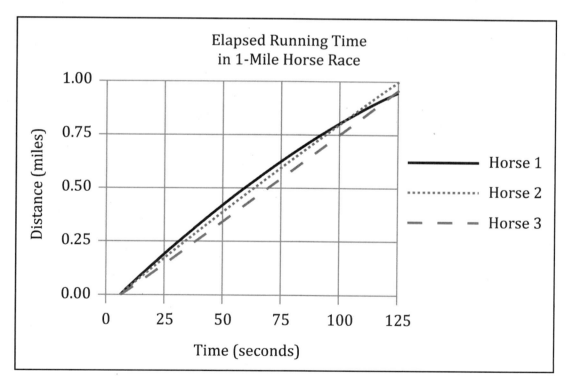

Figure 6.3

602 • SCIENCE INTERPRETATION OF DATA

11. In Figure 6.3, the distances in the horse race are presented in intervals of:

A. 0.25 miles.
B. 0.50 miles.
C. 0.75 miles.
D. 1.00 miles.

12. According to Figure 6.3, which of the following horses won the 1-mile horse race?

F. Horse 1
G. Horse 2
H. Horse 3
J. Cannot be determined from the given information

13. According to Figure 6.3, Horse 3 passed Horse 1 somewhere between:

A. 0.25 miles and 0.50 miles.
B. 0.50 miles and 0.75 miles.
C. 0.75 miles and 1.00 miles.
D. after 1.00 miles.

14. According to Figure 6.3, which of the following horses reached the 0.50-mile marker before 75 seconds?

F. Horse 1
G. Horses 1 and 2
H. Horses 2 and 3
J. Horses 1, 2, and 3

15. According to Figure 6.3, the time it took Horse 1 to complete the 1-mile horse race was:

A. greater than 25 seconds but less than 50 seconds.
B. greater than 50 seconds but less than 75 seconds.
C. greater than 75 seconds but less than 100 seconds.
D. greater than 100 seconds.

EXERCISE 2

DIRECTIONS: Each passage below is followed by questions based on its content. Answer the questions on the basis of what is stated or implied in the corresponding passage. Answers are on page 757.

Passage 1

Most people agree that while reducing energy consumption should be a vital goal, it is important to assess the effectiveness of conservation programs. The results of a long-term study of the results of energy conservation in one community are shown in Figure 6.4.

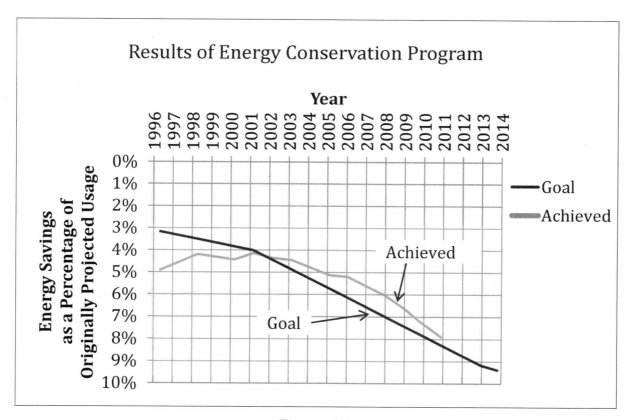

Figure 6.4

604 • SCIENCE INTERPRETATION OF DATA

1. In Figure 6.4, the results of the energy conservation program are presented by comparing the:

    A. amount of energy used with the amount of energy saved.
    B. percent actual energy savings with the percent of savings goal.
    C. percent of energy actually used with the percent of energy conserved.
    D. energy efficiency of conservation with the cost of energy consumed.

2. In Figure 6.4, the vertical scale represents the energy savings as a percent of:

    F. anticipated energy usage.
    G. actual energy consumption.
    H. anticipated energy savings.
    J. energy wasted.

3. According to Figure 6.4, in which of the following years did the community achieve a 6% energy savings?

    A. 2001
    B. 2002
    C. 2006
    D. 2008

4. According to Figure 6.4, in which of the following years did the goal for energy savings equal the achieved energy savings?

    F. 1996
    G. 2002
    H. 2006
    J. 2008

5. According to Figure 6.4, the goal for energy savings in 2008 was:

    A. 4%.
    B. 5%.
    C. 6%.
    D. 7%.

Passage 2

The stone crab, *Menippe mercenaria*, (Figure 6.5), is harvested from the waters around Florida. Only the claw is harvested. By law, the claw must be removed and the de-clawed crab returned to the water. Approximately 20% to 25% of all stone crabs harvested in this way are able to regenerate a new claw suitable for harvesting again within a year. In order to determine whether the stone crab is a sustainable resource, scientists are seeking to determine whether an increase in the number of traps used by crabbers causes a decline in the harvest of stone crabs. Figure 6.6 presents the findings of the scientists.

Dorsal View of Male Stone Crab
(*Menippe mercenaria*)

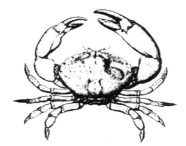

Figure 6.5

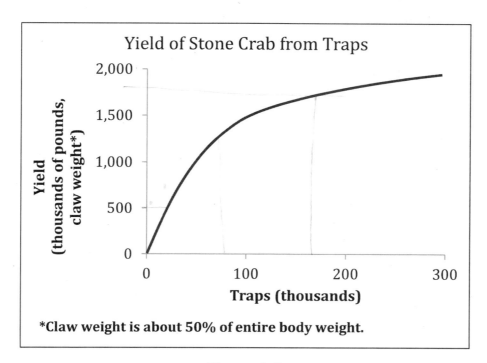

Figure 6.6

6. In Figure 6.6, the yield of stone crab from the traps is given in measurements of:

   F. pounds of crab.
   G. pounds of crab claw.
   H. thousands of crabs.
   J. thousands of pounds of crab claw.

7. According to Figure 6.6, 500 thousand pounds of crab would yield approximately how many pounds of claw?

   A. 250 thousand pounds
   B. 500 thousand pounds
   C. 1 million pounds
   D. 2 million pounds

8. According to Figure 6.6, an increase in the number of traps is associated with:

   F. a decrease in the yield.
   G. an increase in the yield.
   H. no net change in the yield.
   J. a disruption of the yield.

9. According to Figure 6.6, the use of 75,000 traps yielded:

   A. less than 500,000 pounds claw weight.
   B. more than 500,000 pounds but less than 1,000,000 pounds claw weight.
   C. more than 1,000,000 pounds but less than 1,500,000 pounds claw weight.
   D. more than 1,500,000 pounds claw weight.

10. According to Figure 6.6, a yield of 1,750,000 pounds claw weight required:

    F. fewer than 100,000 traps.
    G. between 100,000 and 200,000 traps.
    H. between 200,000 and 300,000 traps.
    J. more than 300,000 traps.

Passage 3

The spectral power distribution (SPD) of a light source is the energy output per unit wavelength. It is measured using a spectroradiometer, which separates the broadband radiation emitted from a source into small wavelength intervals. The radiant energy from the source is measured for each interval. An SPD may be expressed in artificial units based on a particular wavelength such as 555 or 560 nanometers. Figure 6.7 shows the SPD of a High Intensity Discharge (HID) used as a headlamp in cars.

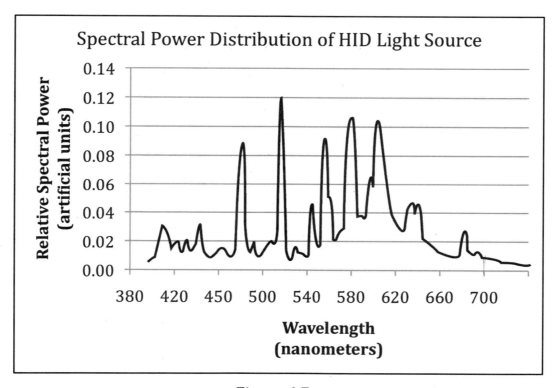

Figure 6.7

11. In Figure 6.7, the horizontal scale represents:

    A. power distributions measured in wavelengths.
    B. wavelengths of light measured in nanometers.
    C. relative special power measured in nanometers.
    D. relative special power measured in artificial units.

12. In Figure 6.7, the artificial units of relative spectral power are presented in intervals of:

    F. 0.02.
    G. 0.14.
    H. 2.
    J. 60.

13. According to Figure 6.7, the wavelength of light with the greatest relative spectral power is:

    A. more than 420 but less than 460 nanometers.
    B. more than 500 but less than 540 nanometers.
    C. more than 540 but less than 580 nanometers.
    D. more than 580 but less than 620 nanometers.

14. According to Figure 6.7, light with a wavelength of 700 nanometers has a relative spectral power of:

    F. less than 0.02.
    G. more than 0.02 but less than 0.04.
    H. more than 0.04 but less than 0.06.
    J. more than 0.06.

15. According to Figure 6.7, light with wavelength longer than 420 nanometers but shorter than 450 nanometers has a relative spectral power of:

    A. less than 0.2.
    B. less than 0.4.
    C. greater than 0.4.
    D. greater than 0.6.

Science **Interpretation of Data**

Unit 7 | **Practice**

INSIDE THIS UNIT:
– Exercise 1 – – Exercise 2 –

EXERCISE 1

DIRECTIONS: Each passage below is followed by questions based on its content. Answer the questions on the basis of what is stated or implied in the corresponding passage. Answers are on page 757.

Passage 1

The pH scale is used to measure the strengths of acids and bases. The conventional pH scale ranges from 0 (most acidic) to 14 (most basic). A pH of 7.0 is neutral. A pH less than 7.0 is acidic, and a pH greater than 7.0 is basic. Pure water is neutral, with a pH of 7.0. Vinegar and lemon juice are acidic substances, while soap (lye) and ammonia are basic. Table 7.1 summarizes pH levels for a variety of common substances.

TABLE 7.1		
	Substance	pH
Base	Lye	13.0
	Bleach	12.5
	Ammonia	11.0
	Milk of Magnesia	10.5
	Baking Soda	8.3
	Human Blood	7.4
Neutral	Pure Water	7.0
Acid	Milk	6.6
	Coffee	4.9
	Malt Beverages	4.0
	Orange Juice	3.0
	Vinegar	2.2
	Lemon Juice	2.0

1. According to Table 7.1, the pH of ammonia is:

   A. 3.0.
   B. 4.5.
   C. 8.3.
   D. 11.0.

2. According to Table 7.1, the pH of vinegar is:

   F. 2.0.
   G. 2.2.
   H. 8.3.
   J. 12.4.

3. According to Table 7.1, which of the following substances is the most acidic?

   A. Lye
   B. Pure water
   C. Milk
   D. Lemon juice

4. According to Table 7.1, which of the following substances is the most basic?

   F. Lye
   G. Bleach
   H. Baking soda
   J. Human blood

5. According to Table 7.1, which of the following substances is basic?

   A. Milk
   B. Baking soda
   C. Coffee
   D. Orange juice

Passage 2

Between 1969 and 1972, six Apollo missions brought back 382 kilograms (842 pounds) of lunar rocks and regolith (broken rocks and dust). Study of the rock and regolith samples from the moon has provided information about the chemical make-up of the moon's surface. Figure 7.1 shows a chemical analysis of the moon samples.

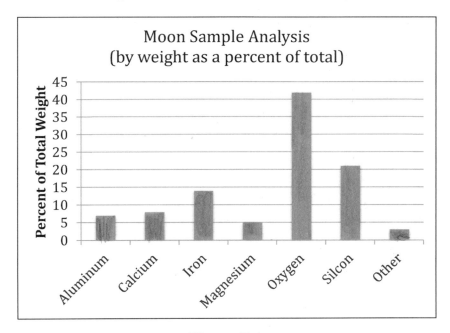

Figure 7.1

6. In Figure 7.1, the contents of the moon samples are given in measurements of:

    F. grams.
    G. percentages.
    H. kilograms.
    J. pounds.

7. According to Figure 7.1, which of the following is the most abundant element, by weight, in the moon samples?

    A. Aluminum
    B. Iron
    C. Oxygen
    D. Silicon

8. According to Figure 7.1, which of the following elements is the least abundant, by weight, in the moon samples?

    F. Aluminum
    G. Calcium
    H. Iron
    J. Magnesium

9. According to Figure 7.1, silicon constitutes what percent of the moon samples by weight?

    A. Less than 10 percent
    B. More than 10 percent but less than 20 percent
    C. More than 20 percent but less than 25 percent
    D. More than 25 percent but less than 30 percent

10. According to Figure 7.1, iron constitutes approximately what percent of the moon samples by weight?

    F. 5 percent
    G. 6 percent
    H. 7 percent
    J. 14 percent

Passage 3

Most objects absorb electromagnetic radiation and convert that radiation into heat that is then re-radiated (emitted). A radiation curve provides information about the particular way that the energy emitted by an object varies with the wavelength of the radiation. Figure 7.2 shows the radiation curve for an object at different temperatures. For any given temperature, there is a specific wavelength at which the intensity of the emitted radiation is the greatest. This is called the peak wavelength. The shape of a radiation curve is dependent on temperature: the hotter the object, the shorter the peak wavelength.

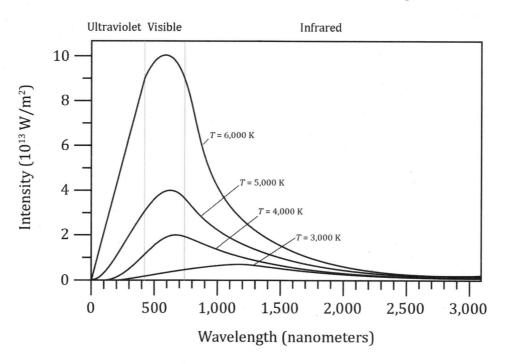

Figure 7.2

11. In Figure 7.2, the wavelengths of the emissions are given in measurements of:

    A. meters.
    B. kelvin.
    C. degrees.
    D. nanometers.

12. According to Figure 7.2, visible light is electromagnetic radiation at wavelengths of approximately:

    F.   0 to 200 nanometers.
    G.   200 to 400 nanometers.
    H.   400 to 750 nanometers.
    J.   1,000 to 1,200 nanometers.

13. According to the graph in Figure 7.2, the object with the peak wavelength with the greatest intensity had a temperature of:

    A. 3,000 K.
    B. 4,000 K.
    C. 5,000 K.
    D. 6,000 K.

14. According to Figure 7.2, the object with a peak wavelength in the infrared light range had a temperature of:

    F. 3,000 K.
    G. 4,000 K.
    H. 5,000 K.
    J. 6,000 K.

15. According to Figure 7.2, the wavelength at which all four objects had intensities that were the closest is:

    A. 500 nanometers.
    B. 1,000 nanometers.
    C. 1,500 nanometers.
    D. 2,500 nanometers.

Passage 4

The total distance required to stop a moving vehicle depends on the time it takes to react and the time it takes for the vehicle to stop once the brakes are applied, as illustrated in Figure 7.3. The distance a vehicle travels between the time a driver realizes that the brakes should be applied and when they are applied is called the reaction distance. The distance a vehicle travels between the time that the brakes are applied and the time the vehicle comes to a complete stop is called the braking distance. The sum of the reaction distance and braking distance is the total stopping distance.

Figure 7.3

A driver's initial speed, reaction distance, and braking distance were recorded for six trials. The results are recorded in Table 7.2. All trials were conducted under dry driving conditions.

TABLE 7.2			
Stopping Distance Under Dry Driving Conditions			
Initial Car Speed (kilometers/hour)	Reaction Distance (meters)	Braking Distance (meters)	Total Stopping Distance (meters)
30	5.3	5.5	10.8
50	9.2	14.8	24.0
60	11.0	21.4	32.4
80	14.7	28.0	52.7
100	18.3	59.4	77.7
120	22.0	85.5	107.5

16. The unit of measure for all distances listed in the table is:

    F. meters.
    G. feet.
    H. kilometers.
    J. kilometers per hour.

17. The maximum speed for which reaction distance, braking distance, and total stopping distance are given is:

    A. 60 kilometers/hour.
    B. 80 kilometers/hour.
    C. 100 kilometers/hour.
    D. 120 kilometers/hour.

18. The reaction distance for a vehicle traveling 60 kilometers per hour is:

    F. 11.0 meters.
    G. 14.7 meters.
    H. 21.4 meters.
    J. 32.4 meters.

19. The braking distance for a vehicle traveling 100 kilometers per hour is:

    A. 18.3 meters.
    B. 59.4 meters.
    C. 77.7 meters.
    D. 205.7 meters.

20. The total stopping distance for a vehicle traveling 50 kilometers per hour is:

    F. 85.5 meters.
    G. 28.0 meters.
    H. 24.0 meters.
    J. 14.8 meters.

EXERCISE 2

DIRECTIONS: Each passage below is followed by questions based on its content. Answer the questions on the basis of what is stated or implied in the corresponding passage. Answers are on page 757.

Passage 1

As a solar-powered aircraft gains altitude, it rises through the dense but gradually thinning lower atmosphere. From sea level to 12 kilometers, cooler air produces a decrease in the operating temperature of the solar cells. However, at altitudes above 12 kilometers, the thinner air provides less air flow over the solar panel to cool the cells, and the operating temperature of the cells rises. Figure 7.4 shows the change in the operating temperature of the solar cells as the aircraft gains altitude.

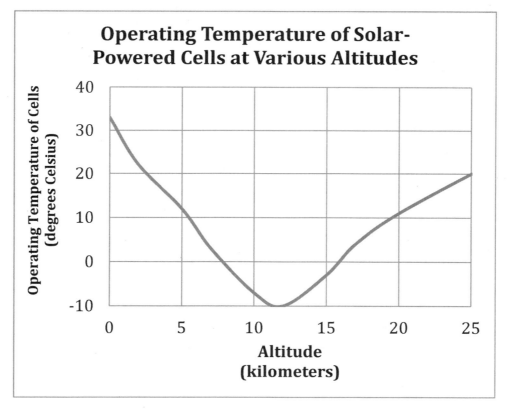

Figure 7.4

1. Figure 7.4 provides information about:

   A. the efficiency of solar cells at various altitudes.
   B. the operating temperature of solar cells at various altitudes.
   C. air flow over and around a solar aircraft at various altitudes.
   D. the air temperature at various altitudes.

2. In Figure 7.4, the vertical scale represents:

   F. altitude in kilometers.
   G. temperature in kilometers.
   H. altitude in degrees.
   J. temperature in degrees Celsius.

3. According to Figure 7.4, the operating temperature of the solar cells at 12 kilometers is approximately:

   A. −10 degrees Celsius.
   B. 0 degrees Celsius.
   C. 12 degrees Celsius.
   D. 32 degrees Celsius.

4. According to Figure 7.4, the maximum operating temperature of the solar cells occurs at an altitude of:

   F. 0 kilometers.
   G. 10 kilometers.
   H. 12 kilometers.
   J. 25 kilometers.

5. According to Figure 7.4, the solar cells operate at a temperature of 10 degrees Celsius at altitudes of approximately:

   A. 6 kilometers only.
   B. 12 kilometers only.
   C. 6 kilometers and 19 kilometers.
   D. 6 kilometers, 12 kilometers, and 19 kilometers.

Passage 2

Per capita estimates of the food supply provide information on the amount of food and nutrients available for consumption. These estimates are useful for assessing trends in food and nutrient consumption over time, monitoring the potential of the food supply to meet the nutritional needs of Americans, and examining relationships between food availability and diet-health risk. Figure 7.5 provides historical information about certain nutrients in the food supply.

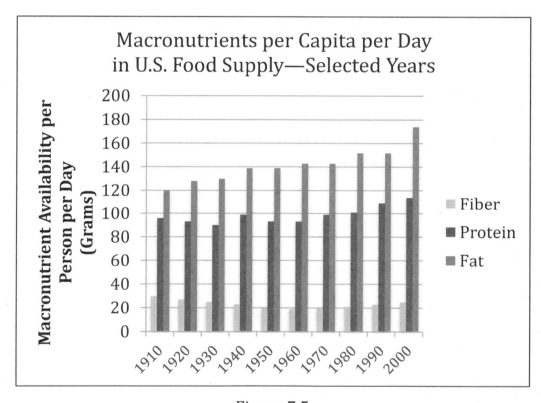

Figure 7.5

6. In Figure 7.5, the amounts of macronutrients are given in measurements of:

F. milligrams.
G. years.
H. kilograms.
J. grams.

7. According to Figure 7.5, the per capita per day amount of protein in the food supply in 1940 was approximately:

A. 25 grams.
B. 100 grams.
C. 115 grams.
D. 140 grams.

8. According to Figure 7.5, in what year did the per capita per day amount of fat in the food supply first exceed 140 grams?

F. 1940
G. 1950
H. 1960
J. 1970

9. According to Figure 7.5, in what year was the per capita per day amount of fat in the food supply equal to 120 grams?

A. 1910
B. 1950
C. 1970
D. 2000

10. According to Figure 7.5, from 1910 to 2000 the per capita per day amount of fiber in the food supply:

F. increased and then decreased.
G. increased, then decreased, and then increased.
H. decreased and then increased.
J. decreased, then increased, and then decreased.

Passage 3

The strength of the earth's gravitational field decreases as distance from the center of the earth increases. The earth's rotation about an axis through its north and south poles causes it to bulge out slightly at the equator. Thus, an object located at the North Pole is approximately 21 kilometers closer to the center of the earth than an object at the equator. The strength of gravity varies by latitude on the earth's surface (Table 7.3). Additionally, the height above sea level, or altitude, affects the gravitational field strength (Table 7.4).

TABLE 7.3		
Gravitational Field Strength at Various Points on the Earth's Surface at Sea Level		
Degrees Latitude North (°N)	Gravitational Field Strength (newtons/kilogram)	Distance to the Center of the Earth (kilometers)
0 (Equator)	9.7805	6,378
15	9.7839	6,377
30	9.7934	6,373
45	9.8063	6,367
60	9.8192	6,362
75	9.8287	6,358
90 (North Pole)	9.8322	6,357

TABLE 7.4				
Gravitational Field Strength at Three Locations				
Degrees Latitude North (°N)	Gravitational Field Strength at Sea Level (newtons/kilogram)	Location	Altitude (meters)	Gravitational Field Strength at Indicated Altitude (newtons/kilogram)
42	9.8035	Chicago	182	9.8029
28	9.7919	Mt. Everest	8,848	9.7647
32	9.7950	Dead Sea	−397	9.7962

11. According to the information provided, an object located at the North Pole is:

    A. closer to the center of the earth than an object located at the equator.
    B. farther away from the center of the earth than an object located at the equator.
    C. just as far from the center of the earth as an object located at the equator.
    D. sometimes closer and at other times farther from the center of the earth than an object located at the equator.

12. All of the measurements in Table 7.3 were taken at:

    F. sea level.
    G. the equator.
    H. the North Pole.
    J. latitude 0°N.

13. According to the information provided, the unit of gravitational field strength is:

    A. kilograms.
    B. newtons.
    C. kilograms/newton.
    D. newtons/kilogram.

14. In Table 7.4, the altitude of the given locations is reported in:

    F. degrees.
    G. meters.
    H. kilometers.
    J. newtons.

15. In Table 7.3, the distance from points on the earth's surface to its center is reported in:

    A. meters.
    B. kilometers.
    C. newtons.
    D. kilograms.

16. According to Table 7.3, the gravitational field strength at latitude 45°N is:

    F. 9.7839 newtons/kilogram.
    G. 9.7934 newtons/kilogram.
    H. 9.8063 newtons/kilogram.
    J. 9.8192 newtons/kilogram.

17. According to Table 7.4, the Dead Sea is located:

    A. above sea level.
    B. at sea level.
    C. below sea level.
    D. on the equator.

18. According to Table 7.4, the strength of the gravitational field at latitude 28°N and an altitude of 8,848 meters is:

    F. 9.8035 newtons/kilogram.
    G. 9.7919 newtons/kilogram.
    H. 9.7950 newtons/kilogram.
    J. 9.7647 newtons/kilogram.

Science **Scientific Investigation**

Unit 8 | **Describing Experiments**

INSIDE THIS UNIT:
– Introducing Simple Scientific Investigations and Experiments – – Extracting Information from Simple Experiments – – Exercise –

Non-Negotiable Skill:

Find basic information describing
simple experiments.

Introducing Simple Scientific Investigations and Experiments

In Units 1 through 7, you learned about the different kinds of graphs that can be used to present scientific data. There are tables, plots, bar graphs, line graphs, pie charts, and even some oddball presentations. In those units, you were primarily concerned with looking for basic information in the table or graph or finding a single piece of data. As you've seen, scientific presentations are usually accompanied by textual information. Thus far, any accompanying information simply explained the origin and purpose of the data presentation.

We've been focused on data reporting—how to read tables and graphs, extract values, and manipulate data—and reading background information. Another important skill is the ability to understand and describe experiments. This skill is no different from that developed in the Interpretation of Data units: find the needed information in the accompanying text.

Simple Investigation

A group of science students investigated the movement of the sun by measuring the length of the shadow cast by the flagpole in front of their school. The students used a meter stick to measure the shadow and gathered data every hour. Figure 8.1 summarizes their findings.

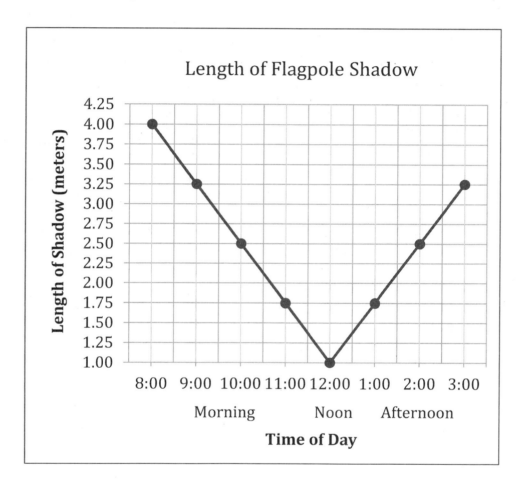

Figure 8.1

1. The students measured the length of the flagpole shadow:

   A. every day.
   B. every hour.
   C. once a day.
   D. at all times.

2. The length of the flagpole shadow was measured in units of:

   F. meters.
   G. feet.
   H. yards.
   J. hours.

3. The purpose of the investigation was to measure:

   A. the height of the flagpole.
   B. the rate at which the sun moves across the sky.
   C. the shadow cast by a flagpole in moonlight.
   D. the shadow cast by a flagpole in sunlight.

4. According to Figure 8.1, the flagpole shadow was shortest at:

   F. 1:00 in the morning.
   G. 8:00 in the morning.
   H. 12:00 noon.
   J. 3:00 in the afternoon.

5. According to Figure 8.1, the flagpole shadow was longest at:

   A. 4:00 in the morning.
   B. 8:00 in the morning.
   C. 12:00 noon.
   D. 3:00 in the afternoon.

6. According to Figure 8.1, at 2:00 in the afternoon, the length of the flagpole shadow was:

   F. 1.25 meters.
   G. 2.0 meters.
   H. 2.5 meters.
   J. 10.25 meters.

Other passages present descriptions of simple science experiments, in which some things (variables) are controlled to determine the impact on other things (other variables). We'll start with two very simple biology experiments.

Simple Experiment 1

Students in a biology class wanted to determine the effect of different lighting conditions on plant growth. They planted 10 bean seedlings in individual pots. They placed five of the pots in full light and the remaining pots in partial darkness. All pots received the same amount of water. The students measured the height of the seedlings every five days, averaged the heights, and entered the information in a log. At the end of the experiment, they created a graph to summarize their findings (Figure 8.2).

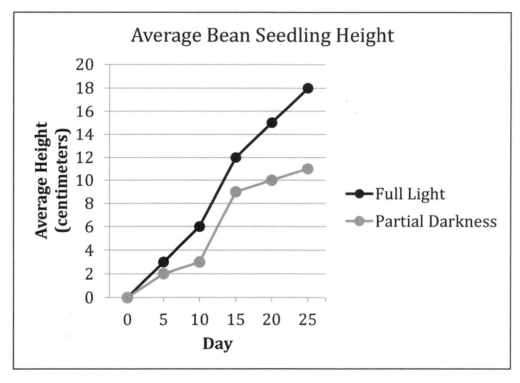

Figure 8.2

7. The purpose of the experiment was to:

   A. calculate the amount of light to which bean seedlings were exposed.
   B. investigate how light conditions affect the growth of bean seedlings
   C. determine the effect of different fertilizers on the growth of bean seedlings.
   D. analyze the different growth rates of two types of bean seedlings.

8. The students measured the results of the experiment by:

   F. counting the number of seedlings planted.
   G. measuring the height of the seedlings.
   H. counting the days since planting.
   J. measuring the amount of light to which the seedlings were exposed.

9. Throughout the experiment, which of the following was constant for each group of bean seedlings?

   A. Seedling height
   B. Average seedling height
   C. Number of days since planting
   D. Light conditions

10. According to Figure 8.2, on which of the following days was the average full light seedling height greater than the average partial darkness seedling height?

    F. Days 5 and 10
    G. Days 5 and 15
    H. Days 10, 20, and 25
    J. Days 5, 10, 15, 20, and 25

Simple Experiment 2

A scientist investigated the effect of alcohol on a northern leopard frog (*Rana pipiens*). The frog was placed into a laboratory dish filled with fresh running water supplied by a hose. All sources of external stimuli such as movement or direct, non-ambient lighting were blocked. Once the frog had been still for five minutes, the water was turned off and a second hose filled the dish with a 0.50 M (molarity) methanol in water solution. The scientist recorded the duration of time until a reaction in the frog (such as a twitch) was observed. The dish was purged with fresh running water until the frog was again still for five minutes. The experiment was repeated for four additional concentrations of methanol: 0.55 M, 0.60 M, 0.65 M, and 0.70 M.

The entire experiment was repeated using ethanol in water solutions of the same concentrations. The experimental results are summarized in Figure 8.3.

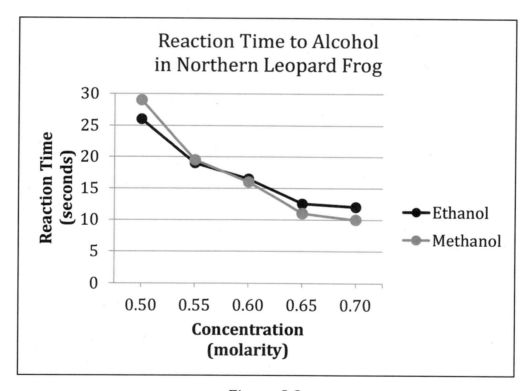

Figure 8.3

11. The experiment measured the reaction time of a frog to:

A. the same concentration of one type of alcohol.
B. the same concentration of two types of alcohol.
C. various concentrations of one type of alcohol.
D. various concentrations of two types of alcohol.

12. In the experiment, the alcohol solutions are described in terms of:

F. flow time (seconds).
G. concentration (molarity).
H. reaction time (seconds).
J. volume (milliliters).

13. The scientist measured the reaction time of the frog in:

A. molarity.
B. milliseconds.
C. seconds.
D. liters.

14. Which of the following is kept constant for the entire experiment?

F. Number of frog specimens tested
G. Concentration of ethanol in water
H. Concentration of methanol in water
J. Volume of fresh running water used to purge the dish

15. What is the correct sequence of the following steps in this experiment?

I. Wait for the frog to be still for five minutes.
II. Fill the dish with alcohol water solution.
III. Record the length of time until the frog moves.
IV. Fill the dish with fresh running water.

A. I, II, IV, III
B. I, IV, II, III
C. IV, I, II, III
D. IV, II, I, III

Extracting Information from Simple Experiments

Every scientific investigation or experiment begins with a question. Consider an antacid tablet that fizzes when dropped in water. One might wonder, "Does the temperature of the water affect the time it takes for the tablet to react?"

To answer the question, you could devise an experiment to test the validity of a stated hypothesis. A hypothesis attempts to answer the question asked. For example, "Antacid tablets react faster in warm water." The experiment may prove or disprove the stated hypothesis, but either way, the question about the observed phenomenon is answered: "Yes, the temperature of the water affects the time it takes an antacid tablet to react."

Simple experiment passages often begin with a brief introduction to the phenomenon being studied. The purpose of the experiment and its relation to the phenomenon may also be stated. Then, an experiment passage will describe in detail the testing protocol. This may include descriptions of tools and functions of these tools (more on this in Unit 10), methods used, and which variables are held constant (controlled) and which are observed. We'll talk more about independent (controlled) and dependent variables and controlled experiments in Level 2. For now, it's enough to know that for any given set of observations or measurements, an experiment controls all variables except for one so that the impact of that one variable can be determined.

In our antacid example, to test the impact of water temperature on tablet reaction time, all variables except temperature must be controlled (type of tablet, amount of water, size of tablet, etc.). Only the temperature of the water is varied in order to determine its impact on reaction time.

Some experiments benefit from the use of a control experiment, typically a parallel setup that uses the same materials but without manipulation of a variable. A control helps rule out the possibility that the result would have happened even if the one variable hadn't been adjusted.

Now, let's look at a case study based on our antacid example.

Case Study

A group of students investigated how water temperature affects the time it takes for an effervescent antacid tablet to react completely with water. Using a thermometer, they adjusted the tap water to a temperature of 20°C before filling a glass beaker with 200 mL of water. A student started the timer when a tablet was dropped into the water and stopped the timer when the tablet finished reacting, as indicated by the cessation of any observable gas production (fizzing bubbles). To minimize experimental variation, three trials were conducted and the results were averaged.

The experiment was repeated for three additional tap water temperatures: 5°C, 15°C, and 35°C. The same size and brand tablets were used in all trials. Table 8.1 shows the experimental results.

Table 8.1: Effect of Water Temperature on Antacid Reaction Time

Water Temperature	Total Time for Tablet to Dissolve (seconds)			
	Trial 1	Trial 2	Trial 3	Average
5°C	102	108	106	105
15°C	55	60	58	58
20°C	41	39	38	39
35°C	33	36	35	35

1. According to the passage, the purpose of the experiment is to:

   A. measure how much an antacid tablet changes the temperature of 200 mL of water.
   B. determine how water temperature affects the time it takes an antacid tablet to react completely.
   C. determine which temperature of water best improves the ability of antacid tablets to calm an upset stomach.
   D. test different brands of antacid tablets to determine which reacts fastest.

   The correct answer is (B). The questions asks for the purpose of the experiment. This information is located in the first sentence of the passage: "how water temperature affects the time it takes for an effervescent antacid tablet to react completely."

UNIT 8 | DESCRIBING EXPERIMENTS • 633

2. How many antacid tablets are needed for the entire experiment?

   F. 9
   G. 12
   H. 16
   J. 24

   The correct answer is (G). Four water temperatures are investigated: 5°C, 15°C, 20°C, and 35°C. For each temperature, three trials are completed. Therefore, a total of $3 \times 4 = 12$ tablets are needed for the entire experiment.

3. Which of the following is a complete and accurate list of the materials used in this experiment?

   A. Antacid tablets, beaker, thermometer, and water
   B. Antacid tablets, fume hood, thermometer, and water
   C. Antacid tablets, beaker, thermometer, timer, and water
   D. Antacid tablets, beaker, thermometer, timer, water, and electronic balance

   The correct answer is (C). This question asks for a list of all the materials needed to complete the experiment. For each trial, an antacid <u>tablet</u> is dropped in a <u>beaker</u> containing <u>water</u> at a specific temperature as determined using a <u>thermometer</u> and a <u>timer</u> used to measure the time it takes the tablet to react completely. Identical tablets were used, so it was not necessary to use an electronic balance to weigh them.

4. What is the correct sequence of the following steps in this experiment?

   I. Drop the antacid tablet in the water.
   II. Fill the beaker with water.
   III. Determine the temperature of the water.

   F. I, II, III
   G. II, III, I
   H. II, I, III
   J. III, II, I

   The correct answer is (J). The passage states that the students used a thermometer to determine when the tap water reached the desired temperature, after which 200 mL of tap water was added to a beaker. Then, the tablet was dropped into the beaker.

634 • SCIENCE SCIENTIFIC INVESTIGATION

5. The time from when the timer is started to when it is stopped represents the total time:

A. that the antacid tablet is in the water.
B. that the antacid tablet produces bubbles.
C. between when the antacid tablet is dropped into the water and when the production of bubbles stops.
D. between when the antacid tablet is dropped into the water and when the bubbles first appear.

The correct answer is (C). The passage states that the students started the timer when the antacid tablet was dropped into the beaker and stopped the timer when bubble production was no longer observed. Note that (B) is not correct because the passage does not say whether the tablets begin producing bubbles immediately upon being dropped in the water or after some time.

6. According to the passage, which of the following is the same in every trial?

F. The volume of water in the beaker
G. The required time for the antacid tablet to begin producing bubbles
H. The required time for the antacid tablet to react completely
J. The water temperature

The correct answer is (F). Each trial uses 200 mL of water in a beaker, so water volume is a constant in this experiment. The time required for each tablet to begin producing bubbles is not measured. The time required for each tablet to react completely is the variable that changes due to changes in water temperature. Note that while the water temperature *is* the same for every repeated trial at a given temperature, it is *not* the same for all the trials in the experiment.

7. According to the passage, which of the following is NOT the same for the entire experiment?

   A. The brand of the antacid tablets
   B. The size of the antacid tablets
   C. The volume of water in the beaker
   D. The water temperature

   The correct answer is (D). The second paragraph of the passage states that the brand and size of the tablets are the same in every trial. Moreover, as covered in the previous item, the volume of water in the beaker is the same in every trial. However, over the course experiment, four different water temperatures are investigated: 5°C, 15°C, 20°C, and 35°C.

8. According to the passage, the student stopped the timer when:

   F. the water temperature began to decrease.
   G. the water temperature began to increase.
   H. bubbles were no longer observed.
   J. bubble production stopped.

   The correct answer is (J). According to the passage, the students stopped the timer when bubbles were no longer observed being produced, that is, when the fizzing stops. Note that this is different from bubbles not being observed. It is possible that bubbles remain in the water (clinging to the side of the beaker) after the tablet reacts completely.

9. Which of the following best explains why three trials are completed for each water temperature?

   A. Averaging data over several trials improves accuracy.
   B. Each student wants an opportunity to time a trial.
   C. Different size tablets are used in each trial.
   D. Different volumes of water are used in each trial.

   The correct answer is (A). According to the passage, three trials are completed for each temperature to "minimize experimental variation" by averaging: the greater the number of data points included in an average, the more accurate the measurement.

636 • SCIENCE SCIENTIFIC INVESTIGATION

10. According to Table 8.1, which of the following statements is accurate?

    F. Antacid tablets react faster in colder water.

    G. Antacid tablets react faster in warmer water.

    H. Water temperature does not affect the time it takes an antacid tablet to react completely.

    J. Antacid tablets do not react completely with water regardless of temperature.

The correct answer is (G). The data in Table 8.1 shows that the warmer the water was (increasing temperatures), the faster the tablets reacted completely (decreasing times).

Summary

- Passages based on simple experiments or observations can be from any subject in the sciences: biology, physics, chemistry, earth sciences, astronomy, geology, and so on. The only requirement is that the text be "scientific."

- Science experiment passages typically have three main parts: introduction, experiment description, and results.

- All Level 1 science questions test reading comprehension: the key to solving questions about experiment descriptions is to find the needed information in the text (and/or data presentation).

EXERCISE

> **DIRECTIONS:** The passage below is followed by questions based on its content. Answer the questions on the basis of what is stated or implied in the passage. Answers are on page 757.

The ability of a substance (solute) to dissolve in a liquid (solvent) is referred to as its solubility. During a chemistry experiment, a student compared the solubility of common table salt in four liquids: water, mineral oil, vegetable oil, and rubbing alcohol.

The student numbered and labeled four flasks. In each flask, he poured 100 mL of one of the liquids and added 1 tablespoon of table salt. Each flask was stoppered and shaken for one minute. The student then noted whether the salt dissolved completely, partly, or not at all in each of the four liquids.

The experiment was repeated using the same liquids to test the solubility of four other substances: table sugar, baking soda, Epsom salt, and powdered chalk. Table 8.2 summarizes the experimental results.

	Table 8.2: Solubility Observations of Common Substances				
	Table Salt	Table Sugar	Baking Soda	Epsom Salt	Powdered Chalk
Water	Totally dissolved	Totally dissolved	Totally dissolved	Totally dissolved	Did not dissolve
Mineral Oil	Did not dissolve	Did not dissolve	Did not dissolve	Did not dissolve	Did not dissolve
Vegetable Oil	Did not dissolve	Did not dissolve	Did not dissolve	Did not dissolve	Did not dissolve
Rubbing Alcohol	Small amount dissolved	Small amount dissolved	Small amount dissolved	Small amount dissolved	Did not dissolve

638 • SCIENCE SCIENTIFIC INVESTIGATION

1. The purpose of the experiment is to:

   A. compare the solubility of common solutes in common solvents.
   B. compare the solubility of common solvents in common solutes.
   C. determine whether common solutes react with common solvents.
   D. determine whether common solvents react with common solutes.

2. How much vegetable oil is needed for the entire experiment?

   F. 100 mL
   G. 400 mL
   H. 500 mL
   J. 2,000 mL

3. What is the correct sequence of the following steps in this experiment?

   I. Add the solute to the flask.
   II. Stopper and shake the flask.
   III. Add the solvent to the flask.
   IV. Label the flask.

   A. I, III, II, IV
   B. III, I, IV, II
   C. IV, I, III, II
   D. IV, III, I, II

4. How many tablespoons of table salt are needed for the entire experiment?

   F. 3
   G. 4
   H. 16
   J. 20

5. The relative solubilities of how many solutes are tested in this experiment?

   A. One
   B. Two
   C. Four
   D. Five

6. The relative dissolving abilities of how many liquids are tested in this experiment?

   F. One
   G. Two
   H. Four
   J. Five

7. Which of the following is NOT constant for each part of the experiment testing the relative solubility of a given solute?

   A. The type of solvent in each of the flasks
   B. The quantity of solute in each flask
   C. The length of time each flask is shaken
   D. The quantity of solvent in each flask

8. Which of the following is NOT required for this experiment?

   F. Baking soda
   G. Vegetable oil
   H. Bunsen burner
   J. Test tubes

9. According to the experimental results, which solute(s) did not dissolve in any of the solvents?

   A. Rubbing alcohol only
   B. Epsom salt and powdered chalk only
   C. Vegetable oil and mineral oil only
   D. Powdered chalk only

10. According to the experimental results, which solvent(s) did not dissolve any of the solutes?

    F. Mineral oil and vegetable oil only
    G. Powdered chalk and baking soda only
    H. Vegetable oil only
    J. Powdered chalk only

Science **Scientific Investigation**

Unit 9 | **Describing Experiments Practice**

INSIDE THIS UNIT:
– Exercise –

EXERCISE

DIRECTIONS: Each passage below is followed by questions based on its content. Answer the questions on the basis of what is stated or implied in the corresponding passage. Answers are on page 757.

Passage 1

An estuary is a semi-enclosed area where two or more bodies of water meet and mix. Heron Marsh is a freshwater estuary where the Sugar River and the Ottawa River meet the largest lake in the area, Spring Lake. The region has a high density of farms, and farmers apply fertilizers to their fields in the spring. After heavy rains, fertilizer runoff drains into the two rivers, which in turn drain into Heron Marsh and then Spring Lake.

A team of scientists investigated whether freshwater estuaries, such as Heron Marsh, help to filter chemicals from river water before feeding into the larger lake. The scientists collected water samples at various locations in Heron Marsh (Figure 9.1) for nine consecutive days following a heavy spring rainstorm. The samples were then tested for nitrate, a chemical found in fertilizers known to cause adverse health effects in infants and children. The results are shown in Table 9.1.

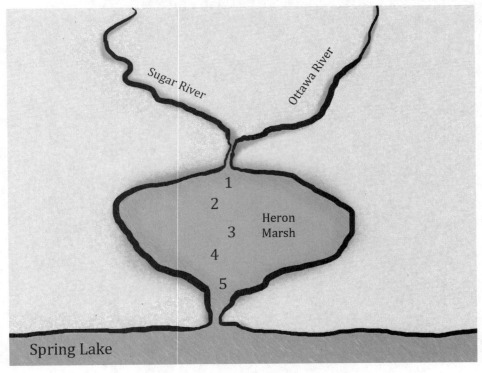

Figure 9.1

UNIT 9 | DESCRIBING EXPERIMENTS PRACTICE • 643

Table 9.1: Heron Marsh Nitrate Concentration Levels (parts per million)									
Station	Days after Storm								
	1	2	3	4	5	6	7	8	9
1	7.1	7.3	10.5	13.2	11.8	10.4	8.8	7.8	7.6
2	0.3	0.5	3.2	6.5	8.8	9.1	7.2	7.0	5.0
3	0.4	0.5	0.5	2.2	4.2	10.3	9.3	7.1	6.5
4	0.4	0.5	1.6	2.5	4.0	4.1	4.2	4.2	3.8
5	0.3	0.6	0.6	2.0	3.4	3.3	3.6	3.3	2.5

1. The purpose of the investigation was to:

A. observe the direction of water flow in the Heron Marsh watershed area.
B. determine the nitrate concentration levels at various locations in Spring Lake.
C. determine the nitrate concentration levels at various locations in Heron Marsh.
D. determine the number of chemicals in the water at various locations in Heron Marsh.

2. Which of the following is the best description of a freshwater estuary?

F. An enclosed area where two bodies of saltwater meet and mix
G. An enclosed area where two or more rivers meet and mix with a lake
H. A semi-enclosed area where two bodies of water meet and mix
J. A semi-enclosed area where two or more rivers meet and mix with a freshwater lake

3. During which season was the testing conducted?

A. Spring
B. Summer
C. Autumn
D. Winter

644 • SCIENCE SCIENTIFIC INVESTIGATION

4. At how many locations in Heron Marsh were water samples taken for testing?

   F. One
   G. Three
   H. Five
   J. Nine

5. Which testing location is closest to where the two rivers drain into Heron Marsh?

   A. Station 1
   B. Station 2
   C. Station 3
   D. Station 5

6. The nitrate concentrations found in the water samples are reported in units of:

   F. grams.
   G. parts per million.
   H. grams per milliliter.
   J. parts per billion.

7. Which of the following is a correct representation of water flow in the Heron Marsh watershed area?

   A. Heron Marsh → Spring Lake → Ottawa River
   B. Ottawa River → Heron Marsh → Spring Lake
   C. Spring Lake → Ottawa River → Sugar River
   D. Heron Marsh → Spring Lake → Sugar River

8. According to Table 9.1, which testing location had the highest nitrate concentration levels the first day after the storm?

   F. Station 1
   G. Station 2
   H. Station 3
   J. Station 5

9. According to Table 9.1, how many days after the storm did nitrate concentration levels peak at Station 3?

   A. Four
   B. Six
   C. Seven
   D. Nine

10. According to Table 9.1, the nitrate concentration levels at all testing locations following the storm:

   F. first increased, then decreased.
   G. increased only.
   H. remained unchanged.
   J. decreased only.

Passage 2

Stream tables are used to investigate how sediment, vegetation, and flowing water interact to form stream channels. A stream table is a long rectangular tray, elevated at one end, with a hole for drainage at the other end (Figure 9.2). A water supply is connected to the elevated end. Various materials and objects can be placed in the table to study the impact on water flow.

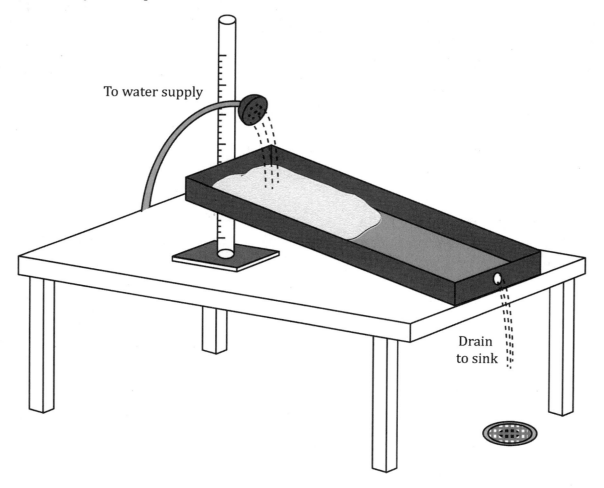

Figure 9.2

A student used a stream table approximately one meter in length to study how steepness affects the velocity of flowing water. She filled the upper two-thirds of the tray with sand approximately 2 centimeters deep. She set the elevation of the water supply end of the table to 5 centimeters. With a small shovel, she carved a channel in the sand from the upper end of the tray to where the sand ends.

After placing a small cork ball at the elevated end of the channel, she turned on the water to a preset steady rate. She started a timer when the ball began to move and

646 • SCIENCE SCIENTIFIC INVESTIGATION

stopped the timer when the ball reached the end of the channel. To minimize experimental variation, she conducted four trials and calculated the average.

The student repeated the experiment, using the same cork ball, for three additional table elevations: 10 centimeters, 15 centimeters, and 20 centimeters. The results are reported in Table 9.2.

Table 9.2: Experimental Results					
Height of Elevated Table End (centimeters)	Cork Travel Time (seconds)				
	Trial 1	Trial 2	Trial 3	Trial 4	Average
5	35	31	35	28	32
10	26	27	23	25	25
15	18	19	18	22	19
20	12	13	9	14	12

11. According to the passage, the purpose of the experiment is to determine how:

   A. sand affects velocity of water flow.
   B. steepness affects turbulence of water flow.
   C. steepness affects velocity of water flow.
   D. steepness affects the length of time before the ball begins to move.

12. Approximately how deep was the sand in the stream table?

   F. 2 centimeters
   G. 5 centimeters
   H. 10 centimeters
   J. 1 meter

13. Which of the following was NOT needed for this experiment?

   A. Small shovel
   B. Beaker
   C. Sand
   D. Timer

14. How many cork balls were used in the entire experiment?

   F. One
   G. Two
   H. Three
   J. Four

15. The experiment was repeated for how many different elevations of the stream table end?

    A. One
    B. Three
    C. Four
    D. Five

16. Which of the following was constant for each repetition of the experiment?

    F. The speed at which the ball travels the length of the channel
    G. The flow rate of the water supply
    H. The velocity of the water flow through the stream table
    J. The elevation of one end of the stream table

17. What is the correct sequence for the following steps in this experiment?

    I. Start the timer.
    II. Turn on the water supply.
    III. Place the ball in the channel.

    A. I, III, II
    B. II, III, I
    C. III, I, II
    D. III, II, I

18. According to the passage, the student started the timer when:

    F. the ball was placed in the channel.
    G. the ball began to move.
    H. the water was turned on.
    J. the water was turned off.

19. According to the passage, the student stopped the timer when:

    A. the water was turned off.
    B. the ball reached the end of the table.
    C. the ball reached the end of the channel.
    D. the last of the water reached the end of the channel.

20. Which of the following best explains why four trials were completed for each elevation of the stream table end?

    F. Each trial used water at different temperatures.
    G. Each trial used balls of different sizes.
    H. Each trial used balls of different materials.
    J. Averaging data over several trials improves accuracy.

Passage 3

Ocean acidification occurs when an ocean uptakes carbon dioxide from the atmosphere. The dissolved carbon dioxide forms carbonic acid, which in turn increases the acidity of the seawater. The acidity (or basicity) of a liquid is measured on the pH scale: the lower the pH, the greater the acidity (Figure 9.3).

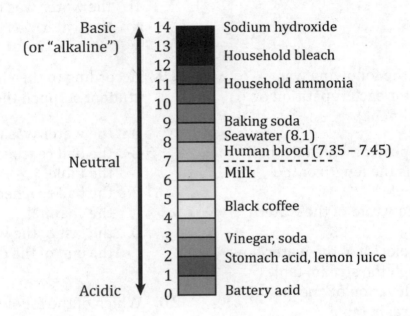

Figure 9.3

To investigate the effects of acidity on marine animals with shells, a group of students exposed seashells to solutions of varying pH. The students made four test solutions in beakers by diluting household vinegar with distilled water and using litmus paper to determine when the four desired pH values were reached: 3.0, 4.0, 5.0, and 6.0. Each beaker contained 250 mL of test solution. The experiment control was a fifth beaker containing 250 mL of distilled water (pH 7.0).

Students used an electronic balance to weigh each of the five similarly shaped seashells. A shell was placed in each beaker, and the test solution entirely covered the shells. The beakers were covered with aluminum foil, placed in a cool, dark corner of the laboratory, and left undisturbed for 24 hours.

At the conclusion of 24 hours, the remnants of the seashells were removed from the beakers using tweezers. To evaporate any moisture, the remnants were placed in a drying oven for one hour at 225°F. After being removed from the oven and allowed to cool, the remnants were weighed. Table 9.3 shows the results.

UNIT 9 | DESCRIBING EXPERIMENTS PRACTICE • 649

Table 9.3: Experimental Results			
	pH	Seashell Mass (grams)	
		Initial	Final
Vinegar Solutions	3.0	4.83	0.00
	4.0	2.78	2.35
	5.0	2.28	2.23
	6.0	3.40	3.37
Water	7.0	4.17	4.17

21. The purpose of the experiment is to determine:

   A. the change in pH of vinegar when various amounts of water are added.

   B. if seashells disintegrate when heated in an oven for long periods at low temperatures.

   C. whether vinegar evaporates faster than distilled water.

   D. the effect of acidity on the disintegration of seashells.

22. According to the passage, lower pH corresponds to:

   F. greater acidity.
   G. lesser acidity.
   H. greater basicity.
   J. neutral solutions.

23. According to the given information, seawater is naturally:

   A. acidic.
   B. neutral.
   C. slightly basic.
   D. very alkaline.

24. Which of the following correctly describes the difference between the test solutions and the control used in this experiment?

   F. The control is diluted vinegar of pH 7.0 and the test solutions are vinegar diluted with distilled water to various pH values.

   G. The control is distilled water and the test solutions are vinegar diluted with milk to various pH values.

   H. The control is tap water and the test solutions are vinegar diluted with tap water to various pH values.

   J. The control is distilled water and the test solutions are vinegar diluted with distilled water to various pH values.

650 • SCIENCE SCIENTIFIC INVESTIGATION

25. According to the passage, the seashells soaked in the vinegar solutions for:

A. 8 hours.
B. 16 hours.
C. 24 hours.
D. 24 days.

26. According to the passage, the students weighed the seashells:

I. before the shells were soaked.
II. after the shells were soaked.
III. after the shells were dried.

F. I and II only
G. I and III only
H. II and III only
J. I, II, and III

27. How many seashells are required for this experiment?

A. One
B. Four
C. Five
D. Ten

28. Which of the following is the same throughout this experiment?

F. The volume of solution in each beaker
G. The volume of vinegar in each solution
H. The mass of the seashell in each beaker
J. The pH of each vinegar solution

29. Which of the following correctly describes the seashells before they were soaked in the solutions?

A. Each shell had the same mass and shape.
B. Each shell had a different mass and shape.
C. Each shell had the same mass but a different shape.
D. Each shell had the same shape but a different mass.

30. According to the passage, the seashells were placed in the drying oven to:

F. determine if the shells would disintegrate when heated.
G. neutralize the acid on the shells.
H. activate the acid on the shells.
J. evaporate moisture on the shells.

Science **Scientific Investigation**

Unit 10 | **Experimental Tools and Methods**

INSIDE THIS UNIT:

– Understanding Tools and Their Functions –
– Exercise –

Non-Negotiable Skill:

Understand tools and their functions in simple experiments.

Understanding Tools and Their Functions

Experiments involve laboratory apparatuses and other equipment. Scientific equipment is highly specialized and has its own nomenclature. In science class, you'll encounter the following common laboratory equipment:

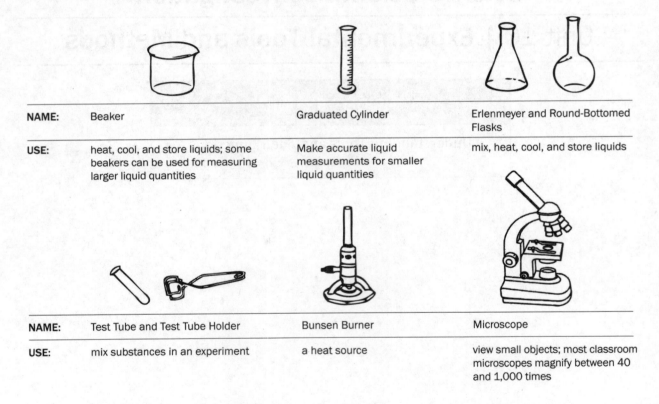

NAME:	Beaker	Graduated Cylinder	Erlenmeyer and Round-Bottomed Flasks
USE:	heat, cool, and store liquids; some beakers can be used for measuring larger liquid quantities	Make accurate liquid measurements for smaller liquid quantities	mix, heat, cool, and store liquids

NAME:	Test Tube and Test Tube Holder	Bunsen Burner	Microscope
USE:	mix substances in an experiment	a heat source	view small objects; most classroom microscopes magnify between 40 and 1,000 times

The questions presented in Units 8 and 9 asked about experimental design and procedures. Units 10 and 11 further develop this category by focusing on the scientific tools of simple experiments and their functions.

Fortunately, you are not going to be asked to memorize a list of technical names. As you take science classes that involve lab work, you'll pick up the terminology. For now, we'll concentrate on common tools and typical functions of those tools in simple experiments. At Level 1, all questions about tools and their functions can be answered by finding the required information in the text, figure, and/or data presentation.

Let's start with a couple of case studies. When reading through the passages, pay particular attention to the tools, their uses, their design, and any noted units of measurement.

Case Study 1

The compound ethylene glycol is mixed with water and used as antifreeze/coolant in car engines because the ethylene glycol-water solution boils at a higher temperature and freezes at a colder temperature than pure water. A group of students conducted an experiment to examine the relationship between the concentration of ethylene glycol in an ethylene glycol-water solution and its boiling point.

In 250 ml beakers, the students mixed ethylene glycol with distilled water to create three solutions of concentrations 25%, 50% and 75% ethylene glycol. A fourth beaker containing only distilled water served as a control. Each beaker and its contents were heated on a hot plate. The temperature of each solution was monitored using a temperature probe connected to a computer with data collection and graphing programs. The data program collected temperature readings from the probe every 15 seconds for 10 minutes. The graphing program graphed the heating curves of the solutions (Figure 10.1). The plateau of each heating curve represents the boiling point of that solution.

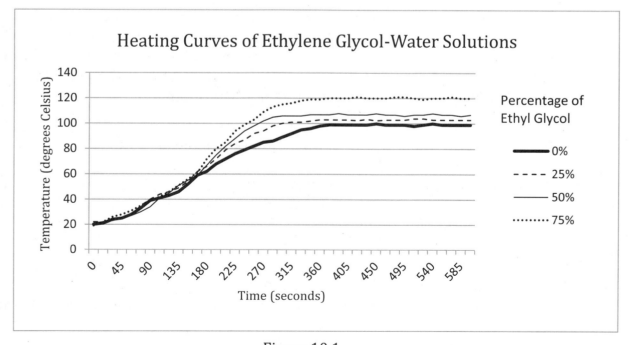

Figure 10.1

654 • SCIENCE SCIENTIFIC INVESTIGATION

1. The purpose of the experiment is to determine:

   A. how the concentration of ethylene glycol in an ethylene glycol-water solution affects the freezing point of the solution.
   B. how the concentration of ethylene glycol in an ethylene glycol-water solution affects the boiling point of the solution.
   C. the concentration of ethylene glycol in four different ethylene glycol-water solutions.
   D. how the water temperature affects the dissolution of ethylene glycol in ethylene glycol-water solutions.

   The correct answer is (B). According to the end of the first paragraph, the purpose of the experiment was to "examine the relationship between the concentration of ethylene glycol in an ethylene glycol-water solution and its boiling point."

2. According to the passage, which of the following is a complete and accurate list of the equipment and tools used in this experiment?

   F. Temperature probe, beakers, and hot plate
   G. Computer, thermometer, beakers, and hot plate
   H. Computer, temperature probe, beakers, and electronic balance
   J. Computer, temperature probe, beakers, and hot plate

   The correct answer is (J). According to the passage, beakers were used to hold the solutions, a hot plate was used to heat the solutions, a temperature probe was used to measure the temperatures, and a computer was used to collect and graph the data. Note that (G) is incorrect because the passage specifically says "temperature probe," not "thermometer."

3. In this experiment, the purpose of the temperature probe is to:

   A. record and graph the solution temperatures.
   B. stir the solution until thoroughly mixed.
   C. heat the solution to boiling point.
   D. measure the temperature of the solution.

   The correct answer is (D). According to the second paragraph, the temperature probe measured the temperature of the solution. Note that the computer was responsible for recording (and graphing) the solution temperatures but not for measuring them.

UNIT 10 | EXPERIMENTAL TOOLS AND METHODS • 655

4. In this experiment, the purpose of the hot plate is to:

F. record and graph the solution temperatures.
G. provide an interface between the temperature probe and computer.
H. heat the solution to boiling point.
J. heat the ethylene glycol before adding it to the water in the beaker.

The correct answer is (H). According to the second paragraph, the purpose of the hot plate was to heat the ethylene glycol-water solutions to their boiling points.

5. The most likely units of measurement for the temperature probe in this experiment are:

A. degrees Celsius.
B. degrees Fahrenheit.
C. kelvin.
D. milliliters.

The correct answer is (A). This information is not found in the text of the passage itself but in the graph. According to the y-axis label of the graph, the temperature measurements are given in degrees Celsius.

Case Study 2

During chemistry class, a student measured four properties of an unknown liquid: boiling point, freezing point, water solubility, and density.

The student filled a 250 mL beaker with hot tap water and centered it over a Bunsen burner in a fume hood using a ring stand with an iron ring and wire gauze to hold the beaker. Using a utility clamp also connected to the ring stand, a test tube containing 10 mL of the unknown liquid was immersed in the hot water bath. As the burner heated the water bath, the student monitored the sample until the water bath began to boil. A thermometer was used to measure the temperature of the sample in the test tube when the water bath began to boil (100°C). The sample was not observed to boil, indicating a boiling point in excess of 100°C.

Next, the student filled a 250 mL beaker with ice and added salt to lower the ice bath temperature below 0°C. She immersed a second test tube containing 10 mL of the unknown liquid in the ice bath and occasionally used a stirrer to mix the contents of the test tube to maintain a uniform temperature. As the ice bath cooled the sample, the student monitored the sample until it began to form crystals, indicating the freezing point. A thermometer was used to measure the freezing point of the sample (17°C).

To test the solubility of the unknown liquid in water, the student mixed 10 mL of distilled water with 10 mL of the unknown liquid in a third test tube. After corking the test tube with a stopper to prevent spilling, she shook it to mix the contents thoroughly and then allowed the contents to settle. She observed the unknown liquid form a layer on top of the water, indicating that the liquid is not soluble in water.

Finally, the student used an electronic scale to measure the mass of an empty 10 mL graduated cylinder. After adding 10 mL of the unknown liquid to the cylinder, the student again measured its mass. She calculated the density of the liquid by dividing the mass of the sample by its volume (0.9 g/mL).

6. Which of the following is the most likely unit of measurement for the electronic scale in this experiment?

   F. Milliliters
   G. Grams
   H. Grams/milliliter
   J. Degrees Celsius

   The correct answer is (G). According to the last paragraph, the density is equal to mass (as determined by the scale) divided by volume (as determined using the graduated cylinder). Since the density is given as 0.9 g/mL, the scale units are grams (and the graduated cylinder units are milliliters).

7. Which of the following is the most likely unit of measurement for the thermometer in this experiment?

   A. Milliliters
   B. Grams
   C. Grams/milliliter
   D. Degrees Celsius

   The correct answer is (D). The measurements given for the temperature data are in units of degrees Celsius, such as 100°C.

UNIT 10 | EXPERIMENTAL TOOLS AND METHODS • 657

8. Which of the tests in this experiment does NOT require a test tube?

   F. Boiling point
   G. Melting point
   H. Solubility
   J. Density

   The correct answer is (J). According to the experimental description, the student used a test tube in the first three tests: boiling point, freezing point, and solubility. Only the fourth test, density, used a graduated cylinder to hold the liquid sample rather than a test tube (so the volume of the sample can be accurately measured).

9. Which of the following was used for the boiling point test?

   A. Bunsen burner
   B. Stopper
   C. Electronic balance
   D. Ice

   The correct answer is (A). The stopper was used in the solubility test. The electronic balance was used in the density test (to measure mass). Ice was used in the freezing point test. Only the Bunsen burner was used in the boiling point test (to heat the water bath).

10. Which of the following was NOT used for both the boiling point test and the freezing point test?

    F. Thermometer
    G. Beaker
    H. Stirrer
    J. Test tube

    The correct answer is (H). Both the boiling test and the freezing test required a thermometer to measure the temperature of the water and ice baths, respectively. Both required a beaker to hold the baths. The passage only describes the stirrer as being used (to keep the sample contents uniform) in the freezing point test.

658 • SCIENCE SCIENTIFIC INVESTIGATION

11. For which test in this experiment was an electronic scale used?

    A. Boiling point
    B. Freezing point
    C. Solubility
    D. Density

    The correct answer is (D). According to the final paragraph, an electronic scale was used to measure the weight of the graduated cylinder before and after 10 mL of the unknown liquid was added to the graduated cylinder.

12. During the experiment, the student used the Bunsen burner to:

    F. indirectly heat the liquid sample during the freezing point test by melting the ice in the ice bath.
    G. indirectly heat the liquid sample during the boiling point test by heating the water in the water bath.
    H. directly heat the liquid sample during the boiling point test.
    J. directly heat the water in the test tube during the solubility test.

    The correct answer is (G). As covered in question #9, the Bunsen burner was used during the boiling point test to heat the water bath, which in turn heated the contents of the test tube, that is, the unknown liquid sample.

13. The stirrer was used during the freezing point test to:

    A. lower the temperature of the ice bath
    B. raise the temperature of the ice bath
    C. prevent the ice from melting.
    D. maintain uniform temperature in the liquid sample.

    The correct answer is (D). As covered in question #10, the stirrer was used in the freezing point test to keep all the unknown liquid in the test tube the same temperature as it approached the freezing point.

14. The stopper was used during the solubility test to:

    F. maintain a constant temperature in the test tube while it was shaken.
    G. hold the thermometer in place while the test tube was shaken.
    H. prevent the liquid sample from spilling while the test tube was shaken.
    J. prevent any gases from escaping the test tube while it was shaken.

    The correct answer is (H). The solubility test is discussed in the fourth paragraph. It states that the stopper was used to cork the test tube to prevent its contents from spilling while the student shook it.

15. Which of the following was used in both the boiling point test and the freezing point test?

    A. Electronic scale
    B. Stirrer
    C. Thermometer
    D. Ice

    The correct answer is (C). During the boiling point test, the student attempted to determine the temperature at which the unknown liquid boils. During the freezing point test, she determined the point at which the unknown liquid freezes. She used a thermometer to measure the temperatures in each case.

16. According to the passage, the purpose of the utility clamp in the boiling test was to hold the:

    F. beaker over the Bunsen burner.
    G. test tube over the Bunsen burner.
    H. test tube while it was immersed in the hot water bath.
    J. thermometer while it was immersed in the test tube.

    The correct answer is (H). The boiling test is discussed in the second paragraph. It states that the utility clamp was connected to the ring stand and used to hold the test tube while it was immersed in the hot water bath.

660 • SCIENCE SCIENTIFIC INVESTIGATION

17. The purpose of sprinkling salt on the ice in the beaker used for the freezing point test was to:

A. lower the temperature of the ice bath.
B. raise the temperature of the ice bath.
C. prevent the ice from melting.
D. maintain uniform temperature of the liquid in the test tube.

The correct answer is (A). The freezing point test is discussed in the third paragraph. It states that salt was added to the ice to "lower the ice bath temperature below 0°C."

18. Which of the following is the best description of a test tube?

F. A thin glass tube, closed at one end, used to hold small amounts of material
G. A narrow-necked glass container, typically conical, used to hold reactants or prepare samples
H. A wide mouthed cylindrical glass container used for stirring, mixing, and heating liquids
J. A narrow mouthed cylinder used to measure a volume of liquid accurately.

The correct answer is (F). This question tests students' understanding of basic experimental tools, in this case, a test tube. The test tubes used in the first three parts of the experiment were used to hold a small amount of liquid (10 mL) that had been poured into the test tubes. (F) is the description that best matches this use. Note that (J) describes the graduated cylinder in the density test.

19. The reason for using a graduated cylinder, rather than a test tube, to hold the sample of unknown liquid in the density test was to:

A. allow for accurate measurement of the volume of the sample.
B. prevent the sample from spilling on the electronic scale.
C. allow for accurate measurement of the mass of the sample.
D. calibrate the electronic scale before and after the sample was weighed.

The correct answer is (A). The density test requires accurate measurements of the volume and mass of the sample (as determined by weighing the graduated cylinder without and with 10 mL of the sample). A graduated cylinder allows for accurate measurements of small volumes of liquids.

Now, let's have a quick peek at the next level of Interpretation of Data and Scientific Investigation skills. This advanced problem requires comparison of the experimental results with an additional data presentation to identify the unknown liquid in the experiment. Give it a try!

20. Based on the experimental results, the unknown liquid is most likely which one of the four chemicals listed in the table below?

Substance	Density (g/mL)	Freezing Point (°C)	Boiling Point (°C)	Solubility in Water
Ethanol	0.8	−117	78.5	Soluble
Linoleic Acid	0.9	−5	230	Insoluble
Ethyl Acetate	0.9	−83.6	77.2	Insoluble
Oleic Acid	0.9	16.3	286	Insoluble

F. Ethanol
G. Linoleic acid
H. Linoleic acid
J. Oleic acid

The correct answer is (J). According to the passage, the student determined the boiling point of the unknown liquid is greater than 100°C, the freezing point is 17°C, the density is 0.9 g/mL, and the liquid is insoluble in water. The only substance in the table that approximates these values is oleic acid.

Summary

- Read the passage carefully and answer the question asked.

- Most tools in scientific experiment passages will be easily recognizable, such as Bunsen burners, test tubes, scales, graduated cylinders, flasks, ring stands, etc. If the tool in question happens to be more uncommon, the passage will describe its design and function.

- The answer to every Level 1 question about tools and their functions is located in the passage and any associated data presentations, figures, or diagrams.

EXERCISE

DIRECTIONS: Each passage below is followed by questions based on its content. Answer the questions on the basis of what is stated or implied in the corresponding passage. Answers are on page 758.

Passage 1

Nutrition scientists determine the amount of energy, or calories, contained in food by using a bomb calorimeter. A bomb calorimeter (Figure 10.2) measures the heat created by a sample burned under a pressurized oxygen atmosphere in a closed chamber, or bomb, surrounded by water in an outer chamber under controlled conditions. The bomb is filled with oxygen to ensure that the sample burns completely. An insulating air jacket around the outer chamber prevents energy loss from the water bath and a stirrer in the water bath ensures the temperature is uniform.

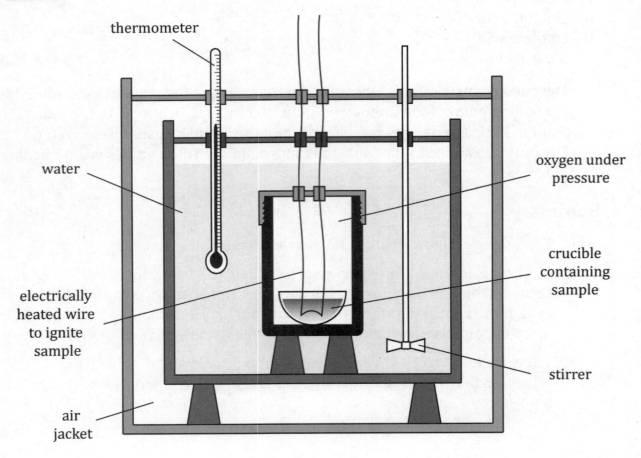

Figure 10.2

A small 1-gram sample of food is weighed in a crucible and placed in the bomb. The sample burns (combusts) when ignited by an ignition wire connected to an electric current. The heat produced by the burning sample warms the water bath. A thermometer in the outer chamber measures the temperature change of the water. The amount of kilocalories (kcal) in the sample is determined from the temperature change: a kilocalorie is defined as the amount of heat needed to raise the temperature of 1 liter of water by 1°C.

1. Which of the following best describes a bomb calorimeter?

   A. An ignition device connecting a food sample to a device that measures electric current
   B. An instrument used to measure the heat produced by the combustion of something
   C. An insulating air jacket use to prevent energy loss
   D. A device that measure the energy output of bombs

2. According to the passage, the inner chamber of the bomb calorimeter is completely filled with pressurized oxygen to:

   F. insulate the calorimeter.
   G. generate the current flowing through the ignition wire.
   H. ensure that the food burns completely.
   J. ensure that the heat is equally distributed in the inner chamber.

3. According to the passage, the function of the insulating air jacket is to:

   A. prevent heat loss from the water bath during testing.
   B. keep the water from overheating during testing.
   C. keep the food sample from overheating during testing.
   D. provide oxygen for the combustion of the food.

4. The thermometer in a bomb calorimeter directly measures the temperature of the:

   F. food.
   G. oxygen.
   H. water in the outer container.
   J. air in the room where testing is conducted.

5. The function of the stirrer in a bomb calorimeter is to:

   A. ensure that oxygen is evenly distributed in the bomb.
   B. ensure that the food sample is pulverized before testing.
   C. remove smoke from the inner container.
   D. stir the water in the outer chamber to maintain consistent temperature throughout the water bath.

6. The function of the ignition wire in a bomb calorimeter is to:

   F. calibrate the thermometer.
   G. raise the temperature of the water bath.
   H. ignite the oxygen in the bomb.
   J. ignite the food sample in the bomb.

7. What is the correct sequence of the following steps in determining the calories in food?

   I. Turn on the electric current.
   II. Place the food sample in the bomb.
   III. Measure the temperature change of the water bath.

   A. I, II, III
   B. II, I, III
   C. II, III, I
   D. III, II, I

8. According to the passage, when a completely burned food sample in a bomb calorimeter raises the temperature of a 1-liter water bath by 10°C, how many kilocalories are in the food sample?

   F. 0
   G. 1
   H. 10
   J. 100

Passage 2

A student conducted an experiment to determine the percentage of salt in a salt/sand mixture contained in a glass vial. To determine the weight of the mixture, the vial was weighed using an electronic scale before and after it was emptied into a 250 mL beaker. Then, 150 mL of distilled water was added to the beaker and the contents stirred for several minutes to ensure the salt had completely dissolved. The student separated the sand from the saltwater by pouring the mixture through a funnel fitted with filter paper. Water from a squeeze bottle was squirted in the beaker a few times to ensure all the contents were poured through the filter.

The wet sand and filter paper were placed in a drying oven under low heat to evaporate any remaining moisture. When the sand and paper were dry, the sand was scraped from the paper with a spatula and weighed on the electronic scale.

The saltwater was poured into an evaporating dish positioned on a ring stand over a Bunsen burner and heated until all the water boiled away. Finally, the salt was scraped from the dish and weighed on the scale. Table 10.1 summarizes the experimental data and results.

Table 10.1: Experimental Data and Results	
	Mass (g)
Glass Vial + Original Sand/Salt Mixture	56.14
Glass Vial	45.02
Original Sand/Salt Mixture	11.12
Dry Sand (evaporated)	7.18
Dry Salt (evaporated)	3.17
Recovered Sand/Salt Mixture	10.35
Percentage of Mixture Recovered	93.1%
Percentage of Salt in Mixture Recovered	30.6%

9. The purpose of this experiment is to determine the percentage of:

   A. salt in a salt/sand mixture by volume.
   B. salt in a salt/sand mixture by weight.
   C. sand in a salt/sand mixture by volume.
   D. sand in a salt/sand mixture by weight.

10. The purpose of the filter paper is to:

    F. allow the saltwater to pass through while preventing sand from passing through.
    G. allow water to pass through while preventing salt and sand from passing through.
    H. allow sand to pass through while preventing salt from passing through.
    J. allow sand and water to pass through while preventing salt from passing through.

11. Which of the following two tools perform essentially the same function in this experiment?

    A. The filter paper and the evaporating dish
    B. The drying oven and the Bunsen burner
    C. The squeeze bottle and the filter paper
    D. The spatula and the funnel

12. Which of the following perform essentially the same function in this experiment?

    F. The filter paper and the funnel
    G. Water from the squeeze bottle and the spatula
    H. The evaporating dish and the drying oven
    J. The Bunsen burner and the beaker

13. Which of the following is the best description of the spatula used in this experiment?

    A. An appliance used to remove moisture from materials by heating at low temperatures
    B. A small gas burner with an open hot flame
    C. A tool used to separate particles from liquids
    D. A tool used to scoop small amounts of material

14. Which of the following statements is supported by the data in Table 10.1?

    F. A small amount of salt was unrecovered.
    G. A small amount of sand was unrecovered.
    H. A small amount of material was unrecovered, but it is not possible to determine if it was sand or salt or both.
    J. A small amount of salt was present in the sand at the end of the experiment.

15. Which of the following best accounts for the recovered salt and sand weighing less than the original mixture?

    A. Some saltwater solution spilled out of the evaporating dish while boiling.
    B. The filter paper had a small tear that allowed some sand to flow through into the conical flask.
    C. The sand was still moist when it removed from the heating oven.
    D. Too much water was sprayed into the beaker to remove all the sand.

Science **Scientific Investigation**

Unit 11 | **Experimental Tools and Methods Practice**

INSIDE THIS UNIT:
– Exercise –

EXERCISE

DIRECTIONS: Each passage below is followed by questions based on its content. Answer the questions on the basis of what is stated or implied in the corresponding passage. Answers are on page 758.

Passage 1

Hydrodistillation is a method used for extracting essential oils from plants. The leaves, stems, and seeds of a plant are mixed with distilled water. The mixture is transferred to a round-bottomed flask, centered over a Bunsen burner, and slowly heated to boiling. The vapor from boiling, containing both steam and plant oils, passes through the inner tube of a glass condenser. Water flowing through the outer tube of the condenser cools the vapor, causing it to condense into a liquid, or distillate, which is collected in an Erlenmeyer flask (Figure 11.1).

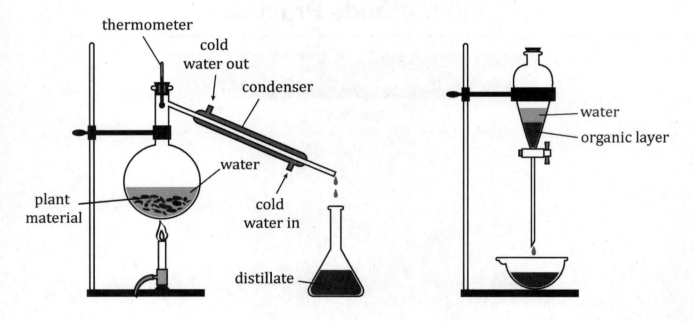

Figure 11.1   Figure 11.2

To separate the water from the plant oils, the distillate is poured into a separation funnel, an organic solvent is added, and the mixture is shaken for several minutes. The solvent, which does not mix with water, dissolves the plant oils and settles below the water layer because of its higher density. This organic layer, containing the solvent and plant oils, is drained from the funnel into an evaporating dish

(Figure 11.2). The dish is placed in a fume hood and left until the solvent evaporates, leaving behind the essential plant oils.

1. Which of the following is a complete and accurate list of the components in the distillate in Figure 11.1?

   A. Water
   B. Water and plant oils
   C. Water and organic solvent
   D. Water, plant oils, and organic solvent

2. Which of the following is a complete and accurate list of the components in the organic layer in Figure 11.2?

   F. Organic solvent
   G. Water and organic solvent
   H. Organic solvent and plant oils
   J. Water, plant oils, and organic solvent

3. Which of the following is NOT a property of the organic solvent used in the extraction process shown in Figure 11.2?

   A. Denser than water
   B. Dissolves the plant oils better than water does
   C. Evaporates slower than plant oils do
   D. Does not mix with water

4. Which of the following represents an Erlenmeyer flask?

   F.
   G.
   H.
   J.

5. Which of the following represents an evaporating dish?

   A.
   B.
   C.
   D.

6. Which of the following represents a round-bottom flask?

F.

G.

H.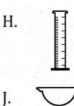

J.

7. Which of the following is used to separate the components of the distillate?

A. Organic solvent and a condenser
B. A fume hood and Bunsen burner
C. A Bunsen burner and a condenser
D. A separation funnel, fume hood, and organic solvent

8. Which of the following are used to separate the components of the organic layer?

F. A separation funnel and an evaporating dish
G. Organic solvent and a separation funnel
H. A fume hood and an evaporating dish
J. A Bunsen burner and a separation funnel

9. According to the procedure described, a Bunsen burner is used to:

A. condense the vapor from the boiling plant/water mixture.
B. evaporate the water from the distillate.
C. evaporate the solvent from the organic layer.
D. vaporize the plant oils from the plant/water mixture.

10. The function of the cool water flowing through the outer tube of the condenser is to:

F. cool and liquefy the vapor.
G. add water to the distillate collected by the receiving flask.
H. separate the plant oils from the water vapor.
J. separate the plant oils from the seeds, leaves, and stems.

Passage 2

Geologists identify mineral specimens using a range of properties including color, luster, and density. Often, color and luster (the quality and quantity of light reflected from the surface) are not sufficient identifiers. Not many minerals have a fixed color since small amounts of impurities can drastically change a mineral's color, and some minerals exhibit a range of lusters. Furthermore, the density of a mineral, defined as a sample's mass divided by that sample's volume, can be a difficult test to perform in the field. In addition to a digital scale, to determine mass, accurate liquid volume measurements are required both before and after the sample is added to a graduated cylinder to determine the displaced volume. Two additional tests are easy to do with simple tools in the field and can often make identification definitive: streak and hardness.

A mineral's streak is its color when ground to a powder. Minerals that occur in a range of colors always have the same streak, so streak is a more reliable indicator than color. To perform a streak test, a specimen is scraped across a small rectangular piece of unglazed ceramic tile, called a streak plate, to create a powdered streak of the specimen.

A mineral's hardness can also be a reliable indicator for the majority of minerals because most samples of the same mineral have similar hardness. The Mohs hardness test compares the resistance of a mineral to being scratched with that of ten reference minerals of different hardness, ranging from very soft (talc) to very hard (diamond). For example, a mineral with a hardness value of "4" on the Mohs scale (Table 11.2) is easily scratched by a butter knife and has a hardness similar to fluorite, whereas a mineral with a hardness value of "5" is just barely scratched by the same knife and so has a hardness similar to apatite. A scratch must be a distinct groove cut in the mineral surface that can be felt by touch, not simply a mark on the surface that wipes away.

674 • SCIENCE SCIENTIFIC INVESTIGATION

Table 11.1: Mohs Hardness Scale		
Hardness	Reference Mineral	Scratch Test
1	Talc	Powdered by fingernail
2	Gypsum	Scratched by fingernail
3	Calcite	Scratched by copper penny
4	Fluorite	Easily scratched by butter knife
5	Apatite	Just scratched by butter knife
6	Orthoclase	Scratched by steel file
7	Quartz	Scratches glass easily
8	Topaz	Easily scratches quartz
9	Corundum	Easily scratches topaz
10	Diamond	Cannot be scratched

The reference minerals (or any other material of known hardness) can also be used to perform the scratch test. For example, if a sample of quartz produces a scratch on an unknown mineral specimen, the unknown mineral is softer than or equal in hardness to quartz; if the unknown is not scratched, it is harder than quartz.

Hardness picks are also commonly used for testing small specimens or for testing small grains embedded in rock. Each pick has a sharp point made of a material of known hardness, such as plastic (hardness of 2), copper (hardness of 3), and various alloys (hardness of 4 through 9).

11. Which of the following mineral identification tests requires a ceramic tile?

A. Color
B. Hardness
C. Streak
D. Luster

12. According to the passage, which of the following properties requires no special equipment for its determination?

F. Color
G. Density
H. Streak
J. Hardness

13. Which of the following tools is commonly used for testing hardness of small mineral grains embedded in rock?

    A. Reference minerals
    B. Ceramic tile
    C. Quartz
    D. Hardness picks

14. According to the given information, a steel file would be used for determining:

    F. hardness.
    G. streak.
    H. luster.
    J. color.

15. A mineral specimen is determined to have a hardness of 6. According to Table 11.2, which of the following tools succeeded in scratching it?

    A. Fingernail
    B. Copper penny
    C. Butter knife
    D. Steel file

16. Which of the following tools does NOT indicate a hardness of 3 on the Mohs hardness scale?

    F. Calcite
    G. Butter knife
    H. Hardness pick with copper point
    J. Copper penny

17. Which of the following sets of tools can all be used to indicate a hardness of 3 on the Mohs hardness scale?

    A. Fingernail, copper penny, and hardness pick with plastic tip
    B. Fluorite, calcite, and hardness pick with plastic tip
    C. Copper penny, calcite, and hardness pick with copper tip
    D. Fluorite, gypsum, and hardness pick with alloy tip

18. According to the information provided, which property of a mineral specimen requires the tools and measurement depicted in the figure below?

    F. Mass
    G. Volume
    H. Hardness
    J. Streak

19. According to the information provided, which property of a mineral specimen requires the tools and measurement depicted in the figure below?

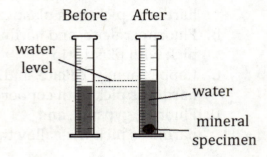

A. Mass
B. Hardness
C. Volume
D. Luster

20. According to the information provided, which property of a mineral specimen requires the tools and measurement depicted in the figure below?

F. Color
G. Luster
H. Hardness
J. Streak

Passage 3

Paper chromotography is a method of separating the components of a mixture, allowing the individual parts to be identfied. Chromotography is used to identify all sorts of substances in police work.

Using paper chromotography, a forensic technician analyzed the ink found on a note left at a crime scene. A small quantity of the note's ink was transferred to a sheet of filter paper, 1 centimeter from the sheet bottom. Additionally, one dot each from four leading brands of black markers were also applied to the filter paper, 1 centimeter from the sheet bottom. The filter paper was placed in a beaker containing a shallow layer of solvent formulated with ethanol, acetone, and water, so that just the edge of the paper—but not the ink dots—was in the solvent.

As the filter paper absorbed the solvent, the various color components of the ink spots dissolved and "climbed" the paper with the solvent. The distance a component climbs the paper depends on its attraction to the paper: the stronger the attraction, the smaller the distance.

The filter paper was removed from the beaker after the solvent had been absorbed to approximately three-quarters the height of the paper. The technician determined the retention factor (R_f) for each ink component (Table 11.2), defined as the component distance divided by the solvent distance. By comparing the R_f values of the four crime scene ink components with the ink components of the four tested markers, the technician identified the brand of marker used to write the note found at the crime scene as Brand C.

Table 11.2: Ink Component Retention Factors (R_f)					
Ink Component	Crime Scene Ink	Brand A Marker	Brand B Marker	Brand C Marker	Brand D Marker
Yellow	0.28	x	0.91	0.28	0.11
Magenta	0.18	0.42	0.72	0.18	0.81
Green	x	0.98	x	x	x
Blue	0.95	0.62	0.68	0.95	0.95

Note: An "x" indicates that color ink component was not detected.

21. According to the passage, paper chromatography is a method used for:

    A. calculating the solubility of a substance in water.
    B. separating the components of a solvent.
    C. separating the components of a mixture.
    D. mix the components of a solution with a solvent.

22. The purpose of this experiment is to:

    F. separate ink samples into their various color components to identify an unknown ink sample.
    G. combine ink samples to determine which combination matches an unknown ink sample.
    H. determine the length of time it takes an unknown ink sample to separate into its various color components.
    J. determine the length of time it takes the color components of an unknown ink sample to climb the paper.

23. In this experiment, the term "ink component" refers to the:

    A. weight of the ink.
    B. height of the ink on the filter paper.
    C. four brands of marker tested.
    D. various colors in the ink.

24. According to Table 11.2, how many different color ink components did each marker contain?

    F. One
    G. Two
    H. Three
    J. Four

25. According to the passage, which of the following is the process by which the solvent climbs the filter paper?

    A. Dissolution
    B. Absorption
    C. Distillation
    D. Retention

26. According to the passage, the height to which an ink component climbs the filter paper is determined by the:

   F. absorption rate of the solvent by the filter paper.
   G. ink component color.
   H. degree to which the ink particles are attracted to the filter paper.
   J. type of solvent used.

27. The solvent used in the experiment is made with:

   A. water, acetone, and ethanol.
   B. acetone, ethanol, and ink.
   C. water, acetone, and ink.
   D. water, ethanol, and ink

28. In the experiment, the purpose of the solvent is to:

   F. speed the absorption of the ink components by the filter paper.
   G. break down the filter paper in order to absorb the inks.
   H. dilute the inks so they could be tested several times.
   J. dissolve the inks into their various components.

29. Which of the following is NOT needed for this experiment?

   A. Beaker
   B. Ruler
   C. Filter paper
   D. Electronic scale

30. The forensic technician determined the crime scene ink was from a Brand C marker because:

   F. both the crime scene ink and the Brand C marker did not have a green ink component.
   G. the ink components of the crime scene ink had the same retention factors as those of the Brand C marker.
   H. the ink components of the crime scene ink had different retention factors than those of the Brand C marker.
   J. the ink components of the Brand C marker had different retention factors than those of the other brand markers.

Science Evaluation of Models, Inferences, and Experimental Results

Unit 12 | Understanding Models

INSIDE THIS UNIT:
– Extracting Information from Text Describing Conceptual Models – – Exercise –

Non-Negotiable Skill:

Find basic information describing conceptual models.

Extracting Information from Text Describing Conceptual Models

In Units 8 through 11, our science coverage expanded to include text that often accompanies data presentations, typically in the context of simple descriptions of scientific investigations or experiments. Again, the skill tested was the same: find information in the text that describes the experiment. Sometimes that information was located in the data presentation.

Now, we move on to scientific models. A model is a physical, conceptual, or mathematical representation of a real phenomenon that is difficult to observe directly. Models may provide simplified methods for calculations or simplified explanations for observed phenomenon. Regardless, the tested skill continues to be one of comprehension: find basic information in the text that describes the model.

Let's begin with a couple of case studies.

Case Study 1

Many ponds undergo a regular yearly process called thermal stratification. A thermally stratified pond has a noticeable difference in temperature, or temperature gradient, as the water gets deeper. Water is densest at 39°F, becoming less dense at temperatures above and below 39°F. Therefore, at the end of a cold winter, the bottom layer in a deep pond is 39°F, the overlying layers of water are colder, and ice, which is less dense than water, is on the surface.

In early spring, the sun eventually warms the water near the surface to 39°F. Now, with uniform water temperature and density, the water thoroughly mixes in a phenomenon called spring turnover.

As the pond continues to warm through late spring into summer, the water layers near the surface become warmer than the water at the bottom. The thermal stratification of the pond is most pronounced at this point. The warm, upper layer is called the epilimnion, the cold, lower layer is called the hypolimnion, and the relatively narrow layer in between is called the thermocline. The thermocline is characterized by a steep temperature gradient from top to bottom.

As fall arrives, the pond's upper layers cool until reaching the same temperature as the deepest layers, at which point the water mixes thoroughly in the fall turnover.

Finally, as fall becomes winter, the colder upper layer becomes less dense, causing the pond to become stratified once again. A layer of ice forms on the pond surface, the pond is sealed, and the stratification is preserved until spring.

1. According to the passage, a thermally stratified pond is one that has:

    A. different temperatures during each season.
    B. layers of water at different temperatures.
    C. different water levels during each season.
    D. ice on its surface in the winter.

    The correct answer is (B). According to the first paragraph, "a thermally stratified pond has a noticeable difference in temperature… as the water gets deeper."

2. According to the passage, thermal stratification of a pond is most pronounced in:

    F. spring.
    G. summer.
    H. fall.
    J. winter.

    The correct answer is (G). The third paragraph states that the thermal stratification of a pond is the most pronounced as late spring turns into summer due to the sun warming the upper layers of the pond, while the bottom layers stay relatively cool.

3. According to the passage, what condition causes spring and fall turnovers in ponds?

    A. Water near the pond surface is colder than water near the bottom.
    B. Water near the pond surface is warmer than water near the bottom.
    C. Water near the pond surface is less dense than water near the bottom.
    D. All water in the pond has the same temperature.

The correct answer is (D). The passage describes both spring and fall turnovers, in which the water in a pond mixes thoroughly. This mixing occurs because there are no stratified layers, as temperature, and thus density, are uniform throughout.

4. According to the passage, which of the following is true of a thermally stratified pond in summer?

   F. The epilimnion is the coldest water layer.
   G. The hypolimnion is the water layer nearest the pond surface.
   H. The thermocline has a large temperature gradient across it.
   J. The thermocline is the thickest water layer.

   The correct answer is (H). The third paragraph states that the epilimnion is the warm upper layer, the hypolimnion is the cold lower layer, and the thermocline the thinner layer in between. As such, the thermocline has a large temperature gradient, or difference, across it.

5. According to the passage, a thermally stratified pond in summer:

   A. mixes easily.
   B. has the warmest layer of water near the bottom.
   C. has the coldest layer of water near the bottom.
   D. has the densest layer of water near the top.

   The correct answer is (C). The third paragraph discusses thermally stratified ponds in summer. The thermal stratification of a pond is most pronounced in summer, when the coldest layer is near the bottom, as the sun warms the top layer.

6. According to the passage, a thermally stratified pond in winter:

   F. mixes easily.
   G. has the coldest layer of water near the bottom.
   H. has the densest layer of water near the top.
   J. has the densest layer of water near the bottom.

   The correct answer is (J). A thermally stratified pond has a temperature gradient across the layers. Whether the top layer or the bottom layer is the warmest (summer and winter, respectively), the bottom layer is the densest in both summer and winter.

7. According to the passage, why is the water at the bottom of a deep pond in the middle of a cold winter always 39°F?

   A. Water freezes at 39°F.
   B. Water has its greatest density at 39°F.
   C. Water has the lowest density at 39°F.
   D. Water evaporates the slowest at 39°F.

   The correct answer is (B). This question is a variation on the previous one. The first paragraph states that water is the densest at 39°F. Therefore, the bottom layer is always 39°F in the middle of a cold winter.

8. According to the passage, the steepest water temperature gradient in summer corresponds to:

   F. the temperature at which water is its densest.
   G. the temperature of a pond in spring or fall.
   H. the change in water temperature across the epilimnion.
   J. the change in water temperature across the thermocline.

   The correct answer is (J). The end of the third paragraph states that the thermocline is "characterized by a steep temperature gradient from top to bottom."

Case Study 2

Thunderstorms are characterized by a series of sudden electrical discharges that result in flashes of light (lightning) and trembling sound waves (thunder). The simplified model of a single thunderstorm cell has three stages: developing, mature, and dissipating.

During the developing stage, parcels of warm, humid air rise from the earth's surface (updrafts) because they are less dense than the surrounding air. As the air parcels rise, the water vapor they contain cools and begins to condense into small droplets. As temperatures continue to drop the higher the air parcels rise, some of the droplets freeze into small ice crystals.

It is thought that the collisions of these ice crystals result in a re-distribution of electric charge. After many such collisions, large areas of electric charge build up within the cloud, and this contributes to the formation of lightning in the next stage.

The mature stage of the thunderstorm begins when the droplets and ice crystals get so large that the updraft can no longer hold them up and they begin to fall as precipitation. Electrical discharges occurring within the cloud during this time may involve the ground (cloud-to-ground lightning), the air (cloud-to-air lightning), or another cloud (cloud-to-cloud lightning). The rapid expansion and heating of air caused by lightning produces the accompanying loud clap of thunder.

During the mature stage, humid air continues to rise in the form of updrafts, while at the same time, the falling precipitation brings colder air down from above (downdrafts). The colder air forms wind gusts that spread across the earth's surface. Sometimes the spreading cold air gusts can initiate new thunderstorms tens or even hundreds of miles away. It is during the mature stage that tornadoes and hail are most likely.

The dissipating stage is the final stage in the life cycle of a thunderstorm. It occurs when the cooler air downdrafts begin to cut off the supply of warm, humid air updrafts that fed the thunderstorm in the first place. Precipitation soon stops, but lightning remains a danger.

9. According to the model, how many stages are in the life cycle of a single cell thunderstorm?

   A. Two
   B. Three
   C. Four
   D. Five

   The correct answer is (B). As stated in the end of the first paragraph, a single cell thunderstorm has a life cycle of three stages: developing, mature, and dissipating. The rest of the passage discusses each of these stages.

10. According to the model, which of the following is thought to contribute to the formation of lightning?

    F. Collision of ice crystals
    G. Collision of rain droplets
    H. Updrafts of warm air particles
    J. Downdrafts of cold air particles

    The correct answer is (F). Following the introduction to the model of thunderstorms in the first paragraph, the passage goes on to discuss the developing stage. The third paragraph then discusses how the collision of the ice crystals in the first stage are thought to contribute to the formation of lightning in the second stage due to the creation of large areas of electric charge built up from the collisions.

11. According to the passage, what is the cause of thunder?

    A. Collision of ice crystals
    B. Updrafts of warm air particles
    C. Rapid expansion and heating of air by lightning
    D. Increases of electric charge in the cloud

    The correct answer is (C). The first paragraph describes thunder as "trembling sound waves," but this isn't an answer choice, so you'll have to dig a little deeper. The last sentence of the fourth paragraph states that the "rapid expansion and heating of air caused by lightning" produces the thunder that we hear following lightning.

12. According to the passage, lighting is possible during which stages of the thunderstorm life cycle?

    F. Developing and mature
    G. Developing and dissipating
    H. Mature and dissipating
    J. Developing, mature, and dissipating

    The correct answer is (H). The third paragraph refers to the collision of ice crystals in the first stage as contributing to the formation of lighting, but then it clearly states that lighting doesn't actually occur until the mature stage. The fourth paragraph also states that the lighting doesn't occur until the precipitation begins to fall, during the mature stage. Then, the last paragraph says that lighting remains a danger during the dissipating stage. Therefore, lighting is possible during the mature and dissipating stages.

13. According to the passage, updrafts consist of air that is:

    A. cool and dry.
    B. warm and dry.
    C. cool and humid.
    D. warm and humid.

The correct answer is (D). The first sentence of the second paragraph defines updrafts as parcels of warm, humid air that rise because they are less dense than the surrounding air.

14. According to the passage, tornadoes are mostly likely to occur during which stage(s) of the thunderstorm life cycle?

   F. Mature
   G. Developing and dissipating
   H. Mature and dissipating
   J. Developing, mature, and dissipating

   The correct answer is (F). The last sentence of the fourth paragraph states, "tornadoes and hail are most likely" to occur during the mature stage. Tornadoes are not mentioned elsewhere in the passage, so there is nothing to support choice (H) or (J).

15. According to the model, which of the following leads to the final stage in the thunderstorm life cycle?

   A. Warmer air downdrafts
   B. Cooler air downdrafts
   C. Warmer air updrafts
   D. Cooler air updrafts

   The correct answer is (B). The last paragraph states that the dissipating, or final, stage in the thunderstorm life cycle begins when the cooler air downdrafts that formed in the mature stage begin to cancel out the warmer air updrafts that fed the developing stage in the first place.

Summary

- Models are physical, conceptual, or mathematical representations of real phenomenon that are difficult to observe directly.

- Scientific passages based on conceptual models may or may not include diagrams or data presentations.

- The key to solving Level 1 items based on models is the same as for all other Science Level 1 items: read carefully and answer the question asked by locating the information in the text and/or accompanying figure(s).

EXERCISE

DIRECTIONS: Each passage below is followed by questions based on its content. Answer the questions on the basis of what is stated or implied in the corresponding passage. Answers are on page 758.

Passage 1

Paleontologists use biomechanic principles to estimate the speed of dinosaurs from trackways fossilized in sedimentary rock. To calculate a dinosaur's speed, three variables factor into the equation: the dinosaur's stride length, the dinosaur's hip height, and the acceleration due to gravity (approximately 9.8 meters per second-squared). Stride length is the distance between two successive prints of the same foot (Figure 12.1). Hip height for dinosaurs is estimated to have ranged from 3.6 to 4.3 times the foot length. Foot length is the straight line distance from the tip of the longest toe to the back of that same foot. For convenience, an average value of 4 times the foot length is often used for estimating a dinosaur's hip height.

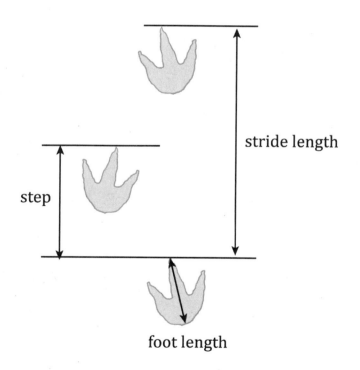

Figure 12.1

690 • SCIENCE EVALUATION OF MODELS, INFERENCES, AND EXPERIMENTAL RESULTS

1. According to the passage, which of the variables used in estimating a dinosaur's speed is the same for all dinosaurs?

   A. Acceleration due to gravity
   B. Foot length
   C. Stride length
   D. Hip height

2. According to the passage, which measurement is used in estimates of dinosaur hip height?

   F. Stride length
   G. Hip length
   H. Acceleration due to gravity
   J. Foot length

3. In addition to acceleration due to gravity, what other two variables are needed to calculate the speed of dinosaurs based on fossilized trackways?

   A. hip height and foot length
   B. hip length and step length
   C. stride length and step length
   D. stride length and hip height

4. According to the passage, if the hip height of a particular dinosaur is unavailable, which of the following formulas could be used to approximate the hip height?

   F. 2 × foot length
   G. 4 × foot length
   H. 4 × stride length
   J. foot length ÷ 4

5. According to the passage, the acceleration due to gravity is:

   A. approximately 3.6 meters per second-squared.
   B. approximately 4.3 meters per second-squared.
   C. approximately 9.8 meters per second-squared.
   D. variable.

6. According to the passage, the stride length is best defined as the distance:

   F. from hip to ground.
   G. between two successive foot prints of opposite feet.
   H. between two successive footprints of the same foot.
   J. between the tip of the longest toe and the heel of the same foot.

Passage 2

As the earth formed, it went through a geological process called differentiation, by which heavy materials sunk to the planet's core while lighter materials remained closer to the surface. Due to this differentiation, the present interior structure of the earth is arranged by density in four major layers: the heaviest materials (iron and nickel) are found in the inner and outer core, and the less dense materials (rocks) are found in the mantle and crust (Figure 12.2).

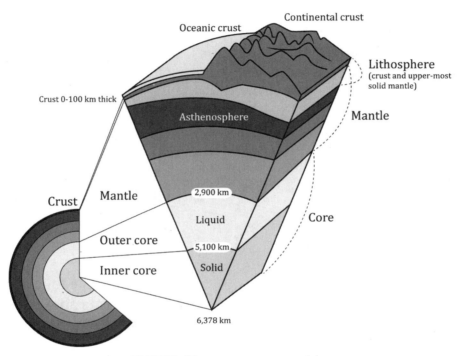

NOTE: Figure not to scale

Figure 12.2

The dense inner core is composed largely of solid iron and nickel and is extremely hot (between 5,000°C and 7,000°C). The decay of radioactive elements is mostly responsible for the heat of the inner core. The outer core consists mostly of molten iron, with significant amounts of nickel and sulfur. The movement of the molten "ocean" of metals in the outer core creates the earth's magnetosphere.

The mantle is the thickest of the four major layers of the earth. It consists of hot rock that flows very slowly under pressure. The ability to flow is especially pronounced in an upper layer of the mantle called the asthenosphere. Above the asthenosphere is a cooler, rigid region of the mantle.

Finally, the earth's "skin" is made up of two types of crust: oceanic and continental. Oceanic crust is thinner, younger, and denser than continental crust. The rigid upper layer of the mantle and the crust are collectively referred to as the lithosphere.

7. According to the passage, the earth's layers are distinguished based on differences in:

   A. density.
   B. temperature.
   C. levels of radioactive elements.
   D. thickness.

8. According to the passage, how many major layers does the earth's interior have?

   F. Three
   G. Four
   H. Eight
   J. Ten

9. According to the passage, the earth's magnetosphere is generated in the:

   A. outer core.
   B. inner core.
   C. mantle.
   D. crust.

10. According to Figure 12.2, what is the approximate distance to the center of the earth?

    F. 2,900 km
    G. 5,000 km
    H. 6,400 km
    J. 7,000 km

11. Which of the following layers of the earth is the thickest?

    A. Outer core
    B. Inner core
    C. Mantle
    D. Crust

12. Which of the following statements about the earth's crust is NOT supported by the model?

    F. Both the continental crust and the oceanic crust are part of the lithosphere
    G. The continental crust is thicker than the oceanic crust.
    H. The continental crust is less dense than the oceanic crust.
    J. The continental crust is younger than the oceanic crust.

Passage 3

Kepler's first law of planetary motion, or the law of ellipses, describes the elliptical orbits of the planets as they revolve around the sun. Given two points, or foci, an ellipse is defined as the locus of points such that the sum of the distances to each focus point is constant. In the orbit of a planet, the planet follows the path of an ellipse with the sun at one focus point (Figure 12.3). Perihelion is the point at which a planet makes its closest approach to the sun and aphelion is the point at which the planet is at its greatest distance from the sun.

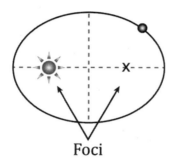

Figure 12.3

Kepler's second law of planetary motion, or the law of equal areas, states that an imaginary line drawn from the center of the sun to the center of a planet will sweep out equal areas in equal time. For example, in Figure 12.4, a planet travels from point A to point B in the same time it takes the same planet to travel from point C to point D, and the two shaded areas are equal in size. This also means that a planet travels fastest at perihelion and slowest at aphelion. Thus, the orbital speed of the planet from point A to point B is much slower than the orbital speed of the planet from point C to point D.

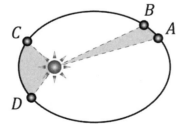

Figure 12.4

13. According to Kepler's first law of planetary motion, the shape of a planet's orbit around the sun is:

A. a circle.
B. a triangle.
C. an ellipse.
D. a straight line.

14. According to the passage, another name for Kepler's second law of planetary motion is the law of:

F. equal areas.
G. ellipses.
H. periods.
J. imaginary lines.

15. Which of Kepler's laws is illustrated in Figure 12.3?

A. The law of gravity
B. The law of ellipses
C. The law of equal areas
D. The law of periods

16. Which of Kepler's laws is illustrated in Figure 12.4?

F. The law of gravity
G. The law of ellipses
H. The law of equal areas
J. The law of periods

17. According to Kepler's first law of planetary motion, where is the sun located in a planet's orbit?

A. The sun is located at the center of the planet's orbit.
B. The sun is located at the perihelion of the planet's orbit.
C. The sun is located at the aphelion of the planet's orbit.
D. The sun is located at one of the foci of the planet's orbit.

18. According to the passage, perihelion is the point at which a planet:

F. is farthest from the sun.
G. is closest to the sun.
H. has its spring equinox.
J. has its fall equinox.

19. According to Kepler's second law, a planet at aphelion travels at:

A. the same orbital speed as when the planet is at perihelion.
B. the same orbital speed as when the planet is at a focus point.
C. its fastest orbital speed.
D. its slowest orbital speed.

20. According to Kepler's second law, if the earth's perihelion occurs in early January and its aphelion occurs in early July, the earth has its greatest orbital speed in:

F. January.
G. April.
H. July.
J. October.

Science Evaluation of Models, Inferences, and Experimental Results

Unit 13 | Understanding Models Practice

INSIDE THIS UNIT:
– Exercise –

EXERCISE

DIRECTIONS: Each passage below is followed by questions based on its content. Answer the questions on the basis of what is stated or implied in the corresponding passage. Answers are on page 758.

Passage 1

Epidemiologists use the chain of infection model (Figure 13.1) to investigate patterns and causes of infectious disease and injury in humans. The chain of infection starts with the reservoir, a habitat where an infectious agent lives. Examples of reservoirs include humans, insects, rodents, soil, and dirty water. The agent is what causes a disease. For infectious diseases, the agent is usually a microbe, such as a virus, bacteria, or fungus.

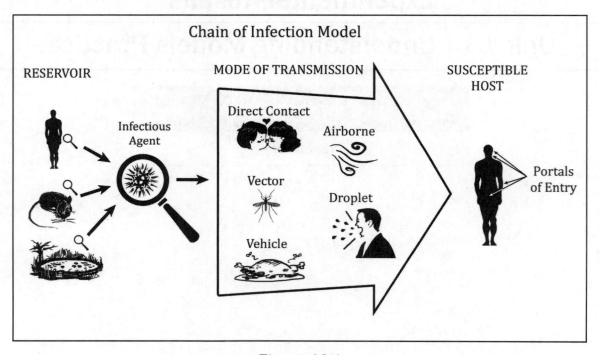

Figure 13.1

An infectious agent can be transmitted from a reservoir to a susceptible host by numerous modes, including direct person-to-person contact, droplets (sneezing or coughing), vectors (insects, worms), inanimate vehicles (contaminated food, needles), or via dust or other particles in the air. The agent can enter the susceptible host through several portals of entry, including the mouth and nose or by syringe. Finally, a susceptible host who becomes ill from an infectious agent may become a reservoir in a new cycle of the chain of infection.

1. According to the passage, epidemiologists are primarily concerned with the study of:

   A. hereditary disorders.
   B. infectious diseases.
   C. human nutrition.
   D. water quality.

2. According to the passage, the habitat of an infectious agent in the first stage of the chain of infection model could be:

   F. a human.
   G. bacteria.
   H. contaminated air.
   J. contaminated food.

3. According to the passage, the mode of transmission of an infectious agent in the chain of infection model could NOT be:

   A. a susceptible host.
   B. insects.
   C. contaminated air.
   D. contaminated food.

4. According to the passage, which of the following is NOT an example of an infectious agent?

   F. Contaminated air
   G. Bacteria
   H. Fungus
   J. Virus

5. According to the passage, which of the following is NOT an example of a reservoir in the chain of infection model?

   A. Dirty water
   B. Fungus
   C. Human
   D. Rodent

6. Bacterial conjunctivitis, more commonly known as pink eye, is caused by direct contact with the eye secretions of an infected person. The mode of transmission in the chain of infection model for bacterial conjunctivitis is:

   F. a human.
   G. a virus.
   H. bacteria.
   J. eye secretions.

7. According to the chain of infection model, a possible portal of entry for an infectious agent into a susceptible host is:

   A. from the mouth of another human.
   B. through the nose of the susceptible host.
   C. by droplets.
   D. by contaminated air.

8. Guests at a picnic eat potato salad contaminated with *Salmonella* bacteria. According to the chain of infection model, the portal of entry for the food poisoning outbreak that results is:

   F. contaminated air.
   G. *Salmonella* bacteria.
   H. the guests' mouths.
   J. the potato salad.

9. Malaria is a disease thought to be caused in humans by a bite from the female mosquito of the genus *Anopheles*. In the chain of infection model for malaria, the mosquito represents:

   A. a susceptible host.
   B. an infectious agent.
   C. the mode of transmission.
   D. the reservoir.

10. Which of the following is LEAST likely to be the mode of transmission of an infectious agent from reservoir to susceptible host if both are human?

    F. Contaminated air
    G. Direct contact
    H. Droplets
    J. Rodents

Passage 2

The collision model of chemical reactions explains the observed rate laws for both one-step and multi-step reactions. The model assumes that for any step in a reaction to occur, the reactant particles must collide with enough energy to overcome the mutual repulsion of their outer shell electrons. If the energy requirement, or activation energy, for a collision is high, only a small percentage of total collisions will result in product being formed at room temperature.

An energy diagram tracks the total energy of a system during a chemical reaction. A collision between reactant particles with sufficient kinetic energy to "climb over" the activation energy "hill" results in the reaction of those particles to form the products. In an exothermic reaction (Figure 13.2), the products have less chemical potential energy than the reactants had at the beginning of the reaction, so energy is released as heat or light. In an endothermic reaction (Figure 13.3), the products have more chemical potential energy than the reactants had at the beginning of the reaction, so the system must absorb energy from the surroundings for the reaction to occur.

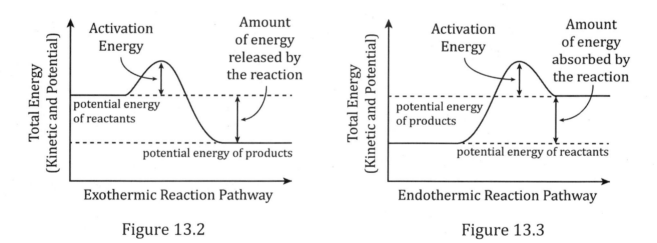

Figure 13.2   Figure 13.3

The collision model also explains why factors such as reactant concentration, reactant surface area, and system temperature affect chemical reaction rates. Increases in reactant concentrations and/or surface area (such as, powdered reactants instead of granular) increase collision frequency (number of collisions per unit time), which increases the probability of collisions having the activation energy, so the reaction rate increases. Increased system temperature increases particle speeds and energies, which also increases the probability of collisions having the activation energy, and again the reaction rate increases.

11. According to the collision model, the minimum energy required for reactants to form products in a chemical reaction is the:

    A. activation energy.
    B. heat of reaction.
    C. product energy.
    D. reactant energy.

12. According to the passage, reactant particles at higher temperatures:

    F. move slower.
    G. move faster.
    H. have outer shell electrons with weaker electrical repulsion.
    J. have outer shell electrons with stronger electrical repulsion.

13. According to the passage, if a reaction has a high activation energy, the percentage of all collisions between reactant particles that result in a reaction is:

    A. almost zero.
    B. small.
    C. large.
    D. infinite.

14. According to the passage, an endothermic chemical reaction:

    F. proceeds at a faster rate than does an exothermic chemical reaction.
    G. proceeds at a slower rate than does an exothermic chemical reaction.
    H. releases energy in the form of heat or light.
    J. requires absorption of energy from the system's surroundings.

15. According to the passage, an exothermic chemical reaction:

    A. proceeds at a faster rate than does an endothermic chemical reaction.
    B. proceeds at a slower rate than does an endothermic chemical reaction.
    C. releases energy in the form of heat or light.
    D. requires absorption of energy from the system's surroundings in the form of heat.

16. According to the collision model, in the chemical reaction between reactants A and B to form product C, if a particle of reactant A collides with a particle of reactant B and the particles do not have sufficient energy to meet the reaction energy requirement, then:

   F. the surface area of particles of both reactants A and B will increase.
   G. the concentration of reactants A and B will decrease.
   H. the particles of reactants A and B will react to form particles of product C.
   J. particles of reactants A and B will not react.

17. According to the collision model, which of the following two conditions would both contribute to an increase in chemical reaction rate?

   A. Lower reactant concentration and higher temperature
   B. Lower reactant concentration and lower temperature
   C. Higher reactant concentration and higher temperature
   D. Higher reactant concentration and lower temperature

18. A chemist who wants to slow the rate of a chemical reaction should:

   F. use powdered reactants instead of granular reactants.
   G. decrease the system temperature.
   H. increase the system temperature.
   J. increase the reactant concentrations.

19. According to the collision model, if the chemical potential energy of the reactants is more than the chemical potential energy of the products, then the system:

   A. releases energy during the chemical reaction.
   B. requires additional energy for the chemical reaction to occur.
   C. absorbs energy during the chemical reaction.
   D. will not change unless reactant concentrations are increased.

20. According to the collision model, increasing the surface area of reactant particles:

F. decreases particle speed and thus increases the probability of collisions having the activation energy required for reaction.
G. decreases frequency of collisions and thus decreases the probability of collisions having the activation energy required for reaction.
H. increases particle energy and thus increases the probability of collisions having the activation energy required reaction.
J. increases frequency of collisions and thus increases the probability of collisions having the activation energy required for reaction.

Passage 3

Sunspots are regions on the surface of the sun where the solar magnetic field is particularly strong. The sunspots appear dark because they are several thousand degrees Celsius cooler than the surrounding regions. Sunspots follow an approximate 11-year cycle, in which the percentage of the sun's surface covered by the spots waxes and wanes (Figure 13.4).

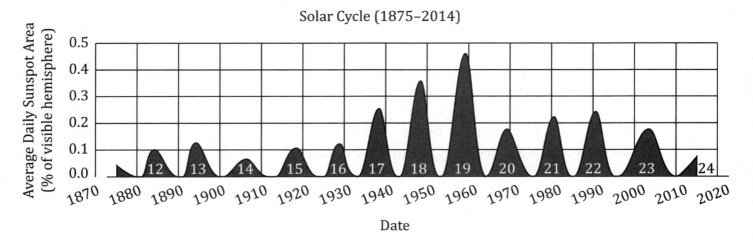

Note: The solar sunspot cycle numbers represent consecutive numbering of the cycles since 1755, when the recording of the sunspot activity began.

Figure 13.4

Sunspot locations generate a "butterfly" diagram (Figure 13.5) when plotted as a function of time and latitude (angular distance north or south from the equator). At the beginning of a cycle, sunspots appear in bands at mid-latitudes between the equator and the poles. As the cycle progresses, the sunspot bands widen and then narrow, so as the cycle ends, the sunspots are clustered near the equator.

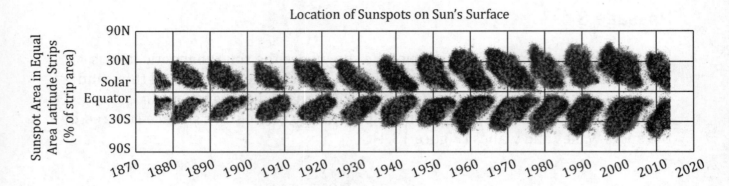

Figure 13.5

Like all stars, the sun is composed of mostly plasma. Plasma is similar to a gas, except the atoms are made up of free electrons and ions. Other examples of plasmas include fluorescent light bulbs, neon signs, and the auroras. Because the sun is not composed of rigid materials, different regions are free to rotate at different rates. Plasma near the equator rotates at the fastest rate.

The Babcock model theorizes that the butterfly pattern observed during a solar sunspot cycle is caused by the sun's magnetic field lines being "dragged" at a faster rate by the rotating plasma near the equator than the slower rotating plasma near the poles. According to the model, this causes a wrapping effect, in which the magnetic field lines near the equator move closer together, strengthening the magnetic field and causing it to become twisted and tangled. At these points, the magnetic field erupts on the surface as sunspots (Figure 13.6). This process of sunspot formation and migration from mid-latitudes to the equator continues until the solar magnetic field reverses after approximately 11 years.

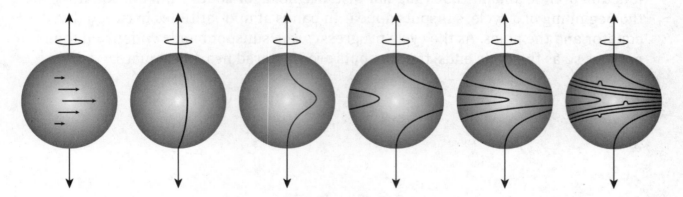

Figure 13.6

21. According to the passage, the temperature of a sunspot is:

    A. several thousand degrees Celsius cooler than the surrounding region.
    B. several hundred degrees Celsius cooler than the surrounding region.
    C. several hundred degrees Celsius warmer than the surrounding region.
    D. several thousand degrees Celsius warmer than the surrounding region.

22. According to the passage, approximately how long is a solar sunspot cycle?

    F. 1 year
    G. 10 years
    H. 11 years
    J. 150 years

23. According to the passage, the sun is composed of mostly:

    A. solid.
    B. liquid.
    C. gas.
    D. plasma.

24. According to the passage, the strongest regions of the sun's magnetic field have:

    F. few sunspots and the magnetic field lines are far apart.
    G. few sunspots and the magnetic field lines are close together.
    H. many sunspots and the magnetic field lines are far apart.
    J. many sunspots and the magnetic field lines are close together.

25. During which solar sunspot cycle shown in Figure 13.4 did sunspots cover the greatest percentage of the sun's visible surface?

    A. 12
    B. 17
    C. 19
    D. 22

26. Solar maxima are those periods in a solar sunspot cycle with the greatest number of sunspots. According to Figure 13.4, approximately what percentage of the sun's visible surface was covered with sunspots during the solar maximum of solar sunspot cycle 21?

F. 0.1–0.2%
G. 0.2–0.3%
H. 0.3–0.4%
J. 0.4–0.5%

27. Solar minima are those periods between solar sunspot cycles with the fewest number of sunspots. According to Figures 13.4 and 13.5, in approximately which year did the solar minimum occur during the period from 1990 to 2000?

A. 1990
B. 1992
C. 1996
D. 2000

28. According to Figure 13.5, in approximately which year of solar sunspot cycle 23 were sunspots found at the greatest distance from the sun's equator?

F. 1998
G. 2000
H. 2005
J. 2010

29. According to Figures 13.4 and 13.5, the sun is currently in solar sunspot cycle:

A. 11.
B. 23.
C. 24.
D. Cannot be determined from the given information

30. According to the passage, the Babcock model:

F. explains how the sun produces energy in its core.
G. describes a mechanism that explains observed solar sunspot patterns.
H. demonstrates that the sun has different rotation rates at different locations.
J. theorizes that the sun's plasma generates magnetic fields.

SCIENCE MASTERY TEST 1

> **DIRECTIONS:** Each passage below is followed by questions based on its content. Answer the questions on the basis of what is stated or implied in the corresponding passage. Answers are on page 758.

Passage 1

Blizzards are dangerous storms. Occasionally, blizzards strike suddenly, filling the previously calm air with snow driven by strong winds that reduce visibility from miles to feet in minutes. The National Weather Service issues warnings that help to reduce the chance of individuals being surprised or stranded by blizzards. Table 14.1 provides information about the number of blizzards that occurred in selected states over a 10-year period.

Table 14.1: Number of Blizzards (1957–1967)	
State	Number of Blizzards
Colorado	1
Illinois	3
Iowa	12
Kansas	6
Minnesota	14
Missouri	2
Montana	11
Nebraska	17
North Dakota	24
South Dakota	23
Wisconsin	8
Wyoming	2

1. According to Table 14.1, Montana had how many blizzards from 1957 through 1967?

   A. 3
   B. 11
   C. 14
   D. 17

2. According to Table 14.1, which of the following states had 23 blizzards from 1957 through 1967?

   F. Iowa
   G. Minnesota
   H. Wyoming
   J. South Dakota

708 • SCIENCE

3. According to Table 14.1, which of the following states had the fewest blizzards from 1957 through 1967?

    A. Colorado
    B. Illinois
    C. Nebraska
    D. Wisconsin

4. According to Table 14.1, which of the following states had the most blizzards from 1957 through 1967?

    F. Iowa
    G. Nebraska
    H. North Dakota
    J. South Dakota

5. According to Table 14.1, which of the following pairs of states had the same number of blizzards from 1957 through 1967?

    A. Illinois and Wisconsin
    B. Wisconsin and Nebraska
    C. North Dakota and South Dakota
    D. Missouri and Wyoming

Passage 2

Irrigation increases crop production in areas experiencing insufficient rainfall or drought conditions. However, irrigation also affects the quantity and quality of water available for other uses. In order to determine the effect of present irrigation practices on water supply and quality, researchers studied the historical usage of water for irrigation purposes. Table 14.2 presents data on the number of irrigated farms and the number of irrigated acres from 1900 to 1980.

Table 14.2: Irrigated Farms and Irrigated Acreage (1900–1980)		
Year	Number of Irrigated Farms	Number of Irrigated Acres (millions)
1900	121,209	10.12
1920	240,118	11.46
1940	301,106	15.07
1960	297,248	43.98
1980	258,129	46.27

SCIENCE MASTERY TEST 1 • 709

6. In Table 14.2, the amount of irrigated acreage is given in measurements of:

   F. acres.
   G. thousands of acres.
   H. millions of acres.
   J. tens of millions of acres.

7. According to Table 14.2, in 1940, the number of irrigated farms was:

   A. 240,118.
   B. 301,106.
   C. 11,460,000.
   D. 15,070,000.

8. According to Table 14.2, in 1960, there were approximately how many irrigated acres?

   F. 43.98
   G. 4,398
   H. 297,248
   J. 43,980,000

9. According to Table 14.2, the year with the greatest number of irrigated farms was:

   A. 1920.
   B. 1940.
   C. 1960.
   D. 1980.

10. According to Table 14.2, the number of irrigated farms between 1960 and 1980:

    F. decreased.
    G. increased significantly.
    H. increased slightly.
    J. remained unchanged.

Passage 3

An astronomical unit (AU) is a unit of length equal to about 92,955,807 miles. It is defined as the mean distance between Earth and the Sun over one Earth orbit. When someone speaks of the distance of a planet from the Sun, this usually means the "mean distance" since the planets are not the same distance from the Sun at every point in their orbits. Astronomers often use the astronomical unit to refer to the mean distance of a given planet from the Sun. Table 14.3 summarizes the mean distances of the planets from the Sun in both miles and astronomical units.

Table 14.3: Distance of Planets from the Sun		
Planet	Mean Distance From Sun (millions of miles)	Mean Distance (AU)
Mercury	36.0	0.39
Venus	67.1	0.72
Earth	92.9	1.00
Mars	141.5	1.52
Jupiter	483.4	5.20
Saturn	886.7	9.54
Uranus	1,782.7	19.18
Neptune	2,794.3	30.06

11. Based on the given information, 1 AU is equal to approximately:

A. 1.0 million miles.
B. 36.0 million miles.
C. 92.9 million miles.
D. 2,794.3 million miles.

12. According to Table 14.3, the mean distance of Mercury from the sun is:

F. 0.39 AU.
G. 0.72 AU.
H. 36.0 AU.
J. 67.1 AU.

13. According to Table 14.3, the planet farthest from the Sun is a mean distance from the Sun of:

A. 0.39 AU.
B. 30.06 AU.
C. 36.0 AU.
D. 2,794.3 AU.

14. According to Table 14.3, which of the following planets is a mean distance of 483.4 million miles from the Sun?

F. Venus
G. Earth
H. Mars
J. Jupiter

15. According to Table 14.3, which of the following planets is a mean distance of 9.54 AU from the Sun?

A. Mars
B. Jupiter
C. Saturn
D. Neptune

Passage 4

The measure of the acidity of a substance is called the pH. Lower pH values indicate acidic solution. Acid rain can lower the pH of a body of water. Some types of plants and animals are able to tolerate acidic waters. Others, however, are acid-sensitive and die as the pH declines. If the pH of the water is lower than the minimum pH a species can tolerate, the species cannot survive. Table 14.4 shows the minimum pH for the survival of various species.

Table 14.4: Minimum pH for Survival	
Species	Minimum pH for Survival
Bass	5.5
Clams	6.0
Crayfish	5.5
Frogs	4.0
Mayflies	5.5
Perch	4.5
Salamanders	5.0
Snails	6.0
Trout	5.0

16. According to Table 14.4, perch will not survive if the pH of water drops below a minimum value of:

F. 4.0.
G. 4.5.
H. 5.0.
J. 5.5.

17. According to Table 14.4, snails will not survive if the pH of water drops below a minimum value of:

A. 4.5.
B. 5.0.
C. 5.5.
D. 6.0.

18. According to Table 14.4, which of the following species is able to tolerate the lowest pH?

F. Clams
G. Crayfish
H. Trout
J. Frogs

19. According to Table 14.4, in order to survive, which of the following species must have water with the same minimum pH as clams?

A. Bass
B. Perch
C. Salamanders
D. Snails

SCIENCE MASTERY TEST 1 • 713

20. According to Table 14.4, which of the following species is able to survive in water with a pH of 4.0?

F. Frogs
G. Bass
H. Salamanders
J. Snails

Passage 5

Striped bass (*Morone saxatilis*) are native to the Atlantic coastline. The striped bass is an important game fish. By 1982, the population had declined to less than 5 million worldwide, but efforts by anglers and management programs to rebuild the stock have been successful. Marine biologists monitor striped bass and keep records of the length and weight of the fish caught. Table 14.5 summarizes the size of the striped bass (length and weight) by the age of fish caught in a recent year.

Table 14.5: Average Size of Striped Bass (length and weight)										
Age (years)	1	2	3	4	5	6	7	8	9	10
Length (inches)	12.5	15.0	18.5	22.0	24.5	27.0	29.5	31.5	33.5	35.5
Weight (pounds)	1.25	2.6	4.1	5.7	7.4	9.6	11.7	13.8	16.1	18.8

21. In Table 14.5, the average length of the striped bass caught is given in measurements of:

A. inches.
B. years.
C. pounds.
D. fish.

22. According to Table 14.5, the average weight of a striped bass 5 years old was:

F. 5.7 pounds.
G. 7.4 pounds.
H. 9.6 pounds.
J. 24.5 pounds.

23. According to Table 14.5, the average length of a striped bass 8 years old was:

A. 11.7 inches.
B. 12.75 inches.
C. 24.5 inches.
D. 31.5 inches.

24. According to Table 14.5, at what age do striped bass have an average weight of 9.6 pounds?

F. 3 years
G. 6 years
H. 9 years
J. 10 years

25. According to Table 14.5, at the age when striped bass have an average length of 22 inches, what is their average weight?

   A. 4.0 pounds
   B. 5.7 pounds
   C. 18.5 pounds
   D. 24.5 pounds

Passage 6

Cladophora is a branching, green filamentous species of algae found naturally along the shoreline of most of the Great Lakes. Research has linked large spikes in the populations of *Cladophora* (called blooms) to high levels of phosphorous in the water. Phosphorus, which acts as a nutrient for the algae, enters the Great Lakes as a result of the run-off of fertilizer and the discharge of sewage and detergents into the water. Researchers monitor the levels of phosphorus in the water. Figure 14.1 is the record of phosphorus levels at a monitoring station near Chicago from 2005 through 2010.

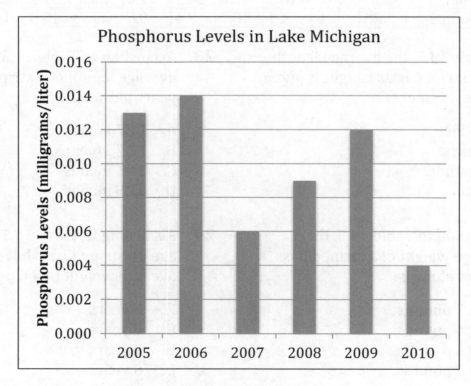

Figure 14.1

SCIENCE MASTERY TEST 1 • 715

26. In Figure 14.1, the phosphorus levels are given in measurements of:

    F. milligrams.
    G. liters.
    H. milligrams per liter.
    J. grams.

27. According to Figure 14.1, phosphorus levels at the monitoring station were highest in which of the following years?

    A. 2006
    B. 2007
    C. 2008
    D. 2009

28. According Figure 14.1, phosphorus levels at the monitoring station were lowest in which of the following years?

    F. 2007
    G. 2008
    H. 2009
    J. 2010

29. According to Figure 14.1, in 2006, the phosphorus level at the monitoring station was:

    A. 0.004 milligrams per liter.
    B. 0.006 milligrams per liter.
    C. 0.013 milligrams per liter.
    D. 0.014 milligrams per liter.

30. According to Figure 14.1, from 2006 to 2010, the phosphorus levels recorded at the monitoring station:

    F. decreased, increased, and then decreased.
    G. decreased and then remained constant.
    H. increased and then remained constant.
    J. increased, decreased, and then increased.

Passage 7

Human rabies cases are rare. However, the disease can be transmitted to humans through contact with an infected animal. Because of the seriousness of rabies (the disease is almost always fatal if not treated before symptoms appear), animals suspected of being rabid should be tested. Figure 14.2 shows the number of positive tests out of the total number of cases of suspected animal rabies.

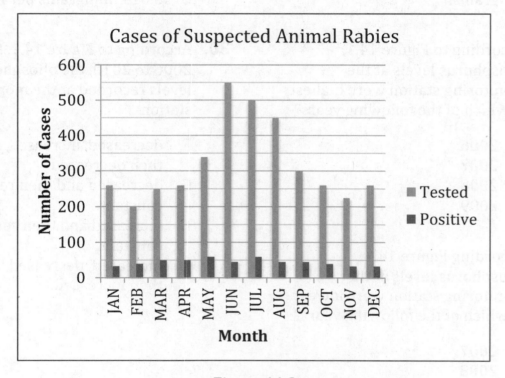

Figure 14.2

31. According to Figure 14.2, the greatest number of rabies tests were conducted in:

A. January.
B. February.
C. May.
D. June.

32. According to Figure 14.2, the fewest number of rabies tests were conducted in:

F. February
G. June
H. August.
J. September.

33. According to Figure 14.2, how many rabies tests were conducted in December?

A. Fewer than 100
B. Between 100 and 200
C. Between 200 and 300
D. More than 300

34. According to Figure 14.2, how many rabies tests conducted in December were positive?

F. Fewer than 50
G. Between 50 and 100
H. Between 100 and 150
J. More than 150

35. According to Figure 14.2, the number of rabies tests conducted from January to February:

A. increased by approximately 50.
B. decreased by approximately 50.
C. decreased by approximately 100.
D. decreased by approximately 150.

Passage 8

Federal law states that the minimum acceptable time (in seconds) from the notification (typically a chime) that an elevator car has answered a call until the door of the car starts to close must be calculated in the following way:

$$\text{Time} = \frac{\text{distance}}{1.5 \text{ feet/second}}$$

Distance is measured from the farthest call button controlling an elevator car to the centerline of the elevator door. The formula applies for distances of 8 feet or more. For any distances less than 8 feet, the minimum acceptable notification time is 5 seconds. To implement this requirement, an engineer created the graph in Figure 14.3.

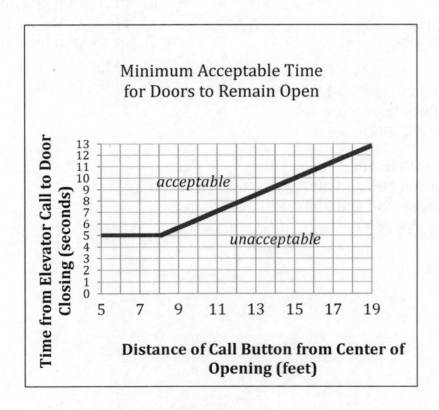

Figure 14.3

36. In Figure 14.3, the horizontal scale represents the distance between the:

F. farthest call button and the center of the elevator door.
G. farthest call button and the call button nearest to the center of the elevator door.
H. center of the elevator door and the location of the passenger who called for the elevator.
J. the nearest call button and the center of the elevator car.

37. For an elevator system that is already installed, the information provided in Figure 14.3 can be used to determine the:

A. minimum time the door should remain open.
B. maximum time the door should remain open.
C. minimum size of the elevator car.
D. minimum rate of travel of the elevator car.

38. According to Figure 14.3, for an elevator with the farthest call button 15 feet from the center of the elevator door, the minimum time required for the door to remain open is:

F. 5 seconds.
G. 6 seconds.
H. 10 seconds.
J. 13 seconds.

39. According to Figure 14.3, for an elevator with the farthest call button 6 feet from the center of the door, the minimum time required for the door to remain open is:

A. 5 seconds.
B. 6 seconds.
C. 7 seconds.
D. 8 seconds.

40. According to Figure 14.3, if the distance from the farthest call button to the center of the elevator door is 14 feet, a door remaining open for 7 seconds is:

F. acceptable.
G. unacceptable.
H. the minimum acceptable.
J. the maximum acceptable.

Passage 9

Research conducted by the United States Department of Agriculture indicates that, on average, people today have available a much greater daily supply of Calories than was available 40 years ago. The total available food supply, however, is not an accurate measure of the amount of food actually consumed. In order to determine how much is actually consumed, it is necessary to know how much remains after spoilage and other losses. Figure 14.4 summarizes the data on average daily per capita food supply in the US for 1970 through 2000.

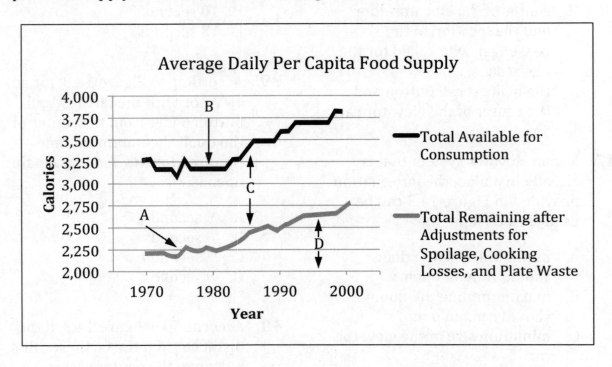

Figure 14.4

41. In Figure 14.4, the vertical axis representing the average daily per capita food supply is presented in intervals of:

A. years.
B. 250 Calories.
C. 10 years.
D. 1,000 Calories.

42. In Figure 14.4, which of the lettered features (A, B, C, or D) indicates the amount of the average daily per capita food supply that is <u>lost</u> to spoilage, cooking losses, and plate waste?

F. A
G. B
H. C
J. D

43. According to Figure 14.4, in 1970, the total average daily per capita food supply available for consumption was:

A. more than 2,750 Calories but less than 3,000 Calories.
B. more than 3,000 Calories but less than 3,250 Calories.
C. more than 3,250 Calories but less than 3,500 Calories.
D. more than 3,500 Calories but less than 3,750 Calories.

44. According to Figure 14.4, in 1995, the total average daily per capita food supply remaining after spoilage, cooking losses, and plate waste was:

F. more than 2,250 Calories but less than 2,500 Calories.
G. more than 2,500 Calories but less than 2,750 Calories.
H. more than 2,750 Calories but less than 3,000 Calories.
J. more than 3,000 Calories but less than 3,250 Calories.

45. According to Figure 14.4, the total average daily per capita food supply available for consumption first exceeded 3,500 Calories:

A. between 1970 and 1980.
B. between 1980 and 1990.
C. between 1990 and 2000.
D. after 2000.

Passage 10

Solubility refers to the ability of a substance (such as an ionic solid) to dissolve in another substance (such as water). Solubility is usually reported as the maximum number of grams of a substance that can dissolve in 100 grams of water. The solubility of ionic solids, such as sodium chloride (NaCl) and potassium nitrate (KNO$_3$), is dependent on water temperature. Figure 14.5 provides solubility curves for these two substances.

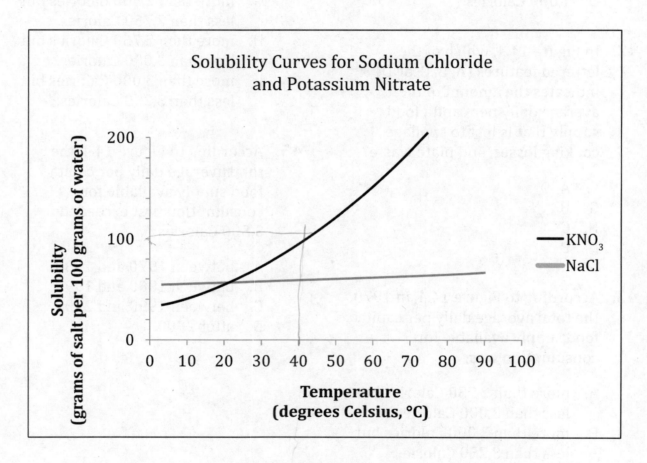

Figure 14.5

46. In Figure 14.5, temperature is given in measurements of:

F. degrees Fahrenheit.
G. degrees Celsius.
H. grams of salt.
J. grams of water.

47. In Figure 14.5, the maximum temperature for which solubility information is provided is:

A. 15°C.
B. 30°C.
C. 100°C.
D. 200°C.

48. According to Figure 14.5, approximately how many grams of potassium nitrate will dissolve in 100 grams of water at 40°C?

F. 40 grams
G. 60 grams
H. 100 grams
J. 120 grams

49. According to Figure 14.5, 200 grams of potassium nitrate will dissolve in 100 grams of water at approximately:

A. 50°C.
B. 75°C.
C. 100°C.
D. 125°C.

50. According to Figure 14.5, the solubilities of sodium chloride potassium nitrate in 100 grams of water are equal at approximately:

F. 0°C.
G. 25°C.
H. 38°C.
J. 85°C.

SCIENCE MASTERY TEST 2

DIRECTIONS: Each passage below is followed by questions based on its content. Answer the questions on the basis of what is stated or implied in the corresponding passage. Answers are on page 759.

Passage 1

A student performs an experiment to investigate how different types of floor surfaces affect the rolling distance of a marble. He uses PVC tubing and connectors to construct a ramp for launching a steel marble onto the floor (Figure 15.1). He tests five different floor surfaces: tile, newspaper, thin carpet, rubber mat, and a plastic sheet. The start point for the marble on the ramp is 12 centimeters above the floor and the marble's launch point is at the other end of the ramp, level with the floor.

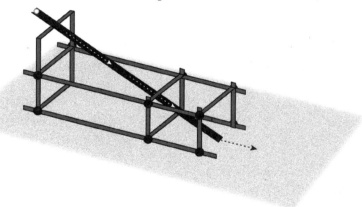

Figure 15.1

For each floor surface, the student releases the marble from rest at the start point. After the marble rolls to a stop on the floor surface, he uses a tape measure to determine the distance from the launch point to the stop point. To minimize the effect of random experimental variations, four trials are conducted for each floor surface and the results averaged. Table 15.1 summarizes the experimental data.

| Table 15.1: Experimental Results ||||||
Floor Surface	Trial 1	Trial 2	Trial 3	Trial 4	Average
Tile	590	611	604	598	601
Newspaper	406	412	420	398	409
Thin Carpet	76	73	66	74	72
Rubber Mat	153	158	152	163	156
Plastic Sheet	565	578	574	562	570

1. Based on the information given, which of the following diagrams is a correct representation of this experiment?

A.
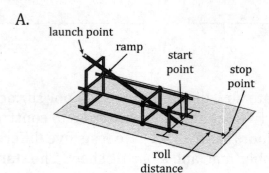

B.
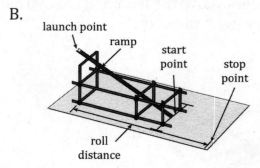

C.
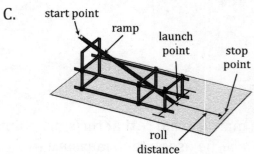

D.
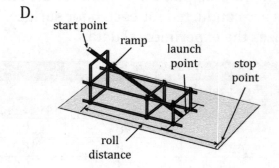

2. According to the passage, the purpose of the experiment is to investigate how:

F. the ramp elevation affects the speed of a rolling marble.
G. the type of tubing used to construct the ramp affects the distance a marble rolls.
H. the type of marble affects the distance it rolls.
J. the type of floor surface affects the distance a marble rolls.

3. At what height above the floor does the student release the marble in each trial?

A. 0 centimeters
B. 1 centimeters
C. 12 centimeters
D. 30 centimeters

4. Which of the following does the student measure in every trial of this experiment?

F. Acceleration due to gravity
G. Ramp height
H. Ramp length
J. Roll distance

5. Which of the following is NOT constant for this entire experiment?

   A. Roll distance
   B. Acceleration due to gravity
   C. Ramp length
   D. Type of PVC tubing

6. Which of the following does the student change for each set of trials in this experiment?

   F. Ramp length
   G. Floor surface
   H. Roll distance
   J. Type of marble

7. Which of the following is a complete and accurate list of the equipment and tools needed for this experiment?

   A. Marble, PVC tubing, floor surfaces, and tape measure
   B. Marble, PVC tubing, floor surfaces, and connectors
   C. Marble, PVC tubing, connectors, floor surfaces, and tape measure
   D. Marble, connectors, tape measure, and computer

8. According to Table 15.1, on which of the following floor surfaces does the marble roll the shortest distance?

   F. Thin carpet
   G. Tile
   H. Rubber mat
   J. Plastic sheet

9. According to Table 15.1, on which of the following floor surfaces does the marble roll the longest distance?

   A. Newspaper
   B. Tile
   C. Rubber mat
   D. Plastic sheet

10. Which of the following best explains why four trials are completed for each floor surface?

    F. Different ramp elevations are used in each trial.
    G. Different types of marbles are used in each trial.
    H. Averaging data over several trials minimizes the effect of random experimental variations.
    J. Averaging data over several trials magnifies the effect of random experimental variations.

Passage 2

A motion sensor is an electronic sensing device that measures the distance from the sensor to a moving object by bouncing ultrasonic sound waves off the object and timing the echoes of the returning waves. A student uses a motion sensor to measure and record her position as she moves back and forth in front of the sensor (Figure 15.2). The sensor transmits the data to a computer, which plots the distance every 0.2 seconds (Figure 15.3).

In Figure 15.3, as time increases, an increase in distance indicates that the student is walking away from the sensor, and a decrease in distance indicates that she is walking towards it. Furthermore, since speed is defined as the distance traveled per unit time, the greatest distance covered in the same amount of time corresponds to the greatest speed.

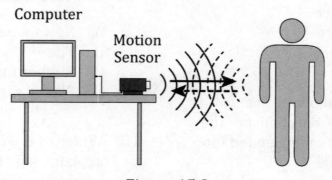

Figure 15.2

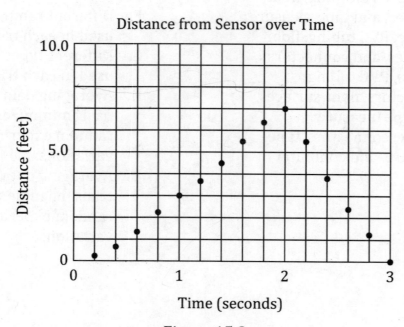

Figure 15.3

11. Which of the following is the best description of the motion sensor in this experiment?

A. A computer program that graphs the distance of an object as a function of time
B. A diagnostic medical imaging system for visualizing muscles, tendons, and internal organs
C. A device that emits ultrasound waves and measures their absorption by moving objects
D. A device that emits ultrasound waves and detects the difference in bounced echoes to determine the distance to a moving object

12. How many data points are collected during this experiment?

F.   5
G. 10
H. 15
J. 30

13. The units of measurement for distance in this experiment are:

A. feet.
B. meters.
C. seconds.
D. kilometers.

14. In this experiment, time is measured in units of:

F. milliseconds.
G. seconds.
H. feet.
J. kilometers.

15. According to the passage, which of the following is a complete and accurate list of the equipment and tools used in this experiment?

A. Motion sensor and computer
B. Motion sensor, computer, and speaker
C. Motion sensor, computer, and meter stick
D. Motion sensor, computer, speaker, and meter stick

16. According to the passage, the computer plots the distance data every:

F.   0.1 second.
G.   0.2 second.
H.   1 second.
J. 10 seconds.

17. According to Figure 15.3, the distance of the student from the sensor at 0.8 seconds is approximately:

A. 1 foot.
B. 2 feet.
C. 3 feet.
D. 4 feet.

18. According to Figure 15.3, what is the farthest in one direction that the student walks before turning around?

F. 1 foot
G. 3 feet
H. 7 feet
J. Cannot be determined from the given information

19. According to Figure 15.3, the student:

A. walks with the greatest speed away from the sensor.
B. walks at equal speeds both toward and away from the sensor.
C. does not move during the experiment.
D. walks with the greatest speed toward the sensor.

20. During which of the following time intervals in Figure 15.3 does the student walk the slowest?

F. 0–1 second
G. 1–2 seconds
H. 2–3 seconds
J. Cannot be determined from the given information

Passage 3

A student group constructs simple pendulums by connecting solid iron bobs to the ends of wires connected to a hook in the ceiling. They investigate the effects of both bob weight and wire length on the pendulum period. One period is defined as the time it takes the pendulum to swing away from and back to its original position—from A to C (through B) and back to A (Figure 15.4).

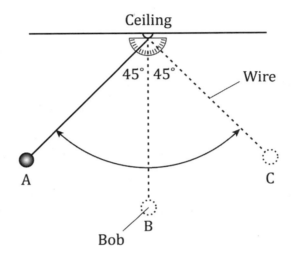

Figure 15.4

The students begin with a pendulum made with a 0.5-pound bob and a wire 1 foot in length. A student pulls the pendulum back to a 45° angle with respect to the pendulum's resting position, as indicated by a protractor. A stopwatch is used to record the time for 10 complete swings of the pendulum. The value obtained is then divided by 10 to calculate the time for a single swing of the pendulum. The experiment is repeated for 1.0-pound and 1.5-pound bobs. Each of the three bobs is used again with wires 2 feet and 3 feet in length. The experimental results are summarized in Table 15.2.

Table 15.2: Experimental Results			
Pendulum Period (seconds)			
	Bob Weight (pounds)		
Wire Length (feet)	0.5	1.0	1.5
1	1.1	1.1	1.1
2	1.6	1.6	1.6
3	3.3	3.3	3.3

21. The effect(s) of which of the following variable(s) on the period of a pendulum is (are) investigated in this experiment?

    A. Wire length
    B. Bob weight
    C. Bob weight and wire length
    D. Bob weight, bob starting position, and wire length

22. How many pendulum bob and wire combinations are tested in this experiment?

    F. One
    G. Three
    H. Six
    J. Nine

23. In addition to the hook in the ceiling, which of the following is a complete and accurate list of the equipment and tools needed for this experiment?

    A. Bobs and wires
    B. Bobs, wires, and a stopwatch
    C. Bobs, wires, a stopwatch, and a computer
    D. Bobs, wires, a stopwatch, and a protractor

24. Which of the following correctly represents the pendulum position when the stopwatch is started?

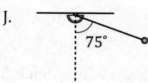

25. Which of the following correctly describes the pendulum position when the stopwatch is stopped?

    A. The pendulum is perpendicular with the floor.
    B. The pendulum is at its starting position after swinging 10 times.
    C. The pendulum is at the farthest point from its starting position.
    D. The pendulum is at its starting position after swinging twice.

26. In this experiment, the pendulum period is measured in units of:

F. feet.
G. pounds.
H. seconds.
J. degrees.

27. According to Table 15.2, the period of the pendulum constructed from a 1.5-pound bob and 2-foot wire is:

A. 1.1 seconds.
B. 1.5 seconds.
C. 1.6 seconds.
D. 3.3 seconds.

28. According to Table 15.2, the period of the pendulum is the least for a wire of length:

F. 1 foot.
G. 2 feet.
H. 3 feet.
J. 5 feet.

29. According to Table 15.2, which of the following had an effect on the period of the pendulum?

A. bob weight
B. wire length
C. both bob weight and wire length
D. neither bob weight nor wire length

30. Which of the following best describes the data in Table 15.2?

F. Longer wires result in shorter pendulum periods, but bob weight has no impact.
G. Longer wires results in longer pendulum periods, but bob weight has no impact.
H. Both longer wires and heavier bobs results in longer pendulum periods.
J. Both longer wires and lighter bobs result in longer pendulum periods.

Passage 4

An object's potential energy (PE) depends on its height; its kinetic energy (KE) depends on its speed; and its total mechanical energy (TME) is the sum of the potential and kinetic energies. All three quantities are measured in joules (J). As an object falls and gains speed due to the acceleration of gravity, potential energy is converted into kinetic energy. Measuring an object's height and speed at different points as it falls allows calculations of the object's potential, kinetic, and total mechanical energies.

Students use a motion sensor to measure the position and velocity of a ball as it falls. A ball is dropped from a pre-measured height of 2 meters onto a protective screen, below which a motion sensor is positioned (Figure 15.5). The motion detector records the position of the ball at 0.1-second intervals as it falls. Students then input the mass of the ball into the computer program. Using the data from the students and motion sensor, the program calculates the potential, kinetic, and total mechanical energies of the ball as a function of height above the sensor. The results are graphed in Figure 15.6.

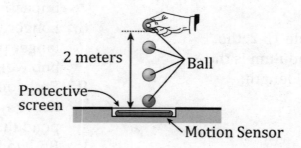

Figure 15.5

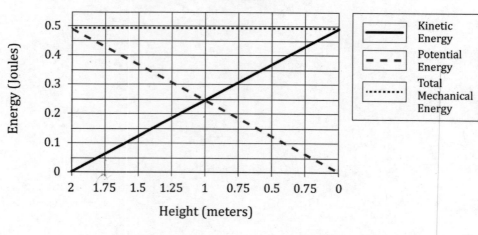

Figure 15.6

31. According to the passage, the location of the protective screen is:

A. below the motion sensor.
B. on the sides of the motion sensor.
C. between the ball and the students.
D. on top of the motion sensor.

32. In this experiment, the ball is dropped from a height of:

F. 0 meters.
G. 0.5 meter.
H. 1 meter.
J. 2 meters.

33. According to the passage, potential, kinetic, and total mechanical energies are given in units of:

A. seconds.
B. meters.
C. joules.
D. meters per second.

34. In this experiment, the computer program calculated which properties of the falling ball?

F. Mass, kinetic energy, and potential energy
G. Kinetic energy, potential energy, and total mechanical energy
H. Kinetic energy only
J. Total mechanical energy only

35. According to the passage, which of the following equations correctly represents the calculation for total mechanical energy (TME), where KE and PE are the kinetic and potential energies, respectively?

A. $TME = KE + PE$
B. $TME = KE \times PE$
C. $TME = 2(KE + PE)$
D. $TME = KE/PE$

736 • SCIENCE

36. According to the passage, which of the following is a complete and accurate list of the equipment and tools needed for this experiment?

    F. Motion sensor, ball, and protective screen
    G. Motion sensor, ball, protective screen, and computer
    H. Motion sensor, ball, protective screen, and tape measure
    J. Motion sensor, ball, and computer

37. According to Figure 15.6, the ball's potential energy is greatest for a height above the sensor of approximately:

    A. 0 meters.
    B. 0.5 meter.
    C. 1 meter.
    D. 2 meters.

38. According to Figure 15.6, the ball's kinetic energy at a height of 1.75 meters is approximately:

    F. 0.06 joules.
    G. 0.18 joules.
    H. 0.42 joules.
    J. 0.49 joules.

39. According to Figure 15.6, the height above the sensor for which the ball's kinetic energy is equal to its potential energy is approximately:

    A. 0 meters.
    B. 0.5 meter.
    C. 1 meter.
    D. 2 meters.

40. According to Figure 15.6, as the ball drops, its:

    F. potential energy decreases, kinetic energy increases, and total mechanical energy remains constant.
    G. potential energy increases, kinetic energy decreases, and total mechanical energy remains constant.
    H. potential energy increases, kinetic energy increases, and total mechanical energy increases.
    J. potential energy decreases, kinetic energy decreases, and total mechanical energy remains constant.

Passage 5

The atom is the basic unit that makes up all elements. In simple terms, an atom is composed of a positively charged nucleus surrounded by a cloud of negatively charged electrons. The atomic number of an atom corresponds to the number of protons in the nucleus, which, for a neutral atom, is equal to the number of electrons.

The Bohr model of the atom was an early attempt to describe the arrangement of electrons about an atom's nucleus. The model states that electrons are found in shells about the nucleus. Each shell has a maximum number of electrons that it can hold. The outermost shell—called the valence shell—is particularly important to understanding the chemical behavior of an atom. Atoms with full valence shells are stable and do not react with other atoms.

Ionization energy refers to the energy needed per unit of charge to remove an electron from an atom. Once an electron is removed, the atom is said to be ionized and it has an overall positive electric charge. Elements with complete valence shells (noble gases) have high ionization energies: they tightly hold onto their electrons. The same is true for elements with valence shells that are almost complete. On the other hand, elements with only one electron in the outer valence shell (alkali metals) have low ionization energies; it is relatively easy to remove the lone valence electron. Figure 15.7 illustrates the first ionization energies (the energy required to remove the first valence electron) of the elements.

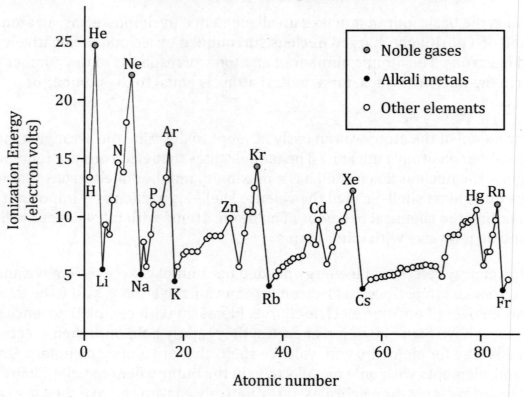

Figure 15.7

41. According to the passage, the Bohr model describes:

A. the arrangement of protons in the atomic nucleus.
B. the arrangement of protons and neutrons in energy levels surrounding the atomic nucleus.
C. the arrangement of electrons in energy levels in the atomic nucleus.
D. the arrangement of electrons in energy levels surrounding the atomic nucleus.

42. According to the passage, which of the following best describes a valence electron?

F. An electron in the innermost electron shell of an atom
G. An electron in the outermost electron shell of an atom
H. An electron with low ionization energy
J. An electron with high ionization energy

43. According to the Bohr model, an atom is most difficult to ionize when:

    A. its outer electron shell is full.
    B. its outer electron shell is not full.
    C. its inner electron shell is full.
    D. its inner electron shell is not full.

44. According to the Bohr model, which of the following determines an atom's chemical properties?

    F. The valence electrons
    G. The protons
    H. The binding energy of the electrons
    J. The number of completed electron energy shells

45. The atomic number of a helium atom is 2. According to the given information, how many electrons does a neutral helium atom have?

    A. Zero
    B. One
    C. Two
    D. Four

46. Atomic ionization energy is measured in units of:

    F. electron volts.
    G. atomic number.
    H. angstroms.
    J. seconds.

47. According to Figure 15.7, which of the following is not a noble gas?

    A. Argon (Ar)
    B. Helium (He)
    C. Neon (Ne)
    D. Sodium (Na)

48. According to Figure 15.7, which of the following elements has the greatest first ionization energy?

    F. Francium (Fr)
    G. Helium (He)
    H. Hydrogen (H)
    J. Radon (Rn)

49. According to Figure 15.7, as atomic number increases, the first ionization energy of an alkali metal:

    A. increases, then decreases.
    B. decreases, then increases.
    C. remains approximately the same.
    D. Cannot be determined from the given information.

50. According to the given information, approximately how much energy is required to remove the first valence electron from a nitrogen (N) atom?

    F. 5 electron volts
    G. 10 electron volts
    H. 15 electron volts
    J. 25 electron volts

Post-Assessment

INSIDE THIS UNIT:
– Post-Assessment Administration – – How to Use the Post-Assessment Reports –

Post-Assessment Administration

At the end of the course, you will take a second previously administered EXPLORE test. Use the bubble sheet your teacher gives you to record your answers. When you take the test, bring the following items to the classroom, in addition to anything else your teacher instructs you to bring:

1. Sharpened, soft-lead No. 2 pencils

2. A calculator that is approved for use on the test. This includes any four-function, scientific, or graphing calculator, except for those with the following features:

   - Built-in computer algebra systems

   - Pocket organizers or PDAs

   - Handheld or laptop computers

   - Electronic writing pad or pen-input devices

   - Calculators built into any electronic communication device, such as a cell phone

   - Models with a QWERTY (typewriter) keypad (Calculators with letters on the keys are permitted as long as the keys are not arranged in a QWERTY keypad.)

   You may use the following types of calculators if you make these modifications:

   - Models with paper tape: the paper must be removed.

   - Models that make noise: the sound feature must be turned off.

   - Models that have an infrared data port: the port must be covered with duct tape, electrician's tape, or another heavy, opaque material.

   - Models that have a power cord: the power cord must be removed.

You may NOT use the following calculator models:

- Texas Instruments: Any model number beginning with TI-89 or TI-92 or the TI-NSpire or TI-NSpire CAS

- Hewlett-Packard: HP 48GII, HP Prime or any model number beginning with HP 40G, HP 49G, or HP 50G

- Casio: Algebra fx 2.0, fx-CP400, ClassPad 300, ClassPad 330 or any model number beginning with CFX-9970G

(For more detailed information on calculator usage, go to http://actstudent.org/faq/calculator.html.)

3. A watch (to pace yourself as you work through each test section)

As you take the test, remember the following points about marking the bubble sheet:

- The bubble for each answer choice must be completely darkened. If the letter within the bubble can be read through the pencil mark, then it is not dark enough. Mechanical pencils, even with No. 2 pencil lead, often fail to leave a dark mark.

- Stay within the lines.

- When erasing pencil marks, be sure to erase the marks completely. Do not leave any stray marks.

- When changing an answer, over-darken the final answer choice after completely erasing the original mark. This extra density tends to offset the residue left over from the original answer choice.

- Circle the answer choices in the test booklet. Towards the end of the section, or after you complete a group of items, transfer the selected answers as a group to the answer form. This saves time and reduces the number of errors on the answer form.

Strategic test-taking:

- Code items in the margin of the test booklet as easy or difficult before beginning to answer them. When pressed for time, you can skip to items that you are more likely to answer correctly.

744 • POST-ASSESSMENT

- Make notes and calculations directly in the test booklet.

- Underline key words in Reading passages.

If your program has ordered post-assessment Student Summary reports, you will receive one of these reports with your post-assessment results. This report will help you determine the areas in which you need continued study. Refer to the "How to Use the Pre-Assessment Reports" section on page 2 to learn more about how to read and use the Student Summary report.

How to Use the Post-Assessment Reports

Approximately six business days after you take the post-assessment, you will receive Student Summary and Student Item Analysis reports that explain your test results. You and your teacher will use these results to evaluate your individual strengths and weaknesses. Review the details of the sample reports on pages 3–4 of this book so that you are familiar with their contents.

Appendix | **Answer Key**

INSIDE THIS UNIT:
– English – – Math – – Reading – – Science –

ENGLISH

Unit 1 | Topic Development
EXERCISE (p. 16)

1. A	4. F	7. D	10. F	13. D	16. H	19. A
2. F	5. A	8. H	11. A	14. F	17. A	20. F
3. C	6. H	9. D	12. H	15. A	18. J	

Unit 2 | Transition Words and Phrases
EXERCISE (p. 33)

1. A	5. D	9. D	13. A	17. C	21. B	25. D
2. H	6. G	10. G	14. F	18. H	22. G	
3. A	7. C	11. C	15. C	19. B	23. C	
4. H	8. J	12. G	16. F	20. G	24. J	

Unit 3 | Practice
EXERCISE (p. 40)

1. A	5. D	9. A	13. A	17. B	21. D	25. B	29. A
2. H	6. F	10. H	14. F	18. F	22. H	26. F	30. G
3. C	7. C	11. C	15. A	19. D	23. A	27. B	
4. J	8. J	12. J	16. J	20. G	24. J	28. J	

Unit 4 | Clarity in Sentences
EXERCISE (p. 58)

1. D	5. D	9. D	13. D	17. A	21. C	25. B
2. G	6. H	10. H	14. F	18. H	22. G	
3. C	7. B	11. B	15. C	19. A	23. D	
4. J	8. G	12. H	16. G	20. J	24. F	

ANSWER KEY • 747

Unit 5 | *Clarity in Noun and Pronoun Usage*
EXERCISE (p. 68)

1. D	5. A	9. C	13. C	17. A	21. D	25. C
2. F	6. G	10. G	14. G	18. G	22. F	
3. D	7. B	11. A	15. D	19. B	23. B	
4. J	8. H	12. J	16. H	20. H	24. J	

Unit 6 | *Practice*
EXERCISE (p. 74)

1. D	5. B	9. A	13. A	17. C	21. A	25. A	29. A
2. F	6. H	10. J	14. G	18. F	22. G	26. F	30. G
3. B	7. C	11. D	15. A	19. C	23. C	27. B	
4. J	8. G	12. H	16. G	20. G	24. J	28. J	

Unit 7 | *Conjunctions and Punctuation*
EXERCISE (p. 89)

1. B	5. C	9. A	13. D	17. C	21. A	25. D
2. F	6. G	10. J	14. H	18. G	22. J	
3. A	7. B	11. C	15. B	19. D	23. A	
4. J	8. J	12. F	16. H	20. H	24. F	

Unit 8 | *Verb Tense*
EXERCISE (p. 101)

1. B	5. A	9. A	13. C	17. A	21. A	25. B
2. H	6. G	10. J	14. F	18. J	22. H	
3. C	7. D	11. B	15. A	19. C	23. D	
4. G	8. H	12. G	16. J	20. J	24. G	

Unit 9 | *Practice*
EXERCISE (p. 108)

1. C	5. A	9. A	13. D	17. C	21. C	25. B	29. D
2. H	6. F	10. J	14. G	18. G	22. J	26. G	30. G
3. A	7. D	11. D	15. A	19. B	23. C	27. A	
4. J	8. H	12. G	16. H	20. H	24. F	28. G	

Unit 10 | *Past Participles*

EXERCISE (p. 127)

1. B	5. A	9. D	13. B	17. B	21. B	25. D
2. H	6. F	10. H	14. F	18. F	22. H	
3. A	7. C	11. B	15. D	19. B	23. C	
4. J	8. G	12. H	16. F	20. J	24. F	

Unit 11 | *Adjectives*

EXERCISE (p. 137)

1. C	5. C	9. C	13. C	17. C	21. A	25. D
2. H	6. G	10. F	14. J	18. F	22. G	
3. B	7. A	11. B	15. D	19. B	23. C	
4. G	8. J	12. F	16. F	20. F	24. J	

Unit 12 | *Commas*

EXERCISE (p. 148)

1. A	5. B	9. C	13. B	17. C	21. E	25. E
2. J	6. J	10. F	14. F	18. F	22. H	
3. D	7. A	11. D	15. B	19. A	23. D	
4. G	8. J	12. H	16. H	20. K	24. G	

Unit 13 | *Practice*

EXERCISE (p. 154)

1. C	5. D	9. A	13. C	17. A	21. B	25. D	29. B
2. F	6. G	10. J	14. G	18. J	22. H	26. G	30. G
3. C	7. A	11. A	15. D	19. B	23. B	27. C	
4. H	8. H	12. J	16. F	20. J	24. F	28. J	

English Mastery Test 1 (p. 163)

1. C	5. A	9. D	13. A	17. D	21. D	25. D
2. F	6. H	10. F	14. H	18. G	22. G	
3. D	7. D	11. A	15. A	19. B	23. C	
4. J	8. F	12. H	16. G	20. H	24. G	

ANSWER KEY • 749

English Mastery Test 2 (p. 171)

1. A	5. A	9. D	13. A	17. B	21. D	25. C
2. G	6. J	10. F	14. G	18. F	22. J	
3. C	7. A	11. B	15. A	19. D	23. A	
4. J	8. H	12. H	16. H	20. G	24. H	

MATH

Unit 1 | Basic Manipulations

EXERCISE (p. 183)

1. E	5. C	9. E	13. A	17. E	21. E	25. D	29. A
2. J	6. J	10. K	14. G	18. G	22. H	26. G	30. K
3. D	7. B	11. D	15. B	19. C	23. E	27. B	
4. J	8. G	12. F	16. K	20. F	24. H	28. K	

Unit 2 | Fractions

EXERCISE (p. 195)

1. D	5. C	9. E	13. E	17. A	21. A	25. A
2. G	6. H	10. H	14. G	18. G	22. G	
3. C	7. E	11. B	15. C	19. C	23. E	
4. K	8. J	12. G	16. J	20. G	24. J	

Unit 3 | Number Lines

EXERCISE (p. 204)

1. C	5. B	9. A	13. A	17. B	21. E	25. C
2. J	6. H	10. H	14. G	18. K	22. G	
3. E	7. D	11. C	15. D	19. D	23. A	
4. F	8. K	12. K	16. H	20. H	24. H	

Unit 4 | One- and Two-Step Problems
EXERCISE (p. 215)

1. E	5. E	9. C	13. E	17. D	21. B	25. E
2. K	6. K	10. F	14. J	18. F	22. G	
3. B	7. A	11. C	15. E	19. B	23. B	
4. F	8. F	12. G	16. K	20. G	24. F	

Unit 5 | Basic Expressions
EXERCISE (p. 223)

1. D	5. D	9. A	13. B	17. D	21. C	25. A
2. H	6. J	10. F	14. F	18. H	22. G	
3. C	7. C	11. D	15. A	19. E	23. A	
4. H	8. G	12. F	16. J	20. K	24. G	

Unit 6 | Basic Equations
EXERCISE (p. 235)

1. C	5. B	9. D	13. D	17. D	21. B	25. A
2. H	6. H	10. H	14. J	18. H	22. H	
3. B	7. A	11. E	15. D	19. B	23. E	
4. H	8. H	12. K	16. J	20. G	24. G	

Unit 7 | Practice
EXERCISE (p. 238)

1. E	5. C	9. C	13. B	17. B	21. D	25. D	29. C
2. H	6. H	10. J	14. K	18. K	22. G	26. J	30. K
3. D	7. D	11. C	15. B	19. E	23. E	27. B	
4. H	8. G	12. F	16. K	20. G	24. H	28. J	

Unit 8 | Pattern Identification
EXERCISE (p. 247)

1. D	5. A	9. E	13. E	17. D	21. C	25. E
2. H	6. H	10. J	14. K	18. J	22. G	
3. C	7. C	11. D	15. B	19. D	23. C	
4. G	8. J	12. K	16. J	20. J	24. H	

Unit 9 | **Length and Distance**

EXERCISE (p. 261)

1. C	5. A	9. B	13. D	17. B	21. A	25. B
2. F	6. H	10. G	14. H	18. G	22. H	
3. A	7. C	11. E	15. D	19. E	23. D	
4. J	8. H	12. J	16. F	20. H	24. J	

Unit 10 | **Perform Common Unit Conversions**

EXERCISE (p. 272)

1. C	5. B	9. D	13. E	17. D	21. B	25. A
2. K	6. K	10. K	14. F	18. K	22. K	
3. C	7. E	11. C	15. C	19. A	23. C	
4. H	8. J	12. K	16. F	20. G	24. F	

Unit 11 | **Averages**

EXERCISE (p. 280)

1. D	5. B	9. C	13. C	17. D	21. B	25. B	29. D
2. H	6. H	10. F	14. J	18. H	22. F	26. H	30. G
3. D	7. C	11. A	15. B	19. D	23. A	27. B	
4. H	8. G	12. F	16. G	20. H	24. G	28. G	

Unit 12 | **Charts and Tables**

EXERCISE (p. 296)

1. B	5. D	9. E	13. E	17. E	21. D	25. D
2. H	6. K	10. H	14. F	18. K	22. J	
3. D	7. B	11. B	15. C	19. E	23. E	
4. H	8. F	12. H	16. F	20. J	24. J	

Unit 13 | **Practice**

EXERCISE (p. 304)

1. B	5. D	9. D	13. D	17. B	21. E	25. C
2. G	6. H	10. G	14. K	18. G	22. K	
3. D	7. A	11. E	15. C	19. B	23. A	
4. G	8. J	12. K	16. F	20. J	24. G	

Math Mastery Test 1 (p. 309)

1. A	5. E	9. A	13. E	17. D	21. E	25. D	29. C
2. J	6. H	10. K	14. G	18. F	22. F	26. H	30. K
3. A	7. B	11. A	15. D	19. C	23. C	27. B	
4. K	8. F	12. J	16. G	20. G	24. H	28. G	

Math Mastery Test 2 (p. 313)

1. D	5. C	9. E	13. C	17. A	21. A	25. D
2. G	6. H	10. J	14. K	18. G	22. G	
3. D	7. B	11. D	15. B	19. B	23. D	
4. J	8. F	12. G	16. H	20. G	24. G	

READING

Unit 1 | Main Idea
EXERCISE (p. 321)

1. D	5. C	9. D	13. A	17. C	21. B	25. C	29. D
2. F	6. H	10. F	14. G	18. J	22. F	26. J	30. F
3. B	7. C	11. C	15. A	19. A	23. D	27. A	
4. G	8. G	12. G	16. G	20. J	24. G	28. H	

Unit 2 | Specific Details
EXERCISE (p. 339)

1. A	5. D	9. B	13. B	17. D	21. B	25. C
2. H	6. G	10. H	14. G	18. F	22. J	26. J
3. D	7. B	11. B	15. C	19. A	23. C	27. A
4. F	8. H	12. J	16. F	20. H	24. F	28. G

Unit 3 | Practice
EXERCISE (p. 348)

1. B	5. A	9. A	13. B	17. C	21. A	25. B
2. H	6. G	10. H	14. H	18. F	22. J	
3. C	7. D	11. D	15. A	19. C	23. A	
4. G	8. F	12. H	16. J	20. J	24. G	

ANSWER KEY • 753

Unit 4 | Events and Relationships

EXAMPLE PASSAGE 1 (p. 358)
1. D
2. F
3. B

EXAMPLE PASSAGE 2 (p. 361)
1. D
2. G
3. B

EXERCISE (p. 363)

1. A	5. D	9. B	13. A	17. A	21. C	25. B	29. A
2. G	6. J	10. F	14. H	18. H	22. J	26. H	30. F
3. D	7. B	11. A	15. D	19. B	23. C	27. D	
4. F	8. H	12. H	16. G	20. G	24. J	28. G	

Unit 5 | Vocabulary

EXERCISE (p. 382)

1. B	5. A	9. B	13. D	17. D	21. B	25. C	29. D
2. G	6. G	10. F	14. H	18. H	22. H	26. G	30. F
3. C	7. D	11. A	15. A	19. B	23. D	27. A	
4. J	8. H	12. H	16. F	20. F	24. J	28. G	

Unit 6 | Practice

EXERCISE (p. 392)

1. C	5. B	9. D	13. A	17. D	21. A	25. B	29. A
2. J	6. G	10. G	14. H	18. J	22. H	26. H	30. F
3. C	7. A	11. A	15. B	19. C	23. A	27. C	
4. J	8. J	12. G	16. G	20. G	24. F	28. J	

Unit 7 | Implied Ideas and Conclusions

EXAMPLE PASSAGE 1
(p. 404)
1. *
2. J
3. A
4. J
5. A

EXAMPLE PASSAGE 2
(p. 408)
6. H
7. A
8. F
9. B
10. H

EXAMPLE PASSAGE 3
(p. 411)
11. C   16. J
12. G   17. C
13. D   18. H
14. G   19. B
15. A   20. F

754 • Appendix

EXERCISE (p. 414)

1. B	4. J	7. A	10. F	13. A	16. G	19. A
2. G	5. C	8. J	11. D	14. H	17. C	20. J
3. C	6. G	9. D	12. G	15. B	18. J	

Unit 8 | *Purpose of Sentences*

EXERCISE (p. 431)

1. D	4. G	7. B	10. F	13. B	16. F	19. D
2. G	5. A	8. G	11. B	14. F	17. A	20. F
3. C	6. G	9. B	12. J	15. A	18. G	

Unit 9 | *Practice*

EXERCISE (p. 444)

1. C	5. D	9. B	13. A	17. D	21. A	25. B	29. D
2. H	6. F	10. G	14. G	18. G	22. F	26. F	30. G
3. B	7. B	11. D	15. B	19. B	23. C	27. B	
4. F	8. G	12. H	16. G	20. G	24. H	28. J	

Unit 10 | *Practice*

EXERCISE (p. 460)

1. B	5. D	9. A	13. D	17. D	21. C	25. B	29. C
2. G	6. F	10. J	14. F	18. G	22. J	26. F	30. G
3. D	7. C	11. B	15. D	19. C	23. B	27. B	
4. H	8. J	12. H	16. F	20. F	24. H	28. F	

Unit 11 | *Practice*

EXERCISE (p. 472)

1. B	5. A	9. C	13. A	17. C	21. A	25. D	29. A
2. F	6. G	10. G	14. G	18. H	22. J	26. H	30. F
3. A	7. B	11. A	15. C	19. A	23. A	27. B	
4. F	8. H	12. F	16. H	20. J	24. G	28. G	

ANSWER KEY • 755

Unit 12 | Analyzing Arguments
EXERCISE (p. 489)

1. D	3. B	5. A	7. B	9. B
2. H	4. J	6. F	8. H	10. F

Unit 13 | Analyzing Paired Passages
EXERCISE (p. 500)

1. A	4. F	7. C	10. F	13. C	16. G	19. D
2. F	5. A	8. F	11. B	14. F	17. C	20. G
3. D	6. J	9. A	12. G	15. B	18. F	

Reading Mastery Test 1 (p. 509)

1. B	5. A	9. A	13. D	17. D	21. A	25. B	29. A
2. F	6. J	10. H	14. G	18. G	22. H	26. G	30. F
3. B	7. B	11. C	15. C	19. B	23. D	27. D	
4. H	8. F	12. F	16. J	20. H	24. H	28. J	

Reading Mastery Test 2 (p. 519)

1. A	4. H	7. A	10. H	13. B	16. J	19. B
2. G	5. B	8. F	11. A	14. G	17. D	20. H
3. A	6. G	9. B	12. H	15. A	18. G	

SCIENCE

Unit 1 | Tables

EXAMPLE PASSAGE (p. 533)
1. A
2. J
3. B
4. H
5. A

EXAMPLE PASSAGE (p. 535)
1. A
2. J
3. B
4. H
5. A

EXERCISE (p. 537)

1. C	8. H	15. B
2. H	9. D	16. H
3. C	10. G	17. A
4. G	11. A	18. F
5. C	12. F	19. C
6. J	13. B	20. J
7. A	14. J	

756 • APPENDIX

Unit 2 | *Tables Practice*
EXERCISE 1 (p. 546)

1. C	3. B	5. D	7. D	9. B	11. B	13. B	15. D
2. G	4. F	6. G	8. F	10. F	12. H	14. F

EXERCISE 2 (p. 551)

1. A	3. C	5. C	7. C	9. C	11. B	13. C	15. D
2. H	4. J	6. F	8. J	10. F	12. H	14. F

Unit 3 | *Bar Graphs*
EXAMPLE PASSAGE (p. 561)

1. A
2. J
3. B
4. H
5. A

EXERCISE (p. 563)

1. D	8. J	15. C
2. J	9. B	16. J
3. B	10. G	17. C
4. H	11. B	18. F
5. A	12. H	19. A
6. J	13. C	20. J
7. C	14. G	

Unit 4 | *Bar Graphs Practice*
EXERCISE 1 (p. 572)

1. C	3. D	5. C	7. D	9. A	11. A	13. B	15. D
2. G	4. G	6. G	8. J	10. F	12. J	14. F

EXERCISE 2 (p. 577)

1. A	3. D	5. C	7. D	9. A	11. B	13. C	15. D
2. J	4. F	6. H	8. H	10. G	12. G	14. H

Unit 5 | *Line Graphs*
EXAMPLE PASSAGE (p. 587)

1. A
2. J
3. B
4. H
5. A

EXERCISE (p. 589)

1. B	8. J	15. A
2. J	9. D	16. G
3. C	10. F	17. C
4. F	11. C	18. F
5. B	12. J	19. D
6. H	13. D	20. J
7. D	14. G	

Unit 6 | Line Graphs Practice

EXERCISE 1 (p. 598)

1. C	3. C	5. C	7. C	9. C	11. A	13. C	15. D
2. G	4. H	6. F	8. G	10. H	12. G	14. J	

EXERCISE 2 (p. 603)

1. C	3. D	5. D	7. A	9. C	11. B	13. B	15. B
2. F	4. G	6. J	8. G	10. H	12. F	14. F	

Unit 7 | Practice

EXERCISE 1 (p. 610)

1. D	4. F	7. C	10. J	13. D	16. F	19. B
2. G	5. B	8. J	11. D	14. F	17. D	20. H
3. D	6. G	9. C	12. H	15. D	18. F	

EXERCISE 2 (p. 617)

1. B	4. F	7. B	10. H	13. D	16. H
2. J	5. C	8. H	11. A	14. G	17. C
3. A	6. J	9. A	12. F	15. B	18. J

Unit 8 | Describing Experiments

SIMPLE INVESTIGATION (p. 625)

1. B   5. B
2. F   6. H
3. D
4. H

SIMPLE EXPERIMENT 1 (p. 627)

7. B
8. G
9. D
10. J

SIMPLE EXPERIMENT 2 (p. 629)

11. D   15. C
12. G
13. C
14. F

EXERCISE (p. 637)

1. A   6. H
2. H   7. A
3. D   8. H
4. G   9. D
5. D   10. F

Unit 9 | Describing Experiments Practice

EXERCISE (p. 642)

1. C	5. A	9. B	13. B	17. D	21. D	25. C	29. D
2. J	6. G	10. F	14. F	18. G	22. F	26. G	30. J
3. A	7. B	11. C	15. C	19. C	23. C	27. C	
4. H	8. F	12. F	16. G	20. J	24. J	28. F	

758 • APPENDIX

Unit 10 | *Experimental Tools and Methods*
EXERCISE (p. 662)

1. B	3. A	5. D	7. B	9. B	11. B	13. D	15. A
2. H	4. H	6. J	8. H	10. F	12. G	14. H	

Unit 11 | *Experimental Tools and Methods Practice*
EXERCISE (p. 670)

1. B	5. D	9. D	13. D	17. C	21. C	25. B	29. D
2. H	6. G	10. F	14. F	18. F	22. F	26. H	30. G
3. C	7. D	11. C	15. D	19. C	23. D	27. A	
4. F	8. H	12. F	16. G	20. J	24. H	28. J	

Unit 12 | *Understanding Models*
EXERCISE (p. 689)

1. A	4. G	7. A	10. H	13. C	16. H	19. D
2. J	5. C	8. G	11. C	14. F	17. D	20. F
3. D	6. H	9. A	12. J	15. B	18. G	

Unit 13 | *Understanding Models Practice*
EXERCISE (p. 696)

1. B	5. B	9. C	13. B	17. C	21. A	25. C	29. C
2. F	6. J	10. J	14. J	18. G	22. H	26. G	30. G
3. A	7. B	11. A	15. C	19. A	23. D	27. C	
4. F	8. H	12. G	16. J	20. J	24. J	28. F	

Science Mastery Test 1 (p. 707)

1. B	8. J	15. C	22. G	29. D	36. F	43. C	50. G
2. J	9. B	16. G	23. D	30. F	37. A	44. G	
3. A	10. F	17. D	24. G	31. D	38. H	45. C	
4. H	11. C	18. J	25. B	32. F	39. A	46. G	
5. D	12. F	19. D	26. H	33. C	40. G	47. C	
6. H	13. B	20. F	27. A	34. F	41. B	48. H	
7. B	14. J	21. A	28. J	35. B	42. H	49. B	

Science Mastery Test 2 (p. 725)

1. C	8. F	15. A	22. J	29. B	36. G	43. A	50. H
2. J	9. B	16. G	23. D	30. G	37. D	44. F	
3. C	10. J	17. B	24. F	31. D	38. F	45. C	
4. J	11. D	18. H	25. B	32. J	39. C	46. F	
5. A	12. H	19. D	26. H	33. C	40. F	47. D	
6. G	13. A	20. F	27. C	34. G	41. D	48. G	
7. C	14. G	21. C	28. F	35. A	42. G	49. C	

ERROR CORRECTION AND SUGGESTION FORM • 761

Cambridge *Non-Negotiable Skills, Level 1, 6th Edition*
Error Correction and Suggestion Form

Name/Location: _____ Day Phone: _____ E-mail Address: _____

Part of Materials: ☐ Student Text, Specify Subject: _____ Page: _____ Item: _____
                     ☐ Teacher's Guide, Specify Subject: _____ Page: _____ Item: _____
Error/Suggestion: _____
_____
_____

Part of Materials: ☐ Student Text, Specify Subject: _____ Page: _____ Item: _____
                     ☐ Teacher's Guide, Specify Subject: _____ Page: _____ Item: _____
Error/Suggestion: _____
_____
_____

Part of Materials: ☐ Student Text, Specify Subject: _____ Page: _____ Item: _____
                     ☐ Teacher's Guide, Specify Subject: _____ Page: _____ Item: _____
Error/Suggestion: _____
_____
_____

Part of Materials: ☐ Student Text, Specify Subject: _____ Page: _____ Item: _____
                     ☐ Teacher's Guide, Specify Subject: _____ Page: _____ Item: _____
Error/Suggestion: _____
_____
_____

Part of Materials: ☐ Student Text, Specify Subject: _____ Page: _____ Item: _____
                     ☐ Teacher's Guide, Specify Subject: _____ Page: _____ Item: _____
Error/Suggestion: _____
_____
_____

Part of Materials: ☐ Student Text, Specify Subject: _____ Page: _____ Item: _____
                     ☐ Teacher's Guide, Specify Subject: _____ Page: _____ Item: _____
Error/Suggestion: _____
_____
_____

Mail form to Cambridge Educational Services, Inc. or fax form to 1-847-299-2933. For teacher's assistance, call 1-800-444-4373 or e-mail solutions@CambridgeEd.com. Visit our Web site at www.CambridgeEd.com.